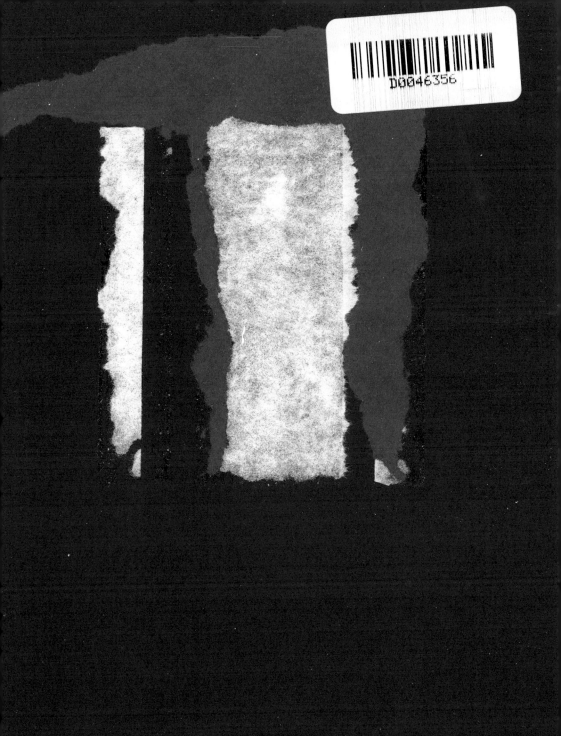

The
HANDICAPPER'S
CONDITION
BOOK

The HANDICAPPER'S CONDITION BOOK

An Advanced Treatment of Thoroughbred Class

JAMES QUINN

WILLIAM MORROW AND COMPANY, INC.

New York

The author would like to thank *The Daily Racing Form, Inc.*, for granting written permission for its copyrighted material to be reproduced throughout this book.

Portions of this book first appeared in THE HANDICAPPER's CONDITION BOOK by James Quinn, published by GBC Press, 630 South 11th Street, Box 4115, Las Vegas, Nevada, © 1981 by James Quinn.

Library of Congress Cataloging-in-Publication Data

Quinn, James, 1943–
   The handicapper's condition book.

  Bibliography: p.
  1. Horse race betting.   2. Thoroughbred horse.
I. Title.
SF331.Q547   1986   798.4'01   86-5255
ISBN 0-688-05931-7

Printed in the United States of America

First Edition

1 2 3 4 5 6 7 8 9 10

BOOK DESIGN BY BERNARD SCHLEIFER

Preface

WITHIN A YEAR OF its original publication in 1981, publisher John Luckman (GBC Press, Las Vegas, NV) called *The Handicapper's Condition Book* a standard in the field. The book eventually became Luckman's all-time best-seller.

Just as rewarding to its author, in book reviews and critical essays of periodicals and newspapers, in critiques and official ratings supplied to subscribers by consumer protection newsletters, and in personal correspondence, I have yet to find a negative reaction to the book's content or methodology, even among professionals and devotees of the pastime who do not particularly adhere to the principles and practices of class handicapping. The book more than satisfied a felt need. It struck a nerve.

Many of my correspondents have testified that the book has improved their handicapping in fundamental ways and has contributed significantly to a greater level of financial success. A gentleman from the San Francisco area gave the book full credit for his cashing a Pick-Six ticket worth $376,000 at Santa Anita, saying an 8-to-1 shot in a classified allowance race he could not have spotted otherwise had keyed the killing. The winner and his brother-in-law, in fact, had flown from northern California to Santa Anita just to wager on the horse, a morning-line longshot, because it fit the book's selection criteria so well. The lucky reader singled the horse as well on a $128 Pick-Six card. He sent me a photostat of the huge check but neglected to include a 10 percent finder's fee.

And in an especially sweet moment for me, when I accidentally bumped into the industry executive I have admired most for many years, F. E. (Jimmy) Kilroe, Director of Racing at Santa Anita Park, a

cultivated man, member of The Jockey Club, and the principal ar-
chitect of Thoroughbred racing in southern California for three dec-
ades, at the deli counter in a local supermarket, he told me, "I've
read that book of yours, and I think it is a first-class job."

Luckman had told me once, "If a major New York house wants to
pick this up for wider distribution, you'll get no resistance from me."

Thus, I am pleased to present this revised edition for William
Morrow and Company of New York. The opportunity for revision is
in fact timely. Major trends in the sport identified in the first edition
have accelerated—the faster development of younger horses, a proliferation of stakes, international racing, embarrassingly small
fields, and, regrettably, the general decline in the quality of overnite
competition.

In response, the original manuscript has been amplified considerably. An important new section in the chapter on stakes and
handicaps gives handicappers the inside track on international racing—the only source of this material on record, so far as I am aware.
The intention is to give regular handicappers a leg up on success in
the races that feature foreign horses. Evaluating the records of foreign-bred and foreign-raced horses intelligently, and knowing the
local conditions of eligibility under which the imports regularly
shine, has become perhaps the most generous source of conspicuous
overlays in the game. This book now tells handicappers everything
they need to know, and in Appendix 2 readers will find complete
lists of the graded and "listed" stakes currently programmed in
seven countries, including the United States, identified by grade
designations, purse values, and eligible ages.

In another ripe addition, evidence lately produced can help
handicappers deal more effectively than ever with the most unpredictable of races, the routes for two-year-olds. That thin section has
been beefed up with solid new data.

A third new section discusses the claiming-race conditions at
small tracks much more thoroughly than before. In several other
sections up-to-date data from studies of pace, form cycles, and dosage have been incorporated into the basic guidelines.

The new version also contains several updated illustrations,
though several others remain the same. Where sample races appear
outdated, handicappers can be confident the points they illustrate
are timeless, or current at the least. The examples in the original
manuscript were carefully selected, and some have served the text
remarkably well.

Numerous readers of the first edition suggested that the dozens of selection and elimination profiles would serve the purpose better if they were accessible from a single depository. Appendix 1, also new, supports that cause. It represents a ready-reference resource for the selection-elimination guidelines for twenty variations of eligibility conditions. I hope handicappers will find its substance and format conveniently useful.

Finally, I wish to give a special nod to handicapping author Tom Ainslie, a mentor, who played an important role in the publication of the original manuscript. I sent the finished draft of Part 1 to Ainslie, inquiring whether the material was "publishable." He assured me it was not only fit for publication, but should be a tremendous help to handicappers everywhere. Thus, I pushed on. Eventually, Ainslie's bare-knuckles critique of the lead chapter of Part 2 forced me to grapple with my ideas about nonclaiming three-year-olds until they had been refined and reshaped such that readers might actually comprehend the messages. The chapter was reworked six times.

No less important at the time, Ainslie's enthusiastic public endorsement of the book gave it instant credibility as a work of substance and helped it gain firm footing in the marketplace.

Five years following its debut, *The Handicapper's Condition Book* promises its readers that its guidelines work. They have been demonstrably effective now for thousands of practitioners and should remain so for many, many seasons to come.

Foreword

HANDICAPPERS WHO have tested their mettle at racetracks and have emerged from the experiences even more devoted to the pastime form the audience this book seeks. The text is advanced. It relates eligibility conditions to past performances. Its purpose is to put in relatively sophisticated hands a handicapper's condition book, a full season's edition that helps handicappers place bets, even as condition books issued by racetracks help horsemen place horses.

If race conditions are written with particular kinds of horses in mind—and they are—players profit when able to recognize the past-performance profiles of horses best suited to the conditions. Such players can concentrate on animals for which the race was written, appreciate the unlikelier chances of others. The approach gets the work done faster, and better.

To players well grounded in the fundamentals of handicapping, those with two or three seasons of profitable or improving play under the belt, *The Handicapper's Condition Book* promises even better days ahead. The book will cut down your handicapping time, polish your methods, illuminate betting opportunities previously ignored or misapprehended, and boost the all-important rate of return on the invested dollar.

Because my own experience grew mainly on the southern California circuit, many of the handicapping examples come from Santa Anita or Hollywood Park. But as my occasional excursions to Aqueduct, Keystone, Arlington Park, Longacres, Meadowlands, and Golden Gate Fields have indicated, the book's ideas and practices are widely applicable. If your track sits on a major circuit, this book is for you. Players at minor tracks, where conditions of eligibility are more restricted, will find here a handy tool for dealing specifically and comprehensively with the basic run of races carded everywhere. A new section on claiming races at small tracks should make the book more valuable to handicappers there.

Handicapping may be the most challenging and exciting of hobbies, to be sure. I've been at it now for more than a decade and can still feel the stir of a new season. But it's painstaking, too, hard work, and for most players, however studied or practiced, a losing proposition. An understanding of which conditions of eligibility favor which horses helps enormously.

Once *Daily Racing Form* has been opened, what could be more gratifying than reading the conditions of eligibility for a race to be run the next afternoon, reviewing the entries, and recognizing the horse perfectly suited to the conditions?

That horse figures to win.

Contents

PREFACE   5

FOREWORD   9

PART 1
Eligibility Conditions
and Past Performances

1 Openers   15

2 Maidens   29

3 Nonwinners Allowances   57

4 Stakes and Handicaps   78

5 Classified Allowances   107

6 Claimers   121

7 Starters   145

PART 2
Eligibility Conditions
and Developing Horses

8 Nonclaiming Three-Year-Olds   159

9 To Separate Contenders: Total Performance
   Handicapping   187

10 Three-Year-Olds and Up   208

11 Two-Year-Olds   228

REFERENCES   249

APPENDICES

1 Selection and Elimination Guidelines for Twenty
     Variations of Eligibility Conditions   251

2 A Compilation of the Graded and Listed Stakes of Can-
     ada, England, France, Germany, Ireland, Italy, and the
     United States by Grade Designations, Purse Values, and
     Eligible Ages   283

Part 1

Eligibility Conditions and Past Performances

CHAPTER 1

Openers

THOROUGHBRED RACING changed profoundly and for all times during the 1970s. The lives of owners, breeders, horsemen, and racetrack executives were shaken by unabating inflation and surpassing competition for the gaming dollar. Hallowed traditions have been slipping away ever since. Those slow of mind or foot already have fallen far behind. Much the same has befallen this book's hero, the handicapper, who struggles on against ever-increasing odds.

For openers, the claiming game, once the player's bread and butter, has been altered drastically, and not in the interests of handicappers. The stakes programs too have changed, expanding greatly, but this in the interest of alert handicappers. Allowances have hardly escaped the overhaul, but classified allowances still provide the likeliest bonanzas for informed, perceptive handicappers. At all levels of competition the fields grow smaller and the odds get correspondingly tighter.

More than ever, professional handicappers and their sidekicks, serious hobbyists, must pay attention to the changing conditions under which the competition proceeds. When professional handicappers of southern California open the *Form* to an allowance race, for four-year-olds and up, nonwinners of $2,500 twice other than maiden or claiming, they anticipate the contenders will exhibit past performance profiles vastly different from the contenders for these purses of just a few years ago. At least one is likely to be foreign-bred or foreign-raced, with victories or earnings superior to minor nonwinner allowance conditions. Yet those animals remain eligible for today's race, their overseas performances notwithstanding, and

15

may pulverize the chronic nonwinners from the homeland that normally populate these events. In New York, New Jersey, Maryland, Illinois, and other centers where state-bred programs have materialized, apparent contenders under nonwinner allowances might not figure at all, their earlier easy victories and average earnings having accumulated in homebred races characterized by higher purses but cheaper horses.

An approach to handicapping that begins with a shrewd comprehension of a race's conditions of eligibility and the kinds of horses they attract remains a fertile and vital area of exploration for seasoned handicappers, whether they have concentrated on this aspect of the game or not. In many situations traditional practices no longer apply, and handicappers who have not kept in step with a changing game will have more trouble than ever keeping the books in order.

THE CHANGING CONDITIONS OF PLAY

The following conditions, interrelated, have led to fundamental alterations in the conditions of racing.

1. The rapid and general inflation of the 1970s.

Not surprisingly, a decade of escalating inflation has held out severe consequences for all concerned. Purses for owners and horsemen have gone up, but not enough. Competition for horseflesh among racetracks now features million-dollar bonuses for horses able to win a series of stakes races in New York, Chicago, New Jersey, and southern California, and in New Jersey developing three-year-olds can qualify for a two-million-dollar bonus, the latter program having already eroded the traditional prestige of racing's Triple Crown. Breeders' Cup Event Day in late fall has displaced as definitive the flagship stakes of several major tracks with seven races carrying purses of a million dollars or more. Of interest to handicappers, inflation has contributed to (a) a staggering increase in the number of racing days, races, and number and kind of wagering opportunities, (b) a corresponding decline in the quality of the competition, especially overnite competition, (c) modifications in purse structures such that better purses more often go to the younger horses or state-bred horses, and (d) a declining emphasis on the claiming game for older horses.

The larger number of racing days and opportunities has meant even more than a general weakening in the competitive quality.

More racing has been accompanied by a hotly unpopular situation among the players—the small field. Given alternative opportunities, horsemen tend instinctively to avoid the kind of competition in which their horses are more likely to lose. The resulting practices, shipping and scratching, have so reinforced a worsening situation that by 1985 the small field had virtually been institutionalized.

In southern California the six- or seven-horse field has become commonplace, more so as the season progresses. Late declarations, even program scratches, technically improper as practiced, have increased terrifically, partly because overextended horses suffer more ailments, partly because their trainers prefer to go shopping for easier spots. In the rich handicap and stakes races it is no longer unusual for four or five to go postward, with one a stickout at miserly odds. During the eighty-nine days of the 1984–85 season at Santa Anita, the feature race had six horses or less thirty-seven times. No less than sixteen times the day's featured race filled with five horses or four. Two or three entrants are intended solely to pick up the second, third, or fourth shares.

With hundred-granders sprouting up everywhere, unless a race carries the kind of Grade 1 prestige that escalates the winner's breeding value, stables find practical answers to the rhetorical questions: Why run against the division leader? Or against the potential champion? So the real competition goes elsewhere, to another race or another place.

The upshot for players has been noncompetitive fields and lowered odds, balanced indelicately against the greater probability of picking a winner. Even-money shots may figure big, but they hardly contribute to the profit margin, the main reason most noncompetitive races remain unplayable.

2. A dramatically charged emphasis on the development of young Thoroughbreds.

The successful development of young horses leads owners and trainers to better purses, breeding syndications, and ultimately, to the long-sought empire. At major tracks these goals have veritably taken over the game. Unfortunately for handicappers, the less successful development (fantastically more common) of young horses has spread the industrialization of breeding and commercialization of racing among slower, more misshapen animals.

Contemporary southern California reflects national trends. The summer and fall programs have been redesigned to enhance the opportunities for that circuit's nicely bred twos and threes. The spring and early summer session at Hollywood Park has dedicated its innovations to the three-year-old, including additional stakes and conditioned stakes, two major stakes limited to homebreds, additional distance races, additional grass races, additional races restricted to Cal-breds, and an earlier mingling of three-year-olds and older.

Del Mar in late summer and Oak Tree at Santa Anita during fall have sought to extend additional racing opportunities to two-year-olds, but with limited effectiveness so far.

The Handicapper's Condition Book contends nothing has changed the handicapper's game as has modern racing's preoccupation with young horses, notably three-year-olds. For the policies that favor young horses have been stooped and bent under a naturally low ceiling on success. In a typical season the tracks produce a few dozen good ones, and several hundred that are common or worse. Races must be carded for inferior horses too. And hundreds are. State-bred maiden races. Cheaper claiming races for twos and threes. And those awful maiden-claiming sprints that surge upon handicappers field after field. Sophisticated racegoers who have watched daily processions of low-priced three-year-old claiming horses plodding to the wire at six furlongs in the season's spring do not applaud this unhappy circumstance, produced by policies that sponsor so many young horses.

Handicappers have suffered as much as anyone. Claiming events for older horses, the player's store of beatable races, have continued on the decline. So have classified allowance races for older runners, where bright prospects at nice prices have long resided. The classified allowance sprint is practically extinct. Starter races are on the way out. In their place have arrived overnite races for unfashionable three-year-olds, slower and less reliable all.

Handicappers have little recourse but to revise their practices in accord with a changing game. Surely they should sharpen their methods when analyzing young horses. Present and future handicappers will need to understand the three-year-old specifically and comprehensively.

Existing literature on this matter is scarce and faulty. Tom Ainslie, an intelligent, perceptive, and prolific writer and teacher and leading authority on handicapping, long since has alerted handicappers to the charms of the nicely bred, lightly raced, improving three-year-old. In the aggregate, however, Ainslie's writings lump three-year-olds too routinely with older horses. Three-year-olds are distinct. They warrant separate treatment.

Not only is the three-year-old more physically immature, its temperament is relatively fragile and unstable. Its behavior is more erratic and unpredictable. Its experience is relatively little and unreliable. Its abilities and preferences remain under development, under experiment. Not much about it is conclusive or generalizable.

On the track the three-year-old's youthfulness shows throughout the season. Its class varies more widely and unpredictably, and perhaps repeatedly. Its form cycle improves and deteriorates more suddenly and with less reliability. Its distance and pace preferences remain more elusive and problematic. Its responsiveness to riders and to new competitive experiences is more tentative and inexplicable.

Three chapters of this book deal rigorously with the idiosyncrasies and inconsistencies of three-year-olds. The claimers appear first. Then the lead chapter of Part 2 examines better three-year-olds under a full array of racing conditions. A third chapter alerts handicappers to the eligibility conditions under which three-year-olds have a better or poorer chance against older horses. Here the latest evidence reveals some surprises.

3. The increased importation of foreign-bred and foreign-raced horses.

One handicapping colleague never wagers on foreign-bred or foreign-raced horses until they have demonstrated good form under local conditions. He misses opportunities that way, but he doesn't care. My friend remains more comfortable with traditional methods. More relaxed handicappers can enjoy a new edge in nonwinner allowances or certain stakes races.

The number of foreign-bred or foreign-raced horses competing under U.S. conditions has jumped dramatically. A few stables now concentrate almost exclusively on the buying and racing of imports. Despite having won repeatedly overseas, several of the imports remain eligible at some tracks, including those of California, under nonwinner allowance conditions. Imports that have won open or graded stakes at some tracks overseas can enter conditioned stakes here. Alerted handicappers find splendid opportunities now in races that formerly resisted analysis or defied their best efforts. The mutuels are often moderate and sometimes large, the general public being relatively untrusting of the unfamiliar. The expert gets ahead by learning to interpret the past performances of imported horses with confidence and know-how.

4. A proliferation of stakes races and the consequent grading of stakes in terms of their relative quality.

A Grade 1 stakes horse can stampede a group of lower grade runners when in shape to do so. This is axiomatic to successful play.

It pays to know which horses are Grade 1, Grade 2, or lower grade.

Class standouts, properly placed, are still the surest bet at any oval. More than ever the stakes are playable. Whether an added-money feature is conditioned, Grade 1, lower grade, or ungraded, one or two entrants will likely have demonstrated the kind of past performances best suited to the race. A new hierarchy among stakes competitors has been emerging. Finding the suitable entrants has become easier than before, due to new information available in the past performances or results charts.

Regardless of these or other changes in the conditions of play, the great majority of races still run true to form. The best horses usually win. Still true, too, is the underestimated and often unstated proposition that the class of a field is tied tightly to eligibility conditions. In a Grade 1 stakes, the Grade 1 horse romps over the Grade 2 kind, even as $16,000 claiming horses pound the $10,000 brand.

Other differences among eligible horses might be less obvious but no less significant. What follows intends to illuminate the differences.

HOW HANDICAPPERS USE
ELIGIBILITY CONDITIONS

An approach to handicapping which emphasizes the relationships between eligibility conditions and past performances requires players to apprehend which horses are best suited to a particular kind of race.

In the usual case, more than one entrant has achieved a past performance profile suited to the conditions. Under varying conditions, nonetheless, suitable past performance profiles can be drawn and these can be arranged in a kind of ascending or descending order of suitability. Because flexible thinking usually beats rigid rules, the suitable performance profiles are best regarded as interchangeable, depending on variations in eligibility conditions, such as distance or footing, and the relative qualifications of horses fundamentally suited to the race.

Horses whose past performance profiles are best suited to the conditions do not always win, but they are always contenders, and players whose methods ignore this circumstance will find their play characterized by greater error and confusion than is necessary or acceptable. Players who respect the role of eligibility conditions are not easily defeated by fast clockings or impressive performances recorded in races not strongly related to the class of competition under study now.

A consistent four-year-old allowance sprinter wins by ten under classified conditions in June, earning a ninety-five speed rating, its highest ever. Is it a contender two weeks later when entered in a stakes sprint, Grade 2? Hardly.

A three-year-old colt from a leading barn wins a maiden sprint handily in ordinary time first try. Is it a threat when entered next in an allowance sprint for three-year-olds and older, nonwinners other than maiden or claiming? Absolutely.

A fast-working, first-time starting two-year-old colt, trained by the leading trainer, to be ridden by a leading jockey, has been entered in a maiden-claiming sprint at six furlongs, for sale at $20,000. Is the colt a contender? Never.

What about a three-year-old dropping from a $32,000 claiming race to a $25,000 race, same distance? Is it a good thing? Probably not. But a six-year-old gelding so dropping could be a stickout.

Which kind of horse is the likelier winner of a maiden sprint for three-year-olds? A fast-working first-timer from a leading stable? Or a colt that finished second last time out in a similar event? It's the colt that finished second last out.

What kind of past performance profile leaps to mind as a likely winner of a starter race at a classic distance on the turf, for horses that recently started for a $20,000 claiming price or less?

What kind of three-year-old is likely to win a conditioned stakes that bars former stakes winners?

Under what conditions is the older sprinter at better advantage in a middle-distance route?

Dealing knowledgeably, confidently, and effectively with these questions, and with dozens like them, is basic to handicapping. Yet many regular players fail to develop a working knowledge of eligibility conditions. As a result many place big bets on misplaced horses. Misplaced horses usually lose. They lose because their basic quality is not equal to the competition or their racing preferences are suited to other distances or kinds of footing.

Why do so many players ignore or underestimate the role of eligibility conditions? Two reasons, I believe.

One, most players are comparison handicappers. They compare horses' records with one another, a relative comparison, and not with objective standards or criteria, absolute relationships. Relative comparisons are more subjective and less reliable, dependent as they are on personal experiences, beliefs, and preferences. Absolute comparisons are more objective and more reliable, dependent as they are on established facts, percentages, and probabilities.

The first question is not whether Horse A is likely to beat Horse B, but whether A and B treated independently are suited to the kind of competition eligible to race. To answer that question handicappers depend on objective standards, or at least on established principles or guidelines from which such standards can be derived.

If both A and B, studied independently, are suited to the conditions, then the comparative standards and subjective judgments apply, guiding a final decision, which in any case will be more complicated and precarious than would be the case were comparisons and judgments not needed. The exception would be a race in which only one entrant was suited to the conditions, eliminating need for comparisons.

No one regrets this circumstance. The use of comparative judgment makes handicapping the fun, challenge, and personally satisfying endeavor it is. Yet a full-fledged capitulation to comparison handicapping goes too far. That approach picks a potential winner every race. Over time, comparison handicappers suffer from too much action on unplayable races.

To illustrate, consider one of racing's toughest nuts—the allowance race for nonwinners of one or two races other than maiden or claiming.

What kinds of horses appeal to you in these events? Can you imagine their past performance profiles?

Handicappers generally prefer lightly raced younger entrants of better connections that have won impressively and merely are moving through their basic conditions. Alternately, experts discount horses that have competed under similar conditions several times but have failed.

In practice, variations of the two general performance profiles can be numerous and puzzling. A typical field might contain two or three horses that have lost a dozen or more allowance races; two or three others that have lost six to eight allowance races but with an occasional impressive performance; a lightly raced easy maiden winner; a frequently raced maiden winner now showing improvement; and two or three horses that have lost only a few allowance tries, perhaps with impressive performances or clockings.

What to do? Comparison handicappers typically eliminate horses that have lost too many allowance races (unless their recent clockings have been impressively fast), eliminate maiden winners, and compare the leftovers. The remaining four or five are separated by homemade combinations of speed-pace ratings, jockey assignments, stable connections, and size of the odds.

This is sloppy handicapping. By providing more action on poorly placed horses, it lowers the win percentage, the statistic to which the dollar return is most closely sensitive. And a common mistake is to dismiss lightly raced handy maiden winners. By definition these easy winners fit as contenders in allowance races for nonwinners other than maiden or claiming. Where should handicappers expect the horses will win next?

To be sure, allowance races for nonwinners of allowance races often remain unplayable. Handicappers do not yet have enough fundamental information about the horses to permit reliable distinctions. Which can set or overcome the fastest pace? Which are ready to improve? Which possess the classic qualities of willingness and determination?

What will the easy maiden winner do when pressed? Quit? Or dig in and win? Too often handicappers just don't know.

The nonwinner allowances are not hospitable to comparison handicappers. The comparisons do not hold up.

Handicappers unravel these races efficiently by concentrating on horses whose past performance profiles are well suited to allowance races for nonwinners. To that end, handicappers best employ objective standards and eliminate horses whose records do not measure up. If no horse qualifies, pass. The race is too unreliable. If too many horses qualify, pass. The race is too competitive.

Other conditions of eligibility admit horses less puzzling than those eligible to nonwinner allowances. Handicappers who can identify the suitable past performance profiles will find attractive opportunities galore.

The key to handicapping by the conditions is the class factor. More than anything else, eligibility conditions define and limit the quality of the horses eligible. Handicappers benefit by completing two first steps. One, identify horses suited to the class of the race. Two, determine whether one horse enjoys a decisive class advantage in relation to the conditions.

Suppose, for example, the race is a Grade 1 stakes for older horses. Players merely identify entrants that are Grade 1 horses (defined later). Is one a champion or a division leader? If so, players may eliminate the other horses confidently. Why? Handicappers rely on fundamental knowledge. They realize that (a) the differences between Grade 1 horses and lower grade horses are substantial (to put it mildly), (b) Grade 1 races are almost invariably won by

Grade 1 horses, and (c) the upsets that occur in these events are few and unpredictable.

The second reason not enough players pay attention to eligibility conditions is that they associate conditions with the trainer's job. *The Handicapper's Condition Book* argues that eligibility conditions should be as pertinent to handicappers placing bets as to horsemen placing horses.

THE TOUR DE FORCE

The book has two parts. Part 1 identifies the kinds of horses handicappers should expect to win under the various conditions of eligibility that are traditional on major racing cards. Its chapters unfold in a sequence not unlike that followed by many promising thoroughbreds as they progress in their races. As do practically all horses, Part 1 begins with maiden races, ends with claiming races.

Part 2 concentrates on developing horses, three-year-olds whose records do not yet reveal them as horses of a kind, and the juveniles. When the past performances are too few and too unclear, handicappers can relate the qualities of class and form they do reveal to the *quality of performance typically demanded by the various conditions of eligibility.* It's a fascinating approach to the game, and a vastly underplayed one. The important lead chapter shows handicappers how to deal comprehensively and specifically with the special handicapping problems presented by nonclaiming three-year-olds. Can three-year-old winners take the next step successfully? Not unless they can call into play the performance qualities demanded at that level. Handicappers will want to try the systematic handicapping procedures advanced in a companion chapter for analyzing the past performances of developing three-year-olds.

PART 1

Our tour de force looks first at maiden races for older horses, three- and four-year-olds. These races are more predictable than ever, thanks to conclusions supported by the best probability studies of handicapping ever conducted. Next, maiden claiming races get just the once-over they deserve. Handicappers might be surprised by the book's enthusiasm for some of these sluggish races. Contrary to generally accepted opinion, maiden claiming races are beatable.

Maiden winners that have run respectably proceed to the allowance races for nonwinners other than maiden or claiming. Cheaper types sometimes proceed immediately to claiming events.

Nonwinner allowance races can be wickedly difficult. The competition may be restricted to nonwinners of two races, to nonwinners other than maiden or claiming, to nonwinners of a specified winner's share other than maiden or claiming, or to nonwinners two, three, or four times other than maiden or claiming. Under all circumstances handicappers arrive too often at impenetrable barriers. Sensible guidelines do apply, and they do eliminate errors of the grossest kind. These contents cannot assure handicappers they will beat these difficult contests, but they will demolish some myths and bolster the important win percentage.

After two or three victories, still-improving thoroughbreds move from nonwinner allowances to the stakes events. Many first try an increasingly scheduled proposition, the conditioned stakes. There they meet their own kind—unless, that is, an eligible horse is actually another kind. Experts know how to spot the differences and can collect nice rewards for doing so.

Eventually the top thoroughbreds sort themselves out in open and graded stakes competition. Those unable to earn stakes in open events compete in classified allowance races where they make their way against a more restricted competition. Horses that cannot earn monies in either category soon enter the high-priced claiming ranks. Excepting the outstanding individuals, when horses of stakes or classified quality can no longer withstand that caliber of competition, they too descend to the high-priced claiming events. All horses that compete there eventually begin an unevenly patterned descent to their current levels of satisfactory performance, claiming levels at which they win purse monies for their owners and trainers. The descent continues until the racing career ends.

The Handicapper's Condition Book proceeds similarly from the conditioned stakes to open stakes. There are more of both than ever. Here handicappers can take hold of a rare helping hand extended by the industry. Anxious to restore a sense of order in sales rings and on farms, the breeding industry in 1973 began the grading of stakes. Now stakes races can be distinguished as graded or ungraded, and graded events can be distinguished as Grade 1, Grade 2, or Grade 3. Ungraded stakes now are distinguished as listed, open, and restricted.

Handicappers who understand how handily a Grade 1 or Grade 2 stakes horse can dispose of the lower grades when ready to do so have edged toward profit in featured races. Recently at Santa Anita a Grade 1 horse humbled its opposition in a Grade 3 feature and paid $5. Handicappers who recognized the situation had confidence enough to make a sizeable wager, and quickly recovered 150 percent profit.

Next, international racing receives its first full-blown review in American handicapping literature. American horsemen have been importing foreign horses increasingly in recent years. The trend will continue. International racing is a sign of the times. Foreign horses are best understood in terms of the stakes races they exit. This book provides the guidelines. It also lists the graded and listed stakes of Canada, England, France, Germany, Ireland, Italy, and the United States by grade designations, purse values, and eligible ages. This information is available to handicappers nowhere else.

Perhaps the most interesting and penetrating section of Part 1, the chapter classified allowance races, presents the complexities of eligibility conditions which, although relatively restricted, bring together horses of highly diverse abilities and preferences. Here more than anywhere else handicappers survive only on comprehensive skill.

Under classified allowance conditions, the best horse often loses. Just as often it wins. Eligible previous stakes winners often lose; others win. Several times each season first money goes to claiming horses. Handicappers need to know what should happen today, and why. Eligibility conditions give handicapping's fundamentals and their interrelationships a clearer application and priority. Experts find betting bonanzas under classified allowance conditions. Handicapping offers them no greater challenges or rewards.

The tour turns next to the better thoroughbreds' poor brothers and weak sisters, the claiming horses. As most know, these third-rate racers first find a level of competition at which they can earn a purse or two. Then they complete successive cycles of improvement and deterioration, perhaps shuttling from barn to barn, while up and down the claiming scale. The overall pattern, with notable exceptions, becomes one of deterioration, such that last year's $25,000 claimer may carry $12,500 tags this year, and next year may be too disabled to warrant a stall.

Within traditionally broad outlines, the claiming game has changed. First we examine claiming races for older horses. Then we look at similar races for three-year-olds. The idea of price brackets appropriate to the schedule of claiming competition on local circuits is proposed and explained in the context of rapid change. Class rises and drops in claiming races now are understood best in a context of price brackets.

Where this is not particularly true, at smaller minor tracks, we look closely at the claiming competition there. Handicappers might be surprised at the wide array of eligibility conditions characteristic of claiming contests at minor tracks.

Part 1 ends with a quick examination of starter races, a diminishing breed. Where these intriguing events are carded, solid handicappers can expect to win them as regularly as do the consistent horses made eligible to them by maneuvering stables.

PART 2

Part 2, on developing horses, urges handicappers to rely on their understanding of eligibility conditions when the past performances do not yet tell a persuasive story. Even when relative class is not yet understood, horses whose chances are more apparent than real can be revealed as phonies and discarded.

Part 2 begins with a rigorous study of nonclaiming three-year-olds, the most misunderstood thoroughbreds of all. A companion chapter reveals handicapping procedures particularly suited to developing three-year-olds. Similar three-year-olds in competition with their elders follow. Under varying conditions of eligibility, which age is likelier to win?

Part 2 ends with a short chapter on two-year-old racing. Here contemporary change has so far been real but incidental to handicappers. Perhaps the most dramatic occurrence has been numerical increases in juvenile horses and races. Final times still count. Speed handicappers in possession of accurate figures now get more opportunities to dazzle their nonarithmetical friends.

Handicappers put off by calculations of par times, variants, and adjusted speed ratings will be relieved at finding references to the accurate figures of others—transportable figures, adjustable figures, winning figures.

Guidance provided by the eligibility conditions of two-year-old races is limited. Yet the topic merits some exploration. A few pointers will be enlightening and useful to handicappers.

STARTING POINTS

Now as always races are won by fit horses suited to the class and distance of races, provided the pace is favorable or comfortable and nothing about the footing, jockey, weight, or post position figures to nullify basic advantages.

Players unable to handicap a field of thoroughbreds on these fundamentals are best advised to postpone study of this guide until more basic work has been completed. The recommended sources are the writings of Tom Ainslie and his associates, notably Fred Davis, who published *Percentages & Probabilities,* a clear and concise twenty-three-page tool that provides well-grounded handicappers with statistical insights into the utility of numerous characteristics contained in the past performances, and William L. Quirin, who in 1979 extended Davis' research significantly and in 1984 published *Thoroughbred Handicapping: State of the Art,* an interpretive guided tour of the past performance tables. Unlike so much of the statistical evidence published on handicapping, the Davis and Quirin research is sound in method and the samples are representative.

The book assumes fundamental know-how and a few productive rounds of experience. The starting points are these.

The Handicapper's Condition Book should advance the cause of good handicappers everywhere. And I know it will help scores of regular racegoers get back on course or started on a straight one. Personal experience has taught that even ruggedly experienced handicappers do not get a sure enough hold on a race's eligibility conditions. At Santa Anita in 1979, a professional man and handicapping acquaintance bet a fat sum a colt that had lost eight maiden claiming sprints in succession would win on the ninth try against a similar field. He felt supremely confident of that. Why? Because the colt had earned the highest speed rating of its field, had shown satisfactory early speed, had earned improved final times in its last two races, and should benefit by a favorable jockey switch to national leader Chris McCarron.

The poor horse was burned up by the early speed of a first-time starter, and lost miserably.

In 1985, that same professional man could be found at his customary box, making the same kinds of bets he did five years ago—on horses that are desperately outclassed.

No one can win at the races that way. Matters are not so simple. Handicappers who favor these guidelines for working with eligibility conditions will not bet on maiden claiming horses that have lost eight maiden claiming events.

By cutting unnecessary losses, of that kind and numerous others, the win percentage shoots up. So does the return on the invested dollar.

CHAPTER   2

Maidens

MAIDEN RACES FOR OLDER HORSES

OLDER MAIDENS, three-year-olds and up, can be handicapped readily and reliably, even when their past performances are sparse and contain inadequate indicators of their abilities and preferences. Handicappers can rely on the few criteria and standards all older maidens' records should satisfy. Now too we can utilize the powerful statistical findings compiled by Fred Davis in *Percentages & Probabilities*. Davis has removed the major impediment to analyzing races for older maidens successfully—how to evaluate fast-working first-time starters.

After the first quarter of the year, eligibility conditions typically invite three- and four-year-old maidens to compete with one another. Four-year-old maidens automatically become suspect and rarely rate the favoritism of handicappers. But what about three-year-old maidens? Which figure best?

Fred Davis has taken handicappers almost to the cashier's window. In maiden races for three-year-olds and up, Davis found the second place finish last out is a powerful predictor of success next time. Moreover, first-time starters win less than half their rightful share. Consider the facts:

Finish Last Out	% of Starters	% of Winners	Probability
2	9.0	24.6	274%
3	8.2	14.3	172%
Below 3rd	76.0	58.1	77%
1st starters	6.8	3.0	44%

(The probability of winning equals simply the percentage of winners having the characteristic divided by the percentage of starters having the characteristic.)

The data is illuminating. When considering the merits of two maiden contenders, one that finished second last out, the other a first-time starter, handicappers should prefer the horse that finished second last out. These horses represent 9 percent of the starters, but they win approximately 25 percent of the races, almost three times their rightful share. The statistics show too that third-place finishers win almost twice their share. In close analyses, third-place finishers merit support over first-time starters.

The findings do not mean handicappers should stop betting on first-time starting older maidens. A first-timer may win in a breeze and look the part on paper. Earlier in the year, especially, handicappers must respect impressive three-year-olds that debut for leading stables. When confronted with the two types of contenders, however, inseparable on paper, handicappers solve a chronic dilemma by going to the second-last-out horse every time. Those who favor betting on that kind will be working with percentages. They may lose one, two, or a short series of wagers, but they will end the season comfortably ahead.

Notwithstanding statistical advantages, any three-year-old and an occasional four-year-old may have the basic ability to trounce a field of older maidens. Handicappers give high regard to these guidelines and standards:

1. Older maidens should be working out regularly and sharply.

At least one or two works should indicate speed, and at promising distances. For sprints, a speedy work of five furlongs or longer impresses more. For routes, the fast work should occur at six furlongs, preferably a mile.

Once begun, the workouts should occur regularly, every five or six days. A pattern appreciated by many regulars contains a series of alternating speed and stamina works at lengthening distances, followed by a series of three or four "bottom" works, followed perhaps by a short speed blowout just prior to a race. Handicappers who collect workout tabs will notice this and other favored training patterns. Patterns that hide speed. Customers who rely exclusively on the four most recent workouts recorded in the *Form* will not. Professionals bother to collect workout tabs, and do so easily, as the *Form* prints daily workouts at all tracks on a circuit.

A maiden prepares for its debut with a series of ten to twelve serious workouts. If the training persists for too extended a period, involving too many or intermittent workouts for more than two months, handicappers suspect something is wrong physically. Usually, they're right. The first-time status becomes even more problematic.

Too, if an unraced or lightly raced three-year-old has not been working out, or stops working out, handicappers presume something is wrong physically. Most eliminate this kind confidently. The eliminations hold for top barns.

2. The three-year-old usually is preferable to older horses, especially after four months of the season.

Outstanding exceptions are nicely bred, sharp-working four-year-olds that represent leading barns. Classier stables do not carry four-year-old maidens unless the animals can run fast. The better bred these horses, the more likely leading horsemen have catered carefully to nagging problems in hopes of realizing the fashionable breeding value.

3. Among first-time starters, prefer horses bred to show high early speed.

Whether sprints or routes, the great majority of maiden races are won by horses that run on or near the early lead. Handicappers prosper by consulting tabulations of sires whose get go fast. Experts use the *American Racing Manual* as an annual source. They copy the lists of leading sires and leading juvenile sires whose trump is speed. Each season the *Form* updates these tabulations with monthly reports of sire standings. In routes, to be sure, handicappers feel reassurance if the breeding also suggests a dosage of stamina. The lists on these pages identify sires that earned national respect during 1983–84.

4. The rider should be a national or local leader, or one the stable considers particularly suitable to the horse.

Promising maidens almost always attract leaders of the jockey colony. A few are handled by regular stable riders. At times stables match maidens with riders having peculiar talents. When the horse was two and unraced, owner B. J. Ridder and trainer Gordon Campbell deliberately sought Don Pierce to ride California's 1979 candidate for the three-year-old classics, Flying Paster. An expert judge of pace and rugged finisher, Pierce excelled too at developing the raw speed of a young horse by controlling it with strong sensitive hands, rating it kindly, off the early lead if possible, and unleashing it powerfully when the moment arrives. Pierce was teaching as he rode.

Leading Sires—Money Won
January 1–December 31, 1983

Sire	Perf.	Win Perf.	Sts.	1st	2nd	3rd	Unp.	Purses
Halo	69	45	463	86	57	68	252	$2,773,637
Grey Dawn II	92	43	763	97	81	88	497	2,338,825
Targowice	10	7	65	13	8	6	38	2,255,774
Damascus	58	32	368	58	52	45	213	2,094,713
Vice Regent	86	50	703	97	109	85	412	2,052,218
Seattle Slew	25	14	120	31	16	11	62	2,049,715
Mr. Leader	127	74	1,116	161	140	124	691	2,037,833
Full Pocket	119	84	1,140	174	151	148	667	1,972,134
Naskra	117	65	1,050	113	136	143	658	1,952,019
Shecky Greene	116	77	1,012	178	163	127	544	1,940,261
Nodouble	115	67	1,096	141	129	107	719	1,914,795
Al Hattab	81	51	770	109	90	95	476	1,829,529
Tentam	80	48	693	105	99	86	403	1,809,083
His Majesty	48	26	427	77	57	60	233	1,798,682
Nijinsky II	54	30	330	58	49	28	195	1,792,989
Avatar	83	49	693	103	82	84	424	1,719,307
Icecapade	93	50	745	100	89	39	458	1,687,466
Mr. Prospector	86	44	565	89	72	73	331	1,636,646
What Luck	98	66	822	123	106	116	477	1,615,699
Raja Baba	104	60	782	105	108	101	468	1,565,892
Lyphard	38	19	254	41	27	25	161	1,537,533
Sir Ivor	52	27	363	50	50	51	212	1,488,044
Tri Jet	70	43	666	91	72	91	412	1,473,787
Explodent	83	49	720	108	96	78	438	1,470,657
Stop the Music	61	33	420	67	59	54	240	1,429,485
Windy Sands	83	43	725	79	110	85	451	1,415,999
In Reality	62	42	447	77	90	59	221	1,402,512
Ack Ack	76	45	678	82	72	80	444	1,402,351
Norcliffe	74	41	710	91	77	99	443	1,387,363
Exclusive Native	64	30	487	68	49	59	311	1,376,888
Hold Your Peace	97	58	967	106	129	115	617	1,370,248
Bold Forbes	66	36	569	83	79	70	337	1,359,485
Raise a Bid	124	80	1,395	183	173	156	883	1,348,346
Timeless Moment	61	33	467	73	66	60	268	1,346,084
Verbatim	88	46	707	90	68	76	473	1,335,439

Leading Sires—Money Won
January 1–December 31, 1984

Sire	Perf.	Win Perf.	Sts.	1st	2nd	3rd	Unp.	Purses
Seattle Slew	46	23	215	49	30	20	116	$5,361,259
Icecapade	101	60	973	143	125	121	584	4,035,986
Exclusive Native	72	38	553	88	69	74	322	3,219,115
Ole Bob Bowers	93	46	1,019	108	85	117	709	3,099,211
Mr. Prospector	74	52	561	114	75	68	304	2,669,231
Vice Regent	94	61	798	125	97	101	475	2,462,738
Mr. Leader	123	77	1,217	167	142	175	733	2,299,260
Verbatim	98	55	720	103	75	80	462	2,209,834
Naskra	122	79	1,213	159	152	150	752	2,181,580
Damascus	58	34	408	56	47	57	248	2,180,272
Danzig	12	10	73	22	10	15	26	2,146,530
Nodouble	136	76	1,169	149	127	152	741	2,105,573
In Reality	74	48	522	93	72	74	283	2,091,691
Nijinsky II	48	25	274	51	40	35	148	2,089,900
Alydar	42	21	222	42	34	25	121	2,085,001
Full Out	103	71	1,084	139	140	151	654	2,018,903
Raja Baba	101	63	863	127	119	110	507	2,002,680
Full Pocket	136	73	1,078	138	138	127	675	1,922,110
Shecky Greene	107	62	1,016	131	151	125	609	1,875,656
Chieftain	66	38	533	72	76	68	317	1,873,918
His Majesty	50	32	415	77	38	51	249	1,862,324
Tentam	77	51	822	124	122	117	459	1,855,297
Cox's Ridge	37	23	247	37	42	30	138	1,742,351
Cutlass	99	61	841	140	128	114	459	1,667,296
Sovereign Dancer	31	24	236	38	34	34	130	1,650,847
Majestic Light	56	40	414	79	52	52	231	1,629,890
Avatar	82	50	858	105	105	114	534	1,608,258
Hold Your Peace	97	57	959	116	109	96	638	1,593,923
Timeless Moment	63	35	537	75	81	62	319	1,551,165
Norcliffe	81	45	748	82	92	98	476	1,546,877
Valid Appeal	60	44	464	82	67	45	270	1,544,325
Bold Forbes	77	45	688	81	96	72	439	1,527,994
Forceten	46	33	444	91	59	77	217	1,527,013
Sauce Boat	78	52	751	100	101	107	443	1,522,842
Nalees Man	125	75	1,138	150	154	136	698	1,508,935

Sprinters

Some horses are bred to be sprinters, expected to run out of oxygen after traveling more than six or seven furlongs. Physically, such horses are blocky and quite muscular looking. The stallions listed below are known to be sires primarily of sprinters, horses with an abundance of speed and very little stamina:

Blade	Loom
Christopher R	Our Michael
Cutlass	Princely Native
Distinctive	Rollicking
Duck Dance	Shecky Greene
Full Pocket	Time Tested
Hard Work	Tumiga
Insubordination	What Luck
Kaskaskia	

Sprint types often are precocious, and usually do well as two-year-olds before the distances begin stretching out. They are likely candidates to win their racing debuts.

Routers

Other horses can't get going unil they have traveled half a mile or six furlongs. They prefer races over a distance of ground. For some, the longer the better. Physically, they tend to be longer and slimmer than the typical sprinter.

The following stallions tend to produce progeny with little speed and an abundance of stamina:

Big Spruce	London Company
Cougar II	One For All
Good Counsel	Proud Clarion
Grey Dawn	Run The Gantlet
High Echelon	Tom Rofle
Le Fabuleux	

Routers tend to develop more slowly than sprinters. Some come around toward the end of their juvenile season, others not until becoming three-year-olds. Smart handicappers give extra credence to such horses when they stretch out for the first time, especially if they had shown any signs of ability at shorter distances.

Slop Breeding

Certain horses race especially well over wet surfaces. At least they seem to endure such conditions better than most. It seems valid to conclude that the progeny of certain stallions inherit an aptitude for racing under adverse conditions. Particularly noteworthy are the following:

Bagdad	Key To The Mint
Bosun	King's Bishop
Cinteelo	Native Charger
Damascus	Proudest Roman
Graustark	Ridan
Grey Dawn	Spanish Riddle
Herbager	The Pruner
In Reality	Truxton King

HANDICAPPING BY THE CONDITIONS

Country Tune

Dk. b. or br. f. 3, by Bagdad—Loyal Ruler, by Gallant Man
Br.—Blue Seas Music Co (Ky)   1980 12 1 1 0 $8,974
Own.—Bacharach B   **117**   Tr.—Lambert George   1979   5 M 0 2 $2,264

30Dec80-8BM	1 :46³ 1:11² 1:39³sy	30 114	23 79½ 7¹⁶ 7¹⁶	Leonard J²	⑥Alw 55	PsychicPowr,MyviwLdy,Silky'sNurs 7
26Nov80-5BM	6f :22⁴ :46 1:11 ft	11 118	94¾ 42½ 2¹ 1¾	Leonard J⁸	⑥Mdn 85	CountryTune,Muffle,RngoonRosie 12
5Nov80-4BM	1¹⁄₁₆ :46³ 1:11⁴ 1:44 ft	24 117	21½ 2ʰᵈ 21½ 23½	Leonard J⁵	⑥Mdn 75	BerryBush,CountryTun,SpcilEvning 9
22Oct80-4BM	1¹⁄₁₆ :46² 1:11⁴ 1:44⁴ft	8 116	1ʰᵈ 5⁴ 56½ 67½	Marciel G⁶	⑥Mdn 67	SomeonDr.Propht'sProfit,BrryBush 8
20Oct80-4BM	1¹⁄₁₆ :45⁴ 1:10⁴ 1:43³ft	5½ 116	13 12 33 4⁷	Aragon J⁸	⑥Mdn 74	Retracking, Berry Bush, Devilishly 8
4Sep80-4BM	6f :22⁴ :45² 1:10²ft	7½ 116	68½ 7¹¹ 8¹² 8¹³	Aragon J⁹	⑥Mdn 75	WindyCityEnvoy,Rtrcking,Plsu⁻Er 12
2Aug80-3Bmf	1 :46 1:10³ 1:36⁴ft	24 110	2¹ 2½ 2⁴ 46½	Archuleta S¹	Mdn 79	Major Bill, Cholla, Dr. Monty M. 9
24Jly80-6Bmf	6f :23¹ :46¹ 1:10³ft	32 108⁵	43 46½ 5⁸ 5¹¹	Holtkamp W¹²	Mdn 76	Roper, Major Bill, Cholla 12
15Jun80-6Hol	7f :21⁴ :44² 1:22⁴ft	18 115	75 12¹³12¹²12¹²	ShoemkerW¹¹	⑥Mdn 73	LdyOffshor,Mstoctor,ApthcryMss 12
16Apr80-2Hol	1 :46¹ 1:11² 1:37³ft	51 117	63 10⁷¾10¹⁴10²²	Toro F⁵	⑥Mdn 56	PlentyO'Tool,RuthPitchr,WinknEy 10

Nov 21 BM 6f ft 1:16 h   Nov 15 BM 6f ft 1:14⁴ h

Handicappers at Bay Meadows November 26 did not much fancy composer Burt Bacharach's Bagdad filly, but let her victory that day remind us all to stand on alert when an older maiden shows a second-place finish last out. As a predictor of pending victory in races for older maidens, the second-place finish last time is one of handicapping's most powerful probability statistics. It wins approximately 275 percent times its fair share of the races for older maidens.

Having noticed the second-place finish November 5, handicappers might next have credited Country Tune's six-furlong time of the October 2 route. Clearly on the improve, the filly obviously appreciated the return to the sprint distance.

Regardless of its number of previous losses, if an older maiden has been picking it up lately, and finished second last out, handicappers had better pay strict attention to it. I've checked out this angle in southern California. It works. Not only that, the mutuels are sometimes generous, as at Bay Meadows November 26.

Although journeyman jockeys at major tracks can ride almost any horse in the stalls effectively, if a sharp-looking older maiden will be handled by a rider other than the types listed above, handicappers should beware. The maiden may be a runner, but apparently neither the stable nor the jockey agents realize it. In the absence of anticipated jockeys, handicappers should tighten all other guidelines, making certain the signs are favorable, especially the workout pattern.

The next guideline, extensively ignored, cuts predictable losses to the bone, especially when studying sprints.

5. In sprints, require an experienced runner to have earned a speed rating within three seconds of the track record for the distance (eighty-six or better); in routes, require a time within five seconds of the track record (seventy-six or better).

The time requirements remove two barriers to success. One, handicappers avoid slower horses, however close their recent finishes. Two, any first-time starter getting in an experienced horse's way will need to run above-average clockings to win. If speed requirements eliminate all experienced entrants, handicappers can concentrate more confidently on the credentials and connections of new starters. First-time starters may lose more than half their rightful quota of maiden races, but their chances improve to the extent they can get home first without a clock-busting performance.

Exceptions are maidens that have run within a tick or two of the preferred clockings, have demonstrated improved form, and last time out finished second or third while gaining ground in the stretch. So are maidens whose speed ratings, while slightly below preferred clockings, resulted after their involvement in fast early speed duels. If these horses figure to control the early pace, or contest a slower pace, handicappers can prefer them to first starters.

Glorious exceptions are maidens whose final times or pace ratings are simply better than the recorded Form ratings. Handicappers who calculate local par times for older maiden sprints and use these and daily variants to modify recorded times can expect to discover overlays in these races every month. A few lengths makes all the difference.

Par times are merely adjusted average times, sometimes referred to as standard times. To calculate reliable par times, select fifteen recent older maiden sprints. Eliminate the three fastest and two slowest final times. Average the remaining final times. Accept the figure as par for older maiden sprints. Subtract recorded final times to find sprint variants. Adjust final times by adding variants. Do the same for routes.

Handicappers who cannot bother with research or arithmetic can refer to a book that provides par times for all major tracks. *Winning at the Races: Computer Discoveries in Thoroughbred Handicapping,* by William Quirin, also provides explicit and simplified procedures for adjusting par times for one class-distance race to other class-distance races, including races for older maidens.

6. When analyzing maiden races on turf carded at middle distances, prefer horses whose breeding indicates a liking for the footing.

Turf races for older maidens have increased, and will continue to increase, as racing secretaries attempt to offer developing horses opportunities under conditions better allied to their peculiarities. Studies indicate maidens bred for grass will win more frequently on it than will maidens whose families have not so distinguished themselves. As identified by Quirin's probability studies, a number of sires transmit talent on the grass.

Here is a list (as of August 22, 1983) of the top ten grass sires. The criterion is a combination of wagering profitability and consistency from at least fifty starters.

Top Ten Turf Sires

1. Little Current	6. Advocator
2. Stage Door Johnny	7. Star Envoy
3. Exclusive Native	8. Roberto
4. One For All	9. Big Spruce
5. Tell	10. Ambernash

Other Leaders:

Nodouble	Forli
Verbatim	Our Native
Rock Talk	Minnesota Mac

Turf Sires Whose Horses Win More Than Their Share of Grass Races and Show Profit on a Series of $2 Bets

Prince John	T.V. Commercial	Grey Dawn II
Stage Door Johnny	Intentionally	Vent Du Nord
Verbatim	Dr. Fager	Le Fabuleux

Round Table	Mongo	Nijinsky II
Hoist the Flag	Sea-Bird	One For All
Chieftain	Bolero	(Princequillo Line)
Exclusive Native	Herbager	(Prince Rose Line)

Note: Horses by Sir Gaylord, Graustark, Tom Rolfe, and T.V. Lark win more than a fair share but do not show net profits.

Broodmare Sires Whose Horses Win More Than Their Share of Grass Races

Princequillo	Ribot	John's Joy
Prince John	Amerigo	T.V. Lark
Round Table	Intentionally	Mongo
Sir Gaylord	Bolero	

Suspected Turf Sires Whose Horses Do Not Win Enough or Pay Enough

Sir Ivor	Arts & Letters	Assagai
Drone	In Reality	Vaguely Noble
Ribot	Hawaii	John's Joy

Sometimes maidens are entered in turf races under nonwinner allowance conditions. In cheaper circumstances, maidens challenge previous winners in claiming routes on turf. The maidens should be accepted as contenders, subject to more intensive study. The stables probably hope to surprise by taking advantage of breeding for grass. In major racing, several stables frequently employ the tactic—and get away with it.

Who are the most promising young turf sires? They are Caro, Empery, Majestic Light, Top Command, Mississippian, His Majesty, Forceten, High Echelon, Champagne Charlie, Native Royalty, Unconscious, Cannonade, and London Company.

7. When comparing two or more maiden contenders that satisfy the standards of the form, jockey, breeding, speed, and footing factors, handicappers should prefer the horse that finished second last out.

The guideline puts the previously remarked second-place finish in context. Its function: to separate relatively equal contenders.

Though Davis's data did not represent the issues, reason suggests the second-place finish should accumulate added force if the race occurs (a) at the route, (b) during summer or fall, or (c) on a day the second-place entrant will benefit by a jockey switch from journeyman to leader.

Handicappers who conform play to these guidelines can expect to win approximately 40 percent of bets placed on older maidens. Profits run high.

To bolster the higher win percentage, handicappers should keep in mind the following concerning races for older maidens:

1. Open races draw distinctively better fields than do state-bred races—but not always.

Maidens lack class in a categorical sense, but representatives of the best families generally inherit more potential than do others. Unless the circuit runs in Kentucky or Florida, a maiden race limited to state-breds is likelier to fill with several entrants slower or of a quality less than that of horses produced by the prestigious breeding farms of those states.

Maidens moving from open events to the state-bred kind typically challenge less capable rivals. Handicappers possessing results charts can examine recent races to determine if today's sharp-looking specimen has been beaten off by a finely bred colt or two by Kentucky stallions.

Charts review also the possibly unwarranted assumption that an open race was better. State-breds win open events. Kentucky- and Florida-breds do not combine to monopolize thoroughbred class. Horses bred by E. P. Taylor of Canada or sired by stallions such as California's Gummo and Don B. always catch the smart handicapper's attention. Such maidens have inherited potential enough. They can shine in open events stocked with royal Kentucky lineage, and may stand out in state-bred contests.

2. Excuses due to "racing luck" often are more imagined than real.

Trouble can happen, or can be characteristic of horses. Handicappers hesitate to excuse older maidens their poor or unacceptable performances because of racing luck. As likely as not, the trouble has been self-induced or has resulted from incompetent or incomplete training and schooling. Those brands of trouble will likely be repeated. Gate problems or trouble on turns are particularly repetitive.

Exceptions are otherwise-impressive maidens that have broken slowly (not badly—slowly) or started slowly and will now wear blinkers. So are horses in trouble that clearly has resulted from interference by other horses or jockeys.

3. Certain ranking stables are not so interested in winning maiden purses with first-time starters.

Big bettors in southern California consider it elementary that Charles Whittingham's royally bred maidens are not aimed at small purses. Whittingham's youngsters may win these events (they certainly have the ability), but they merely are allowed to win, just as they are allowed to lose.

Rather than risk the development of fine young thoroughbreds by all-out gunnings for maiden shares, Whittingham prefers the horses' early races improve their running styles, teach responsiveness to the rider, and provide evidence of distance and pace preferences, equipment needs, and willingness to keep at it when tiring. To help horses learn and adapt, they are permitted to lose, often at miserly odds.

The same is true of David Whiteley's stable in New York, and presumably, probably to less extent, of stables on every circuit. It pays handicappers to find out which stables move carefully with maidens.

4. Signs of deterioration in the form of older maidens should be accepted at face value.

Cycles of deterioration among three-year-olds may not be so pronounced as among juveniles, but the deteriorating form of older maidens is bad news. No rapid improvement should be predicted. Handicappers should not be misled by the conventional jockey switch or equipment change. The problem probably is more basic.

Not much more is pertinent to races for older maidens. These guidelines get the work done admirably. Class is immaterial. The distance factor, always fundamental, is less decisive among maidens. Since lightly raced horses and new starters are standard fare, probable pace becomes problematic, and pace ratings unreliable, yet analysis of the probable early pace remains a slice of the handicapping regimen every time.

As an interesting illustration, practically prototypical, of the problems handicappers encounter routinely in analyzing fields of older maidens, examine the records of the horses entered in a middle-distance event run at Santa Anita, February 24, 1985.

Handicappers can first find the three five-year-olds and eliminate them from further observation. Five-year-old maidens are not likely to change their status on any given day.

The lightly raced Commander's Song would deserve more atten-

3rd Santa Anita

1⅛ MILES
SANTA ANITA
▲START ▲FINISH

1 ⅛ MILES. (1.45⅘) MAIDEN. Purse $23,000 4-year-olds and upward. Weights 4-year-olds, 117 lbs.; older, 118 lbs. (Non-starters for a claiming price of $32,000 or less preferred.)

Reserve

Own.—Keck H B Jr **117**

Dk. b. or br. c. 4, by Buckfinder—Irish Mail, by Double Jay
Br.—Keck H B (Ky) **1985 4 M 0 3 $10,300**
Tr.—Whittingham Charles **1984 3 M 1 0 $6,200**
Lifetime 7 0 1 3 $16,500

11Feb85-6SA	1⅛	:46^2	1:11	1:50^{1}ft	4	119	6^8	5$^{4\frac12}$	4$^{2\frac12}$	3$^{3\frac14}$	Pincay L Jr^2	Mdn	75-15	Fiscal Win, SpruceHarbor,Reserve	12
30Jan85-6SA	1 1/16	:46^3	1:11^1	1:44^{4}ft	2¾	117	6$^{5\frac34}$	4$^{5\frac12}$	4^6	5^5	McCarron C J^7	Mdn	72-17	UndrAStr,VctorosRlr,NotNcssrlyS	12
16Jan85-6SA	1 1/16	:47^1	1:11^4	1:45^{1}ft	*8-5	117	9^8	6$^{7\frac12}$	4$^{4\frac12}$	3$^{4\frac34}$	Pincay L Jr^3	Mdn	70-20	Ridgeline, Adolfo, Reserve	12
16Jan85—Pinched back, steadied at 7 1/2															
4Jan85-6SA	1 1/16	:46^4	1:11^3	1:45^{1}ft	*4-5	117	5^4	6^5	3^2	3^{nk}	Pincay L Jr^2	Mdn	75-17	Fitzallen, Bestom, Reserve	9
4Jan85—Wide; lugged in badly stretch															
8Dec84-1Hol	1	:46^2	1:12	1:38^{1}sy	3	119	2^1	2$^{\frac12}$	2$^{1\frac12}$	2^2	McCarron C J^2	Mdn	82-10	Cloud Strider, Reserve, Fitzallen	7
8Dec84—Lugged in stretch															
28Nov84-4Hol	1	:46	1:10^2	1:37^{3}ft	2	119	4^5	4$^{6\frac12}$	4$^{5\frac12}$	4$^{5\frac12}$	McCarron C J^4	Mdn	81-05	Traffic Island, Nicholai, Fitzallen	7
18Nov84-2Hol	1	:46^4	1:12^1	1:37^{3}ft	*9-5	114^5	6$^{4\frac12}$	6^{12}	6^{10}	5$^{11\frac34}$	Lozoya D A^8	Mdn	— —	MilanoJunction,TrafficIslnd,Nicholi	8

Feb 20 Hol 5f ft 1:00^2 h **Feb 8 SA 5f ft :59^4 h** **Jan 27 SA 5f ft :59^3 h** **Jan 22 SA 3f ft :38 h**

Spruce Harbor

Own.—Cayer J J (Lessee) **117**

Dk. b. or br. c. 4, by Big Spruce—Oak Harbor, by Polly's Jet
Br.—Braun A & Marjorie (Cal) **1985 1 M 1 0 $4,600**
Tr.—Anderson Laurie N **1984 2 M 0 0**
Lifetime 3 0 1 0 $4,600

11Feb85-6SA	1⅛	:46^2	1:11	1:50^{1}ft	34	119	2$^{\frac12}$	2^{hd}	1$^{\frac12}$	2^3	Hawley S^1	Mdn	75-15	Fiscal Win, SpruceHarbor,Reserve	12
11Feb85—Rank to place, bumped in early stages															
18Mar84-6SA	1 1/16	:46	1:11	1:44^{4}ft	49	118	9^{12}	9^{11}	9^{11}	9^{12}	Lipham T^9	Mdn	65-18	Bean Bag, ParkRow,You'reMyLove	9
4Mar84-2SA	1 1/16	:47^1	1:12^2	1:45 ft	35	118	12^{12}	12$^{9\frac12}$	9$^{8\frac34}$	9$^{11\frac12}$	Meza R Q^4	Mdn	64-17	CoopersHill,Reptrit,LionOfThDsrt	12
4Mar84—Bobbled start, checked at 5/16															

Feb 20 SA 5f ft 1:01^2 h **●Feb 4 SA 1 ft 1:42 h** **Jan 28 SA 4f ft :48^4 hg** **Jan 18 SA 1 ft 1:46^3 h**

Bestom

Own.—Priestley P A **113^5**

B. h. 5, by R Tom Can—Our Best Girl, by Pluck
Br.—Priestley P A (Cal) **1985 2 M 1 0 $4,725**
Tr.—Sena Peter E **1984 1 M 0 0 $1,050**
Lifetime 16 0 2 0 $11,115

16Jan85-6SA	1 1/16	:47^1	1:11^4	1:45^{1}ft	9¾	113^5	4$^{2\frac12}$	5$^{7\frac12}$	5$^{5\frac12}$	5$^{6\frac12}$	Lozoya D A^5	Mdn	68-20	Ridgeline, Adolfo, Reserve	12
16Jan85—Lugged in 7 1/2, checked at 3/8															
4Jan85-6SA	1 1/16	:46^4	1:11^3	1:45^{1}ft	54	118	1$^{\frac12}$	1$^{\frac12}$	1$^{\frac12}$	2^{hd}	Cruz J B^8	Mdn	75-17	Fitzallen, Bestom, Reserve	9
4Jan85—Bumped late															
14Dec84-1Hol	7f	:22^3	:46	1:24^{3}ft	64	122	1^{hd}	1^{hd}	1^{hd}	4$^{5\frac14}$	Cruz J B^6	M32000	79-08	MestroMio,VictoriousRuler,Divldo	12
20Aug83-4Dmr	6f	:22^2	:45^4	1:09^{4}ft	69	117	6^8	6$^{8\frac12}$	6^{12}	5$^{13\frac14}$	Olivares F^3	Mdn	76-20	Trento,Nighthawker,RondsDeJmbe	8
7Aug83-6Dmr	1 1/16	:46^1	1:10^3	1:44^{1}ft	93	116	12^{18}	10^{16}	10^{11}	9^{12}	Ortega L E^4	Mdn	67-18	SwpTheGlss,BeldleFleet,CountySt	12
18Jun83-4GG	1 1/16	:47	1:11	1:43^{4}ft	15	113	1^{hd}	2^1	4^4	4$^{7\frac12}$	Gonzalez R M^2	Mdn	76-13	BrzenSpy,GenerlDynmo,RpidRogue	8
4Jun83-4GG	1 1/16	:47^3	1:12	1:45 ft	10	114	2^1	6^6	4^9	6$^{9\frac12}$	Ramirez O^4	Mdn	68-19	CristlDeLune,EsyMover,GnrlDynmo	7
13May83-6Hol	1 1/16	:49	1:14^1	1:47^{3}ft	39	115	1^1	1^{hd}	1$^{\frac12}$	2^{hd}	ValenzuelaPA^8	M40000	57-30	ChnsonDeGeste,Bestom,HllumLke	11
5May83-2Hol	6f	:22^3	:46^2	1:12^{2}ft	11	110^5	11^{11}	11^{15}	9^{12}	8$^{8\frac34}$	HersheyRWJr^3	M32000	66-27	SmokeyCnyon,RedyGlory,Esclting	12
22Apr83-1SA	6f	:22	:45^1	1:10^{3}ft	54	113^5	4^3	3^5	3$^{5\frac12}$	4$^{5\frac14}$	HrshyRWJr^6	[S]M40000	80-20	LuckyBuddy,CallEddie,BostonMgic	8

Feb 19 SA 6f ft 1:13^3 h **Feb 13 Hol 6f ft 1:18^2 h** **Jan 14 SA 3f ft :35^4 h**

Cineamoblia

Own.—Fluor Est-Port-Taylor **112**

Ch. f. 4, by Stage Door Johnny—Fashion Verdict, by Court Martial
Br.—Welcome Farm (Pa) **1985 0 M 0 0**
Tr.—Gosden John H M **1984 0 M 0 0**
Lifetime 0 0 0 0

Feb 21 SA 4f ft :48^3 hg **Feb 14 SA 1 ft 1:39^3 h** **Feb 8 SA 7f ft 1:26^2 h** **Feb 3 SA 6f ft 1:16^4 h**

Nicholai

Own.—King Fran A **113^5**

Dk. b. or br. g. 5, by Golden Eagle II—Nacht Wind, by Crazy Kid
Br.—Kraai Mrs J (Cal) **1984 9 M 1 1 $7,375**
Tr.—King Fran A **1983 0 M 0 0**
Lifetime 9 0 1 1 $7,375

8Dec84-1Hol	1	:46^2	1:12	1:38^{1}sy	*3-2	117^5	6$^{3\frac34}$	6^7	6$^{9\frac12}$	6$^{12\frac34}$	Dominguez R L^4	Mdn	71-10	Cloud Strider, Reserve, Fitzallen	7
28Nov84-4Hol	1	:46	1:10^2	1:37^{3}ft	13	117^5	1^1	1^2	1^1	2^1	Dominguez R L^2	Mdn	86-05	Traffic Island, Nicholai, Fitzallen	7
18Nov84-2Hol	1	:46^4	1:12^1	1:37^{3}ft	26	117^5	1$^{\frac12}$	2^{hd}	3^1	3$^{3\frac34}$	Dominguez R L^1	Mdn	— —	MilanoJunction,TrafficIslnd,Nicholi	8
30Oct84-3SA	6½f	:22	:45^2	1:18^{4}ft	57	116^5	9^7	10$^{8\frac14}$	7$^{6\frac34}$	5$^{3\frac34}$	DomnguzRL^8	[S]M40000	72-18	CozyCorner,Chariot,KeepCharging	12
30Oct84—Broke slowly															
3Sep84-4Dmr	6f	:22^4	:46	1:11 ft	63	122	4$^{1\frac34}$	6$^{1\frac14}$	6^{10}	6$^{10\frac34}$	Lambert J^{10}	M50000	72-18	NordicSong,BestLedr,Spiritulistic	10
28Jly84-4Dmr	6f	:22^4	:46^1	1:10^{1}ft	62	122	5$^{3\frac14}$	5$^{6\frac12}$	7^{13}	8$^{19\frac12}$	Lamance C^3	Mdn	67-16	Nitro, Best Leader, Stickette	8
19May84-6GG	6f	:22^2	:45^1	1:10^{2}ft	89	122	11$^{9\frac34}$	9^{12}	10^{15}	10^{14}	Lamance C^{11}	Mdn	73-14	CaptainCrozier,Bovig,PetesInnate	12
27Apr84-4GG	6f	:22^2	:45^2	1:09^{2}ft	19	119	5$^{6\frac12}$	6^{11}	6^9	7$^{21\frac12}$	Lamance C^3	Mdn	70-19	SirClaudius,NtiveEnvoy,YYGooGoo	9
13Apr84-5GG	6f	:22^2	:45^2	1:10 ft	29	119	10^{10}	10^{13}	10^{14}	7$^{13\frac14}$	Lamance C^8	Mdn	76-15	ClssicSecretry,ShweHl,HedMyHls	12
13Apr84—Broke in a tangle															

Feb 18 SLR tr.t 1 ft 1:41 h **Feb 13 SLR tr.t 1 ft 1:41 h** **Jan 28 SLR tr.t 7f ft 1:28^3 h** **●Jan 23 SLR tr.t 6f ft 1:16^1 h**

Lion Of The Desert

Ch. c. 4, by Alydar—Azeez, by Nashua
Br.—Jones W L Jr (Ky) 1985 2 M 0 0 $3,225
Own.—Universal Stable 117 **Tr.—Lukas D Wayne** 1984 8 M 3 2 $17,825
Lifetime 10 0 3 2 $21,050 **Turf** 1 0 0 0

17Feb85-3SA 6f :22 :444 1:094ft 5½ 117 21 35 36½ 48¼ Delahoussaye E7 Mdn 81-13 Spotter Bay, Count Geiger, Kinetic 8
31Jan85-6SA 6f :212 :442 1:094ft *9-5 117 42½ 44½ 45½ 47¼ Valenzuela P A6 Mdn 82-15 Sun Master, Billikin, Kinetic 10
31Jan85—Lugged in stretch
20May84-1Hol 6f :222 :452 1:102ft 4 115 2½ 1½ 31 87¼ Meza R Q1 Mdn 78-17 Melodisk,QuackQuackQuck,Billikin 8
20May84—Veered out, bumped start
29Apr84-6Hol 6½f :214 :444 1:163ft 2½ 117 98¼ 78½ 53½ 56¼ Pincay L Jr5 Mdn 81-15 WshIhdMlln,Ddlsck,Agnstthngdm 11
11Apr84-8SA a6½f Ⓣ:211 :4331:142fm 21e 116 75¾119¾1013 89 Toro F8 Baldwin 78-17 DbonrJnor,FrtntPrspct,DstntRydr 11
31Mar84-3SA 6f :22 :452 1:11 ft 4 118 44 43 22 2¾ Valenzuela P A2 Mdn 82-18 RunningDgr,LionOfThDsrt,BndnRd 9
4Mar84-2SA 1$\frac{1}{16}$:471 1:122 1:45 ft 3½ 118 1½ 1hd 1hd 31¾ Pincay L Jr2 Mdn 74-17 CoopersHill,Reptrit,LionOfThDsrt 12
4Mar84—Veered out, bumped after start
19Feb84-2SA 1$\frac{1}{16}$:463 1:113 1:441ft 3¾ 118 2½ 1½ 2hd 35½ Pincay L Jr6 Mdn 74-14 WoodlndWy,OcnViw,LionOfThDsrt 9
28Jan84-2SA 6f :213 :444 1:091ft *3-5 118 21 33 26 29½ Pincay L Jr8 Mdn 82-12 NobleFury,LionOfTheDesrt,T.H.Ang 8
14Jan84-2SA 6f :213 :451 1:113ft *3-2 118 23½ 23½ 21½ 2hd Lipham T3 Mdn 80-19 Artificer,LionOfTheDesert,Ridglin 11
14Jan84—Bumped in stretch
Feb 12 SA 5f ft 1:001 h Feb 6 SA 5f ft :594 h Jan 24 SA 5f ft :593 h Jan 15 SA 5f ft 1:003 h

Commander's Song

Ch. g. 4, by Dust Commander—Char Song, by Charlie's Song
Br.—Hunt N B (Ky) 1985 2 M 0 0 $575
Own.—Summa Stable (Lessee) 117 **Tr.—Scott George** 1984 3 M 1 0 $4,225
Lifetime 5 0 1 0 $4,800

11Feb85-6SA 1⅛ :462 1:11 1:501ft 12 119 1012 88¼ 64½ 54 Stevens G L7 Mdn 74-15 Fiscal Win, SpruceHarbor,Reserve 12
11Feb85—Bobbled at start
31Jan85-6SA 6f :212 :442 1:094ft 15 117 79¾ 811 710 68½ Stevens G L3 Mdn 80-15 Sun Master, Billikin, Kinetic 10
31Jan85—Lugged in backside
22Dec84-3Hol 6f :223 :462 1:121gd 36 120 89¾ 55¼ 44 22½ Stevens G L2 M32000 86-10 Bldewise,Commndr'sSong,TopSdd 12
22Mar84-6SA 6f :214 :444 1:10 ft 5½ 118 89¾ 913 812 713½ Hawley S9 M50000 74-18 BenRedeemed,BargingAhed,Lothr 11
25Feb84-2SA 6½f :214 :444 1:163ft 8 118 86¼ 77¼ 57½ 410¾ Toro F4 Mdn 76-18 Blips, Repatriate, T. H. Ange 9
●Jan 26 SLR tr.t 4f ft :48 h Jan 20 SLR tr.t 5f ft 1:03 h ●Jan 10 SLR tr.t 5f ft 1:012 h Dec 31 SLR tr.t 4f ft :50 h

*King Kutati

B. g. 5, by Kutati—Summer Brocade, by Summer Magic
Br.—Canning D G (NZ) 1985 3 M 0 0 $525
Own.—Canning Joan (Lessee) 118 **Tr.—Whittingham Michael** 1984 3 M 0 0 $500
Lifetime 6 0 0 0 $1,025 **Turf** 1 0 0 0

30Jan85-5SA 1¼Ⓣ:47 1:3612:01 fm 139 115 1220121812251228½ McGurn C8 Aw26000 53-16 VieuxBoucu,FlyingGene,CrroPinto 12
30Jan85—Dwelt at start
16Jan85-6SA 1$\frac{1}{16}$:471 1:114 1:451ft 34 118 118¼11101010 88 McGurn C2 Mdn 67-20 Ridgeline, Adolfo, Reserve 12
4Jan85-6SA 1$\frac{1}{16}$:464 1:113 1:451ft 36 118 914 912 66½ 53 McGurn C9 Mdn 72-17 Fitzallen, Bestom, Reserve 9
8Dec84-1Hol 1 :462 1:12 1:381sy 18 122 74¾ 713 718 719¼ McGurn C5 Mdn 65-10 Cloud Strider, Reserve. Fitzallen 7
8Dec84—Wide 3/8 turn
28Nov84-4Hol 1 :46 1:102 1:373ft 55 122 79 69½ 69 56½ McGurn C6 Mdn 80-05 Traffic Island, Nicholai, Fitzallen 7
12Nov84-4Hol 7f :22 :45 1:231ft 25 122 715 719 617 620¾ Olivares F7 Mdn — — Sticktt,CloudStridr,CommndingViw 7
Feb 18 SA 6f ft 1:14 h Feb 12 SA 5f ft 1:003 h Feb 6 SA 3f ft :352 h Jan 11 SA 5f ft 1:01 h

So Big Much

B. c. 4, by Lt Stevens—Brazen Witch, by Boldnesian
Br.—Bluegrass Farms (Ky) 1985 4 M 0 0
Own.—Suisun Stable Inc 117 **Tr.—Lassiter Harlee W** 1984 0 M 0 0
Lifetime 4 0 0 0

11Feb85-6SA 1⅛ :462 1:11 1:501ft 33 119 11131011 86 65¾ Olivares F11 Mdn 72-15 Fiscal Win, SpruceHarbor,Reserve 12
30Jan85-6SA 1$\frac{1}{16}$:463 1:111 1:444ft 34 117 129½ 98 68 66 Olivares F2 Mdn 71-17 UndrAStr,VctorosRlr,NotNcssrlyS 12
16Jan85-6SA 1$\frac{1}{16}$:471 1:114 1:451ft 38 117 108¼1212 88¾ 66¾ McHargue D G1 Mdn 68-20 Ridgeline, Adolfo, Reserve 12
4Jan85-6SA 1$\frac{1}{16}$:464 1:113 1:451ft 49 117 77½ 89½ 77 65 McHargue D G6 Mdn 70-17 Fitzallen, Bestom, Reserve 9
Feb 21 SA 3f ft :362 h Feb 8 SA 5f ft 1:02 h Jan 28 SA tr.t 4f ft :492 h Jan 23 SA 5f ft 1:013 h

Morse

Dk. b. or br. g. 4, by Star Spangled—Little Moby, by Ballymore
Br.—Humphrey Jr & Farish III (Ky) 1985 1 M 0 0 $1,725
Own.—Proctor W L 117 **Tr.—Johnson Patricia L** 1984 6 M 1 1 $5,900
Lifetime 9 0 2 1 $10,575

11Feb85-6SA 1⅛ :462 1:11 1:501ft *3½e 119 1214 99¼ 52½ 43¼ Steiner J J6 Mdn 75-15 Fiscal Win, SpruceHarbor,Reserve 12
16Nov84-4Hol 1⅛ :483 1:141 1:524ft 3½ 120 910 88 44½ 23 Steiner J J9 M32000 — — RaiseALegend,Morse,Conservatism 9
31Oct84-2SA 1$\frac{1}{16}$:463 1:112 1:444ft 24 117 913 912 56 31½ Steiner J J10 M32000 75-19 TriscaDecc,VictoriousRuler,Morse 11
31Oct84—Steadied at 5/16
19Oct84-2SA 6½f :214 :45 1:171ft 14 118 12121114 912 57¾ Steiner J J6 M32000 76-17 NordicSils,Bldewise.BecuseIt'sTru 12
19Oct84—Bobbled start
8Oct84-4SA 6½f :221 :452 1:18 ft 23 118 86 710 55½ 53 Steiner J J4 M32000 77-16 ContnulChng,BcusIt'sTr,VctorosRlr 8
10Sep84-4Dmr 1$\frac{1}{16}$:471 1:113 1:442ft 9½ 117 75 86½1012 1012¾ DelhoussyeE11 M32000 65-18 Sibilate, Easy Easy, Cum On East 12
20Aug84-6Dmr 6f :222 :454 1:103ft 20 116 911 812 89 78½ DelahoussyeE2 M45000 76-17 Apoplxy,BusnssSchool,NordcSong 10
6Nov83-2SA 6f :223 :462 1:121ft 3½e 118 65¾ 55 36 24½ Steiner J J4 M32000 72-18 Bold Batter Up.Morse,EssentialJoe 7
6Nov83—Bumped after start
26Oct83-4SA 6f :214 :453 1:114ft 62 116 101910171014 57 Steiner J J1 M35000 72-20 LuckyJohnD.,NclrAttck,SmmrPrv 10
26Oct83—Broke slowly, wide
Feb 22 SA 4f ft :50 h Feb 5 SA 1 ft 1:413 h Jan 30 SA 6f ft 1:142 h Jan 8 SA 5f gd 1:013 h

Billikin

Ch. c. 4, by Vice Regent—Alibi IV, by Birkhahn

Br.—Taylor E P (Ont-C)

Own.—Longden & Carr Stables   117

Tr.—Longden John

									1985	2 M	1	0	$4,200
									1984	14 M	3	2	$20,910
				Lifetime	20	0	4	3	$38,855				

17Feb85-3SA	6f :22 :44⁴ 1:09⁴ft	4 117	8¹⁴ 8¹⁴ 7¹² 6¹⁰	Shoemaker W²	Mdn 79-13 Spotter Bay, Count Geiger, Kinetic 8
31Jan85-6SA	6f :21² :44² 1:09⁴ft	7½ 117	8¹¹ 6¹⁰ 5⁷ 2³	Shoemaker W¹	Mdn 86-15 Sun Master, Billikin, Kinetic 10
2Nov84-6SA	6f :21⁴ :44⁴ 1:10 ft	20 119	9¹⁴ 7¹⁴ 7¹⁴ 6¹⁰	Steiner J J⁹	Mdn 78-17 ChmponPlot,SpottrBy,MlnoJncton 9
23Sep84-18M	1½ :47¹ 1:12 1:43²ft	*4-5 115	4³ 3²½ 4²½ 4³½	Diaz A L⁵	Mdn 71-18 Post Flag, Bru Ha Ha, Hapslappy 7
23Sep84—Broke in a tangle					
1Sep84-9Lga	1 :46¹ 1:10⁴ 1:35⁴ft	3½ 114	6⁵½ 7⁵½ 7⁹½ 7³½	Frazier B²	Aw9700 86-12 Knight Skiing,WithSpirit,FleetJoey 7
12Aug84-9Lga	1½ :47 1:11 1:56²ft	50 126	8¹² 8⁷½10¹⁶ 9⁹	Frazier B⁹	Lga Dby 79-25 OfficeSeeker,BbyCnil,ColonlStvns 10
12Aug84—Grade III					
29Jly84-2Lga	6½f :22² :45⁴ 1:17 ft	*2½ 120	4⁵ 3³ 3³ 2¹½	Frazier B²	Mdn 82-17 Holme Run Kid, Billikin, YeslerMill 7
29Jly84—Bobbled at start					
24Jun84-2Lga	6½f :22 :45¹ 1:16⁴ft	*2 120	9⁰¹ 6⁸¼ 4⁸ 4³½	Stevens G L⁷	Mdn 81-19 Morgantar, Old Harp, Yesler Mill 10
20May84-1Hol	6f :22² :45² 1:10²ft	9 115	8⁵ 6⁷ 5⁴ 3²½	Olivares F⁶	Mdn 83-17 Melodisk,QuackQuackQuck,Billikin 8
15Apr84-6SA	1½ :47¹ 1:11⁴ 1:43³ft	3½ 118	42½ 42 22½ 22½	Pincay L Jr⁵	Mdn 80-15 Bronzed Billikin, Tribal King 7
Feb 23 SA 3f ft :37 h		Feb 13 SA 6f ft 1:13⁴ h		Feb 7 SA 5f ft :59⁴ h	Jan 28 SA 6f ft 1:12 h

tion if the gelding had continued its late run February 11 and finished second or third. But it did not; flattened.

Lion of the Desert, the Alydar colt trained by D. Wayne Lukas, is the kind that fools large parts of the crowd all the time. With good early speed and apparently high earnings, the colt is consistently competitive in maiden races but is a sucker horse tried and true. Zero for ten, it has already finished second three times, third twice. This is not the type of second-place finish cited by the Davis research. Lion of the Desert went favored in this race, and lost again.

The contention is reduced readily to Reserve and Spruce Harbor.

Reserve looks vaguely familiar to Lion of the Desert after seven starts. It has flopped three times when favored. That third-place finish February 11 is more likely to set up its backers for another pratfall, as opposed to foreshadowing victory today.

Now look at Spruce Harbor. Lightly raced, from a solid stable, this colt showed tremendous improvement its first race at four, finishing a telltale second after pressing the pace for the first three calls. It was 34 to 1 that day and was rank early, according to its trouble line in the past peformances.

This is exactly the kind of second-place finish handicappers prefer. The kind that represent sudden or dramatic improvement. Spruce Harbor figures to improve next out, and statistics persuade us the improvement is often enough to win. If the price is fair, handicappers have found a likely winner in a race for older maidens. The results chart describes the tons of trouble Spruce Harbor experienced February 24, but the colt regrouped in the stretch and won nonetheless. Winners of this sort are commonplace at all tracks during the first three months of the year especially.

Before proceeding to the next section, which deals interestingly and optimistically with the cheapest, slowest racehorses of all,

THIRD RACE
Santa Anita
FEBRUARY 24, 1985

1 ⅛ MILES. (1.45⅘) MAIDEN. Purse $23,000. 4-year-olds and upward. Weights, 4-year-olds, 117 lbs.; older, 118 lbs. (Non-starters for a claiming price of $32,000 or less preferred.)

Value of race $23,000; value to winner $12,650; second $4,600; third $3,450; fourth $1,725; fifth $575. Mutuel pool $622,909.

Last Raced	Horse	Eqt.A.Wt	PP	St	¼	½	¾	Str	Fin	Jockey	Odds $1
11Feb85 6SA2	Spruce Harbor	b 4 117	2	2	3hd	42	41	51½	12	Hawley S	3.00
17Feb85 3SA4	Lion Of The Desert	4 117	5	5	43½	3½	31	21	2no	Valenzuela P A	2.90
16Jan85 6SA5	Bestom	5 113	3	1	1hd	1hd	1hd	11	3no	Lozoya D A5	22.60
11Feb85 6SA3	Reserve	b 4 117	1	4	7½	83	7hd	4hd	41½	Pincay L Jr	4.10
11Feb85 6SA4	Morse	4 117	8	7	83	7½	86	8	51½	Steiner J J	9.90
11Feb85 6SA5	Commander's Song	4 117	6	6	5hd	64	63	71½	6nk	Stevens G L	8.10
17Feb85 3SA6	Billikin	b 4 117	9	8	62½	52½	52½	6hd	72½	Shoemaker W	4.70
8Dec84 1Hol6	Nicholai	b 5 113	4	3	21½	21½	2½	3½	8	Dominguez R L5	20.90
30Jan85 5SA12	King Kutati	b 5 118	7	9	9	9	9	—	—	McGurn C	47.60

King Kutati, Eased.

OFF AT 2:15. Start good for all but KING KUTATI. Won driving. Time, :23⅖, :47, 1:11⅖, 1:37⅖, 1:51 Track fast.

$2 Mutuel Prices:				
2-SPRUCE HARBOR		8.00	4.20	3.40
5-LION OF THE DESERT			4.80	4.00
3-BESTOM				8.60

Blk. b. or br. c, by Big Spruce—Oak Harbor, by Polly's Jet. Trainer Anderson Laurie N. Bred by Braum A & Marjorie (Cal).

SPRUCE HARBOR broke alertly, lost his action when forced to take up sharply at the clubhouse turn, remained unhurried near the rail for seven furlongs, swung outside the leaders in the upper stretch, closed strongly to gain command and drew clear in the final sixteenth. LION OF THE DESERT, in contention outside the early leaders, bid for the lead entering the stretch but could not finish with the winner. BESTOM set or forced the early pace outside NICHOLAI and lacked the needed response when set down in the drive. RESERVE saved ground around the 'inal turn, rallied between horses in the last furlong and finished strongly. BILLIKIN rallied outside horses leaving the backstretch but flattened out in the stretch. NICHOLAI tired quickly in the final furlong. KING KUTATI dwelt at the start, was away far behind his field and was eased when hopelessly beaten in the final furlong.

Owners— 1, Cayer J J (Lessee); 2, Universal Stable; 3, Priestley P A; 4, Keck H B Jr; 5, Proctor W L; 6, Summa Stable (Lessee); 7, Longden & Carr Stables; 8, King Fran A; 9, Canning Joan (Lessee).

Trainers— 1, Anderson Laurie N; 2, Lukas D Wayne; 3, Sena Peter E; 4, Whittingham Charles; 5, Johnson Patricia L; 6, Scott George; 7, Longden John; 8, King Fran A; 9, Whittingham Michael.

Scratched—Cineamoblia; So Big Much (11Feb85 6SA6).

handicappers benefit by relating the performance profiles described below to the sample race provided.

In descending order of preference, here are the suitable past performance profiles among older maidens:

1. Any lightly raced three-year-old that finished second last time out while earning a satisfactory speed rating.

2. A three-year-old that finished second or third last out, has been showing improved form, and has run the distance within two or three lengths of satisfactory time requirements.

3. A sharp-working three-year-old from a decent stable, bred to show early speed.

In the absence of the above profiles, prefer:

4. A lightly raced four-year-old from a leading stable that finished second last time.

5. Any entrant that finished second last out, provided it has run within four seconds of the local distance record.

In all cases handicappers should not forgive the absence of regular works or suitable jockeys. Improved workouts following a second- or third-place finish deserve extra credit.

MAIDEN CLAIMING RACES

All introductory handicapping texts urge players to avoid maiden claiming races. Nonwinners entered under selling conditions have been convincingly documented as the slowest, cheapest, most inconsistent in the barns. Advising handicappers to choose the least slow among a herd of goats is thought a fool's play. So beginners receive advice to pass, and rightly so.

Yet experienced handicappers can regard maiden claiming competition as racing's bargain basement. Uncompromising consistency of approach beats these slow races and shows substantial seasonal profits while doing so. The approach I have in mind has registered profits on the southern California circuit for five years. During summer 1974 the approach worked well at a minor track, Longacres, near Seattle. The approach works, and it is simple.

The key to success with maiden claiming horses is to suspend classical handicapping procedures. Analyzing maiden claiming events hardly qualifies as handicapping. In practice, the recommended method can be likened to playing a system. It allots little space for analysis or judgment. Handicappers mechanically apply trusty rules. Three guidelines then separate eligible contenders. Patience helps tremendously.

Two rules, negative, guide the critical work at a glance:

1. Eliminate any horse that has lost a maiden claiming race.

2. Eliminate first-time starters.

The two rules eliminate entire fields. So be it. Farewell to the losers.

Horses that have lost under maiden claiming conditions remain unacceptably poor risks for handicappers. No improvement is predictable, nor should it ever be expected.

The conventional excuses do not apply. The colt finished third after taking up at the gate. Handicappers should presume the colt will take up at the gate again. Self-defeating habits characterize maiden claimers. The bad habits are repeated. Exceptions do not alter the situation sufficiently.

First-time starters fool many handicappers in maiden claiming circumstances. These often work out impressively and go postward decidedly favored. The horses sometimes win as underlays, but ordinarily they lose. Young thoroughbreds that show management they can run rarely are offered for sale until their true quality has been understood. Several may be potential stakes winners. One may become a champion. Why would anyone offer horses of potential for sale cheaply? That would be bad economics. Worse, it could become embarrassing to owners.

So handicappers achieve advantage with maiden claiming races by inverting standard practices. The more impressively first-timers have been working out, the faster handicappers should eliminate them. The better their stables, the more likely the horses are wash-outs. If its debut finds a maiden claiming horse mounted by a leading jockey and prepared by a leading trainer, throw the animal out. If the horse has fashionable breeding, forget it.

Turn conventional wisdom upside down. In that way, handicappers take charge of maiden claiming races.

Thinking positively, handicappers can accept as contenders horses moving from open maiden races and satisfying three guidelines.

1. Have raced within three weeks and have worked out since, or have raced within six weeks and have worked out regularly and sharply.

2. Race with a front-running or pace-pressing style, or race in the middle of the pack and have earned a pace rating at least six points higher than any other entrant.

3. In their latest two races at the distance, have earned one of the two top speed ratings in the field.

If a single horse qualifies and will benefit from a jockey switch or equipment change, award extra credit.

If more than one horse qualifies, pass the race, unless one has earned superior speed or pace ratings and figures to like the probable early pace, or unless two qualifiers each go postward at odds of 4 to 1 or higher, which happens several times a season.

Although maidens have not established their class level, the change from open conditions to maiden claiming conditions represents a real change in the quality of the competition. Often the difference is fantastic. In sprints, cheap, slow former maiden claiming losers cannot elude or catch the kind of horse just profiled. The maiden suddenly for sale is dropping from respectable efforts for the win. It should wrestle the lead somewhere prior to the pre-stretch or stretch call, control it, and hold, even if it runs evenly or slows slightly in the drive.

The reliability of this approach has remained relatively constant in southern California for a decade. During Santa Anita 1985 the method proved especially productive. The rate of return on the invested dollar easily exceeded 50 percent. One horse paid $77. It looked like this in the past performance tables:

In House — Ch. c. 3, by Riva Ridge—Hope for All, by Secretariat
Br.—Ringquist Mrs Helen C (Ky) — 1984 3 M 0 0 $425
Own.—Yasuda G — 118 — Tr.—Palma Hector O — $50,000
Lifetime 3 0 0 0 $425

30Dec84-6SA	1 1/16	:491	1:142	1:471sl	38	118	2hd	910	922	923 3/4	Shoemaker W4	Mdn	41-33	BeAHawaiian,ByShoreDrive,Bonhm	9
23Dec84-6Hol	7f	:22	:452	1:242ft	17	118	75 3/4	815	614	617	Shoemaker W8	Mdn	68-08	DoubleDeficit,ByShorDriv,Dondolro	9
16Jun84-6Hol	5f	:223	:461	:583ft	15	116	64 1/4	611	58 1/4	58 1/4	Olivares F7	Mdn	76-16	Pine Belt, Michadilla, G. M.Johnnie	7

Jan 7 SA tr.t 4f ft :471 h — Dec 11 Hol 4f sy :504 h — Dec 5 Hol 5f ft 1:001 h — Nov 28 Hol 5f ft 1:01 h

The nicely bred colt had raced three times and would be making its third start at three. In its latest race In House flashed early speed at the route on a slow strip against nonclaiming maidens. It followed that with its fastest workout, a sharp :47 1/5 on the slower training track. It was dropping into a maiden claiming affair January 11; odds at post were 37 to 1.

Now examine the even-money favorite, ridden by leading jockey Chris McCarron.

Two Hearts — B. c. 3, by Ack Ack—Mairelle, by Wajima
Br.—Barrett Mrs D P (Cal) — 1984 6 M 3 0 $11,100
Own.—Stricklin S — 118 — Tr.—Mitchell Mike — $50,000 — Turf 1 0 0 0
Lifetime 6 0 3 0 $11,100

20Dec84-4Hol	6f	:224	:463	1:123sy	*4-5	118	43 1/4	22 1/4	2hd	2 1/2	McCarron C J5	M50000	85-09	MimiDefi,TwoHerts,ChmpgnMony	10
23Nov84-3Hol	1	:462	1:121	1:383ft	2	118	3 1/2	1hd	2hd	2 1/2	McHargue DG7	M50000	81-19	Ascension,TwoHearts,Chucklecator	8
11Nov84-4Hol	1	ⓣ:461	1:10	1:343fm	60	115	34 1/4	34	44 1/4	74 1/4	Garcia J A8	Bckpsr	90-08	Herat, Sapient, Private Jungle	9
11Nov84—Run in divisions															
18Oct84-6SA	1	:461	1:122	1:39 ft	6 1/2	117	3 1/2	4hd	46	47	DelahoussyeE4	ⓢMdn	66-20	RdDusty,SilvrStrik,Pickin'Rinbows	7
18Oct84—Fanned wide 7/8 turn															
11Oct84-6SA	6f	:221	:451	1:104ft	8	118	2 1/2	3 1/2	2 1/2	26	DelahoussyeE2	M50000	79-18	Mi Dicha, Two Hearts, Bronzino	7
6Sep84-6Dmr	7f	:224	:46	1:234ft	19	118	75 1/4	78	77	59	DelahoussyeE8	M50000	— —	Staff Decision,Gouer,Reformulate	11
6Sep84—Broke slowly, lugged in throughout															

Jan 9 SA 3f ft :362 h — Jan 1 SA 3f ft :37 h — Dec 6 Hol 4f ft :471 h — Nov 30 Hol 5f ft 1:01 h

Many maiden claiming favorites look similar to Two Hearts. What they have in common is repeated losses under maiden claiming conditions, notably at short prices. When leading jockeys climb aboard, the horses go postward as conspicuous underlays. Handicappers should avoid the horses with a vengeance.

Unraced since December 20, twenty-two days, with two short works in between, Two Hearts had every right to disappoint the crowd once again. In House showed good speed from the outset, and in a long hard drive prevailed. Its victory serves as testimony to the rewards that await handicappers who know what to look for in maiden claiming races.

An attractive commodity to handicappers exploring a field of slow horses that repeatedly have collapsed in maiden claiming races is the fast-working first-time starter from a leading or decent barn. The filly below went postward at 7 to 5. To expert eyes it shaped up

SIXTH RACE Santa Anita JANUARY 11, 1985

6 FURLONGS. (1.07$\frac{3}{5}$) MAIDEN CLAIMING. Purse $16,000. Colts and geldings. 3-year-olds. Weight, 118 lbs. Claiming price $50,000; for each $5,000 to $40,000 allowed 2 lbs.

Value of race $16,000; value to winner $8,800; second $3,200; third $2,400; fourth $1,200; fifth $400. Mutuel pool $385,158.

Last Raced	Horse	Eqt.	A.	Wt	PP	St	¼	½	Str	Fin	Jockey	Cl'g Pr	Odds $1
30Dec84 6SA9	In House		3	118	5	4	2^1	1^{hd}	2^2	1no	Pedroza M A	50000	37.50
20Dec84 4Hol2	Two Hearts	b	3	118	8	2	3^2	3$^{1\frac{1}{2}}$	1^{hd}	2$^{2\frac{1}{2}}$	McCarron C J	50000	1.00
	Commuter		3	114	1	10	10	8$^{1\frac{1}{2}}$	6$^{1\frac{1}{2}}$	3^{hd}	Olivares F	40000	47.90
	Dockside Pirate		3	118	2	9	7^{hd}	5^1	5^{hd}	4^{hd}	Toro F	50000	19.40
	Beau's Charm		3	118	6	7	4^{hd}	4^2	3$^{\frac{1}{2}}$	5$^{2\frac{1}{2}}$	Valenzuela P A	50000	6.90
20Dec84 4Hol4	Nobledex	b	3	116	4	5	8^{hd}	6^1	7^2	6$^{\frac{1}{2}}$	Ortega L E	45000	15.00
5Jan85 2SA9	Yucatan	b	3	118	9	3	1^{hd}	2^{hd}	4$^{\frac{1}{2}}$	7$^{1\frac{1}{2}}$	Stevens G L	50000	2.80
24Nov84 6Hol7	Accu Back	b	3	114	10	1	5^{hd}	7^{hd}	8^4	8^6	Hawley S	40000	10.90
21Jly84 2Eng6	Canzone		3	118	7	8	9^4	9$^{2\frac{1}{2}}$	9^3	9^3	Sibille R	50000	16.50
	Jestafisherman		3	114	3	6	6^2	10	10	10	Meza R Q	40000	47.00

OFF AT 3:13. Start good. Won driving. Time, :22, :45$\frac{3}{5}$, :57$\frac{4}{5}$, 1:10$\frac{4}{5}$ Track fast.

$2 Mutuel Prices:			
5-IN HOUSE	77.00	15.60	6.80
8-TWO HEARTS		3.00	2.40
1-COMMUTER			10.80

Ch. c, by Riva Ridge—Hope for All, by Secretariat. Trainer Palma Hector O. Bred by Ringquist Mrs Helen C (Ky).

IN HOUSE, engaged for the early lead outside YUCATAN, brriefly lost the lead to TWO HEARTS in the upper stretch, then gamely came back to prevail. TWO HEARTS, moved to contention outside the leaders going into the far turn, gained a narrow advantage nearing the furlong pole and hung. COMMUTER, bumped and steadied at the start to fall well behind the field, rallied between horses into the stretch and finished well while racing in tight quarters through much of the drive. DOCKSIDE PIRATE was bumped into COMMUTER at the the start, awaited racing room on the far turn, and also finished well. BEAU'S CHARM had no excuses. YUCATAN tired after a half. ACCU BACK was fanned wide into the drive. CANZONE, slow to gain stride at the start, raced widest of all into the stretch. JETAFISHERMAN broke inward to bump DOCKSIDE PIRATE.

Owners— 1, Yasuda G; 2, Stricklin S; 3, Martin Mr-Mrs C; 4, Sarkowsky & Wygod; 5, Golden Eagle Farm; 6, Parks P D & Ruth A; 7, Barrera L S; 8, Ross A or R M or Mildred; 9, Kolbe Barbara T; 10, Sokol E.

Trainers— 1, Palma Hector O; 2, Mitchell Mike; 3, Fanning Jerry; 4, Mandella Richard; 5, Headley Bruce; 6, Moreno Henry; 7, Barrera Lazaro S; 8, Manzi Joseph; 9, Carno Louis R; 10, Nelson Kathleen S.

as the inevitable fast-working first-time starter up for sale in a maiden claiming race, the kind that fools the crowd again and again.

Dear Busia		B. f. 3, by Snow Sporting—She Should Know, by Ole Fols					
		Br.—Ingber B (Cal)		1979	0 M	0	0
Own.—Lipo & Morris	112^5	Tr. Alvarez Fernando	$20,000	1978	0 M	0	0
Jan 7 SA 4f gd :47^2 h	●Dec 29 SA 3f ft :33^2 h	Dec 23 SA 6f ft 1:13^2 h		Dec 5 RC tr.t 6f ft 1:16^4 h			

Dear Busia finished fourth. The results chart noted: "Dear Busia pressed the pace and faded in the final furlong." Hardened handicappers need not be fooled again by the flash of untested training speed entered in maiden claiming affairs.

Dissenters, as always, can point to outstanding exceptions. At Hollywood Park, seasons ago, an unraced colt named Fleet Dragoon won a maiden claiming sprint and was claimed for $40,000. The colt later won the $100,000-added Grade 2 Hollywood Juvenile. Three days afterward it died in its stall.

Most comparable exceptions supply evidence of the truth concerning maiden claiming horses. Unless purchased by barns able to uncover hidden talents, horses started in maiden claiming races at major tracks typically endure abbreviated careers there. The injuries, maladies, or shortcomings that mark them reveal themselves sooner or later, and usually sooner. Handicappers stay on the alert.

When confronted by the past performances of horses that began or won under maiden claiming conditions, handicappers wait for signs of dulling or tailing form. When the signs show, handicappers avoid the horses immediately.

Numerous handicappers distinguish between prices with which maiden claiming horses compete. The dividing line currently appears to be $20,000. There or below the horses are forsaken. Above $20,000 suggests the horses can run, and merely have been valued at fair prices by realistic stables. If other stables want the claim, a fair bargain has been struck. Forget it. The distinction plays too fine. High-priced maiden claiming starters cannot be bet with the confidence of serious wagers. In the long run, such selections will lower the handicapper's win percentage. The dollar return suffers. Who needs it?

At tracks outside of New York and southern California, and painfully so at small tracks, numerous maiden claiming races clutter the weekday cards, and many are filled exclusively by previous maiden claiming losers.

As a rule, handicappers are strongly urged to pass the races. The races drain down the financial reserves relentlessly. Favorites can never, never be tolerated.

Are there any real opportunities in these awful affairs?

A professional who has promoted a technique for coping with these slow races is San Francisco speed-and-pace handicapper Ron Cox. Cox discovered that par times at the selling levels of the maiden claiming scale do not correlate properly with the claiming prices. Instead there were obvious "gaps," as Cox termed them, in the associations between claiming prices and par times.

Consider the following pattern:

Maiden Claiming Selling Prices	Par Times	
$40,000	1:11	2/5
32,000	1:11	3/5
25,000	1:11	4/5
20,000	1:12	2/5
16,000	1:12	3/5
12,500	1:12	4/5
10,000	1:13	
8,000	1:13	3/5
5,000	1:13	4/5

The gaps occur at two selling levels, at $20,000 and $8,000. At these levels the final times are considerably slower than those of the next higher levels. The other class-distance pars correspond evenly to price changes. Cox recommends handicappers pay extra attention to maiden claiming horses that bridge the gaps, or drop from races where average times are significantly faster.

Of course, to implement the strategy handicappers need par times for the various levels of maiden claiming races on the local circuit.

In recent years, trips and track biases have been increasingly invoked as plausible solutions to maiden claiming races that remain mysteries by conventional handicapping practices. Unfortunately, in these terrible races those tactics are largely overestimated. They apply best when the horses expected to benefit have lost just one maiden claiming contest. Repeat losers should be forsaken.

Moreover, reliable trip and bias information is difficult to obtain. Recreational racegoers must rely on professionals who collect the data carefully, and dispense it regularly, either in race-day seminars or as part of weekly information services—for a fee. The small cost, by the way, is well worth the value of the special information.

In this context, a particularly intriguing horse is one dropping into a maiden claiming race following a single terrible humiliation, perhaps two, versus straight maidens. The loss might have looked like this:

```
Naughty N Careless          B. f. 3, by Explodent—Careless Notion, by Jester
                            Br.—Stark R (Cal)                    1985  1 M  0  0
  ST MARTIN E          1155 Tr.—Gosden John H M                  1984  0 M  0  0
Own.—Stark R & Fran              Lifetime    1  0  0  0
20Apr85-6SA    6f :22² :46¹ 1:11²ft  7 112⁵ 10⁹  91²10¹⁵ 816¾  St Martin E⁶  ⑥Mdn 64-19 Prep Charge,NabilaK.,MariaValdez 11
    20Apr85—Pinched back start
   May 3 Hol 4f ft :49¹ h        Apr 28 Hol 4f ft :49² h        Apr 13 SA 7f ft 1:26 h        Apr 7 SA 6f ft 1:13⁴ h
```

Perhaps the horse had a legitimate excuse. Perhaps it also has redeeming value not apparent to the crowd. If the odds will be high, a necessary condition, handicappers might employ that kind of information to excuse the single bad performance. In this way handicappers will be isolating overlays often enough to collect profits over time, maybe high profits.

The following illustration encompasses much of the preceding discussion. The race occurred at Santa Anita 1985, ten days following the race won by In House, a $77 mutuel. Try to find the four contenders.

6th Santa Anita

6½ FURLONGS. (1.14) MAIDEN CLAIMING. Purse $16,000. Fillies. 3-year-olds. Weight, 117 lbs. Claiming price $50,000; for each $5,000 to $40,000 allowed 2 lbs.

Thrill A Minute

Ch. f. 3, by Honest Pleasure—Pardey, by Don B
Br.—Spreen R H Jr (Okla) 1985 1 M 0 0
Own.—Wellman-Pollack-Cass 117 Tr.—Palma Hector 0 $50,000 1984 1 M 0 0 $550
Lifetime 2 0 0 0 $550
5Jan85-3SA 6f :214 :442 1:092ft 19 117 7¾ 711 611 613¼ Pedroza M A2 ⓕMdn 78-12 Layout,MagnificentLindy,FruitTree 8
5Jan85—Veered in, bumped start
22Dec84-6Hol 6f :232 :472 1:121gd 20 118 2½ 34 48½ 513¼ Pedroza M A9 ⓕMdn 74-10 IndnTns,Unscrtl on,ImprssvDrms 10
Jan 14 SA 4f ft :473 h Dec 30 SA 4f sl :494 h Dec 20 Hol 3f sy :382 h Dec 14 Hol 5f ft 1:03 hg

Reckless Miss

B. f. 3, by Whitesburg—Resort Living, by Gallant Romeo
Br.—Robinson W B (Ky) 1984 2 M 0 0
Own.—Franks J R 117 Tr.—Van Berg Jack C $50,000
Lifetime 2 0 0 0
23Dec84-4Hol 6f :222 :461 1:122ft 20 118 812 816 711 64 Wentz M4 ⓕMdn 83-08 AmbrRidge,LorOfZorro,SoulLight 10
30Nov84-4Hol 6f :222 :462 1:123ft 18 118 1112 1010 89 67½ Wentz M12 ⓕM50000 79-11 Ed'sBoldLdy,MiJet,MentlBnkMgic 12
30Nov84—Broke slowly
Dec 14 Hol 5f ft 1:01 hg Dec 8 Hol 4f sy :48 hg

Long Gone Gaelic

Ch. f. 3, by Gaelic Dancer—Keep It Glowing, by Alto Ribot
Br.—Nunez Mr-Mrs M N (Cal) 1985 1 M 0 0 $325
Own.—Maryanski N & R 108[5] Tr.—Williams Harry M $40,000 1984 5 M 0 0 $60X
Lifetime 6 0 0 0 $325
3Jan85-3SA 1 1/16 :48 1:131 1:453ft 35 117 1½ 33½ 48 58½ HnsenRD3 ⓕⓈM32000 65-15 BelleElegant,IrishMessage,Regiwin 8
3Jan85—Lugged out down backstretch
15Dec84-5Hol 1 :451 1:101 1:363ft 58 1135 911 913 914 614½ DominguezRL9 ⓕMdn 77-06 RsUpAndDnc,Mssn,GrbYourSocks 10
29Nov84-6Hol 6f :224 :464 1:121ft 169 118 105¾ 108¾ 910 911¾ Scott J M2 ⓕⓈMdn 77-11 Vivian'sJdeB.,Pirte'sSerende,Dnut 11
3Nov84-8LA 6½f :222 :464 1:20 ft 54 118 75¾ 713 712 610¾ Scott J M9 ⓕMdn 66-11 Kapi Kat, Tacky But True, HaleKea 9
7Oct84-3SA 6f :213 :444 1:102ft 108 117 1214 1017 1020 1017¾ DominguzRL12 ⓕMdn 69-12 Winsome Soon, Fine Spirit,Layout 12
27Sep84-7Pom 6f :221 :464 1:132ft 40 116 78¾ 78 65¼ 53 Scott J M5 ⓕⓈMdn 74-23 CretivePursuit,GirlOfThVlly,MttyD 8
Dec 13 SA 3f gd :383 h

Nuuano Pali

B. f. 3, by Kamehameha—Pegged, by Iron Peg
Br.—Newmarket Stables (Va) 1984 1 M 0 0
Own.—Guidotti R L 117 Tr.—Guidotti Raymond L $50,000
Lifetime 1 0 0 0
28Nov84-6Hol 6f :222 :454 1:11 ft 47 118 56½ 911 915 922¾ Iwai J7 ⓕMdn 72-05 La Lea, Kalatar, Nuclear Winter 9
Jan 12 Hol 4f ft :472 h Dec 14 SA 4f ft :474 h Nov 23 SA 4f ft :483 hg

Serene Fire

Dk. b. or br. f. 3, by Noholme II—Fantastique, by Cornish Prince
Br.—Opstein & Young (Ky) 1984 3 M 1 0 $2,520
Own.—Opstein & Young 117 Tr.—Van Berg Tim $50,000
Lifetime 3 0 1 0 $2,520
6Nov84-5Haw 6f :22 :454 1:132ft *3-2 119 2hd 22 55 66 Kutz D4 ⓕMdn 68-23 Swing Softly, Mabou, Tammy Dove 9
23Oct84-1Haw 6f :214 :454 1:121ft *3-5 119 2½ 2hd 31½ 45¾ Smith M E6 ⓕMdn 74-21 RusticCedr,LdyDnte,Queen'sRvlry 10
16Oct84-3Haw 6f :222 :461 1:112gd 6½ 119 11 11½ 11½ 21½ Smith M E3 ⓕMdn 82-10 Aveen, Serene Fire, Queen Arete 8
Jan 15 SA 6f ft 1:131 h Jan 1 SA 4f ft :512 h Dec 24 SA 5f ft 1:004 h Dec 17 SA 5f ft 1:00 h

Niagara Lady

B. f. 3, by Taylor's Falls—Cool Value, by Cool Moon
Br.—Tom Boy Stable (Ill) 1984 2 M 0 0
Own.—Abtahi-McGaughey-Rochelle 113 Tr.—Stute Melvin F $40,000
Lifetime 2 0 0 0
21Dec84-2Hol 6f :221 :461 1:121m 17 118 25 410 514 918¾ VlenzuelPA1 ⓕM32000 63-11 Clerwy,KnightsCrozr,JustAsPrtty 12
21Dec84—Veered in, bumped at start
8Jun84-6Hol 5f :222 :46 :582ft 12 116 55 65 48 710¾ Guerra W A4 ⓕMdn 74-17 Trunk, Doon's Baby, Renew 10
Jan 16 SA 5f ft 1:003 h Jan 8 SA 5f gd 1:003 h Dec 31 SA 3f ft :372 h Dec 14 Hol 6f ft 1:18 h

Count On Lyn

Ch. f. 3, by Bold Ruckus—Xtra Classy, by Bethel
Br.—Jones B C (Ky) 1985 0 M 0 0
Own.—Pinero Mr-Mrs M 117 Tr.—Marti Pedro $50,000 1984 0 M 0 0
Lifetime 0 0 0 0
Jan 17 Hol 5f ft 1:012 hg Jan 10 Hol 5f ft 1:014 h Dec 21 Hol 5f m 1:011 h Dec 13 Hol 5f gd 1:012 h

Gran Vintage

Gr. f. 3, by Gran Zar—Triple Brandy, by Bold Reasoning
Br.—Thornton & Van Meter Jr (Ky) 1984 4 M 1 2 $6,000
Own.—Four Star Stables & Ozer 117 Tr.—Manzi Joseph $50,000
Lifetime 4 0 1 2 $6,000

17Aug84-4Dmr 6f :22¹ :45⁴ 1:11⁴ft *2 117 65½ 54½ 41½ 31½ VienzuelPA¹¹ Ⓜ M50000 77-18 Suelta,MissBeverlyHills,GrnVintge 11
  17Aug84—Crowded late
3Aug84-6Dmr 6f :23 :47 1:12¹ft 9 115 42 33 32 21½ Sibille R¹ Ⓜ M40000 75-23 SilverPlume,GrnVintg,NightChrgr 18
13Jly84-6Hol 6f :22² :45³ 1:11⁴ft 7 116 46 57½ 41¹ 37½ Sibille R⁶ Ⓜ M40000 71-19 Renew,Stevan'sNaturelie,GrnVintge 7
  13Jly84—Bobbled start
17Jun84-6Hol 5f :22⁴ :46¹ :58⁴ft 39 116 8¹⁵ 8¹⁴ 8¹⁴ 8⁹ Sibille R⁵ Ⓜ Mdn 74-23 Winters'Love,PrincssCbrini,FolkArt 9
  Jan 19 SA 4f ft :49² hg   Jan 14 SA 6f ft 1:12³ h   Jan 9 SA 5f ft 1:01¹ h   Jan 5 SA 4f ft :47² h

Carolyn's Song

Ch. f. 3, by Lyphard's Wish—Traveling Song, by Needles
Br.—Van Hoose J R (Ky)   1985 0 M 0 0
Own.—Sharbil Stable   108⁵   Tr.—Sadler John W $40,000   1984 0 M 0 0
    Lifetime 0 0 0 0
Jan 16 SA 5f ft 1:02² hg   Jan 10 SA 6f ft 1:15³ h   Jan 4 SA 5f ft 1:04¹ h   Dec 29 SA tr.1 4f gd :58² h

Star Pirate

B. f. 3, by Pirate's Bounty—T V Starlet, by T V Lark
Br.—Windy Hill TBA (Cal)   1985 1 M 1 0 $3,000
Own.—Parks R Charlene   115   Tr.—Moreno Henry $45,000   1984 5 M 2 1 $8,400
    Lifetime 6 0 3 1 $11,400
3Jan85-4SA 6f :22¹ :46¹ 1:11⁴ft *2½ 115 2½ 2ⁿᵈ 1½ 2ⁿᵏ Ortega L E⁴ Ⓜ M45000 79-15 Bett'sLady,StarPirate,BountifulLdy 8
14Dec84-3Hol 6f :22⁴ :46² 1:12¹ft *8-5 119 2¹½ 23½ 23 2½ McCrronCJ⁸ Ⓜ M32000 87-08 AnneCuisine,StrPirte,NtiveDotter 12
5Nov84-2SA 6f :22 :45⁴ 1 12 ft 3 117 3ⁿᵏ 3² 47½ 3⁵ McCrronCJ² Ⓜ M40000 73-18 Al'sBigTime,LaurenLeigh,StrPirte 12
19Oct84-6SA 6f :22 :44⁴ 1 10⁹ft 8 117 41½ 6⁸ 9¹⁷ 10¹³½ VienzuelPA¹² Ⓜ Mdn 72-17 Lotta Blue, Danuta,Vivian'sJadeB. 12
8Oct84-6SA 6f :22¹ :45⁴ 1:11³ft *5-5 116 41½ 43 7¹⁰ 7⁸½ ValenzuelPA⁸ Ⓜ Mdn 71-16 B. Elite, Vital Score, Danuta 11
  8Oct84—Wide 3/8 turn
9Sep84-4Dmr 6f :22⁴ :45⁴ 1:11³ft 5½ 112⁵ 2¹½ 2ⁿᵈ 1½ 2ⁿᵒ Fox W I Jr¹ Ⓜ Mdn 80-16 Star's Halo, Star Pirate, B. Elite 9
  9Sep84—Bumped start
Jan 15 SA 6f ft 1:15² h   Jan 1 SA 3f ft :37² h   Dec 26 SA 5f ft 1:03² h   Dec 8 Hol 5f sy 1:02³ h

Bountiful Lady

Dk. b. or br. f. 3, by Pirate's Bounty—Quando Quando, by Pappa Fourway
Br.—Anderson Ranch (Cal)   1985 1 M 0 1 $2,250
Own.—Gough Didi   117   Tr.—Holt Lester $50,000   1984 0 M 0 0
    Lifetime 1 0 0 1 $2,250
3Jan85-4SA 6f :22¹ :46¹ 1:11⁴ft 9½ 117 73½ 75½ 44 32½ DelhoussyE⁸ Ⓜ M50000 76-15 Bett'sLady,StarPirate,BountifulLdy 8
  3Jan85—Wide final 3/8
Jan 16 SA 3f ft :37¹ h   Jan 10 SA 4f ft :49² h   Dec 29 SA tr.1 5f gd 1:02⁴ h   Dec 24 SA 6f ft 1:15¹ hg

Lady Lonestar

Ch. f. 3, by Secretariat—Texas Lark, by Bold Lark
Br.—Welcome Farm (Pa)   1984 1 M 0 0
Own.—Welcome Farm   117   Tr.—Marguelas Steven L $50,000
    Lifetime 1 0 0 0
10Dec84-4Aqu 6f ⊡:22³ :46¹ 1:13 ft 43 117 8⁵½ 11² 11½ 12¹½ 12¹½ 11½½ M gliore R³ Ⓜ Mdn 64-21 BreAssets,StreetSvy,VgulyFoolish 12
Jan 19 SA 4f ft :49 h   Jan 13 SA 6f ft 1:14⁴ hg   Jan 6 SA 5f ft 1:00¹ h   Jan 1 SA 4f ft :49² hg

The possibilities include Thrill A Minute, Serene Fire, Niagara Lady, and Lady Lonestar. The maiden claiming loss suffered by Niagara Lady on December 21 can be excused: mud.

Now check the race's results chart. It is not altogether atypical. Three of the four contenders fought it out. Notice the tightness of the finish, not to mention the odds on each of the first three finishers.

As a postscript, the single wining Pick-Six ticket at Santa Anita on January 21, worth $429,171.20, was cashed by a regular and highly practiced handicapper. The fellow singled Lady Lonestar. How did he pick the long shot? In interviews, the handicapper noted he had clocked the horse in its morning workouts, and it showed high speed, as it had not in its initial start at Aqueduct.

SIXTH RACE Santa Anita JANUARY 21, 1985 — **6 ½ FURLONGS. (1.14) MAIDEN CLAIMING. Purse $16,000. Fillies. 3-year-olds. Weight, 117 lbs. Claiming price $50,000; for each $5,000 to $40,000 allowed 2 lbs.**

Value of race $16,000; value to winner $8,800; second $3,200; third $2,400; fourth $1,200; fifth $400. Mutuel pool $562,120.

Last Raced	Horse	Eqt.	A.	Wt	PP	St	¼	½	Str	Fin	Jockey	Cl'g Pr	Odds $1
10Dec84 4Aqu11	Lady Lonestar		3	117	12	2	21½	22½	21½	1nk	Sibille R	50000	30.40
21Dec84 2Hol9	Niagara Lady		3	113	6	3	1hd	1hd	1hd	2hd	Stevens G L	40000	26.60
6Nov84 5Haw6	Serene Fire		3	117	5	4	41	3hd	31½	31¼	Lauzon J M	50000	8.00
3Jan85 4SA2	Star Pirate		3	115	10	5	3hd	44½	43½	43½	McCarron C J	45000	1.50
23Dec84 4Hol6	Reckless Miss		3	117	2	11	10hd	83½	5½	52½	McHargue D G	50000	11.40
3Jan85 4SA3	Bountiful Lady	b	3	117	11	1	61	7½	72	61½	Delahoussaye E	50000	3.90
17Aug84 4Dmr3	Gran Vintage		3	117	8	6	115	9hd	8hd	71¾	Valenzuela P A	50000	4.30
3Jan85 3SA5	Long Gone Gaelic		3	108	3	7	9hd	12	113	81	Dominguez R L5	40000	56.30
5Jan85 3SA6	Thrill A Minute		3	117	1	8	53½	5½	6hd	9¾	Ortega L E	50000	14.50
	Count On Lyn	b	3	117	7	12	71½	61½	91½	101	Meza R Q	50000	25.20
	Carolyn's Song		3	108	9	10	82	101	10hd	113½	Lozoya D A5	40000	56.10
28Nov84 6Hol9	Nuuano Pali		3	117	4	9	12	111½	12	12	Steiner J J	50000	89.30

OFF AT 3:16. Start good. Won driving. Time, :21⅘, :44⅘, 1:10⅘, 1:17⅘ Track fast.

$2 Mutuel Prices:			
12–LADY LONESTAR	62.80	29.40	13.40
6–NIAGARA LADY		23.00	11.20
5–SERENE FIRE			7.80

Ch. f, by Secretariat—Texas Lark, by Bold Lark. Trainer Morguelan Steven L. Bred by Welcome Farm (Pa).

LADY LONESTAR engaged for the lead outside NIAGARA LADY at once, responded gamely when set down in the drive and prevailed in the closing yards. The latter also responded when challenged in the drive but could not quite last. SERENE FIRE, in good position to the stretch, responded outside the leaders and was gaining at the end. STAR PIRATE had no apparent excuses. RECKLESS MISS saved ground to no avail. BOUNTIFUL LADY dropped back after breaking alertly and was never a factor. GRAN VINTAGE showed little.

Owners— 1, Welcome Farm; 2, Abtahi-McGaughey-Rochelle; 3, Opstein & Young; 4, Parks R Charlene; 5, Franks J R; 6, Gough Didi; 7, Four Star Stables & Ozer; 8, Maryanski N & R; 9, Wellman-Pollack-Cass; 10, Pinero Mr-Mrs M; 11, Sharbil Stable; 12, Guidotti R L.

Trainers— 1, Morguelan Steven L; 2, Stute Melvin F; 3, Van Berg Tim; 4, Moreno Henry; 5, Van Berg Jack C; 6, Holt Lester; 7, Manzi Joseph; 8, Williams Harry M; 9, Palma Hector O; 10, Marti Pedro; 11, Sadler John W; 12, Guidotti Raymond L.

Scratched—Chimes Roman (3Jan85 4SA7).

HANDICAPPING BY THE CONDITIONS

Maiden Races

The preceding chapter contains the directions to finding the nice winner here. Picking the actual winner is difficult and depends on some additional information outside of the past performance tables, a circumstance characteristic of contemporary handicapping practice. Nonetheless, novice and recreational handicappers should be able to spot the phony favorite among the entries, plus the two horses that qualify best under the conditions.

Commentary.

The key to success in this and similar situations is to disregard the chances of Pirate's Coupe, and prepare to bet either Broom Buck or Flashy North Star. The two finished second and third last out. They are therefore statistical probables, as the Davis research has demonstrated.

Interestingly, Pirate's Coupe is trained by Richard Mandella.

6½ FURLONGS (1.14) MAIDEN. Purse $22,000. Colts and geldings. 3-year-olds. Bred in California. Weight, 118 lbs.

Broom Buck — Own.—Hawn W R — 118

Ch. c. 3, by Beau Buck—Mrs Bromley, by Colorado King

Br.—Hawn W R (Cal) — 1985 1 M 1 0 $4,400

Tr.—Johnson Patricia L — 1984 0 M 0 0

Lifetime 1 0 1 0 $4,400

27Mar85-3SA 6½f :22^1 :46 1:18^{2}sl 22 118 8^{6}½ 6^9 4^7 2^{5}½ Shoemaker W^2 Ⓢ Mdn 72-26 ScheerBob,BroomBuck,MrDirctor 12

27Mar85—Broke slowly, bumped after start, steadied at 3/4

Apr 10 SA 3f ft :37^2 h Mar 20 SA 5f ft 1:01^3 hg Mar 14 SA 4f ft :48^4 hg Mar 8 SA 6f ft 1:13^2 h

Captain's Chance — Own.—Bailey & Bailey — 113^5

B. c. 3, by Pappa Martin—Gallentress, by My Captain

Br.—Bailey V (Cal) — 1984 1 M 0 0

Tr.—Stute Melvin F

Lifetime 1 0 0 0

29Dec84-4BM 6f :23 :46^3 1:11^{1}ft 15 118 6^4 7^{7}¾ 7^{8}¾ 7^{15}¾ Hummel C R^4 Ⓢ Mdn 67-27 BrghtAndRght,CntOnBrgn,CrystlTs 8

Apr 8 SA 4f ft :46^4 h Apr 2 SA 6f ft 1:12^3 h Mar 28 SA 5f gd 1:01^1 hg Mar 23 SA 5f ft 1:00 hg

More Thrust — Own.—Sinclair Thoroughbreds — 118

B. c. 3, by Darby Creek Road—Balcony's Bonus, by First Balcony

Br.—Diamond Stable (Cal) — 1985 1 M 0 0

Tr.—Matlow Richard P — 1984 0 M 0 0

Lifetime 1 0 0 0

23Mar85-6SA 6½f :22^1 :45^2 1:16^{3}ft 48 118 2^{hd} 2^{hd} 5^{5}¼ 6^{8}¾ Meza R Q^1 Mdn 78-14 Apalaj,HonestJunny,NotTheRegulr 9

Apr 5 Hol 4f ft :49^3 h Mar 16 Hol 5f ft 1:01^3 hg Feb 27 Hol 6f ft 1:16^2 h Feb 14 Hol 6f ft 1:16^1 h

Majestic Fleet — Own.—Harris & Lewis — 118

Dk. b. or br. c. 3, by Fleet Allied—Miss Patty Dawn, by Harold J

Br.—Lewis D G & Anna Lee (Cal) — 1985 0 M 0 0

Tr.—Landers Dale — 1984 0 M 0 0

Lifetime 0 0 0 0

Entered 10Apr85- 3 SA

Apr 2 SA 5f ft 1:03 h Mar 17 SA 3f ft :36^1 hg Mar 14 SA 7f ft 1:32 h Mar 9 SA 6f ft 1:19 h

I'll Smoke — Own.—Vee Jay Stable — 118

Dk. b. or br. g. 3, by Messenger of Song—Patrisch, by Rising Market

Br.—Johnson J (Cal) — 1985 1 M 0 0 $550

Tr.—Johnson Patricia L — 1984 0 M 0 0

Lifetime 1 0 0 0 $550

30Mar85-6SA 6f :22 :45^3 1:10^{4}ft 10 118 6^{4}¼ 6^{4}¼ 5^{4}¼ 5^{5}¾ Stevens G L^3 Mdn 78-15 Soverignty,ProximCnturi,Costlinr 11

30Mar85—Broke slowly

Apr 10 SA 3f ft :36^2 h Mar 26 SA 3f ft :36^3 h Mar 20 SA 6f ft 1:15^3 h Mar 14 SA 5f ft 1:00^4 hg

Running Debonair — Own.—Rogers J D — 118

B. g. 3, by Debonair Roger—My Princess Rose, by Native Royalty

Br.—Rogers J D (Cal) — 1985 2 M 0 0 $525

Tr.—Threewitt Noble — 1984 0 M 0 0

Lifetime 2 0 0 0 $525

6Feb85-6SA 6½f :22 :45 1:17 ft 4½ 118 1^{hd} 2^{1}½ 3^5 5^{4}¾ McCarron C J^9 Ⓢ Mdn 80-15 TigrOfErn,FlshyNorthStr,DmonSd 12

24Jan85-4SA 6f :21^3 :44^4 1:10 ft 2 118 6^{5}½ 6^{8}¾ 6^{11} 6^{9}¾ McCarron C J^3 Ⓢ Mdn 78-12 Justonofthboys,SlntImpct,HghNtrl 6

24Jan85—Broke slowly

Apr 10 SA 3f ft :37 h Apr 4 SA 6f ft 1:14^3 h Mar 22 SA 6f ft 1:14^3 h Mar 16 SA 6f ft 1:13 h

Flashy North Star — Own.—Harmes-Harmes-Tufeld — 118

B. c. 3, by Canadian Gil—Flashy Diplomat, by Diplomatic

Br.—Harmes T & Dorothy J (Cal) — 1985 7 M 1 2 $10,820

Tr.—Feld Jude T — 1984 0 M 0 0

Lifetime 7 0 1 2 $10,820

6Apr85-3GG 6f :22^2 :45^2 1:10^{2}ft *9-5 118 2^{hd} 4^{1}½ 4^2 3^{1}½ Delgadillo C^6 Mdn 85-13 NtiveAct,PrcticBnds,FlshyNorthStr 8

29Mar85-6SA 6½f :22 :45^2 1:17 ft 4½ 118 2½ 1^{hd} 4^5 11^{12}¾ Pedroza M A^2 M50000 73-20 Tuono,He'sAffirmed,WindfllNtive 12

29Mar85—Veered in, bumped start

14Mar85-6SA 1 :46^3 1:11^3 1:38^{2}ft 6½ 118 1^{hd} 5^{2}½ 5^4 8^{14} Pedroza M A^8 Ⓢ Mdn 62-18 Juli'sMrk,NightGurd,RodOfFortun 10

27Feb85-3SA 6f :21^4 :44^4 1:10^{4}ft 3 118 2^1 2^{hd} 2^{hd} 3^{1}½ Steiner J J^7 Ⓢ Mdn 83-17 ConnptonFt,Jl'sMrk,FlshyNorthStr 9

6Feb85-6SA 6½f :22 :45 1:17 ft 11 118 2^{hd} 1^{1}½ 1^2 2^{2}¾ Steiner J J^3 Ⓢ Mdn 83-15 TigrOfErn,FlshyNorthStr,DmonSd 12

6Feb85—Bumped at start

24Jan85-4SA 6f :21^3 :44^4 1:10 ft 24 118 4^{2}½ 3^{2}½ 3^{2}½ 4^5 Steiner J J^1 Ⓢ Mdn 83-12 Justonofthboys,SlntImpct,HghNtrl 6

24Jan85—Broke slowly

10Jan85-6SA 6f :21^4 :45^2 1:10^{3}ft 6 118 1^{1}½ 1^{hd} 4^4 8^{13}¾ Steiner J J^1 Ⓢ Mdn 71-20 EverBrilliant,Tuono,ChmpgneMoney 9

●Mar 24 SA 3f ft :34 h Mar 8 SA 1 ft 1:41^1 h Feb 25 SA 4f ft :47^2 h Feb 19 SA 6f ft 1:12^2 h

Pirate's Coupe

Own.—Wygod M J   118

B. c. 3, by Pirate's Bounty—Coupe La Mouche, by Grenfail
Br.—Wygod & Weis (Cal)   1985 0 M 0 0
Tr.—Mandella Richard   1984 0 M 0 0
Lifetime   0 0 0 0

Apr 5 SA 5f ft :58⁴ hg   Mar 30 SA 7f ft 1:26³ h   •Mar 21 SA 7f ft 1:25 h   Mar 15 SA 6f ft 1:12³ hg

Boweaver

Own.—Weaver K   118

B. c. 3, by Greco II—Armed for Action, by Johnny Dye
Br.—Levenzon S H (Cal)   1985 1 M 0 0
Tr.—Sylvia Earle K Jr   1984 0 M 0 0
Lifetime   1 0 0 0

27Mar85-3SA 6½f :22¹ :46 1.18³sl 58 11³⁵ 12¹¹12²¹ 9¹⁷ 8¹⁷¼ DominguzRE¹⁰ ⑤Mdn 61-26 ScheerBob,BroomBuck,Mr.Director 12
Mar 14 GD b:1 6f ft 1:15 hg   Mar 9 GD b:1 6f ft 1:14³ h   Feb 24 SA 4f ft :48 hg   Feb 19 GD b:1 5f ft 1:02³ h

Up The Pole

Own.—Rowan L R (Lessee)   118

B. g. 3, by Crystal Water—Why Four, by Coursing
Br.—Rowan L R (Cal)   1984 4 M 1 1 $5,900
Tr.—Canney William T
Lifetime   4 0 1 1 $5,900

3Nov84-3SA   6f :22 :45¹ 1.10⁴ft 4️⃣ 118 2¹½ 3²½ 5⁶ 6¹⁰½ Sibille R¹¹ ⑤Mdn 76-14 JstThFcts,Pckn'Rnbows,RInchATn 11
18Oct84-6SA   1 :46¹ 1.12² 1.39 ft *1 117 2¼ 5¹¼ 7¹⁹ 7¹⁸¼ McCarron C J² ③Mdn 55-29 RdDusty,SilvrStrik,Pickin'Rinbows 7
    18Oct84—Crowded, took up sharply at 1/4
6Oct84-6SA   6f :22 :45³ 1.11²ft 3e117 2ⁿᵈ 2½ 2½ 2ⁿᵈ Sibille R¹¹ ⑤Mdn 81-14 Air Alert, Up The Pole, Calestoga 12
25Aug84-6Dmr 6f :22¹ :45⁴ 1.10³ft 55 117 6²¼ 3¼½ 3³¼ 33¼ Sibille R¹ ⑤Mdn 82-12 FbulousSelction,Cnyonvill,UpThPol 9
Apr 8 SA 5f ft :59 h   Apr 3 SA 7f ft 1.27 hg   •Mar 29 SA 7f gd 1:28 h   Mar 23 SA 6f ft 1:12² hg

Southern California handicappers know Mandella to be unsurpassed with first-starting maidens. From 1978 until 1984 at Santa Anita the trainer scored with 36 percent of his first starters. The dollar profit ranged nicely above 200 percent: remarkable figures. Pirate's Coupe was sent off at 3 to 5. With smashing workouts, the trainer's record, and champion jockey Chris McCarron aboard for its debut, the colt looked appetizing to the crowd and unbeatable to handicappers having access to the trainer data.

Yet Flashy North Star beat the Mandella horse by a neck. Modern speed handicappers would have realized the winner's figures had improved with each start and looked much the best among the horses that had run.

On April 6 at Golden Gate Fields, just five days before, Flashy North Star had competed against a fast-fast pace (better than par both at the fractional call and final time) and had experienced severe trouble in the going. He stayed in there as he had not before—hung tough, as the punters put it. At 9 to 1 its chances against an odds-on first starter looked appealing. Not only was the price right, but also the overbet favorite had tradition and statistics working against its success: inexperience.

Alert, informed handicappers having the crucial information at their command can isolate similar upsets half a dozen times a season. It takes know-how and digging, but it's worth it, as the following results chart confirms.

Another afterthought. When more than one horse satisfies the guidelines for tackling straight maiden races by the conditions, accurately adjusted speed and pace figures can often separate the

SIXTH RACE **Santa Anita** **APRIL 11, 1985** — **6 ½ FURLONGS. (1.14) MAIDEN. Purse $22,000. Colts and geldings. 3-year-olds. Bred in California. Weight, 118 lbs.**

Value of race $22,000; value to winner $12,100; second $4,400; third $3,300; fourths $1,100 each. Mutuel pool $399,672.

Last Raced		Horse	Eqt.	A.Wt	PP	St	¼	½	Str	Fin	Jockey	Odds $1
6Apr85 3GG3		Flashy North Star		3 118	6	3	1½	1hd	1hd	1nk	Delahoussaye E	9.00
		Pirate's Coupe		3 118	7	5	3hd	2 1	2 1½	2 ¾	McCarron C J	.70
6Feb85 6SA5		Running Debonair		3 118	5	4	4 2½	3 ½	3 1½	3nk	Valenzuela P A	11.30
27Mar85 3SA2	DH	Broom Buck		3 118	1	9	7 1	6hd	5 1½	4	Shoemaker W	7.60
29Dec84 4BM7	DH	Captain's Chance		3 113	2	8	8hd	8 2	7 3	4 ½	Dominguez R E5	32.50
30Mar85 6SA5		I'll Smoke		3 118	4	6	5 ½	5 1½	4 2	6 2¾	Stevens G L	8.40
23Mar85 6SA6		More Thrust		3 118	3	7	6 3	7 2½	6 2	7 7	McGurn C	83.00
27Mar85 3SA8		Boweaver		3 118	8	2	9	9	8 2½	8 11	Meza R Q	133.60
30Nov84 3SA6		Up The Pole	b	3 118	9	1	2hd	4 1½	9	9	Pincay L Jr	5.90

DH—Dead heat.

OFF AT 3:52. Start good. Won driving. Time, :21⅘, :45, 1:10⅘, 1:17⅘ Track fast.

$2 Mutuel Prices:			
7–FLASHY NORTH STAR	20.00	5.40	3.80
8–PIRATE'S COUPE		3.00	2.60
6–RUNNING DEBONAIR			4.40

B. c, by Canadian Gil—Flashy Diplomat, by Diplomatic. Trainer Feld Jude T. Bred by Harmes T & Dorothy J (Cal).

FLASHY NORTH STAR engaged for the lead at once, responded when challenged by PIRATE'S COUPE on the stretch turn and outfinished that one in a long drive. PIRATE'S COUPLE prompted the pace outside the winner throughout but hung in the drive. RUNNING DEBONAIR went to the outside for the stretch run but lacked the needed closing kick. BROOM BUCK, slow to gain stride at the start, rallied outside horses in the drive and finished well. CAPTAIN'S CHANCE bore out to be very wide into the stretch and finished with a good late run to just get up for the dead heat. I'LL SMOKE lodged a mild bid on the far turn and flattened out. UP THE POLE prompted the pace wide for three furlongs and tired badly. MAJESTIC FLEET (4) WAS SCRATCHED ON ADVICE OF THE VETERINARIAN. ALL WAGERS ON HIM IN THE REGULAR POOLS WERE ORDERED REFUNDED AND HIS PICK SIX SELECTIONS WERE SWITCHED TO THE FAVORITE, PIRATE'S COUPE (8).

Owners— 1, Harmes-Harmes-Tufeld; 2, Wygod M J; 3, Rogers J D; 4, Hawn W R; 5, Bailey & Bailey; 6, Vee Jay Stable; 7, Sinclair Thoroughbreds; 8, Weaver K; 9, Rowan L R (Lessee).

Trainers— 1, Feld Jude T; 2, Mandella Richard; 3, Threewitt Noble; 4, Johnson Patricia L; 5, Stute Melvin F; 6, Johnson Patricia L; 7, Matlow Richard P; 8, Sylvia Earle K Jr; 9, Canney William T.

Scratched—Majestic Fleet.

qualifiers. As with Flashy North Star, the figures reflect patterns of development—improvement—not apparent to the naked eye.

The same is so of preliminary nonwinners allowance horses, a topic we turn to next.

CHAPTER 3

Nonwinners Allowances

EN ROUTE TO appropriate levels of performance, horses graduate from maiden races to basic allowance conditions. There they meet restricted competition, horses that have never won one or two or three, or maybe four, allowance races.

The conditions of eligibility may look like this:

1 MILE 70 YARDS. (InnerDirt). (1.40) ALLOWANCE. Purse $24,000. 3-year-olds which have never won two races other than Maiden or Claiming. Weights, 122 lbs. Non-winners of a race other than Maiden or Claiming at a mile or over since February 15 allowed 3 lbs. Of such a race since February 1, 5 lbs.

Or like this:

1 1/16 MILES. (Turf). (1.41¾) ALLOWANCE. Purse $15,000. Fillies and mares. 4-year-olds and upward. Non-winners of $3,000 twice other than maiden, starter or claiming. Weights, 4-year-olds, 120 lbs.; older, 121 lbs. Non-winners of one such race at one mile or over since December 15 allowed 3 lbs.

Or like this:

1 1/16 MILES. (Turf). (1.39¾) ALLOWANCE. (Stretch start). Purse $40,000. 4-year-olds and upward which have not won $3,000 three times other than maiden, claiming or starter. Weight, 122 lbs. Non-winners of two such races at a mile or over since February 1 allowed 3 lbs.; such a race since March 1, 5 lbs.

Variations on the theme can be numerous, depending on kinds of restrictions and other factors, including age and time of season. In all cases the racing secretary's purpose limits competition to horses of similar stripes.

In all cases, too, nonwinner allowances extend favorable advancement opportunities to young, lightly raced Thoroughbreds that have recently won and presumably are ready to move up in class by one step. Professional handicappers never discount too quickly the chances of horses that have just lost eligibility at a lower step and now are moving ahead by a step.

But matters can get complicated, and handicappers must stay on alert for performance profiles different from those posed by promising, lightly raced colts and fillies.

Referring back to the three conditions of eligibility listed, handicappers might expect the top race to go to the nicely bred, lightly raced kind of colt that has recently broken maiden status and quickly won an allowance race limited to nonwinners other than maiden or claiming.

But the middle conditions may prove agreeable to a consistent five-year-old mare that has been competing with claiming prices.

And the bottom race likely will be spoils for a four-year-old that already has annexed a stakes.

Diversity aside, the main ingredients of the nonwinner allowances do not mix well for handicappers. The introductory part of this book referred to these races as racing's toughest nuts, and they are. What makes them difficult to crack is clear enough. An axiom of handicapping warns against playing races in which the relative abilities of entrants remain unclear.

The rub with nonwinner allowances is just that. More often than not, fundamental and relative abilities of several horses remain unclear. The races remain mysterious. So they remain unplayable. Opportunities do arise, as should soon become apparent.

As handicappers understand, the term "allowance" designates races in which horses are not for sale and where eligibility and weight assignments vary according to each entrant's recent record. The better the record, the higher the weight. Excepting unusual cases when these events are carded at classic distances, however, weight is rarely a meaningful factor in the handicapping.

Oddly enough, the class factor, which should settle all disputes about these events, too many times is not decisive. Which horses that have run fast in brief careers will also run with willingness and determination when pressed hard throughout the stretch? Handicappers do not yet know. The potential class of several contenders likely will warrant much concern, but will be painstakingly difficult to assess. Last week's five-length winner of a nonwinners once allowance race may finish far back this week, although facing a field defined as only slightly better by today's allowance conditions, for nonwinners twice.

Smart players are cautious. They restrict play to horses having performance profiles suited to the conditions. Below is the array of nonwinner allowances that are run-of-the-mill in major racing, and the kinds of horses that can be expected to win them.

NONWINNERS ONCE

One step removed from maiden ranks horses compete under allowance conditions such as these:

Nonwinners of two races, or

Nonwinners of a race other than maiden or claiming, or

Nonwinners of $2,500 other than maiden or claiming.

Similar, but not the same. The third invites the best (or most diverse) field. The first bars winners of claiming races. The second bars winners of allowance grade races or better. The third admits both claiming race winners and winners of races of allowance grade or better where purses were small enough to afford less than $2,500 to the winners.

Horses that have won six allowance races, perhaps even a handicap, at tracks having relatively small purse structures remain eligible for some nonwinners once or twice allowances at major plants. This form of eligibility has become even more important to stables as the importation of foreigners has increased.

Handicappers are encouraged to stay close to a few suitable profiles. When analyzing races for nonwinners of two, or for nonwinners other than maiden or claiming, handicappers should prefer:

1. Lightly raced maiden winners that have run close once or twice and with fast clockings (speed ratings of eighty-eight or higher in sprints, eighty or higher in routes) under similar allowance conditions.

2. Impressive maiden winners, with stronger preference for the fashionably bred, leading-stable types that have broken maiden ranks first or second time out in fast time, without tiring.

In the absence of these profiles, handicappers should prefer:

NONWINNERS ALLOWANCE CONDITIONS DILEMMA FOR HANDICAPPERS

5th Santa Anita

6 FURLONGS (SANTA ANITA) — START — FINISH

6 FURLONGS. (1.07⅘) ALLOWANCE. Purse $18,000. 4-year-olds and upward. Non-winners of $2,500 other than maiden, claiming, or starter. Weights, 4-year-olds, 120 lbs.; older, 121 lbs. Non-winners of two such races any value since July 21, allowed 3 lbs.; of a race other than claiming since September 25, 6 lbs. (Winners preferred.)

Jim Burke — Own.—Venture Turf — 1105

B. g. 5, by Sette Bello—Honor Jill, by Count of Honor
Br.—White V J (Ky) — 1980 26 5 5 3 $54,000
Tr.—Pappalardo John W — 1979 7 0 1 0 $1,900
Turf 1 0 0 0

27Dec80-5SA	6f	:214 :444 1:092ft	27	1115	12½ 1hd 12 1½	Malgarini TM10	40000	92	Jim Burke, Joe Blot, Reid Street	12
28Nov80-8LA	1 1/16	:453 1:104 1:423ft	4	115	1hd 2½ 45½ 49½	Jones K2	Alw	87	Domineau, HillDrive,DeltaUnlimited	7
16Nov80-5SA	1	:461 1:111 1:364ft	4½	118	11 11 1½ 2½	Pincay L Jr7	32000	84	Desert Hawk,JimBurke,FleetRuler	10
2Nov80-9SA	1⅛	:461 1:102 1:49 ft	4¾	114	1hd 2hd 21 55¼	Jones K6	A25000	78	PierreLMont,ElAbismo,WhiteSprite	8
26Oct80-5SA	6f	:214 :45 1:10 ft	13	117	31 3nk 1½ 1¾	Jones K9	25000	89	Jim Burke, Khal Soon,CactusBlue	10
18Oct80-9SA	1 1/16	:461 1:103 1:43 ft	4	118	2hd 2hd 33 35¼	Valenzuela PA9	25000	80	Tampoy, Protectorate, Jim Burke	10
25Sep80-12Dmf	1 Ⓣ	:452 1:102 1:354fm	6½	1105	25 42½ 75¾ 712	Perez J8	Alw	83	Que Sera, Now and Then,CoboBay	10
17Sep80-6Dmf	1 1/16	:46 1:102 1:432ft	5	115	3½ 3nk 1hd 2nk‡	DelahoussyeE1	20000	83	Deep Blue Water, JimBurke,Brands	7
17Sep80—Dead-heat.										
10Sep80-9Dmr	1	:462 1:111 1:363ft	5¼	116	1hd 12 12½ 12	McCarron C J2	16000	85	Jim Burke, Hank S., AshfordCastle	8
30Aug80-2Dmr	6f	:22 :451 1:092ft	*3-2	117	2hd 1hd 12 13	Pincay L Jr9	c10000	91	JimBurke,CascadeTim,SpeciUohn	12

●Dec 22 SA 5f ft :581 h   Dec 17 SA 3f ft :35 h

Trammel Luck — Own.—Harris Farm — 114

Ch. c. 4, by Wing Out—Egg and I, by Dumpty Humpty
Br.—Harris J C (Cal) — 1980 3 1 1 0 $7,500
Tr.—Gregson Edwin — 1979 0 M 0 0

4Dec80-6BM	6f	:222 :453 1:103m	*6-5	114	56½ 53¾ 67 76¾	Lamance C4	Alw	80	YourBrvLnding,KhlSoon,ShrpFiddl	7
13Sep80-9Dmf	6f	:214 :444 1:091ft	*1	118	21 13 14 17½	Valenzuela P A8	Mdn	92	TrmmlLuck,OhFbulosDy,WilWrttn	11
22Aug80-6Dmr	6f	:22 :441 1:081ft	2½	117	21½ 25 26 210	ValenzuelPA10	Ⓢ Mdn	87	Back'n Time,TrammelLuck,Donald	11

●Dec 27 SA 5f ft :592 h   ●Dec 21 SA 5f ft :572 h   Dec 15 SA 5f ft 1:01 h   Nov 25 SA 5f ft :593 h

Will Win * — Own.—Winchell V H Jr — 115

B. h. 5, by Raise a Native—Our World, by Our Michael
Br.—Winchell V H Jr (Cal) — 1980 3 1 1 0 $10,400
Tr.—Jolly Cecil — 1979 3 M 1 0 $2,400

24Apr80-6Hol	6½f	:214 :442 1:151ft	*2¾	120	2hd 3nk 1hd 42¾	Delahoussaye E2	Alw	91	DonGabriele,MkingHy,JimmytheDip	8
27Mar80-5SA	6½f	:213 :441 1:16 ft	8¼	117	4¾ 1½ 1½ 22½	McHargue D G3	Alw	87	Barnt, Will Win, Seminole Kid	9
7Mar80-6SA	6f	:214 :451 1:10 gd	*7-5	118	15 15 12½ 14	Delahoussaye E6	Mdn	89	Will Win, Forcible,ChieftainsPrince	8
21Oct79-4SA	6½f	:222 :463 1:20 sl	10	118	33½ 14 14 2¾	Cespedes R3	Mdn	69	Motion Perfect, Will Win, Forlion	10
6Oct79-4SA	6½f	:214 :441 1:151ft	21	118	2hd 21½ 510 816	Sim M C3	Mdn	78	Share the Gold,Donald,DancynTim	12
8Sep79-2Dmr	6f	:22 :452 1:10 ft	10	117	98½ 77¾ 78 612	Sim M C7	Mdn	76	Bold Juan, Bergerac, Donald	11

Dec 30 SA 4f ft :484 h   ●Dec 26 SA 6f ft 1:124 hg   Dec 21 SA 6f ft 1:134 h   Dec 16 SA 6f ft 1:14 h

Review the past performances of the above three, entered at Santa Anita under allowances for nonwinners of a race worth $2,500 to the winner of other than maiden or claiming races. The three horses represent a classic problem of handicapping, one which contributes, unnecessarily, to numerous losing bets a season. Which do you prefer?

The five-year-old Jim Burke beat $40,000 claimers five days ago, earning the winner's share of a $22,000 purse. Not only that, the gelding won five of twenty-six for the year, earning $54,000. The other two cannot match those numbers by a long shot. Handicappers relying on those figures and Jim Burke's early speed probably would think highly of the gelding's chances against a field composed of horses which have never won an allowance race. Literally thousands of handicappers fall into the category of player which prefer the likes of Jim Burke in easy allowance races. He just won for a better purse, they'll argue, then cite his consistency and money won and contrast those points against a field of nonwinners. So be it. Yet members of that club are desperately wrong in this case, and assuredly so in many other similar situations.

⁓ Readers of this book will understand that nonwinner allowance races are written for younger, lightly raced horses which have raced impressively so far but whose true class is not fully understood. The nonwinner races not only provide opportunities against a graduated kind of competition, but also the competitive seasoning needed to advance in class against nonclaiming horses.

When confronted by Jim Burke and its like, these handicappers will appreciate first of all that the horse has raced at least thirty-three times, won five times, and earned fifty-six thousand, but *without winning* even a single allowance race. Understanding this, they will recognize Jim Burke as a claiming horse tried and true. They will know too that Jim Burke does not figure to win its first allowance race today if any other entrant qualifies as a genuine allowance runner. So they put Jim Burke's chances on the back burner and scout the field for an allowance horse.

Whether Trammel Luck will beat Will Win is a difficult matter to decide, but either horse figures to handle Jim Burke, or at the least to ruin its chances on the early pace. Both fit the conditions of the nonwinners allowance race snugly. Lightly raced. Fast, impressive races in few tries. Either or both may be on the way to stakes competition. Will Win obviously has had problems staying active, but as a son of Raise A Native it has been carefully guarded, so that it will eventually get the chance to run to its potential. Trammel Luck has been heavily backed all three times, and its disappointment in the mud at Bay Meadows deserves the benefit of the doubt, especially since its other loss occurred in dazzling time against the stakes contender Back'n Time.

I implore handicappers to quit spending money on the likes of Jim Burke in allowance races in which they face impressively quick and determined, lightly raced horses that fit these conditions admirably. Horses of proven claiming caliber cannot beat these conditions unless the field is devoid of allowance quality. This happens. It happens more frequently toward the end of the season, when most of the better horses have already passed their early allowance tests.

When nothing resembling the allowance grade appears, handicappers can profit by backing the Jim Burkes against chronic losers under nonwinners allowance conditions. But first they had better look for the lightly raced, impressively developing horses on the way up. When in doubt, pass the race.

FIFTH RACE
Santa Anita
JANUARY 1, 1981

6 FURLONGS. (1.07⅘) ALLOWANCE. Purse $18,000. 4-year-olds and upward. Non-winners of $2,500 other than maiden, claiming, or starter. Weights, 4-year-olds, 120 lbs.; older, 121 lbs. Non-winners of two such races any value since July 21, allowed 3 lbs.; of a race other than claiming since September 25, 6 lbs. (Winners preferred.)

Value of race $18,000, value to winner $9,900, second $3,600, third $2,700, fourth $1,350, fifth $450. Mutuel pool $206,409. Exacta Pool $423,336.

Last Raced	Horse	Eqt	A	Wt	PP	St	¼	½	Str	Fin	Jockey	Odds $1
24Apr80 ^{6}Hol^{4}	Will Win	b	5	115	4	1	3^{6}	1^{hd}	1^{1½}	1^{hd}	Delahoussaye E	5.50
27Nov80 ^{8}LA^{2}	Channon's Brother	b	4	114	6	6	6	5^{hd}	3^{1}	2^{1½}	Olivares F	3.00
4Dec80 ^{6}BM^{7}	Trammel Luck		4	114	3	2	2^{hd}	2^{3½}	2^{2½}	3^{½}	Valenzuela P A	1.70
31Oct80 ^{7}SA^{9}	El Payaso		5	115	5	4	4^{½}	4^{1½}	4^{½}	4^{2½}	Cordero A Jr	9.10
25Apr80 ^{6}Hol^{1}	Chieftains Prince		5	110	2	5	5^{3}	6	5^{3½}	5^{4}	McGurn C^{5}	16.00
27Dec80 ^{5}SA^{1}	Jim Burke		5	110	1	3	1^{hd}	3^{2½}	6	6	Malgarini T M^{5}	3.00

OFF AT 2:40 PST. Start good. Won driving. Time, :21⅘, :44, :56⅕, 1:09 Track fast.

$2 Mutuel Prices:			
4-WILL WIN	13.00	6.00	3.00
7-CHANNON'S BROTHER		4.40	2.40
3-TRAMMEL LUCK			2.20

$5 EXACTA 4-7 PAID $95.00.

B. h, by Raise a Native—Our World, by Our Michael. Trainer Jolly Cecil. Bred by Winchell V H Jr (Cal).

WILL WIN alternated for the early lead outside rivals, disposed of TRAMMEL LUCK in upper stretch and held off the late charge of CHANNON'S BROTHER while tiring near the finish. The latter, outrun early, raced widest into the stretch and finished with a rush to just miss. TRAMMEL LUCK forced the early pace from between rivals but lacked a closing rally. EL PAYASO never menaced. JIM BURKE alternated for the early lead along the rail, then gave way on the far turn.

Owners— 1, Winchell V H Jr; 2, Colvin & Nadel; 3, Harris Farm, 4, Greene H F; 5, Daley-Hock-Moreno, 6, Venture Turf.

Scratched—Fine Gentleman (13Nov80 ^{7}SA^{6}).

3. Younger horses whose recent efforts or clockings under similar allowance conditions indicate continued or dramatic development.

In allowance races for nonwinners of two, or for nonwinners other than maiden or claiming, handicappers back horses that have registered fast times or impressive performances in few tries. Maiden wins should have been accomplished handily or impressively. If the maiden finish were tight, the time should have been quick. An all-out maiden win in ordinary or slow time can be discounted.

Horses' performances against similar allowance nonwinners should be few, consistent, and impressive. Strong showings in the stretch or high early speed carried to the eighth pole are particularly desirable. Front-runners that have caved in after feeling pressure on the pace can be discounted.

Concerning the third profile, younger horses may struggle against maidens several times, finally win in ordinary fashion, struggle once more versus nonwinner allowance horses, then begin to get their wings flapping. The horses might be maturing or securing the benefits of seasoning, and handicappers had better watch out for them.

A particularly interesting horse is one that was backed strongly in its first few efforts, but lost. Once it gets going, the horse has every right to run the kind of powerful race anticipated by earlier money. It may have been 5 to 1 or better lately, and an overlay now.

At all times handicappers should remain relatively strict about form and jockey standards, with the usual extra credit to top stables, more so if the breeding ranks among the notables.

Instant eliminations include horses whose records reflect the following: repeated opportunities under similar conditions; dull or deteriorating form; fast workouts but noncompetitive races; entry in claiming races without success; a jockey switch from a national or local leader to a journeyman or apprentice (excepting a "hot" apprentice); a come-from-behind style but ordinary speed ratings.

Handicappers' best opportunities arrive any time a single horse shows signs of superior class while the others look dull or ordinary. In late summer or fall, late-starting three-year-olds often look inviting in comparison to older runners that remain chronic losers under nonwinners once allowance conditions. If the classy prospects have merely been maiden winners, the odds may be 5 to 2 or better, scores of racegoers still being unwilling to trust maiden winners entered under allowances. Sophisticated players exploit the crowd's nervousness. Where should fancy maiden winners run next? Against nonwinner allowance horses, of course.

In the absence of the profiles presented, or in the presence of too many suitable but indistinguishable performance profiles, the nonwinner once race is unplayable and should definitely be passed. If handicappers pass the races, they can become more relaxed about observing the competition objectively. Horses on the improve should be watched closely in nonwinner allowance races. There they demonstrate previously uncalled-for signs of class. These are signs handicappers relish.

The ability to get early forward position readily and to show a high turn of speed when the rider asks is one. Another is prolonged stretch drive, especially when challenged inside the 3/16ths pole. A third, and a particularly strong sign, is capacity to set or press fast early fractions, then draw away easily in the stretch. And the best is rapid acceleration and powerful determination when challenged at any key point in the race, more so if challenged repeatedly, and particularly so if pressured throughout the stretch run.

Recently at some major tracks handicappers seeking juicier opportunities in nonwinner allowance races have located intriguing new benefactors. Horsemen have been importing thoroughbreds from around the globe. Most have raced, many impressively. To facilitate the horses' acquaintance with American conditions and counterparts, racing secretaries have carded additional nonwinner allowance races for horses four years old and older. The conditions of eligibility contain a new twist. The conditions grant eligibility to horses that might have won numerous races of allowance grade or better but have not yet won a specified minimum winner's share in those races.

To wit: ". . . nonwinners of $2,500 (or $3,000 or whatever) other than maiden or claiming." By specifying a minimum winner's share the secretaries favor the foreigners. Thoroughbreds imported from England or Ireland or South America or Australia or New Zealand have been racing where purse structures have modest value. Many have won numerous purses, but winner shares have been so small even repeat winners remain eligible for nonwinner allowance shares here. A regularly raced American horse aged four or older and still eligible to nonwinners of $2,500 other than maiden or claiming cannot be too much, especially if the race occurs during the summer or fall. Foreigners have a fat chance to roll.

Handicappers in territories where these conditions exist take fast notice. In concert with performance profiles previously mentioned, in allowance races for four-year-olds and up and limited to nonwinners of a specified winner's share other than maiden or claiming, handicappers should prefer:

4. Any foreign-raced horse that has won races of allowance grade or better more frequently than has been specified in the conditions.

The more consistent the foreigner, the better. Of course, the horses must be fit and suited to the footing and distance. That is, unless the imports exit graded or listed stakes. Any foreign-bred or foreign-raced horse that has finished in-the-money or run close in an important stakes, notably of France or England, has every right to devastate a group of local horses that have yet to win one allowance race. The distance or footing may not be just right; no matter. The class edge is large and can be expected to overcompensate.

NONWINNERS TWICE

When allowance conditions specify ". . . nonwinners twice (or of $2,500 twice) other than maiden or claiming," similar guidelines apply, but with shades of emphasis and priority more hospitable to handicappers. Among the diversity of nonwinner allowances, non-winners twice most often provide handicappers with the least disguised possibilities.

In typical lineups, handicappers find at least one horse that has recently broken the maiden and in few attempts has won an allowance race. If the allowance win looked powerful, the horse may be the classy sort taking just another small step. Handicappers support these horses confidently if the prices are right, or they pass the race. Bets on other horses in the face of lightly raced potential tigers on the way up veritably invite defeat. –

Other fields bring together assorted mixtures. Several horses run consistently with allowance company and have won one allowance race. A few show six to eight allowance performances, with one success. Several have competed lately in claiming races, for purchase prices ($20,000 or higher at major tracks) that suggest consistent earning power. The latter may be aged five or six now, and once won under nonwinner allowances at three or four. A few foreign-raced horses may be entered. By late spring, summer, or fall the age range likely will be three to six.

Handicappers' hands are often tied uncomfortably. What to do? As usual, handicappers prosper by restricting play to the suitable past performance profiles. *The Handicapper's Condition Book* approves of six profiles. When analyzing allowance races for nonwinners twice other than maiden or claiming, handicappers should prefer:

1. Lightly raced impressive younger horses, especially nicely bred improving three-year-olds that recently have won an allowance race impressively or easily in better-than-average time. Or,

2. The same kind of impressive or improving younger horses that have won an allowance event and have lost under nonwinners twice conditions no more than three times while racing competitively. Or,

3. Lightly raced three-year-olds or late-developing four-year-olds that have won an allowance race impressively and were not disgraced when entered in a stakes or handicap.

Naturally, if the field contains three or more horses of suitable profile, a normal event, the race is too contentious, and handicappers must pass, or play the exotics.

In the absence of the above profiles, or in nonwinner twice races restricted to four years old and up, handicappers should prefer:

4. A lightly raced foreign-raced entrant, preferably four, whose

record includes (a) a graded stakes victory, (b) few wins but relatively high earnings, or (c) placings or close finishes in group or listed stakes.

Several powerful foreign-bred or foreign-raced horses remain eligible for nonwinners twice allowance conditions when first they arrive in the states. In longer races, imports often enjoy better seasoning at the distance, especially on turf. Handicappers watch for imports from France, where good horses overseas gather to race for Europe's biggest purses.

HANDICAPPING BY THE CONDITIONS

Nonwinners allowance races may be the toughest kind for handicappers, but those who know what to look for find opportunities such as the following several times each season.

On January 4, 1981, at Santa Anita, the colt profiled below was entered against four-year-olds and up, at one mile and one-sixteenth on the turf, for nonwinners twice other than maiden, claiming, or starter. Handicappers able to accept the workout line as indicative of satisfactory form got a chance at a very good thing. Examine each race in the colt's past performances. Consider its advantages against limited competition of the kind eligible to the January 4 turf route.

Vatza			Ch. c. 4, by Nijinsky II—Shuvee, by Nashua							
			Br.—Stone W (Va)				1980	2 0 1 1	$14,560	
Own.—Bell J A III		**115**	Tr.—Russell John W				1979	4 1 0 1	$12,000	
							Turf	3 1 1 1	$22,960	

14Nov80-3Aqu 1 ①:48¹¹ 1:22¹:37¹fm°4-5 115 6³¼ 55¼ 45 35¼⁴ Maple E⁶ Alw 89 Honey Fox, DiscoCount,Santo'sJoe 7
 ♦14Nov80—Dead heat
7May80-8Aqu 1¹⁄ₓ①:48 1:12¹¹:43²fm 3¼ 113 3⁴ 1hd 2hd 2¼ Maple E⁴⁻ Hl Prnc H 87 Ben Fab, Vatza, Don Daniello 8
310ct79-1Aqu 1¹⁄₈①:48 1:13³¹:514gd 4¼ 120 65¼ 32 11 13¾ Maple E¹⁰ Mdn 85 Vatza, Silver Schuss, Trojan Lark 12
170ct79-4Aqu 1 :47 1:11³ 1:37 ft °6-5 118 52¼ 33¼ 48 4¹³ Maple E³ Mdn 68 Rectory, Philanthropic, TrojanLark 7
40ct79-6Bel 1 :47³ 1:12² 1:37³m 7-5 120 2hd 32 25 4¹³ Maple E³ Mdn 67 Degenerate Jon, Ohno,I'mRegalToo 6
25Aug79-4Sar 6f :22² :45³ 1:103ft °6-5 118 52 42¼ 42 38 Vasquez J² Mdn 79 Southerner,ImpressivePrince,Vatza 8
 Jan 1 SA 6f ft 1:11² h   Dec 27 SA 1 ft 1:40² h   Dec 21 SA 1 ft 1:41² h   Dec 14 SA 7f ft 1:26² h

Handicappers should have noted the following:

1. When first entered on turf, Vatza breezed to the kind of easy victory the earlier betting and its aristocratic breeding had intended of it. The colt was still just two years old.

2. After a six-month layoff, probably due to injury, the colt returned to finish second in a handicap at Aqueduct against the genuine stakes horse Ben Fab. Quite a showing.

3. Following another six months on the sidelines, Vatza returned again, this time running third at odds-on in an Aqueduct overnite allowance route. Perhaps it needed the race.

4. Despite the colt's eligibility to nonwinners once allowances, trainer John Russell has elected to enter under nonwinners twice conditions. Perhaps Russell is confident.

5. The colt's breeding both supports and amplifies all of the above. Sired by chef-de-race Nijinsky II, out of the champion Shuvee, by the champion Nashua, Vatza has absolutely the right to do big things in the sport. Importantly, unless its performances gave strong hint the expectations were justified, which they do, the breeding would not mean a thing.

Other horses in the January 4 race were by Lyhard, Secretariat, Irish Castle, and Ack Ack, but none of these could match Vatza's credentials, or that colt's promise of things to come. Rank in the walking ring and during the post parade, Vatza was taken out of line by jockey Fernando Toro, and jogged to the three-eighths pole, where Toro sat on him near the outer rail for fully five minutes. Vatza settled down, walked calmly to the post, and ran his race.

The promising colt won by nine lengths; paid $9.

More than number of victories, handicappers concentrate now on stakes credentials and earnings. If imports have won or run close in group events or have earned more money than would be typical of allowance nonwinners twice here, they may outclass their rivals decisively. At longer distances the class advantage intensifies. Foreigners that satisfy handicappers' form, distance, and footing standards will occasionally trigger rewarding bets. Astute handicappers will find generous winners among the foreign group.

For an exceptionally outstanding example of the possibilities, examine a middle-distance turf event run at Hollywood Park several summers ago.

No less than five of these ten nonwinners twice eligibles show foreign racing in their past performances. The five are *No Saint, Campodonico, Rachmaninoff, Numa Pompilius,* and *Boots Colonero.* Obviously handicappers equipped to relate their foreign records to current form and conditions will be at some advantage. In this regard, a knowledge of eligibility conditions and the kinds of horses that fit them best is absolutely the key to prosperity.

To begin, it's May, and knowledge of conditions helps handicappers appreciate that horses age five or older still eligible to a race that bars winners of two allowance races had better reveal persuasive excuses for the lack of performance, namely a lack of racing. Let's look first at horses age five and older, and see whether they have a legitimate excuse for remaining eligible today.

8th Hollywood

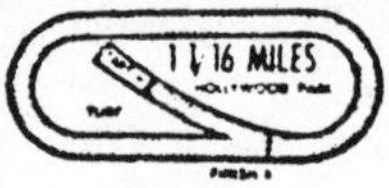

1 1/16 MILES. (TURF). (1.39⅗) ALLOWANCE. Purse $20,000. 4-year-olds and upward. Non-winners of $2,500 twice other than maiden, claiming, or starter. Weight, 120 lbs. Non-winners of such a race at one mile or over since February 14, allowed 3 lbs.; of such a race since December 25, 6 lbs. (Winners preferred.)

Coupled—No Saint and Siempre Uno.

Summit

B. h. 5, by T V Lark—Brown Duchess, by Terrang
Br.—Donaldson & Goldcamp Drs (Ky) 1978 6 1 1 0 $14,250
Own.—Madden P **120** **Tr.—Parker Paul K** 1977 5 1 1 2 $12,175
Turf 3 1 0 0 $7,700

23Apr78-9Hol 1⅜ Ⓣ:494 1:40 2:153fm 7½ 120 53½ 63½ 97¾ 97¾ Pierce D9 Alw 69 Bartlesville, Verdin II, Zor 10
15Apr78-5Hol 1 1/16 :462 1:103 1:422sy 8½ 120 76¾ 3½ 1½ 2nk Pierce D8 Alw 83 Paris, Summit, Siempre Uno 8
1Apr78-9SA 1 1/16 :462 1:11 1:431gd 18 121 1011 64 52 43½ Pierce D10 Alw 83 Protocol, Fig Nooton, Paris 11
18Mar78-7SA 1⅛ Ⓣ:463 1:11 1:484fm 11 121 911 86½ 85½ 88½ Pincay L Jr4 Alw 74 Pomeroy,StrofErinII,GrhmHegney 12
23Feb78-9SA 1⅛ Ⓣ:46 1:102 1:473fm 3½ 116 68 1½ 2½ 1no Pincay L Jr8 Alw 89 Summit, Rising Arc, Thaliard 8
26Jan78-9SA 1 1/16 :463 1:104 1:42 ft 8½ 115 65 64 45½ 48½ Harris W9 Alw 83 RingoTic,PirrLMont,FluorscntLight 9
31Mar77-7SA 1⅛ :463 1:111 1:484ft 2½ 117 66½ 62¼ 42½ 45½ Castaneda M5 Alw 82 Jacks Five, Black Majesty,FoxyHill 7
4Mar77-6SA 1 1/16 :461 1:11 1:424ft *9-5 118 79 43 1½ 13 Pierce D6 Mdn 88 Summit, SavageDance,HillMiracle 10
19Feb77-2SA 1 1/16 :463 1:112 1:423ft *1 117 44 32 34½ 39 Vergara O3 Mdn 80 Theologist, AinfordCastle Summit 11
3Feb77-6SA 1 1/16 :46 1:102 1:424ft *9-5 117 55½ 22 1hd 22½ Vergara O1 Mdn 86 Jacks Five, Summit, Theologist 12
May 6 Hol 6f ft 1:16 h May 1 Hol 5f ft 1:014 h ●Apr 13 Hol 3f ft :342 b Apr 8 SA 5f ft 1:024 h

Pierre La Mont

B. g. 4, by Great Mystery—Two Su Sis, by Andys Glory
Br.—Amlung R (Fla) 1978 7 1 1 2 $18,600
Own.—Siegel Jan **120** **Tr.—Hendricks Byron** 1977 12 3 1 1 $14,536
Turf 11 3 1 3 $25,944

29Apr78-5Hol 1 Ⓣ:47 1:113 1:354fm 5 120 1½ 1½ 1½ 31 Castaneda M1 Alw 90 HppyGelic,NuclerPulse,PirrLMont 10
8Apr78-5SA 1¼ :464 1:354 2:014ft 9 115 11 2½ 54 610 PierceD4 Sn Jcinto H 77 FluorescentLight,Gllpit,ConfdrtYnk 7
8Apr78—Run in two divisions, 5th & 8th races.
2Apr78-5SA 1⅛ Ⓣ:481 1:131 1:504yl 8½ 115 11 1½ 1hd 3nk Pierce D6 Alw 73 Gallapiat, Laredo, Pierre La Mont 10
23Feb78-5SA 1⅛ Ⓣ:471 1:112 1:474fm 3½ 115 11 2½ 11 11 Pierce D6 Alw 88 PierreLMont,Stevor,LicensdToWin 7
26Jan78-9SA 1 1/16 :463 1:104 1:42 ft 9 115 11 2hd 1½ 2hd Pierce D2 Alw 92 RingoTic,PirrLMont,FluorscntLight 9
19Jan78-7SA 1 1/16 :473 1:113 1:432m 18 115 52 43 44 44½ Pierce D1 Alw 80 Bartlesville, Hill Beguin, Zor 6
5Jan78-7SA 1⅛ :474 1:123 1:514sl 20 115 22 22 35½ 412 Pierce D2 Alw 61 BootsColonero,Brtlesville,HillBguin 8
28Aug77-9Dmr 1⅛ Ⓣ:471 1:111 1:502fm 5½ 115 32 31½ 46 710 St Leon G2 A25000 79 VbrntGlow,MovMogul,ThDoublOKd 7
12Aug77-9Dmr 1⅛ Ⓣ:473 1:12 1:504fm 3½ 117 1½ 1hd 2hd 55 St Leon G7 A25000 82 Timely Vision, Vibrant Glow, AuVol 7
21Jly77-9Hol 1⅛ Ⓣ:472 1:114 1:501fm *9-5 119 2½ 1½ 1½ 41 Bailey J D5 A25000 84 The DoubleOKid,DanButcher,Diego 7
Mar 20 SA Ⓣ 1 fm 1:47 h (d) Mar 11 SA 1 ft 1:434 h

*No Saint

B. g. 6, by Bahroona—Dark Mistress, by Underwood
Br.—Dillon M L (NZ) 1978 2 1 0 0 $9,375
Own.—Fogelson E E **120** **Tr.—Whittingham Charles** 1977 8 1 2 1 $3,749
Turf 31 4 8 3 $12,825

16Apr78-6Hol 1 1/16 :464 1:113 1:433ft *1 114 1½ 12 14 16 Shoemaker W4 Alw 77 No Saint, As de Copas, ElReyChico 6
29Mar78-3SA 6½f :221 :45 1:154ft 4½ 114 72¾ 42¾ 43½ 411 Shoemaker W2 Alw 80 TequilaSunrise,Contador,FoxyGrmp 9
11Apr77 ♦ 10Ellerslie(NZ) a1 1:374gd 105 Ⓣ 31½ Tiley N Islington H Carlaw, Battle Fury, No Saint 13
26Mar77 ♦ 11TeAroha(NZ) a7f 1:24 fm 126 Ⓣ 8 Tiley N All Aged Tudor Light, Soliloquy, Chrisarda 16
5Mar77 ♦ 11Ellerslie(NZ) a1 1:344fm 107 Ⓣ 2½ Tiley N City of Papakura H Verax, No Saint, Patronize 18
23Feb77 ♦ 9TeRapa(NZ) a1 1:361gd 25 119 Ⓣ 1no Tiley N Scot H No Saint, Verax, Royal Mallard 18
5Feb77 ♦ 6Matamata(NZ) a1¼ 2:031fm 110 Ⓣ 13 SkltnR Matamata Cup H Fagan's Boy,FreeGold,FastaZecan 18
15Jan77 ♦ 10Avondale(NZ) a1¼ 2:02 fm 127 Ⓣ 13 Tweedie A Wells H Doristoi, NobleBoy SpringWaggon 16
8Jan77 ♦ 7Parawai(NZ) a1¼ 2:023fm 124 Ⓣ 2hd TweedieA Goldfields H Albacore, No Saint, Ellan Vannin 17
3Jan77 ♦ 3Ellerslie(NZ) a1 1:35 fm 124 Ⓣ 43¾ TwdiA Three Thousand H Irish lad, Just Serene, Noble Boy 11
May 9 Hol 3f ft :354 h May 3 Hol 1 ft 1:392 h Apr 28 Hol 3f ft :362 h Apr 22 Hol 3f ft :351 h

Postscript *

B. g. 4, by Speak John—Postal Queen, by Sword Dancer
Br.—Elmendorf Farm (Ky) 1978 4 0 0 0
Own.—Elmendorf **117** **Tr.—McAnally Ronald** 1977 9 3 1 1 $26,990
Turf 1 0 0 0

15Apr78-5Hol 1 1/16 :462 1:103 1:422sy 6½ 118 2hd 1hd 53½ 88 Olivares F6 Alw 75 Paris, Summit, Siempre Uno 8
18Mar78-7SA 1⅛ Ⓣ:463 1:11 1:484fm 11 119 2½ 2hd 62½ 76½ McHargue D G7 Alw 76 Pomeroy,StrofErinII,GrhmHegney 12
5Mar78-8SA 1¼ :454 1:351 2:011sl 7½e 112 53 920 929 941 McCrrnCJ4 SntAnitH 49 Vigors, Mr. Redoy, Jumping Hill 10
8Jan78-5SA 1 1/16 :472 1:114 1:444sl *6-5 120 2½ 78 1115 1117 McHargue D G9 Alw 61 Rojig, Cathy's Reject, Verdin II 12
29Dec77-9SA 1 :48 1:14 1:412m *4-5 114 1½ 1hd 12 15 McHargue D G3 Alw 62 Postscript,ShortVoyg,LicnsdToWin 8
4Nov77-4SA 1 1/16 :454 1:102 1:422ft 7½ 119 1½ 1½ 12½ 15 McHargue DG5 30000 90 Postscript, Best Exit, Molto 6
28Oct77-9SA 1 1/16 :463 1:112 1:45 ft 8-5 117 32 32 11 1¾ McHargue DG5 25000 77 Postscript, Ute City, Tejon Canyon 7

8Oct77-2SA 6½f :214 :443 1:16 ft 8¾ 117 4¾ 2½ 22½ 25 Castaneda M2 20000 85 BouncingDv,Postscript,Fool'sLogc 12
11Jun77-2Hol 6f :213 :443 1:094ft 2½ 114 2½ 56½ 67½ 612 Olivares F2 Alw 78 Bold Logic, Big BadBruce,Rescator 6
30May77-3Hol 6f :22 :444 1:034ft 15 114 31 43½ 46 54¼ Castaneda M1 Alw 86 CrimsonCommnder,SuperJoy,Usurp 7
May 7 Hol 7f ft 1:272 h May 2 Hol 6f ft 1:162 h Apr 25 Hol 4f ft :492 h

Mary's Policy

Own.—Desert Fox Stable-Selesnick 114
Ch. c. 4, by New Policy—Mrs Sanchez, by Sensitivo
Br.—Lazaroff A (Cal)
Tr.—King Hal
1978 5 1 0 1 $10,450
1977 14 2 3 2 $26,850
Turf 4 0 0 2 $7,575

26Mar78-9SA 1⅛ Ⓣ:463 1:112 1:49 fm 34 115 2hd 2hd 21 3¾ Lambert J4 35000 81 ReigningNtive,TrvilII,Mry'sPolicy 12
12Mar78-3SA 7f :223 :452 1:233sl 6½ 121 75½ 1010 1011 1012 McHargueDG3 c25000 73 Repurchase,NightlyCaper,Tenoroc 11
4Mar78-5SA 1⅟₁₆ :47 1:121 1:451m 8 116 53¾ 63¾ 75½ 67¾ McCarron C J4 32000 68 Mr. Irv M., Bold Logic, Repurchase 7
26Feb78-3SA 1⅟₁₆ :463 1:113 1:434ft 4½e115 32½ 3½ 1½ 14 Hawley S3 c20000 83 Mry'sPolicy,PerfectHitter,Mr IrvM 8
19Feb78-1SA 6f :221 :452 1:102ft 35 1105 86 65 67 66½ Chapman T6 25000 80 MediciMn,CtStevens,WindyWhispr 8
4Nov77-4SA 1⅟₁₆ :454 1:102 1:422ft 4½ 1125 59 65 66 511 Chapman T6 30000 79 Postscript, Best Exit, Molto 6
4Jly77-6Hol 1⅟₁₆ Ⓣ:471 1:112 1:421fm 5 109 47 43½ 41 41¾ Hawley S1 Alw 86 Foxy Hill, Flying Kansu, Verdin II 6
19Jun77-5Hol 1⅛ Ⓣ:471 1:113 1:484fm 8 1045 34 42 21½ 31¾ Sellers M S3 Alw 90 TrvilII,ForgtThShowrs,Mry'sPolicy 9
5Jun77-9Hol 1 Ⓣ:464 1:101 1:35 fm 10 1035 72¼ 46½ 58½ 45½ Sellers M S6 Alw 89 ElVctoroso,LckyTrdr,BoldBochrd 10
22May77-1Hol 1 :47 1:113 1:372ft 6 118 85½ 43½ 32½ 1hd Hawley S2 ⓈAlw 79 Mary'sPolicy,Mr Pocle,GranjMimdo 8
May 6 Hol 6f ft 1:143 h Apr 30 Hol 4f ft :493 h Apr 4 SA 5f ft 1:014 h Mar 28 SA 4f ft :48 h

*Campodonico *

Own.—Hirsch C L 1095
Ch. h. 5, by Atlas—Snow Night, by Snow Cat
Br.—Marmol & Troica (Arg)
Tr.—Stute Warren
1978 5 0 0 1 $2,550
1977 7 2 2 1 $5,547
Turf 1 0 0 0

29Apr78-5Hol 1 Ⓣ:47 1:113 1:354fm 34 1095 53½ 74 86 62½ Chapman T M4 Alw 88 HppyGelic,NuclerPulse,PrrLMont 10
15Apr78-5Hol 1⅟₁₆ :462 1:103 1:422sy 13 115 61¾ 72½ 87½ 77½ Toro F7 Alw 76 Paris, Summit, Siempre Uno 8
1Apr78-5SA 1⅟₁₆ :462 1:11 1:431gd 5½ 116 76½ 85 94½ 87½ Pincay L Jr7 Alw 79 Protocol, Fig Nooton, Paris 11
20Feb78-5SA 1⅟₁₆ :462 1:112 1:433ft 13 115 65 84½ 76 35½ Toro F8 Alw 78 DogwoodPssport,Ksk,Cmpodonico 11
28Jan78-7SA 1⅟₁₆ :461 1:102 1:422ft 6 115 45 52¾ 74½ 611 Encinas R1 Alw 79 Pass N' Run,AlphaBoy,StealaMarch 7
20Aug77 ♦8Hipodromo(Arg) a1 1:334ft 2¾ 121 11½ SnguinettiV Stk Campodonico, The Blues, RingoTic 8
7Aug77 ♦5Hipodromo(Arg) a1⅛ 1:492hy *1 126 17 SngttiV PremioTelefonico(Alw) Cmpodonico,FelizVije,ElMisterioso 8
25May77 ♦6Palermo(Arg) a1⅝ 2:35 hy 48 123 911 EncnsR Gran Pr 25 de Mayo Dioico, Hill Beguin, Formico 14
8May77 ♦6Palermo(Arg) a1⅜ 2:18 hy 17 124 310 SngttiV Cl General Belgrano Facistol, Bogart, Campodonico 6
9Apr77 ♦3Palermo(Arg) a1 1:362gd 4½ 115 28 SnguinettiV – Hcp TroproSos,Cmpodonico,NughtyGuy 5
May 10 Hol 3f ft :354 h May 7 Hol 4f ft :474 h Apr 28 Hol Ⓣ 3f fm :361 h (d) Apr 22 Hol 4f ft :48 h

Rachmaninoff

Own.—Silver Star Stable 114
B. c. 4, by Northern Dancer—True Blue, by Jester
Br.—Harbor View Farm (Md)
Tr.—Jackson Evan
1978 1 0 0 0 $450
1977 7 2 3 2 $27,700
Turf 5 1 2 1 $11,335

29Apr78-5Hol 1 Ⓣ:47 1:113 1:354fm 3 115 31½ 31 54 51½ Toro F5 Alw 89 HppyGelic,NuclerPulse,PrrLMont 10
4Jly77-9Hol 1⅟₁₆ Ⓣ:463 1:11 1:42 fm*9-5 115 55½ 64½ 51½ 1no Toro F6 Alw 89 Rchmninoff,ElMorgon,PrsonlityPul 7
26Jun77-6Hol 1⅟₁₆ :451 1:10 1:421ft *8-5 114 32½ 42½ 42½ 25 McHargue D G4 Alw 79 GaelicKing,Rchmnnoff,FigNooton 10
19Jun77-3Hol 1⅛ Ⓣ:463 1:113 1:491fm *1e115 12½ 1½ 11 3hd Pierce D7 Alw 90 MxcnMsc,‡GntlmnGngr,Rchmnnoff 7
29May77-2Hol 1 :46 1:104 1:36 ft *1 114 59 32½ 34 37 Hawley S2 Alw 79 StonePoint,Mr.Pocle,Rachmaninoff 7
8May77-4Hol 1 :46 1:101 1:37 m 2½ 115 2½ 2hd 21 2nk Pierce D4 Alw 81 JunglMission,Rchmnnoff,MnstrlGry 6
1May77-7Hol 1⅟₁₆ :471 1:123 1:464sl 4½ 115 1hd 1hd 21 23 Pierce D9 Alw 58 Postmrk,Rchmninoff,ThDoublOKid 9
10Apr77-4SA 7f :223 :452 1:23 ft 2¾ 118 1½ 11½ 11 11¼ Pierce D3 Mdn 88 Rachmaninoff, Public, Gallahad 6
11Sep76 ♦5Doncaster(Eng) 6f 1:174yl *1 123 Ⓣ 2nk Piggott L Ribero Carriage Way, Rahcmaninoff, Don 8
28Aug76 ♦6Curragh(Ire) 6f 1:141fm*1-2 126 Ⓣ 22½ MrphT Dunmurry (Mdn) LaughingRiver,Rchmninoff,Scbbrd 10
May 7 Hol Ⓣ 5f fm 1:03 b Apr 26 Hol 4f ft :49 b ●Apr 21 Hol Ⓣ 1 fm 1:421 b (d) Apr 14 Hol 7f ft 1:25 h

Siempre Uno

Own.—Tassano & Whittingham C 120
B. c. 4, by Pretense—Dors, by Corporal II
Br.—Flynn E C (Ky)
Tr.—Whittingham Michael
1978 4 2 0 1 $18,400
1977 0 M 0 0

15Apr78-5Hol 1⅟₁₆ :462 1:103 1:422sy *2 120 1hd 2hd 2½ 31¾ Shoemaker W3 Alw 81 Paris, Summit, Siempre Uno 8
30Mar78-5SA 1 :461 1:103 1:362sl *8-5 117 3½ 1hd 2hd 1nk Shoemaker W6 Alw 87 SiempreUno,HppyGelic,WindyDncr 9
10Mar78-7SA 6f :22 :451 1:10 ft 7 117 52½ 63½ 64 64¾ Shoemaker W6 Alw 85 Protocol, Trinative, Ridgemont 9
23Feb78-4SA 6f :221 :451 1:102ft 2 117 31 22½ 23½ 1no Shoemaker W3 Mdn 87 Siempre Uno, Lerky, Firdabee 8
May 8 Hol 5f ft :594 h May 3 Hol Ⓣ 6f fm 1:163 h Apr 26 Hol 5f ft 1:012 h ●Apr 21 Hol Ⓣ 3f fm :374 h (d)

Numa Pompilius

Own.—Cannata C 114
Ch. c. 4, by Dr Fager—Nostrana, by Botticelli
Br.—Batthyany Countess Margit (Fla)
Tr.—Fulton John W
1978 1 0 0 0
1977 8 1 2 0 $11,212
Turf 13 2 3 0 $27,043

11Mar78 ♦5StCloud(Fra) a7½f 1:462gd 3¾ 132 Ⓣ 64½ RssGB Prix Violoncelle(Hcp) Pollira, Sea Moor, Dollar Or 16
23Oct77 ♦6Longchamp(Fra) a1¼ 2:143sf 9-5 123 Ⓣ 716 SmnH Prix de Solferino(Alw) SilverEagle,Salvaro,Watershipdown 8
2Oct77 ♦2Longchamp(Fra) a1⅟₁₆ 2:012gd 7½ 123 Ⓣ 2nk StMrtnY Prixd'Chmpslyss(Hcp) FirstPryer,NumPompilius,Kingdsh 20
6Aug77 ♦4Deauville(Fra) a6½f 1:171gd 33 119 Ⓣ 11 SmnHB PrxMuricedeGhest(Gr3) Flying After,GirlFriend,Polyponder 12
25Jun77 ♦2Longchamp(Fra) a1⅛ 2:023gd 6½ 128 Ⓣ 11 SmnH PirxduMontparnsse(Alw) NumaPompilius,Djadab,Zedon'sSon 5
20May77 ♦5StCloud(Fra) a1⅟₁₆ 2:302sf 4 121 Ⓣ 56¾ SmnHB Prix Lovelace(Alw) Kashneb, Inia, Lestour 5
May 10 Hol 3f ft :352 h May 5 Hol Ⓣ 1 fm 1:443 h (d) Apr 29 Hol 5f ft 1:003 h Apr 23 Hol 1 ft 1:423 h

***Boots Colonero ✻** — B. h. 6, by Snow Boots—Colonia, by Bell Hop

Own.—Agnew D J — 117 — Br.—Haras El Portillo (Arg) — Tr.—Fanning Jerry

1978	4	1	0	0	$7,700
1977	3	0	2	0	$4,800
Turf	2	0	1	0	$2,000

?Apr78-9SA	1 1/16 :46² 1:11 1:43¹gd	77	121	4²	10⁷	10⁷¾	10¹¹	Ramirez R6	Alw	75	Protocol, Fig Nooton, Paris	11
18Mar78-7SA	1⅛ Ⓣ:46³1:11 1:48⁴fm	52	121	6⁶	9⁶¾	11⁷¾	11¹³	Olivares F6	Alw	70	Pomeroy StrofErinII,GrhniHegney	12
15Jan78-6SA	1 1/16 :46² 1:11² 1:44¹sl	*9-5	121	5³½	6⁵½	6¹³	6¹⁴	Cauthen S2	Alw	67	Laredo, Code Three, Ringo Tic	6
5Jan78-7SA	1⅛ :47⁴ 1:12³ 1:51⁴sl	9-5	114	1²	1²	1³	1³	Cauthen S4	Alw	73	BootsColonero,Brtlesville,HillBguin	8
28Dec77-9SA	1 1/16 :49² 1:14⁴ 1:48³m	*3-2	115	1¹½	1³	1²	2no	Cauthen S1	Alw	59	Rojig, Boots Colonero, MinimalArt	5
5Nov77-7SA	1 1/16 :48³ 1:11² 1:44 m	*2½	117	3¹	6⁹½	7¹⁷	7³²	Olivares F4	Alw	50	Sudanes, Dynastic Duke, Thaliard	5
14Sep77-5Dmr	1 1/16 Ⓣ:47²1:12¹1:44²fm	6½	114	3²½	2hd	1hd	2¹	Olivares F5	Alw	86	Laredo,BootsColonero,GranjMimdc	9
8Dec76♦8LaPlata(Arg)	a7f 1:26 ft	*1-2	122				1³	ZptR	Pr CongreveEspecial(Alw)		BootsColonro,Condnsdr,AhElInvct	6
4Jly76♦7LaPlata(Arg)	a1 1:39¹ft	*7-5	126				1¾	CndM	PremioMardeFondo(Alw)		BootsColonro,ElSinRivl,Escndiavc	14
16Apr76♦3LaPlata(Arg)	a5½f 1:07 gd	*1	119				1²½	SndlM	Pr Gran Intriga (Alw)		BootsColonero,MarkedPlay,Yarko	10

May 9 Hol 4f ft :48⁴ h ● May 3 Hol 7f ft 1:26³ h Apr 26 Hol 6f ft 1:16² h Apr 20 Hol 6f ft 1:12³ h

Summit looks acceptable on that score. Laid up shortly after leaving maiden ranks at three (March 4), the gelding beat nonwinners once conditions its second race back. It also indicated a liking that day for turf. It since has run close to nonwinners twice winners, and its loss April 23 can be forgiven—it stayed close for one and one-eighth miles but tired at the marathon distance. Contender.

No Saint has raced twice in the states, winning its last easily. The six-year-old has raced some thirty times in New Zealand, winning enough, but amassing little earnings and a record clearly of nondistinction. It might be a problem today if able to get clear early, but a far safer notion is that it lacks the class to move ahead in nonclaiming company at Hollywood Park.

Campodonico, of Argentina, has not raced very much but has not impressed very much either. It might wake up today, but why bet on it?

Boots Colonero has been humbled in three nonwinners twice races, after daylighting nonwinners once horses when well-backed January 5. The Argentine-bred is either not up to it or terribly off form.

Of the four-year-olds, handicappers prefer them lightly raced, and with sufficient evidence they might yet be able to distinguish themselves in nonclaiming company.

Pierre La Monte beat allowance horses February 23 and has done well enough under today's kind of conditions since, but this gelding is a well-documented claiming horse and not a likely candidate among several allowance winners, particularly if one or more of them will likely contest him early on the pace.

Postscript has early lick but is off form.

Mary's Policy returns to nonwinners allowance competition after a good effort in high-priced claiming company, this two weeks following its claim by the competent Hal King. Its previous allowance record sustains King's new hopes, but its only allowance win occurred in a race restricted to state-breds and lately it has been losing to claiming horses. No play.

Rachmaninoff, Siempre Uno, and *Numa Pompilius,* lightly raced, nicely bred, well-backed in their efforts, each with a note of distinction in its record, are precisely the kind handicappers prefer in these limited events, and indeed the three form the guts of this overnite turf scramble. Does one actually figure to win? Only comprehensive handicapping can decide at this point.

Siempre Uno has no experience on turf, not much seasoning at the distance, barely beat nonwinners once horses, and figures to contest a fast, hotly debated pace. The Pretense colt does not figure to win today.

The contenders are *Rachmaninoff* and *Numa Pompilius.* The previously remarked *Summit* cannot measure up to either and now can be dismissed. *Rachmaninoff,* by the great sire Northern Dancer, finished in-the-money in its seven three-year-old races, winning at a sprint, at today's distance, and on turf. Its turf record is particularly appealing, including its early sprints as the favorite in England and Ireland. Two weeks ago, its first start at four, the colt beat half the field of a turf mile, beaten less than two lengths. It has prepped on turf since. *Numa Pompilius,* by the brilliant Dr. Fager, has won the most money on turf, $27,043, finished second, beaten a neck in an overnite handicap in France, where the best of foreign racing takes place, and was started in a Group 3 event after an easy allowance victory at three. On its return at four, the colt finished sixth of sixteen when strongly backed in a sprint at St. Cloud. It now has arrived in Hollywood, where it has been working splendidly for trainer John Fulton. A close look at its past performances shows that of its three poor efforts, two occurred on soft turf (October 23 it was backed to 9 to 5 against the handicap star Silver Eagle), the other in a Group 3 stakes for which it likely remained unready. The Hollywood turf is firm, and no graded stakes horses will be eligible today. What to do?

Handicappers often are left with indecision after painstaking handicapping of nonwinner allowance races. The May 11 race at Hollywood shaped up as a typical case in point. If forced to choose, *Rachmaninoff's* recent form gets the nod. Whatever edge exists belongs to the Northern Dancer colt. It figures to track the early pace, take the lead into the stretch, and hold. Yet sometimes good fortune strikes for handicappers, and this happened this fortunate day at Hollywood Park. On the track *Rachmaninoff* appeared wet and rank. His edge now blunted, the colt could not be expected to win, and could not be bet at reasonable odds. But *Numa Pompilius*, its chances now improved, could reasonably be bet at unreasonable odds, which it definitely was, thanks to the oversight of the Hollywood crowd.

When *Numa Pompilius* won by a half length with a devastating late rush, the rewards of painstaking, comprehensive handicapping could be collected with much satisfaction. Lest anyone think *Numa Pompilius* lacked the note of distinction remarked as so desirable under nonwinners allowance conditions, during that Hollywood season the colt on June 17 won the $40,000-added Cortez Handicap, at one and three-eighths miles over turf.

When considering the merits of nonwinners once or twice allowance contestants, handicappers are urged to give high regard to foreigners which have sharp current form and have shown they might possess a touch of higher class.

EIGHTH RACE 1 $\frac{1}{16}$ MILES.(turf). (1.39%) ALLOWANCE. Purse $20,000. 4-year-olds and upward. Non-winners of $2,500 twice other than maiden, claiming, or starter. Weight, 120 lbs. Non-winners of such a race at one mile or over since February 14, allowed 3 lbs.; of such a race since December 25, 6 lbs. (Winners preferred.)

Hollywood
MAY 11, 1978

Value of race $20,000, value to winner $11,000, second $4,000, third $3,000, fourth $1,500, fifth $500. Mutuel pool $311,204.

Last Raced	Horse	Eqt.A.Wt PP St	$\frac{1}{4}$	$\frac{1}{2}$	$\frac{3}{4}$	Str	Fin	Jockey	Odds $1
11Mar78 6StC6	Numa Pompilius	4 114 9 9	10	10	10	7$\frac{1}{2}$	1$\frac{1}{2}$	Castaneda M	28.60
15Apr78 5Hol3	Siempre Uno	4 120 8 3	3hd	5$\frac{1}{2}$	7$\frac{1}{2}$	4$\frac{1}{2}$	2nk	McHargue D G	a-1.50
29Apr78 5Hol5	Rachmaninoff	b 4 115 7 4	52	3hd	41	3$\frac{1}{2}$	3$\frac{1}{2}$	Toro F	2.60
26Mar78 9SA3	Mary's Policy	4 114 5 7	9$\frac{1}{2}$	6$\frac{1}{2}$	62	5$\frac{1}{2}$	41	McCarron C J	13.60
16Apr78 6Hol1	No Saint	6 120 3 10	2$\frac{1}{2}$	2$\frac{1}{2}$	21	2$\frac{1}{2}$	5hd	Shoemaker W	a-1.50
29Apr78 5Hol3	Pierre La Mont	b 4 120 2 1	1hd	1$\frac{1}{2}$	1hd	1$\frac{1}{2}$	6$\frac{1}{2}$	Pierce D	4.70
29Apr78 5Hol6	Campodonico	5 109 6 6	7hd	9$\frac{1}{2}$	9$\frac{1}{2}$	9$\frac{1}{2}$	7hd	Chapman T M5	9.50
23Apr78 9Hol9	Summit	b 5 120 1 5	8$\frac{1}{2}$	82	5hd	8hd	8nk	Snyder L	9.20
15Apr78 5Hol8	Postscript	4 117 4 2	6$\frac{1}{2}$	7hd	8$\frac{1}{2}$	6hd	91	Olivares F	33.30
1Apr78 9SA10	Boots Colonero	6 117 10 8	4$\frac{1}{2}$	42	3$\frac{1}{2}$	10	10	Mena F	53.90

a-Coupled: Siempre Uno and No Saint.

OFF AT 5:40 PDT. Start good. Won handily. Time, :22%, :47%, 1:11%, 1:36%, 1:42% Course firm.

$2 Mutuel Prices:

8-NUMA POMPILIUS	59.20	17.40	7.20
2-SIEMPRE UNO (a-entry)		3.20	2.60
7-RACHMANINOFF			3.20

Ch. c, by Dr Fager—Nostrana, by Botticelli. Trainer Fulton John W. Bred by Batthyany Countess Margit (Fla).

NUMA POMPILIUS trailed to the stretch. rallied between horses through heavy traffic, got the lead eagerly on his own courage, then was taken in hand to finish with speed in reserve. SIEMPRE UNO was with the early lead, became shuffled back, found room inside when settled into the stretch and closed under pressure but was no real match for the winner. RACHMANINOFF, saving ground, forced the pace and kept to his task in a good try. MARY'S POLICY made a mild bid to midstretch in the middle of the course, then tired. NO SAINT broke slowly, rushed up and weakened in the late stages. PIERRE LA MONT set the pace and faltered. BOOTS COLONERO raced wide and gave out.

Owners— 1, Cannata Mr-Mrs C; 2, Tassano & Whittingham C; 3, Silver Star Stable; 4, Desert Fox Stable-Selesnick, 5, Fogelson E E; 6, Siegel Jan; 7, Hirsch C L; 8, Madden P; 9, Elmendorf; 10, Agnew D J.

Overweight: Rachmaninoff 1 pound.

Two other profiles deserve special consideration when the nonwinners twice race is limited to four years old and up:

5. Late developing or dramatically improving four-year-olds that have raced exclusively under allowance conditions, especially

horses from leading stables, provided any recent efforts under conditions similar to today's indicate the horses earned above-average speed ratings and did not lose more than 2½ lengths in the stretch.

If that is a mouthful, handicappers benefit if strict with horses four and older that still are eligible to nonwinner twice allowances. More so by spring or later.

6. High-priced claiming horses in top form, particularly claimers that in recent outings have won consistently (two of six) or have run close while competing for purses similar to or better than allowance nonwinners twice purses.

Consistent claiming race winners represent real threats against older allowance bands of chronic nonwinners. If lightly raced improving younger horses are conspicuously missing, and the field contains no attractive imports, hard-knocking claiming horses may find the "allowance" competition quite a comeback. Most of these won an allowance race once, and can do so again when the competition dwindles. This happens more frequently during the first three months of the year, when nonwinners allowance races are carded exclusively for four-year-olds and older. Older horses that have not won one or two allowance races are fair prey for rugged claiming types that long ago did win.

To pursue this line some, decline in the quality of overnite competition makes older claimers better candidates than ever in preliminary nonwinner allowance races. In fact, evidence only two seasons old suggests really top-priced claiming horses have become greater threats than before under classified allowance conditions or even in minor stakes and handicaps. If handicappers fail to find any genuine comers among nonwinner twice entries, but a consistent claiming race winner sticks out, the claiming horse may become the best bet of the day, a likely horse that figures to go off an overlay.

To push the point a bit further still, claiming-horse contenders under nonwinner twice allowance conditions can be found almost regularly the second part of any season in races restricted to fillies and mares. Many owners insist on protective custody for inadequate racehorses valued as potential broodmares. The ladies race forever under nonwinner allowance conditions for which they remain eligible but are not talented enough to escape. At this writing a top breeder among southern California owners races a filly under nonwinner twice allowances and has done so for two seasons. The filly lacks the speed of the allowance sprint, the stamina of its route.

But pity the trainer should he try to sneak the potential broodmare into a claimer. Consistent, high-priced F-claimers can handle these horses, and easily do.

NONWINNERS THREE TIMES

The conditions specify "... nonwinners three times other than maiden or claiming."

Obvious contenders are powerful winners under nonwinner twice conditions. More likely candidates, however, are horses returning to allowance competition following satisfactory efforts in stakes. The statistical studies of Fred Davis indicate the stakes performance warrants priority.

In major racing still-developing horses that win a pair of allowance races often are entered next in a stakes. The stakes event may be restricted or ungraded. No matter. A satisfactory performance, particularly in the stretch, sharpens a horse's edge when entered anew under nonwinner allowances. Davis found that horses entered in stakes but never in claimers constitute 28 percent of allowance race starters, but they win 47.5 percent of the races, 170 percent their rightful share. The finding applies strongly in allowance races for nonwinners three times. So does the corollary finding. Horses entered to be claimed do not win their fair share of these allowances.

When analyzing allowance races for nonwinners three times other than maiden or claiming, handicappers prefer:

1. Impressive winners of two recent allowance races that performed evenly or better in a stakes or handicap.

2. Foreign-raced horses that have won or placed in graded or listed stakes.

If the imports impressed in a Grade 1 race overseas, or won multiple graded or listed events, their chances improve considerably. More on these fascinating horses in the next chapter, on stakes and handicaps.

3. Winners of two allowance races within the past season that have recently performed powerfully in a classified allowance race having a purse higher than today's.

4. Lightly raced impressive winners of two allowance races, provided the horses have never run for a claim.

In the absence of those profiles, handicappers occasionally look for:

5. Consistent claiming horses, aged four or five, that have recently won or finished close while competing for purses similar to or better than today's.

Only better claiming horses can compete. Generally, nonwinners three times allowance races will be won by horses sporting one of the top three profiles. Handicappers must be wary. Regardless of the performances, claiming horses whose best efforts occurred on different footing or at other distances probably are better tossed out.

Not many years ago, claiming horses were taboo under advanced nonwinners allowance conditions. But the general decline in the overall quality of the overnite competition has been felt in the allowance ranks. Again, during the early months of the year, when allowance races are restricted to four-and-up, consistent rugged older claiming types can move into the advanced allowance division and hold their own. Watch for claimers that have been multiple allowance race winners in the past.

NONWINNERS FOUR TIMES

When allowance conditions stipulate ". . . nonwinners four times other than maiden or claiming," handicappers prefer:

1. Stakes winners, preferably of open stakes.

2. Impressive winners of three allowance races that have performed satisfactorily when entered in an open stakes.

The better the stakes competition, the better.

3. Powerful winners of two or more recent allowance races, preferably nicely bred lightly raced colts or geldings from leading stables.

When considering allowances for nonwinners three times or for nonwinners four times, handicappers should expect horses with high potential or high consistency to win. Ordinary horses lose. Contenders should satisfy strict standards of form, speed, and consistency. If an entrant has not negotiated the distance or footing, its chances dwindle sharply. Each season in southern California the best three-year-olds on dirt flounder badly when moved to turf under competitive allowance conditions.

If the probable pace should prove too rigorous or uncomfortable for their running styles, mark the contenders down. Horses challenging the early pace have ability; they do not quit in a wink. Those coming-on later have ability too. They challenge strongly. Only genuinely superior horses survive two stiff challenges in a competitive field.

At major tracks horses shipped from minor circuits can be eliminated unless they have won a definitive stakes on the minor circuit, and impressively. If shippers have won such events, and are managed by sharp stables, accept them.

To conclude on a contradictory and confusing note, handicappers appreciate that a horse's powerful performance in a stakes, however distinguishing the mark, can be entirely misleading. If the stakes performance involved a vicious pace duel, lasting until inside the eighth pole, or demanded an all-out drive from the top of the stretch to the finish, the struggle may have depleted the animal's energies temporarily. It may need freshening. If it comes back too soon, beware. Younger horses of extraordinary quality rebound easily from successive rugged efforts. Others rebound, but not so easily or so soon.

Which reminds handicappers of a point of departure. Nonwinner allowance races are rough. Handicappers scout the past performances for suitable performance profiles. When too many contenders catch the eye, or none do, prudent handicappers pass. Having passed, they watch the action keenly. Such handicappers are betting wisely, on the future.

HANDICAPPING BY THE CONDITIONS

Sample Race

Collectors of results charts will admire the betting coup devised by trainer Larry Rose during October 1980, at Oak Tree at Santa Anita.

Note the conditions of the October 17 chart below, and the performance of the fifth place finisher, Lofty Lover.

Now check the conditions of the October 29 race, twelve days later.

Having tried stakes-placed horses October 17, for nonwinners three times other than maiden or claiming, but remaining eligible October 29 against older horses that have not won even a single allowance race, Lofty Lover can be seen as nose-diving in class for the second race.

The chart on the first race is absolutely the key to profits October 29. Sharp trainers manipulate horses and eligibility conditions. Handicappers just as sharp are not easily fooled.

NINTH RACE
Santa Anita
OCTOBER 17, 1980

1 1/16 MILES. (1.40⅘) ALLOWANCE. Purse $28,000. 3-year-olds and upward which have never won three races of $2,500 other than maiden, claiming or starter. Weights, 3-year-olds, 118 lbs.; older, 122 lbs. Non-winners of $8,800 at one mile or over since July 21, allowed 3 lbs.; of $8,250 other than claiming at any distance since April 7, 5 lbs.; of two races other than maiden, claiming or starter in 1980, 7 lbs.

Value of race $28,000, value to winner $15,400, second $5,600, third $4,200, fourth $2,100, fifth $700. Mutuel pool $172,091. Exacta Pool $370,496.

Last Raced	Horse	Eqt	A	Wt	PP	St	¼	½	¾	Str	Fin	Jockey	Odds $1
22Aug80 ^{8}Dmr^{1}	Beau Moro	b	5	122	5	8	8	8	5^{1}	$2^{1\frac{1}{2}}$	$1^{1\frac{1}{2}}$	Toro F	4.40
21Sep80 ^{11}Dmf^{5}	Accomplice		4	115	6	5	$5^{1\frac{1}{2}}$	5^{1}	1^{hd}	$1^{1\frac{1}{2}}$	2^{6}	McHargue D G	2.20
27Jly80 ^{5}Dmr^{8}	Command Freddy		6	115	1	2	4^{2}	4^{hd}	$3^{1\frac{1}{2}}$	3^{1}	3^{4}	Castaneda M	8.10
21Sep80 ^{8}Dmf^{4}	Rule the Market	b	4	117	8	7	6^{hd}	6^{hd}	8	6^{6}	$4^{\frac{1}{2}}$	Delahoussaye E	2.90
25Sep80 ^{12}Dmf^{4}	Lofty Lover		4	115	3	6	7^{3}	7^{2}	4^{hd}	5^{1}	5^{3}	Pierce D	6.50
18Sep80 ^{11}Dmf^{3}	Gray Dandy		5	115	2	1	$1^{1\frac{1}{2}}$	1^{hd}	$2^{2\frac{1}{2}}$	4^{1}	6^{6}	Mena F	12.80
20Apr80 ^{7}Hol^{8}	O'Bold Raider		4	115	4	3	3^{hd}	2^{hd}	7^{hd}	7^{hd}	7no	Lipham T	8.00
28Sep80 ^{11}Pom^{5}	Cactus Blue		4	114	7	4	$2^{\frac{1}{2}}$	3^{1}	6^{1}	8	8	Malgarini T M^{5}	49.00

OFF AT 5:39 PDT. Start good. Won driving. Time, :23⅕, :47⅕, 1:11⅗, 1:36⅗, 1:43 Track fast.

$2 Mutuel Prices:			
5–BEAU MORO	10.80	4.60	4.20
6–ACCOMPLICE		3.60	2.60
1–COMMAND FREDDY			3.40

$5 EXACTA 5–6 PAID $77.00.

Ro. g, by Peace Corps—Belle Gar, by Beau Gar. Trainer Jones Gary. Bred by Heubeck & Klein (Fla).

BEAU MORO, outrun early, rallied wide on the final turn and into the stretch, overtook ACCOMPLICE in the deep stretch and drew clear. ACCOMPLICE engaged for the lead after five furlongs, drew clear entering the stretch but could not last while drifting out in the final sixteenth. COMMAND FREDDY, in close attendance to the early pace, lacked the needed closing response. RULE THE MARKET never menaced. LOFTY LOVER was outrun. GRAY DANDY was finished after six furlongs.

Owners— 1, Abatti & Lima; 2, Silver Star Stable; 3, Pejsa A W; 4, Siegel Jan; 5, Rose June or L; 6, Hansen & Neishi; 7, Eaves R H; 8, Shoedfeld & Hutchinson.

Scratched—Tantico (7Sep80 ^{7}Dmr^{5}).

FIFTH RACE
Santa Anita
OCTOBER 29, 1980

1 1/8 MILES.(turf). (1.45⅗) ALLOWANCE. Purse $18,000. 3-year-olds and upward which have never won a race of $2,500 other than maiden, claiming or starter. Weights, 3-year-olds, 116 lbs.; older, 120 lbs. Non-winners at one mile or over since July 21 allowed 2 lbs.; since June 1, 4 lbs. (Winners preferred).

Value of race $18,000, value to winner $9,900, second $3,600, third $2,700, fourth $1,350, fifth $450. Mutuel pool $186,538. Exacta Pool $361,051.

Last Raced	Horse	Eqt	A	Wt	PP	St	¼	½	¾	Str	Fin	Jockey	Odds $1
17Oct80 ^{9}SA^{5}	Lofty Lover		4	116	5	3	3^{hd}	3^{2}	3^{1}	$1^{\frac{1}{2}}$	$1^{1\frac{3}{4}}$	Pierce D	5.10
19Oct80 ^{7}SA^{6}	Bronzeador		3	115	3	1	2^{1}	1^{3}	1^{1}	$2^{1\frac{1}{2}}$	2^{2}	Delahoussaye E	5.10
4Sep80 ^{9}Dmr^{2}	Western Mandate	b	4	111	4	2	1^{hd}	2^{1}	2^{hd}	$3^{1\frac{1}{2}}$	3no	Tejada V Jr^{5}	19.50
18Oct80 ^{9}SA^{8}	Deep Blue Water	b	6	120	1	5	9^{hd}	8^{1}	6^{hd}	$5^{2\frac{1}{2}}$	$4^{\frac{1}{2}}$	Lipham T	11.30
19Oct80 ^{7}SA^{3}	Forlaurels	b	3	113	10	6	7^{1}	6^{hd}	4^{hd}	$5^{\frac{1}{2}}$	$5^{1\frac{1}{4}}$	Valenzuela P A	5.10
15Oct80 ^{6}BM^{2}	Irish Frank		4	116	7	7	6^{hd}	7^{3}	8^{1}	6^{1}	$6^{1\frac{1}{4}}$	Wacker D J	14.20
1Sep80 ^{9}Dmr	Pronto Senor		5	118	2	12	12	12	11^{1}	8^{3}	$7^{1\frac{1}{2}}$	Mena F	6.10
17Oct80 ^{4}SA^{2}	Rene Dingle		4	120	6	4	$10^{2\frac{1}{2}}$	10^{1}	9^{2}	$7^{\frac{1}{2}}$	$8^{2\frac{1}{2}}$	Flores R	48.00
18Aug80 ^{8}Dmr^{6}	Dimanche		4	116	9	9	8^{hd}	11^{6}	12	$9^{1\frac{1}{2}}$	$9^{1\frac{1}{4}}$	Shoemaker W	5.90
19Sep80 ^{11}DMF^{4}	Charly n' Harrigan	b	3	114	11	11	$5^{\frac{1}{2}}$	5^{1}	$5^{1\frac{1}{2}}$	10^{1}	$10^{\frac{1}{2}}$	Olivares F	14.20
19Oct80 ^{7}SA^{5}	Royally True	b	3	116	8	8	11^{5}	9^{hd}	10^{3}	12	$11^{1\frac{1}{2}}$	Toro F	9.30
26Apr80 ^{6}Cur^{2}	Musical Boy II	b	3	108	12	10	$4^{1\frac{1}{2}}$	$4^{1\frac{1}{2}}$	7^{hd}	11^{hd}	12	McGurn C	27.40

OFF AT 2:37 PST. Start good. Won driving. Time, :23, :46⅕, 1:11⅖, 1:35⅘, 1:48⅕ Course firm.

$2 Mutuel Prices:			
5–LOFTY LOVER	12.20	7.60	5.20
3–BRONZEADOR		5.40	4.80
4–WESTERN MANDATE			11.60

$5 EXACTA 5–3 PAID $305.00

Ch. c, by High Echelon—Desiring, by Hasty Road. Trainer Rose Larry. Bred by Webb Mrs Lillie F (Ky).

LOFTY LOVER, in close contention outside the leaders from the outset, remained unhurried and saving ground until nearing the far turn, found room to slip inside BRONZEADOR on the stretch turn, got the lead in the upper stretch and drew clear near the end. The latter, rated on the early pace, stayed well away from the rail, then could not resist the winner's closing bid. DEEP BLUE WATER rallied to contention while saving ground into the stretch but also lacked the needed closing kick. FORLAURELS was a bit wide early and offered only a mild rally. PRONTO SENOR, devoid of early speed, failed to reach contention. DIMANCHE showed little.

Owners— 1, Rose June or L; 2, Mamakos & Stubrin; 3, Coelho & Valenti; 4, Najor R; 5, Sutton Place; 6, Roffe & Willis; 7, Alperson Mr-Mrs R; 8, Harris E J; 9, Bernstein & Pratt; 10, Lerner P; 11, Eisenstaedt & Arum; 12 Campbell-Conlin-Cohen et al.

Overweight: Bronzeador 1 pound; Forlaurels 1; Musical Boy II 1.

Scratched—Green Gallant (19Oct80 ^{7}SA^{7}); Sir Spruce (23Oct80 ^{8}SA^{5}).

CHAPTER 4

Stakes and Handicaps

IN STEP WITH the changing numbers at major tracks, stakes programs there have been all revved up. Owners and trainers of commercial and unfashionable horseflesh find more possibilities for black type than ever. Market breeders should continue to prosper. And handicappers can now find solid bets in stakes not available only a few seasons back.

The $100,000-added feature has become so familiar that the shipping of good horses to easier conditions has become routine. With so many spots available, hungry stables size up the local nominations. If the racing looks too rough, they ship out. The tactic is understandable, to win big money or earn breeding credentials.

One consequence of the maneuverings has been lopsided victories of big-time shippers or local division leaders, against small fields, at even money or less. Just a few seasons back the scene included Spectacular Bid's smashing pre-Derby wins at the expense of ordinary three-year-olds in Florida. The other leading eastern colts did not run. In southern California that year, Flying Paster sent that area's second best prospect on airplanes to Louisiana and Arkansas. When he was the undisputed handicap champion at age four, Spectacular Bid won New York's prestigious Marlboro Cup in a walkover. Not another handicap star in the nation bothered to show up. By 1985, the situation had worsened. At every major track today local big shots are more likely than before to find themselves in virtual walkovers to the winner's circle. For handicappers, these selections are simple, but the odds are too low to yield seasonal profits.

The purposes of patient handicappers have been helped nonetheless by two innovations.

One is more conditioned stakes. Sometimes used by top stables as preliminary stops en route to bigger stakes objectives, their prime purpose is to restrict the order of competition, thereby giving more horses a real chance to win.

The second has been the grading of stakes. Essentially a classification scheme, grading is a healthy attempt by the industry's breeding establishment to distinguish the important stakes winners from the other hundreds.

Handicappers at Santa Anita, for example, now can enjoy the spectacle of champions and near-champions competing for that track's eleven Grade 1 titles. They can look forward more eagerly to wagering on events such as the Santa Gertrudes Handicap, a conditioned stakes.

> **SANTA GERTRUDES HANDICAP**   **$ 80,000**
> To be run Saturday, **March 23, 1985**
> For Four Year Olds and Upward Which Have Not Won
> $25,000 Other Than Claiming or Starter in 1984-85
> One Mile and One-Quarter (On the Turf)

The winner of the Santa Gertrudes will not be a Grade 1 horse. These would be ineligible. But it may be a late-developing four-year-old that recently finished close to the winner in a Grade 2 event. Or a five-year-old stakes winner that spent the previous season racing evenly against graded competition but now is being managed more realistically. Or even a marathon turf specialist that lately has been winning classified allowance or high-priced claiming purses, or perhaps another restricted stakes, such a race having a winner's share below $25,000. Nowadays it is more likely than ever to be a foreign horse, maybe even an important stakes winner from a country whose purse structure permits most stakes winners to remain eligible for many restricted U.S. stakes.

Finding opportunities of that kind is a handicapper's fun. The Santa Gertrudes Handicap and its like pop up regularly these days. The payoffs can be rewarding to handicappers that have high regard for eligibility conditions and horses best suited to them.

The Handicapper's Condition Book stresses this point. Handicappers that set out to understand the hierarchies among horses in the stakes divisions of the local circuit will be rewarded splendidly for these efforts throughout the season. At regular intervals they will unearth dandy propositions at fancy odds. Occasionally, these handicappers will encounter standout choices in graded races, and collect on odds better than 3 to 1.

THE CONDITIONED STAKES RACE

Conditioned stakes bar previous stakes winners or winners of a specified amount of first money during a specified time interval. The quality of these fields ranks below that of graded or ungraded stakes open to all runners.

To illustrate, Santa Anita carded fourteen conditioned stakes during its 1985 season. Six were written for three-year-olds; five were for four-year-olds and older. Purse monies were the lowest of the stakes schedule, but none were below $60,000, quite an incentive for all horses that fit the conditions.

The conditions of eligibility look like this:

Santa Catalina Stakes	Three-year-olds, N/W $20,000	One mile and one-sixteenth	$60,000
Santa Ysabel Stakes	Fillies, three-year-olds, N/W $20,000	One mile and one-sixteenth	$60,000
Bolsa Chica Stakes	Three-year-olds, N/W Sweepstakes since December 25	Six furlongs	$60,000
Bradbury Stakes	Three-year-olds, N/W $17,000	One mile and one-eighth	$60,000
Santa Lucia Handicap	Fillies and mares, four-year-olds and up, N/W $25,000 in 1984–85	One mile and one-sixteenth	$80,000
El Monte Handicap	Four-year-olds and up, N/W $25,000 in 1984–85	One mile and one-sixteenth	$80,000
San Marino Handicap	Four-year-olds and up, N/W $25,000 in 1984–85	One mile and one-half (Turf)	$80,000
Providencia Stakes	Fillies, three-year-olds, N/W $20,000	One mile and one-eighth (Turf)	$60,000
La Puente Stakes	Three-year-olds, N/W $20,000	One mile and one-eighth (Turf)	$60,000
San Jacinto Handicap	Four-year-olds and up, N/W $28,000 in 1985	One mile and one-quarter (Turf)	$100,000

Handicappers would expect the San Jacinto Handicap to invite a better field than would the San Marino, the Bolsa Chica to get better horses than the La Puente.

Will the Bradbury Stakes draw the least distinguished field? Perhaps. But it might also draw a lightly raced, improving three-year-old en route to graded stakes open to all comers.

When purse values, specified dates, and ages eligible are highly similar handicappers become more alert to changes of distance and footing.

In general, the fancier entrants are (a) preparing for richer stakes or (b) dropping into easier opportunities. Many successful handicappers tend to prefer the current form and higher odds of the "b" group. Nonstakes winners aged four-and-older are usually the opportunists. Three-year-olds are often preparing for better races, but most of them are sent out to win conditioned events too. Younger horses arrive at conditioned stakes limited to that age by a different design, and this group is treated at length in Chapter 8.

In cases of horses four-and-upward, handicappers first prefer:

1. Horses that recently have finished in-the-money or run close in a Grade 1 or Grade 2 stakes, provided their form remains impressive or continues in the improvement cycle.

2. Horses that have run the most impressive race against the best open stakes competition within recent weeks, provided that sharp form remains intact.

In the absence of the two profiles, handicappers prefer:

3. Any nicely bred lightly raced four-year-old from a leading stable that has won successively and impressively under nonwinner allowance conditions.

This kind of four-year-old merits wholesale scrutiny when entered in conditioned stakes. Notwithstanding its prior lack of stakes activity, if its entire record looks powerful and its breeding, stable, and jockey connections are first-rate, it might be any kind. Any potential star has every right to trounce older horses that remain nonwinners of a stakes or nonwinners of so much first money for a time.

Otherwise, a horse four-or-older that has never raced effectively in added-money competition remains at a disadvantage in stakes, even of the conditioned kind. Then again, in the absence of the profiles above, conditioned stakes conditions are not beyond the reach of:

4. Any highly consistent entrant, including claiming horses, that has won at least two of its latest six races while competing for winner shares only slightly below the specified price in the conditions.

One reason claiming horses have done better in stakes and handicaps lately has been a widespread increase of conditioned stakes. Many better nonclaiming horses are barred.

Notice that previous graded and open stakes winners returning to competition after lengthy layoffs—of a time interval that makes them eligible—do not warrant a recommended profile. The reason is logical.

Their stables normally are using the conditioned stakes as a conditioner. The horses' current form is rarely peaked, and an all-out effort for small money is not happily indulged. Often the distance is not just right. Pace can be more of a problem than when the horses are ready to roll. Unless previous stakes winners look tempting on all the fundamentals, it makes sense to look elsewhere.

In any case, Grade 1 winners pass these contests. Grade 2 winners are always dangerous, and handicappers must pause when these look ready enough. Other previous stakes winners do not merit support unless everything looks just right.

Concerning close finishers in Grade 1 or Grade 2 races, if the finish involved a long, hard drive against ranking competition, the fight may have been too punishing, and handicappers require signs of remaining life. If such a finish occurred just prior to the date specified by the conditions, current form should be peaking. If little recent racing has occurred, latest races must be impressive and workouts must be sparkling, and at longer distances.

The case of impressive stakes performances followed by disappointing losses in overnite competition repeats itself too frequently to be ignored when surveying a conditioned stakes field.

GRADE 1 EVENTS

When the very best of thoroughbreds compete over long distances of dirt or grass for Grade 1 titles, that spectacle surely is worth the price of admission. Do betting opportunities arise? It all depends. In the Santa Anita Handicap of 1984, Bates Motel paid $11.40. Later that season Eclipse filly Heartlight No. 1 dazzled her opponents in the Hollywood Oaks, winning by twelve, and paid $8. At Santa Anita 1979, Affirmed won and paid $4.60, when he should have been 3 to 5. The three figured absolutely. In my opinion, when absolutely Grade 1 horses pay even money or better against opposition of a clearly inferior order, the bets represent solid investment opportunities. When such Grade 1 horses so placed pay 8 to 5 or better, as happens, handicappers collect the wind-fall profits.

To explain. A Grade 1 champion or division leader combines the qualities of speed, stamina, willingness, determination, and courage in optimal degrees. When in shape and suited to the distance and footing, unless challenged by a horse of similar standing, it wins. As handicappers appreciate and have experienced consistently, these horses can easily trounce even their toughest foes, and do so when well meant. When well meant and entered in races of lower grades, the genuine Grade 1 horses stand out. The others hardly stand a chance.

The case is so solidly behind the Grade 1 horse that only a single guideline is appropriate:

1. Except by accident, Grade 1 races are won by Grade 1 horses.

To attempt a definition that holds, a Grade 1 horse (a) has won two or more Grade 1 races, or (b) has won one such event, plus Grade 2 events while beating off its competition definitively.

So superior is this kind that the handicapping consists almost entirely of evaluating the current form and running styles of Grade 1 entrants. When only a single Grade 1 horse has been entered, handicappers check the odds and decide whether a serious wager is warranted.

Liking long shots, many players prefer to shop around in the face of a single Grade 1 horse. Having experienced its happening before, they're hoping the big shot won't run. Even when correct about the Grade 1 entrant, those who shop tend to select the wrong long shot. Besides being few in number, the upsets that do occur in these events are unpredictable. I know of no way of beating Grade 1 races systematically except by backing Grade 1 stickouts intelligently.

Many players can benefit from Grade 1 races by having patience with the following discussion. The experience of one player hardly generalizes. Yet Grade 1 races are personal favorites and the notebook consistently shows a surplus. By remembering their appraisals should begin and end with Grade 1 horses, handicappers can find favorable betting opportunities consistent with these considerations.

If the Grade 1 entrant is the only horse of its kind in the field and the odds pay even money or better, make the play. Winning more than half the bets guarantees profits.

If two or more Grade 1 horses are taking part, but none is a national champion or clearly superior division leader, handicappers make seasonal profits only by limiting play to Grade 1 overlays. In this context, overlay means odds higher than natural odds. If the field contains three relatively equal Grade 1 horses, any is an overlay at odds greater than 2 to 1.

If a clearly superior Grade 1 horse has questionable form or distance, footing or pace preferences not favored by today's conditions, pass the race or link it to others in exotic bets.

Now for the high kicker. If a superior Grade 1 entrant has lost its last race and nothing about its physical condition or training pattern looks suspicious, handicappers should set themselves to jump up the bet this time.

When a genuinely top thoroughbred loses, handicappers can expect some residual value. The price next time will be better.

No horse wins them all. Angle Light beat Secretariat in Aqueduct's Wood Memorial just before that legend's unforgettable classics. Unless beaten by comparable horses, Grade 1 standouts do not often lose high-grade races in succession.

For a riotously delightful example of how this angle can work for handicappers, examine the partial record of the marvelous handicap and turf champion, Exceller.

Exceller won seven Grade 1 stakes during 1978. When at 6 to 5 he lost the Century Handicap at Hollywood Park on April 30, the stage was set for collection of windfall profits. In his next race, the Hollywood Turf Invitational, Exceller breezed to within a length of the track distance record at an incredible 5 to 2!

The best was yet to come. The stage was reset when at 9 to 5 Exceller chased Seattle Slew around Belmont Park in the September 30 Woodward Handicap. Two weeks later, in the definitive Jockey Club Gold Cup, at a more comfortable mile-and-one-half, Exceller ran his patented race, coming from far out of it to overcome a gutty

Slew (which had never really shown us that kind of class before) in as glorious a stretch run as any racing fan will ever see. Hard to imagine, but Exceller was sent off at 7 to 2 by the sophisticated New Yorkers and paid $9.40 for every two. No handicapper ever received a fancier price on as noble a horse under such appropriate Grade 1 conditions. The September 30 loss, so predictable, helped set the overlay.

To continue. If the Grade 1 horse loses twice in succession, when it had figured to win, handicappers should presume something has gone wrong. Eliminate the stars until they show previous form.

This angle backfired at Santa Anita 1979. The great Affirmed was on display. Santa Anita's unique Strub Series, three closely scheduled graded stakes limiting entry to new four-year-olds, had been regarded as a tour de force for 1978's Triple Crown Champion and Horse of the Year. Yet Affirmed finished third in the seven-furlong Malibu Stakes, second in the nine-furlong San Fernando Stakes. In the San Fernando, Affirmed could not gain favorable early position and was just up for second, a labored effort all the way.

When Affirmed dipped to 4 to 5 in the betting for the Grade 1 mile and one-quarter Strub Stakes, I bet confidently on a late-developing hard-hitting gelding named Johnny's Image, trained by Bobby Frankel and sent off at 13.9 to 1. Johnny's Image ran its best race yet in that Strub but could finish only a faraway second, four lengths in front of the third horse. Affirmed returned to its championship form, and won going away by ten.

As a delightful footnote, a twice-burned public remained skeptical when Affirmed returned next, in the Grade 1 $300,000-added Santa Anita Handicap, this open to older handicap horses, including Exceller and Tiller. Expert confident handicappers were not caught napping when this exquisite champion paid $4.60 after an easy record-breaking five-length victory.

No handicapper who understands the dominant characteristics that combine in the superior Grade 1 thoroughbred can afford to lose money by betting against the highly predictable outcomes of Grade 1 races. It will be a perpetual mystery to me how hardened horseplayers can forsake Grade 1 champions at 3 to 2 odds, then rush to unload their pockets with both hands, having been persuaded by the inside dope dished out daily about some first-time-starting three-year-old maiden speedball that goes postward in a light lather at 7 to 5 or less, and finishes up the track.

It happens all the time.

NORTH AMERICAN CLASSICS

Sadly, the general decline in the quality of American racing has touched the Grade 1 events as well. Although by 1985 only 114 of these events existed, The Breeders' Cup Event Day races (seven stakes each offering a million or more in purse monies), and five series of three stakes races, each offering a million-dollar bonus to any horse that sweeps the series, have rocked the foundations of the country's most traditional races. As a result, the Grade 1 designation no longer guarantees that even a single established Grade 1 horse will appear in the entries. Several Grade 1 races at Santa Anita and Belmont Park have already gone barren of authentic Grade 1 competition. It's a sign of the times.

In any season hereafter numerous Grade 1 stakes will be won by horses without the accustomed credentials. The winners will not be the genuine Grade 1 jewels. Some will be absolute imposters. Handicappers therefore can expect to experience a more painstaking task in differentiating among former Grade 1 winners. Which are the true champions and division leaders? Which are a cut below?

One reliable barometer is to identify the winners and runners-up of the nation's most prestigious stakes: the classics. Classics can be defined as stakes that signify the best of what has been traditional. When analyzing Grade 1 races, handicappers should consider whether the entrants have won or placed in any of the stakes below:

Name of Race	Track
Alabama Stakes	Saratoga
Arlington Budweiser Million	Arlington Park
Beldame Stakes	Belmont Park
Belmont Stakes	Belmont Park
Brooklyn Handicap	Belmont Park
Champagne Stakes	Belmont Park
Charles H. Strub Stakes	Santa Anita
Coaching Club American Oaks	Belmont Park
Hollywood Gold Cup	Hollywood Park
Hollywood Futurity	Hollywood Park
Jockey Club Gold Cup	Belmont Park
Kentucky Derby	Churchill Downs
Marlboro Cup Invitational	Belmont Park
Metropolitan Handicap	Belmont Park
Preakness Stakes	Pimlico

Name of Race	Track
San Juan Capistrano Handicap	Santa Anita
Santa Anita Handicap	Santa Anita
Travers Stakes	Saratoga
Turf Classic	Aqueduct
Vanity Handicap	Hollywood Park
Vosburgh Stakes	Aqueduct
Yellow Ribbon Stakes	Santa Anita
Young America Stakes	The Meadowlands

New traditions sometimes becomes classics instantly, and surely this has been so of the seven Breeders' Cup Event Day races:

Breeders' Cup Juvenile
Breeders' Cup Juvenile Fillies
Breeders' Cup Sprint
Breeders' Cup Mile
Breeders' Cup Distaff
Breeders' Cup Turf
Breeders' Cup Classic

The Breeders' Cup races move annually and all are contested under weight-for-age conditions.

Finally, bonus money lures the best horses to the racetracks involved in the series offering the windfalls. In 1985, Kentucky Derby winner Spend A Buck legitimized the Jersey Derby at Garden State Park as a new tradition beckoning the best of three-year-olds, when its owners chose to skip the classic Preakness Stakes and run for an unprecedented two-million-dollar bonus. Handicappers can be more impressed by the horses that win races in the million-dollar bonus series. The general competition should be keener. Here are the races to watch for:

The New York Handicap triple:
   Marlboro Cup Invitational–Woodward Stakes–Jockey Club Gold Cup
The handicap triple on the turf:
   Rothman's International–Turf Classic–Washington D.C. International
The Mid-American triple:
   The Arlington Classic–The American Derby–The Secretariat Stakes, three long-distance tests for three-year-olds at Arlington Park

The Hollywood Park triple:
    The Californian–Hollywood Park Gold Cup–Sunset Handicap
The Garden State triple, plus the Kentucky Derby:
    Cherry Hill Mile–Garden State Stakes–Jersey Derby

At Garden State, three-year-olds earn a one-million-dollar bonus by winning any two in the New Jersey series, plus the Kentucky Derby; two million extra awaits any three-year-old that wins the four races.

In the short time the bonus series have been conducted, three horses have cashed out as all-time one-day money-winners. Spend A Buck swept the Garden State series in consummate style during its inaugural 1985 running. In 1984, the marvelous French filly champion All Along easily won the three handicap turf classics. In 1984 too, Slew o' Gold became the first horse ever to win the New York handicap triple, bagging a cool million extra for the feat.

LOWER GRADE STAKES

Grade 2, Grade 3, and ungraded but open features, which account for 95 percent or more of all stakes run in North America, provide glorious opportunities for profit but generally are not so hospitable to handicapping as their conditioned and Grade 1 counterparts. Open as they are to all interested runners, lower grade stakes attract several horses that are relatively evenly matched. First prize may go to the best horse, but it may go as well to the horse in the peak of form, or best suited to the distance and footing, or most favorably treated by the early pace. The handicapping is conventional, comprehensive, and difficult. Nonetheless, a new subcategory of open stakes, the listed (L) stakes, not well known to racegoers, not only helps handicappers get to the guts of numerous stakes races more quickly but also provides us with another valuable source of overlays. Handicappers merely need access to the vital information. More on this momentarily.

GRADE 2 STAKES

Regardless, the Grade 2 stakes can attract handicappers when any of the following past performance profiles characterizes one of the entrants:

    1. A well-meant Grade 1 horse.

2. A multiple Grade 2 stakes winner that has run competitively in open stakes competition within the past three months, preferably in Grade 1 company.

In any open stakes a Grade 1 horse holds the edge, but this can be blunted or nullified if current form proves difficult to assess *and* the distance is uncomfortable, the footing inappropriate, or the early pace unfavorable. If conditions are not just right, the Grade 1 entrant may be prepping for better races. Yet many Grade 2 races offer $100,000-added or higher purses. So do some ungraded stakes at major plants. Naturally, purses of that size can stir the connections of Grade 1 horses. They may send their pride and joy after the money.

A Grade 2 horse has won two or more Grade 2 stakes and has raced competitively under Grade 1 conditions. If no other horse of comparable credentials lines up, handicappers may have found a solid bet.

In the absence of the above two profiles, handicappers prefer:

3. A recent persuasive winner of a Grade 3 or listed stakes, notably of a purse comparable to or greater than today's.

Handicappers should not trifle with the Grade 2 stakes horses. Only 105 Grade 2 races are carded in this country. The races confer prestige and value on their winners, outstanding racehorses that cannot beat the cream of the crop. As a rule, Grade 2 winners can be expected to dominate lower grade stock, even as Grade 1 horses dominate them. It is not a close situation.

For that reason, when Grade 3 or open stakes graduates tackle Grade 2 conditions, they had better arrive there with extra-added attractions, such as distance, form, and pace advantages, or perhaps the convenient absence in the field of an authentic Grade 2 animal.

GRADE 3, LISTED, AND OPEN STAKES

Below Grade 2, class differentials in the stakes divisions are too often neither distinguishing nor dominant. Formerly, handicappers could fairly be advised to lump Grade 3 stakes and open stakes in a pool and insist potential winners be identified based on class differences *in combination with* advantages on other factors. That ended abruptly in 1983, the moment the industry began to distinguish open stakes as listed or not.

Now handicappers are strongly advised to be on the lookout for the newest category of stakes races, the listed stakes. These important races should be judged as (a) practically interchangeable with Grade 3 stakes and (b) far superior to open stakes that are not listed.

Listed stakes, to clarify, are races judged just below graded stakes in prestige and quality but sufficiently prestigious and definitive of themselves to be listed on the pages of international sales catalogs. To be eligible, purse values cannot dip below $50,000. In 1983, U.S. racing presented 286 listed stakes. Purses ran as high as a quarter-million, and several exceeded $100,000. As well, several were limited to state-bred horses, a restriction always of interest to handicappers. State-bred stakes are normally inferior to open stakes, even the unlisted kind.

Listed stakes deserve the special attention of handicappers for three compelling reasons. One, few racegoers are even aware this category of stakes exists. Two, listed winners can regularly throttle their open but unlisted counterparts. Three, *Daily Racing Form* does not yet designate the listed stakes appearing in the past performance tables. At a breakfast seminar of mid-1985, the author asked a gathering of more than a hundred practiced handicappers how many knew what a listed stakes was. No one knew; no one. As handicappers appreciate, meaningful information that is not well distributed represents a source of overlays, the only horses by which talented handicappers can prosper.

Grade 3 and listed stakes bring together horses that have won graded and ungraded events of varying prestige and purses, perhaps repeatedly. The horses have ability and winning habits, and often can prove difficult to separate. Size of winning purses is an index of relative quality. Other matters being relatively equal, prefer the horses that have won the richest races. Trainers are most attracted by the size of the purse, from which they make a living.

A close evaluation of the demonstrated class of the top two or three finishers in previous stakes is another reliable index. It so happens that the cry of the hardboots—"he didn't beat nothin' "—is a valid benchmark of class appraisal in stakes races much of the time. Manner of victory can be significant but it can also be entirely misleading. Quality of the opposition counts. It counts most often in the older stakes divisions where class maneuvers have been horizontal—a change to the same level of competition. The comparisons take on greater significance when purses exceed $50,000. They can be decisive when horses exiting the lower-grade races they have won have also impressed in Grade 1 or Grade 2 events.

Fred Davis has helped again. Although Davis' statistics indicate second-place finishers last out are better risks in the next races than are winners last out, last-out winners are better bets in stakes and handicaps.

Whether the stakes race is Grade 3, listed, or open at $50,000-added or richer, handicappers prefer these distinguishing profiles:

1. A well-meant Grade 2 horse.

2. Previous Grade 3 or listed winners, especially of higher purse values, and nicely suited to the distance, footing, and probable pace.

3. Grade 1 or Grade 2 close runners-up within the past six months.

The first profile belongs to a high-grade horse. In form, it likely wins. The second is a distinguished stakes winner particularly well suited to today's conditions. The third recognizes the dominant attributes of the highest grade stakes, and the horses that win them. Runners-up of these events are dropping in class, usually, and have every right to pickle a lower-grade group.

When considering open but ungraded, unlisted stakes, handicappers supplement the above three profiles with two others:

4. Previous open stakes winners in sharp form and very well suited to the distance, footing, and probable pace.

When class distinctions become less than decisive, handicappers can settle for horses that have a *class edge* and look outstanding on the other fundamentals.

In the absence of the above, prefer:

5. Any horse that has finished close in a richer recent stakes while gaining ground or pressing the leaders throughout the stretch.

Reliable eliminations include any horse five or older that has never won a stakes; four-year-olds that do not ordinarily compete in stakes, and effectively; any horse four or older that won a conditioned event at two or three but since has never finished in-the-money in an open stakes; foreign-raced horses that have not won a Group Pattern event or finished in-the-money in a Group 1 race.

Importantly, handicappers must also understand that established Grade 1 horses are almost never well intended when entered in Grade 3, listed, or open stakes. Winning lower-grade stakes enhances a Grade 1 horse's value not a bit. When these situations arise, Grade 1 big shots are usually prepping for later Grade 1 races. They should be expected to run well but lose.

At other times Grade 1 stats whose performances against their own kind have been suspiciously dull will be lowered into a Grade 3 or ungraded stakes. Trainers do not yet understand the poor performance or current form of their stars. They know the horses should win easily at the lower levels, and need to find out if they do. Odds on the Grade 1 dropdowns will be low. Handicappers should abstain or at times prefer horses that appear outclassed. If form is that suspicious or problematic, the Grade 1 horses will have excellent excuses for losing in the cheaper fields. Good handicappers know what's happening and can sometimes bet wisely against the class.

If events are ungraded unlisted, are valued at less than $50,000, and none of the above profiles are prominent, handicappers can weigh the merits of classified allowance and high-priced claiming entrants. These can be accepted if (a) the distance is their best and (b) they should be advantaged by the pace. Of horses four and older, two additional helpful hints. In-the-money finishes in conditioned stakes that bar previous stake winners do not qualify horses as acceptable in open stakes. Finally, winners of overnite handicaps do not qualify as contenders in graded stakes.

A complete list of the graded and listed U.S. stakes of 1985 by grade designations, purse values, and eligible ages can be found in Appendix 2. In the same way the appendix lists the graded and listed races of Canada, England, France, Germany, Ireland, and Italy, which brings us to our next topic, arguably the modern handicapper's most generous supply of overlays and long shots.

The following is a list of racetracks in the United States and Canada that programmed at least one graded stakes race in 1985.

Track	Gr. 1	Gr. 2	Gr. 3	Total
Belmont Park	29	14	10	53
Aqueduct	13	9	24	46
Santa Anita	18	10	17	45
Hollywood Park	14	9	15	38
Arlington Park	7	6	6	19
Saratoga	6	9	2	17
Del Mar	2	6	5	13
Meadowlands	2	6	5	13
Monmouth Park	3	5	4	12
Gulfstream Park	3	4	4	11
Hialeah	3	4	3	10
Woodbine	1	1	8	10
Keeneland	2	3	3	8
Laurel	3	0	4	7
Pimlico	1	2	4	7
Ak-Sar-Ben	0	1	6	7
Bay Meadows	0	1	6	7

Track	Gr. 1	Gr. 2	Gr. 3	Total
Oaklawn Park	3	2	1	6
Churchill Downs	2	0	4	6
Golden Gate Fields	0	2	4	6
Louisiana Downs	1	1	2	4
Tropical Park (at Calder)	0	2	2	4
Fair Grounds	0	1	3	4
Sportsman's Park	0	0	3	3
Garden State Park	0	0	3	3
Atlantic City	1	1	0	2
Longacres	0	1	1	2
Keystone	0	1	1	2
Hawthorne	0	1	1	2
Suffolk Downs	0	1	1	2
Exhibition Park	0	0	2	2
Detroit Race Course	0	1	0	1
Thistledown	0	1	0	1
Arapahoe Park	0	0	1	1
Latonia	0	0	1	1
Penn National	0	0	1	1
Tampa Bay Downs	0	0	1	1
Turf Paradise	0	0	1	1
Calder Race Course	0	0	1	1
Fairmount Park	0	0	1	1
Bowie	0	0	1	1
Totals	114	105	162	381

INTERNATIONAL RACING

When Santa Anita Park opened its doors for the 1984–85 season, its 2,100 stalls filled with approximately five hundred foreign horses. They competed every racing day in stakes, classified allowance races, and the nonwinners allowance series. To a lesser extent, the trend has been developing at all major tracks. International racing is a sign of the times.

European racing remains far more aristocratic than its American counterpart. Horsemen and stables on the continent still concern themselves mightily with the improvement of the breed. Geldings cannot even enter Grade 1 races in Europe. That purpose ceased to prevail in the U.S. following the widespread commercialization of the stud in the sixties and outrageously in the seventies. North America now cards approximately 75,000 races; Europe cards less than 15,000. France programs the largest number overseas, approximately 4,200. England runs 2,900. Ireland sports a bloody 720, hardly a week's worth of action in the U.S.

This being so, European racing programs are designed exclusively toward the finer development of nicely bred young stock, much of it, by the way, purchased at American auctions. The practical consequence of interest to U.S. handicappers are two: (1) the great majority of foreign races are stakes races, and (2) stakes opportunities on the continent for horses four and older below the top echelons are virtually nonexistent.

Increasing numbers of those older horses of Europe wind up in the states. More stables than ever concentrate on the buying and racing of imports, and bloodstock agents of any repute consider it practically *de rigeur* that they schedule a buying tour of England, France, and Ireland as part of the annual routine. In the U.S. past performance tables, the foreign horses' records reflect their participation in a sequence of stakes races. Some are graded, but most are not. No purse values are reported. Eligible ages are unknown. Significantly, the listed stakes remain undistinguished from the rest.

The handicapper's need is basic—for information. Information about the graded and listed stakes the invaders have been contesting abroad. How do the foreign horses compare with their American counterparts? How do they compare with one another?

Specifically, handicappers need to know the relative quality of the stakes foreign-breds and foreign-raced horses have won or almost won. They need to know the grade designations, purse values, and eligible age groups. *Daily Racing Form* prints the grade designations for the graded stakes of all foreign countries, but no notation yet differentiates listed stakes from the relatively unimportant others.

Because virtually all foreign races appear in the past performance tables as stakes, particularly crucial for handicappers wanting overlays is the distinction among foreign races between listed stakes and the unlisted kind. The latter are equivalent to U.S. overnite races. Some of the juiciest wagering opportunities of all occur when foreign horses change from listed stakes overseas to allowance or minor stakes conditions here.

The European preoccupation with stakes racing translates into the American horseplayer's obsession when examining the records of foreign horses under U.S. conditions of eligibility. In all cases the operative guideline is this: find the foreign horse that has *a decisive class advantage under today's conditions.* Not only does the situation arise frequently, but the classy horses regularly pay huge dividends, the general public still being basically untrustworthy of the unfamiliar.

To carry the point to its logical conclusion, where decisive class advantages are found, the bets are placed. If not found, handicappers should wait and see. Look elsewhere for the contention today.

Before presenting the specific opportunities handicappers should look to exploit, here are four global guidelines for evaluating foreign horses as a group and for comparing them both to one another and to U.S. horses:

1. All graded stakes of Canada, England, France, Germany, Ireland, Italy, and the United States are considered equivalent by the selection committees grading them.

That is, a Grade 1 race of Italy is equivalent to a Grade 1 race of France is equivalent to a Grade 1 race of the United States. The equivalence does not extend to other countries, i.e., Argentina, Chile, other countries of South America, Australia, New Zealand, or South Africa. Gradings of those stakes are normally submitted by local jurisdictions or by representatives of national jockey clubs, and handicappers should regard the races as generally lower in value and status.

Importantly, handicappers should understand that the equivalence accorded all graded stakes of similar designation from the seven countries reviewed by the formal selection committees, while generally reliable, is a far safer assumption for breeders evaluating prospective matings or buyers inspecting yearlings for sale than for handicappers analyzing the past performances of a field of racehorses. This is particularly true for graded races below Grade 1, as well as all listed stakes.

To explain. Unlike owners and breeders of stakes horses, whose return on investment depends primarily on the breeding value their horses can accrue, stable trainers make their living from the 10 percent commission on their horses' earnings. Thus, trainers are most strongly attracted by the size of the purse. For that reason stakes within a graded category, that is, Grade 2 or Grade 3, are best differentiated by purse values. This is also the most reliable means for distinguishing Grade 3 stakes and open ungraded stakes. Likewise, all listed races should definitely be differentiated by handicappers on purse size.

A trainer's key and self-interested role in the selection of stakes opportunities for horses of that quality contributes to our second global guideline.

2. In general, Grade 1 races excepted, the bigger the purse, the better the competitive quality of the stakes race.

Of the exception, a Grade 1 race offers owners and trainers so much in added value and prestige that no lower grade stakes title of a higher purse value could fairly compensate them as well. Thus, the Grade 1 designation beats Grade 2 of a higher purse. The guideline holds when judging horses of similar age from the seven countries.

In practice, and reliably when evaluating the stakes programmed in this country, handicappers will not often be misled, as Grade 1 stakes normally carry much higher purses than any lower grade stakes. There is an occasional notable exception. As stakes races must be programmed for two years before they are eligible to be graded, racing associations seeking to extend their visibility and prestige nationally have lately fallen into a common practice whereby a big-ticket race is offered to a certain age group, and promoted to the extreme, the track hoping to entice the best horses of that age from all corners of the U.S., and thereby earn the Grade 1 distinction. An illustration is the $500,000-guaranteed Super Derby, for three-year-olds, an invitational offered by Louisiana Downs in late September. After two runnings the Super Derby was designated Grade 3; after three years it was Grade 2. It is now Grade 1. The purse remained the same, but better horses competed for it year after year.

All other stakes races can be fairly differentiated by purse values, including comparisons between countries and gradings, as of a Grade 3 stakes of France and a Grade 2 race of Italy, or of Grade 2 races of England and France, respectively. The richer races are usually the better races. Handicappers who consult Appendix 2 will discover that France typically offers the highest purses. Thus, France attracts more of the better stables and horses.

3. The North American Graded Stakes Committee and the International Pattern Race Committee do an outstanding job of evaluating the thousands of stakes races programmed in the seven countries.

Thus, the stakes races graded or listed by the two committees can be accepted by handicappers as being decidedly superior in competitive quality and prestige than the hundreds of others. If an ungraded stakes of England has been listed in the book's Appendix, and another has not, the listed race is almost certainly the superior race. The same is true of all the U.S. stakes races.

As in this country, horsemen in foreign countries honor their classics by pointing the best horses of every generation toward them. Handicappers should recognize the classics of foreign programs when they see the names. If winners or close runners-up from the classics listed below appear in U.S. races below Grade 1, they can be considered at advantage. They are likewise acceptable in Grade 1 competition here.

	Purses	Ages
The Best of Canada:		
Rothman's International	$405,000	3up
E. P. Taylor Stakes	162,000	3up
Queen's Plate (R)	121,500	3yo
Canadian Oaks	105,250	3yo
The Best of England:		
Benson and Hedges Gold Cup	165,000	3up
Epsom Derby	165,000	3yo
King George VI and Queen Elizabeth Stakes	244,200	3up
One Thousand Guineas	99,000	3yo
St. Leger Stakes	165,000	3yo
Two Thousand Guineas	99,000	3yo
William Hill Futurity	53,625	2yo
The Best of France:		
Arc de Triomphe	637,500	3up
Prix Diane	204,000	3yo
Prix Ganay	114,750	4up
Grand Criterium	127,500	2yo
Prix Ispahan	114,750	3up
Prix Lupin	127,500	3yo
Poule d'Essai des Poulains	127,500	3yo
Poule d'Essai des Pouliches	127,500	3yo
Saint Cloud	255,000	3up
Prix Vermeille	178,500	3yo
The Best of Germany:		
Baden Stakes	126,000	3up
Deutsches Derby	126,000	3yo
Europa Handicap	168,000	3up
The Best of Ireland:		
Irish Sweeps Derby	70,000	3yo
Irish St. Leger	42,000	3up
The Best of Italy:		
Italian Derby	154,000	3yo
Emilio Turati	84,000	3up
Coppa d' Oro (also Jockey Club)	140,000	3up
Tesio	70,000	3–4yo
Di Milano	140,000	3up
Roma	84,000	3up

4. The gradings, listings, and purse values of stakes races of the various foreign countries can be used effectively to predict those horses' performances in U.S. classified and nonwinners allowance races.

As noted, handicappers become most interested when decisive class advantages preside. The classic case is a change from graded or listed stakes competition of Europe to classified and nonwinners competition here. The following selection and elimination guidelines should guide the handicapping process when foreign horses are prominent in U.S. overnite competition.

If the race is a classified allowance or advanced nonwinners allowance (nonwinners three times or four times other than maiden or claiming) race, handicappers should:

1. **Favor** Grade 1 and Grade 2 winners and close runners-up of England, France, Germany, Ireland, and Italy.

2. **Favor** listed stakes winners of Canada, England, France, and Italy, notably horses that have won or finished close consistently in listed and graded stakes.

3. **Accept** high consistency-high earnings Grade 1 winners of South American countries, of Australia, and of New Zealand.

The top profile is obvious, the second far more advantageous to handicappers; prices will be better. In fact, the move from a listed stakes to classified or nonwinners allowance competition presents alerted handicappers with perhaps the most generous overlays of all.

Note that Ireland is missing from the countries cited in the second profile. Handicappers should understand that the purse structures of Ireland are the lowest of Europe. Listed stakes of Ireland typically have purses ranging from $8,000 to $14,000, with many below $10,000. If horses bred in Kentucky, England, or France can be found racing in Ireland, handicappers can presume the horses did not pass muster in the homeland and have been shipped to Ireland, where the competition will be softer. Good horses bred in Ireland, conversely, have long since been sent elsewhere to compete for better purses.

The third profile is also instructive. Until they prove otherwise, the only horses from South America, South Africa, Australia, and New Zealand acceptable under U.S. conditions are multiple Grade 1 winners of high consistency and high earnings. To be acceptable in U.S. stakes, at least one of the Grade 1 wins overseas should have been definitive, usually by numerous lengths in quick time, marking the horses as clearly superior to the stakes competition in their own country. Otherwise, handicappers should wait to see.

To continue with the international profiles:

4. **Accept** Grade 2 horses of England, France, Ireland, and Italy, **notably** those that have finished in-the-money or up close in Grade 1 races.

5. **Accept** consistent Grade 3 horses of England and France, **provided** the distance and footing are favorable, and current form is acceptable.

6. **Eliminate** Grade 2 and Grade 3 horses of Argentina, Chile, South Africa, Australia, and New Zealand.

7. **Eliminate** winners of ungraded foreign stakes listed in the Appendix, **unless** the horses have also finished fourth or better in a Grade 1 stakes; if from England or France, accept finishes third or better in a Grade 2.

8. **Eliminate** all foreign winners of stakes not listed in Appendix 2.

If the U.S. race is a nonwinners allowance race, for nonwinners once or twice other than maiden or claiming:

1. **Favor** winners or runners-up of Grade 1, Grade 2, Grade 3 and listed races of England, France, Germany, Ireland, and Italy, **notably** three-year-olds or lightly raced four-year-olds on the improve, or nicely suited to the distance or footing.

2. **Accept** winners or runners-up of Grade 1 races of Argentina, Chile, South Africa, Australia, and New Zealand, **notably** three- and four-year-olds.

3. **Eliminate** all winners of foreign stakes not listed in Appendix 2.

4. **Eliminate** all horses of Argentina, Chile, South Africa, Australia, and New Zealand that have not started in a Grade 1, **unless** they have won a Grade 2 race.

5. **Regardless of number 3 above,** if horses are from England or France, **accept** those which have more victories than the conditions allow **and** relatively high earnings; that is, have won noticeably more money than U.S. horses on today's circuit that have never won one or two allowance races.

It's useful to reiterate the significance of the **decisive class advantage** as the key to handicapping success. Many foreign horses racing in this country for the first few times, especially when entered in overnite races, will be entered at unfamiliar distances or on unfamiliar footing (dirt). Moreover, current form will often be problematic. The horses may not have competed for months.

The class advantages promoted here can be accepted as overcompensating. That is, the horses can be expected to win regardless. Handicappers should tolerate the uncertain form, the unfamiliar footing, the uncomfortable distance. After all, the horses hold a decisive class advantage. They figure to win. Happily, where form appears short, or distance and footing unfamiliar, the odds will probably be higher. The public will think the foreign horses will be racing at a disadvantage, when actually they have a tremendous advantage. They represent the class of the field, and the differences are relatively great.

Inversely, where class advantages do not exist, or are not great, handicappers should show higher regard for problems associated with form, distance, and footing, and readily mark the foreign horses down.

HANDICAPPING BY THE CONDITIONS

Sample Races

Below is an actual race situation involving two foreign horses competing in the same U.S. overnite race at Santa Anita in 1984. Neither colt had raced in months. By referring to the stakes listings in Appendix 2, handicappers can determine which horse best outclasses the conditions of eligibility.

ALLOWANCE, nonwinners four times other than maiden or claiming.

Those who picked Orixo are badly mistaken. Its Hermitage win at three June 8 is unlisted; it finished last when favored in England's Grade 2 St. James Place, a $49,500 stakes restricted to three-year-olds, and subsequently ran badly in the unlisted Van Geest Stakes. After winning the unlisted Mining Supply Stakes at two, Orixo finished second of five in a Grade 1 event as a long shot. But the full record hardly supports the placing in a five-horse field, and as handicappers should appreciate, two-year-old performance not repeated at three does not translate readily into the four-year-old season.

Ice Hot's record tells a different tale. Last out the colt won the Pin stakes, a listed race at Longchamp, France's flagship oval. The Pin purse was only $25,500, but the race was open to older horses. Ice Hot also placed in the listed Table stakes, a $33,150 race open to older, and was beaten just four lengths in the Grade 3 $38,250 Daphnis stakes for threes. Its single poor performance was a thirteenth in the listed Deauville stakes. Entered in two unlisted stakes, it won one, was beaten three-quarters in the other. All of this was accomplished at age three.

Having won a listed stakes in France, placed in another, and finished close in a Grade 3 stakes, the consistent Ice Hot looked more tempting than Orixo, notably so at the odds, and Ice Hot won handily at Santa Anita, paying $12.80. Orixo, the 5-to-2 favorite under Chris McCarron, was no factor in the race.

In three additional 1984 Santa Anita examples, an English colt named Airfield was sent out by leading trainer Charles Whittingham against horses that had never won two allowance races. In its most recent races on the continent Airfield had finished second twice in listed stakes of England. The colt might just as well have dropped into the Santa Anita allowance race from a listed stakes in the U.S. It won smashingly; paid $18.60.

In an especially notable situation, an Irish-bred horse, Minnelli, paid $13.60 after beating sprinters that had not yet won even one allowance race. Minnelli had finished second of fifteen in Ireland's Moyglare stakes, now a Grade 1 sprint, no less, having the second highest purse in that country. In the minor Santa Anita sprint, the Irish import was nothing short of a stickout.

And finally, in an extraordinary overlay, the filly Bid for Bucks, which had finished fifth of seventeen, beaten just four lengths, in France's classic Diane Stakes (Grade 1), purse an equivalent $204,-000 here, and had placed in another listed French stakes to boot, was sent to the post at Santa Anita versus nonwinners of two allowance races at 16 to 1. Under Bill Shoemaker, the stakes-placed French filly won breezing; returned $35. The predictable Exacta

8th Santa Anita

1 ¼ MILES. (TURF). (1.57⅗) 4th Running of THE YELLOW RIBBON INVITATIONAL STAKES (Grade I). Purse $200,000. Fillies and mares. 3-year-olds and upward. By invitation with no nomination or starting fees. The winner to receive $120,000, with $40,000 to second, $24,000 to third, $12,000 to fourth and $4,000 to fifth. Weights, 3-year-olds, 119 lbs.; older, 123 lbs. The Oak Tree Racing Association will invite a representative field of fillies and mares to compete. The field will be drawn by the closing times of entries. A trophy will be presented to the owner of the winner. Invitations: Thursday, October 30, 1980. (Weight for age.)

Coupled—Kahaila and Sisterhood.

Queen to Conquer

B. f. 4, by King's Bishop—Beat It, by Silnet

Own.—Wimborne Farm (Lessee) 123

Br.—Stokes R (Ky) 1980 4 1 0 1 $84,700

Tr.—Whittingham Charles 1979 9 2 1 3 $34,027

Turf 15 4 1 4 $121,095

26Oct80-8SA 1⅛Ⓣ:461 1:101 1:46 fm 2½ 121 67½ 64¾ 68½ 49 ShmrW9 ⒻLs Plms H 86 Ack'sScrt,AThosndStrs,PrncssToby 9

31Aug80-8Dmr 1⅛Ⓣ:473 1:113 1:492fm 9 115 75¾ 52¾ 31½ 11½ ShmrW10 ⒻRamonaH 94 QntoConqr,AThsndStrs,WshngWll 13

21Aug80-8Dmr 1 1/16Ⓣ:48 1:124 1:441fm 8-5 118 77 52 32½ 4½ ShoemkrW10 ⒻHcp0 87 Petron'sLove,EpicValu,DelindSue 12

8Aug80-5Dmr 7½fⓉ:231 :463 1:294fm 11 114 916 912 95 32 ShoemakerW10 ⒻAlw 90 PcosPppr,ButyHour,QuntoConqur 10

13Oct79♦2Ascot(Eng) a1½ 2:401gd 11 118 Ⓣ 77 TylorB ⒻPrincess Royal(Gr.3) Alia, Crystal Queen, Odeon 11

6Oct79♦2Newmarket(Eng) 1¼ 2:093fm 8 116 Ⓣ 611 EddryP ⒻSun Chariot(Gr.2) Topsy, Bonnie Isle, Odeon 8

21Sep79♦3Newbury(Eng) 1⅜ 2:23 gd 2 116 Ⓣ 13 EddryP ⒻCap R Price Plate QuntoConqur,L'I!DuRv,IdlHourQun 4

21Jly79♦3Curragh(Ire) 1½ 2:333fm 50 126 Ⓣ 33½ SnbrnW ⒻIrishGuinesOaks(Gr1) Godeti,Producer,QueentoConquer 13

27Jun79♦3Salisbury(Eng) 1½ 2:351gd 6 109 Ⓣ 23 WinterP Bibury Cup H Lindoro,QuentoConqur,MlicicusRd 9

1Jun79♦2Kempton(Eng) 1½ 2:373yl 3½ 115 Ⓣ 313 Lynch J Kingfisher H ConcrtHll,Shftsbury,QuntoConqur 13

Nov 6 SA Ⓣ5f fm 1:02 h (d) Nov 1 SA 3f ft :364 b Oct 23 SA Ⓣ5f fm 1:014 h (d) ●Oct 18 SA 1 ft 1:402 h

Bold 'n Determined *

B. f. 3, by Bold and Brave—Pidi, by Determine

Own.—Saron Stable 119

Br.—Layton Dr G (Ky) 1980 11 9 1 0 $631,303

Tr.—Drysdale Neil 1979 4 4 0 0 $108,240

25Oct80-7Kee 1⅛:473 1:112 1:491ft *1-3 119 31 2hd 1hd 1nk DlhossyE5 ⒻSpinster 91 Bold'NDtrmind,LovSgn,LklyExchng 6

16Oct80-7Kee a7f 1:261ft *1-9 120 1hd 11 12 16¾ DelahoussyeE1 ⒻAlw 92 Bold'NDetermined,VitViw,Shwn'sGl 6

10Sep80-8Bel 1 :461 1:104 1:352ft 10 122 22½ 1hd 2hd 1no DlhssyE1 ⒻMaskette 91 Bold'NDtrmind,GnuinRisk,LovSign 5

28Jun80-8Bel 1½:494 2:314ft *6-5 121 2hd 1hd 3½ 1hd DlhssE2 ⒻCcAmrOks 61 Bold'NDtrmnd,Ern'sWord,FrwllLttr 7

8Jun80-8Bel 1⅛:461 1:111 1:493sy *1-2 121 33 1½ 2hd 2hd DlhssE8 ⒻMothrGoos 79 SgrAndSpc,Bld'NDtrmnd,Ern'sWrd 8

24May80-8Bel 1 :444 1:093 1:364ft *2-5 121 2½ 11 12 12¾ DelhoussyE7 ⒻAcorn 84 Bold'NDtrmnd,MtyLvly,SgrAndSpc 8

2May80-8CD 1 1/16:483 1:133 1:444ft *3-5 121 1½ 1hd 11½ 11½ DlhossyE2 ⒻKy Oaks 84 Bold'NDtrmnd,MtyLvly,HnstAndTr 8

5Apr80-9OP 1 1/16:464 1:114 1:451ft *1 121 1hd 1½ 11½ 12¼ DlhoussyE3 ⒻFantasy 82 Bold'NDtrmnd,StnRbr,HonstAndTr 7

9Mar80-8SA 1 1/16:45 1:093 1:411ft 3½ 115 210 22 3½ 1½ DlhssE6 ⒻSta Susana 95 Bold'nDetermined,StrtBllt,TblHnds 7

23Feb80-8SA 7f :213 :441 1:222ft 2 121 64¼ 67 44½ 42 DlnossyE1 ⒻSta Ynez 89 Table Hands, Street Ballet, HazelR. 7

Nov 8 SA Ⓣ3f fm :354 h (d) ●Nov 4 SA Ⓣ7f fm 1:274 h (d) Oct 30 SA Ⓣ4f fm :50 b (d) Oct 15 Kee 3f ft :35 b

A Thousand Stars

Dk. b. or br. m. 5, by Hoist the Flag—Heavenly Body, by Dark Star

Own.—Clore A 123

Br.—Clore A (Ky) 1980 8 2 2 1 $94,650

Tr.—Whittingham Charles 1979 11 0 4 1 $55,728

Turf 30 5 9 5 $248,518

26Oct80-8SA 1⅛Ⓣ:461 1:101 1:46 fm *3-2 119 2½ 21 21½ 22¼ DlhssE6 ⒻLs Plms H 95 Ack'sScrt,AThosndStrs,PrncssToby 9

31Aug80-8Dmr 1⅛Ⓣ:473 1:113 1:492fm 4½ 118 2½ 1hd 1½ 21½ DlhssE11 ⒻRamona H 92 QntoConqr,AThsndStrs,WshngWll 13

9Aug80-8Dmr 1 Ⓣ:462 1:102 1:344fm 4 115 2½ 2hd 1hd 1no DlhoussyE4 ⒻPlm: H 101 AThousndStrs,WishngWll,DvonDtty 9

11Jly80-8Hol 1 1/16Ⓣ:463 1:101 1:401fm *6-5 117 12 12 1½ 31 Shoemaker W1 ⒻAlw 97 LovYoDr,PrncssToby,AThosndStrs 8

28Jun80-8Hol 1⅛Ⓣ:471 1:112 1:472fm 2¾ 117 75 73¾ 53 73¼ ShmrW2 ⒻBev HillsH 90 CountryQun,WishingWll,ThVryOn 10

15Jun80-8Hol 1 1/16Ⓣ:473 1:111 1:413fm 3¼ 118 73¾ 74½ 66½ 62 ShmrW5 ⒻWilshire H 89 WishingWell,Sisterhood,LoveYouDr 9

31May80-8Hol 1 1/16:453 1:091 1:401ft 2½ 119 32 45½ 48 412 ShmkrW1 ⒻMilady H 82 ImageofReality,It'sIntheAir,Fondre 5

14May80-7Hol 1 1/16Ⓣ:47 1:11 1:41 fm *4-5 113 2hd 1hd 12½ 14 Shoemaker W2 ⒻAlw 94 AThousndStrs,SmllrBickr,DlindSu 10

8Nov79♦5StCloud(Fra) a1 1:53 sf 10 120 Ⓣ 15 LgouttP Pr Perth (Gr 3) Tannenberg,MadCaptain,GoldEyes 15

23Oct79♦6Longchamp(Fra) a1¼ 2:113gd *2 118 Ⓣ 22½ PquetP Prix Point du Jour ReinedeSab,AThousndStrs,Louksor 5

Nov 6 SA Ⓣ5f fm 1:00 h (d) ●Oct 21 SA 1 ft 1:393 h ●Oct 16 SA 7f ft 1:25 h Oct 1 SA 4f ft :481 b

Princess Toby *

Ch. m. 5, by Tobin Bronze—Scoop Time, by Correspondent

Own.—Breliant W 123

Br.—Breliant W (Ky) 1980 12 3 2 2 $100,200

Tr.—Bucalo John 1979 15 4 2 1 $75,250

Turf 20 4 3 3 $132,275

26Oct80-8SA 1⅛Ⓣ:461 1:101 1:46 fm 5 117 56½ 33 34½ 36¼ HwleyS3 ⒻLs Plms H 91 Ack'sScrt,AThosndStrs,PrncssToby 9

31Aug80-8Dmr 1⅛Ⓣ:473 1:113 1:492fm 20 116 86¾ 84 1310 1311 Hall DC4 ⒻRamona H 83 QntoConqr,AThsndStrs,WshngWll 13

31Jly80-8Dmr 1 1/16Ⓣ:483 1:122 1:431fm *6-5 116 22½ 2½ 2½ 1¾ Hawley S2 ⒻAlw 93 PrincessToby,TrckRobbery,MoreSo 6

11Jly80-8Hol 1 1/16Ⓣ:463 1:101 1:401fm 11 122 811 510 43½ 2¾ Hawley S2 ⒻAlw 97 LovYoDr,PrncssToby,AThosndStrs 8

13Jun80-8Hol 1 1/16:452 1:084 1:411ft 5 122 66 79½ 715 716 ShmkrW4 ⒻMkt Bskt 73 Splendid Girl, Picea, Canonization 7

26May80-8GG 1⅜Ⓣ:48 1:373 2:15 fm 5½ 120 1010 77½ 614 915 Diaz A1 ⒻYrba Bna H 78 MirzyDotes,Sisterhood,SmllrBickr 11

11May80-7Hol 1 1/16Ⓣ:463 1:111 1:412fm 2¾ 119 57½ 2½ 1½ 14¾ Hawley S8 ⒻAlw 92 PrincessToby,LittleNana,ElegnceII 8

4May80-9Hol 1⅛Ⓣ:464 1:102 1:474fm 15 117 109¾ 98¼ 99½ 87¾ HwleyS3 ⒻGamely H 83 WishngWll,CountryQun,ImgofRlty 12

13Apr80-7Hol 1 Ⓣ:462 1:101 1:341fm 10 119 66 42 25 24 Hawley S6 ⒻCnvence 94 Wishing Well, Princess Toby,Celine 8

5Apr80-8GG 1 1/16:47 1:103 1:431m *2¼ 120 32 33 34 3¾ HlIDC4 ⒻGldn PppyH 86 Fondre,MissMargiMc,PrincessToby 5

Nov 2 SA 7f ft 1:282 h Oct 21 SA 5f ft 1:05 h ●Oct 14 SA 1 ft 1:42 h Oct 5 SA 7f ft 1:263 h

*Kahaila

Dk. b. or br. f. 3, by Pitcairn—Chaldea, by Tamerlane

Own.—Summa Stb & Feldman et al	119	Br.—Molony M (Ire)	1980	8 1 2 1	$37,009
		Tr.—Wheeler Robert L	1979	4 M 0 1	$750
			Turf	12 1 2 2	$37,759

11Oct80♦2Ascot(Eng)	1½	2:414sf	5	115	Ⓣ	54¾	CookP	ⒻPrincess Royal(Gr3)	Karamita, Bonnie Isle, Saint Osyth	8
19Aug80♦4York(Eng)	1½	2:361gd	55	126	Ⓣ	34½	EddrP	ⒻYorkshire Oaks(Gr1)	Shoot a Line, Vielle, Kahaila	7
31Jly80♦3Goodwood(Eng)	1½	2:384gd	8	127	Ⓣ	615	PgttL	Wm Hill Southern H	Hareas, Peppery, Boon	7
5Jly80♦4Haydock(Eng)	1½	2:373gd	33	123	Ⓣ	25	RmndB	ⒻLancashre Oaks(Gr3)	Vielle, Kahaila, The Dancer	6
22May80♦4Goodwood(Eng)	1¼	2:032gd	50	120	Ⓣ	57½	Starkey G	ⒻLupe	Vielle, Norfolk Gal, Glen Dancer	8
7May80♦4Chester(Eng)	a1½	2:371gd	14	126	Ⓣ	920	RmndB	ⒻCheshire Oaks (Gr3)	Shoot aLine,LittleBonny,OffShore	13
25Apr80♦3Newcastle(Eng)	1¼	2:131fm	8	120	Ⓣ	27	RymondB	X Y Z H	Fine Sun, Kahaila, NavigationalAid	9
18Apr80♦7Thirsk(Eng)	1	1:423fm	3½	116	Ⓣ	11½	Duffield G	ⒻStraitlace	Kahaila, Souliotissa, Octavia	12

*Benicia

B. f. 3, by Lyphard—Bashi, by Stupendous

Own.—Head Mrs A	119	Br.—Head A (Ire)	1980	9 2 2 2	$115,379
		Tr.—Head Alec	1979	2 1 1 0	$29,140
			Turf	11 3 3 2	$144,519

20Oct80♦4StCloud(Fra)	a1 5/16	2:211gd	*7-5	124	Ⓣ	11½	Head F	ⒻPr de Flore(Gr3)	Benicia, Good To Beat, Indigene	9
5Oct80♦5Longchamp(Fra)	a1⅛	1:521fm	*6-5	121	Ⓣ	41½	Head F	ⒻPr de l'Opera(Gr2)	Hortensia, Mooningraver,Wildidea	10
21Sep80♦2Longhchamp(Fra)	a1½	2:134gd	*3-5	121	Ⓣ	11	Head F	ⒻPr de Liancort	Benicia, Trephine, Liane de Pougy	5
24Aug80♦5Deauville(Fra)	a1	1:404gd	3	124	Ⓣ	32	Head F	ⒻPr de la Calonne	Safita, Exactly So, Benicia	8
17Aug80♦5Deauville(Fra)	a1¼	2:084gd	*3-5	121	Ⓣ	42½	HeadF	ⒻPr de Psyche(Gr3)	Sovereign Dona, Trevita, Wild Idea	6
23Jun80♦2Longchamp	a1¼	2:142sf	4¾	123	Ⓣ	2hd	Head F	ⒻPr de Mallert (Gr2)	Luth de Saron, Benicia, Hortensia	8
15Jun80♦4Chantilly(Fra)	a1 5/16	2:10 gd	4e	128	Ⓣ	55¾	PquetP	ⒻPr de Diane(Gr1)	Mrs Penny, Aryenne, Paranete	14
25May80♦4Longchamp(Fra)	a1¼	2:044gd	2¾	128	Ⓣ	31	Head F	ⒻPr St Alary	Parante, Safita, Benicia	8
20Apr80♦4Longchamp(Fra)	a1 5/16	2:033gd	*6-5	128	Ⓣ	2hd	Head F	ⒻPr Vanteaux(Gr3)	Luth de Saron, Benicia, Paranete	13

Lady Marion X

B. f. 3, by Table Run—Yakima Princess, by Rare Bike

Own.—Clark D M & D G	119	Br.—Clark D M & D G (Wash)	1980	11 5 2 0	$98,630
		Tr.—Harris Ben	1979	8 3 3 2	$23,988
			Turf	1 1 0 0	$31,800

16Oct80-8BM	1 1/16 Ⓣ	:4821:1241:442fm	8¾	112	811	76½	32	14	Frazier B5	Ascot H	86	LdyMrion,KneCounty,HilowdEnvoy	8
21Sep80-9Lga	1 3/16	:473 1:114 1:554m	*3-2	118	59½	56	31½	11	BzeG4	ⒻBelle Robt H	95	LadyMarion,RightChilly,NavirFlme	6
7Sep80-9Lga	1⅛	:472 1:12 1:50 m	*2¾	117	811	63½	31½	2½	Baze G7	ⒻAlki H	82	SnowPearl,LadyMarion,NavirFlme	11
30Aug80-9Lga	1⅛	:473 1:122 1:501gd	*2¼	119	1010	86¼	31½	14½	BzeG3	ⒻSacajawea H	82	LdyMrion,DneRu,KingsEsterQuen	11
20Aug80-9Lga	1	:463 1:12 1:362ft	3½	116	710	41¼	13	19½	Baze G7	ⒻAlw	87	LadyMrion,PrunePicker,ClssicCper	9
2Aug80-9Lga	1 1/16	:46 1:11 1:431ft	3½	116	3½	21	713	914	Baze G12	ⒻM Dnu H	72	DneRu,GillieGirl,KingsEsterQueen	14
19Jly80-9Lga	1	:454 1:11 1:372ft	5¾	117	67½	32	57½	44¼	BzG6	ⒻBetsy Ross H	77	GmeCookie,DneRu,KingsEsterQun	11
10Jly80-9Lga	6½f	:213 :44 1:151ft	*3-4	120	2hd	2hd	32	55¾	Baze G5	Alw	87	KngsEstrQn,YllwUndrwng,DmndVll	5
21Jun80-9Lga	6½f	:213 :44 1:153ft	4¾	120	55½	58	46	52¾	Baze G3	ⒻMsh	88	DustyFlower,Havdsher,LovelyWine	9
3Jun80-8Lga	6½f	:22 :444 1:154sy	*9-5	120	1hd	11½	16	11½	Baze G2	ⒻAlw	90	LdyMrcn,YllwUndrwng,NllOfthNrth	8

Nov 6 SA Ⓣ 4f fm :462 h (d)   Oct 28 BM 5f ft 1:00 h   Oct 15 BM Ⓣ 4f fm :52 h (d)   Oct 10 BM 4f ft :474 h

Ack's Secret

B. f. 4, by Ack Ack—Escandinhas, by Birikil

Own.—Fogelson E E	123	Br.—Fogelson E E (Ky)	1980	7 4 0 2	$91,312
		Tr.—Whittingham Michael	1979	12 1 6 1	$27,475
			Turf	5 1 2 0	$50,200

26Oct80-8SA	1⅛ Ⓣ	:4611:1011:46 fm	14	114	1½	11	11½	12¼	VlnlPA8	ⒻLs Plms H	97	Ack'sScrt,AThosndStrs,PrncssToby	9
17Oct80-8SA	a6½f Ⓣ	:211 :4331:133fm	3½	117	32	43	45½	44	DlhssE5	ⒻAtmn DysH	87	GretLdyM.,Evyostling,Convenintly	11
14Sep80-11Dmr	1 1/16	:444 1:093 1:431ft	*3	118	3nk	1½	11½	32	VlnzlPA4	ⒻEncnts H	82	Fresca, Miss Magnetic,Ack'sSecret	8
25Aug80-9Dmr	1 1/16	:46 1:11 1:422ft	3	114	12	12	15	16½	VlnzlPA1	ⒻJun Drlng	88	Ack'sSecret,FrenchRose,PlesingStr	7

25Aug80—Run in two divisions, 8th & 9th races

17Aug80-7Dmr	1	:452 1:11 1:371ft	*3-5	115	4¾	41½	34½	33¾	Valenzuela PA5	ⒻAlw	78	EmeraSnds,She'sSwope,Ack'sScrt	5
30Jly80-7Dmr	6f	:221 :451 1:101ft	*1	122	21	22	1hd	13¾	Valenzuela PA3	ⒻAlw	87	Ack's Secret, Ilusao,FoolMeNever	10
18Jly80-5Hol	6f	:214 :443 1:091ft	4¾	119	3½	12	12	12¾	Valenzuela PA2	ⒻAlw	91	Ack'sScrt,ProudstB,LittlMssLovly	10
17Sep79-11Pom	1 1/16	:464 1:12 1:443ft	3-2	114	515	512	514	518	CmpsR1	ⒻCTBAMrin	71	MjesticBlde,CntteToo,Lucky'sMiss	5
9Aug79-9Dmr	1	:46 1:113 1:372ft	*1	114	43¾	23	59	616	Pierce D5	ⒻAlw	65	‡Eve's Image, Doaadola,NiceHonor	8
29Jly79-7Dmr	1	:454 1:103 1:363ft	*7-5	116	52¾	31½	42	3¾	Pierce D6	ⒻAlw	84	‡HoldMeFst,FirstVictory,Ack'sScrt	7

29Jly79—Placed second through disqualification

Nov 6 SA Ⓣ 5f fm 1:00 h (d)   ●Nov 1 SA Ⓣ 3f fm :352 h (d)   ●Oct 23 SA Ⓣ 5f fm 1:004 h (d)   Oct 13 SA 5f ft :58 h

Sisterhood

B. m. 5, by Exclusive Native—Lost Horizon II, by Court Harwell

Own.—Summa Stable	123	Br.—Newstead Farm (Va)	1980	11 2 4 0	$154,175
		Tr.—Wheeler Lin	1979	13 3 0 2	$111,616
			Turf	28 9 4 2	$326,110

31Aug80-8Dmr	1⅛ Ⓣ	:4731:1131:492fm	18	117	33	31½	52½	53	LiphmT8	ⒻRamona H	91	QntoCongr,AThsndStrs,WshngWll	13
9Aug80-8Dmr	1 Ⓣ	:4621:1021:344fm	6½e	118	54	53½	87	75¾	SnoemkrW5	ⒻPlmr H	96	AThousndStrs,WishngWll,DvonDtty	9
28Jun80-8Hol	1⅛ Ⓣ	:4711:1121:472fm	9½e	119	43	31	42	52	PircD10	ⒻBev Hills H	91	CountryQun,WishingWll,ThVryOn	10
15Jun80-8Hol	1 1/16 Ⓣ	:4731:1111:413fm	15e	119	42½	63	42	2nk	PiercD1	ⒻWilshire H	91	WishingWell,Sisterhood,LoveYouDr	9
26May80-8GG	1⅜ Ⓣ	:48 1:3732:15 fm	*7-5e	121	22	32	24	26	PircD11	ⒻYrba Bna H	87	MirzyDotes,Sisterhood,SmllrBickr	11
4May80-9Hol	1⅛ Ⓣ	:4641:1021:474fm	5	120	65	75¾	55	43¼	PierceD6	ⒻGamely H	88	WisnngWll,CountryQun,ImgofRlty	12
23Mar80-8SA	1¼ Ⓣ	:4721:36 2:002fm	3½	118	25	21½	21½	11	PncLJr2	ⒻSta Brb H	85	Sisterhood,Petron'sLove,Relaxing	10
12Mar80-8SA	1⅛ Ⓣ	:46 1:1111:482gd	3	118	48½	53½	2½	21	PncLJr5	ⒻSta Ana H	84	TheVeryOne,Sisterhood,MirzyDotes	8
29Feb80-8SA	1⅛ Ⓣ	:4611:1021:474fm	*6-5	119	44	54¾	2½	11¾	Pincay L Jr6	ⒻAlw	88	Sisterhood, Little Nana,DonaYsidra	8
10Feb80-7SA	a6½f Ⓣ	:211 :4331:132fm	*2	117	76¾	87¾	74	42¾	Pincay L Jr7	ⒻAlw	89	Ole Rumor, NotAFlaw,HappyHolme	9

Nov 1 SA Ⓣ 1⅛ fm 1:564 h (d)   Oct 25 SA Ⓣ 1 fm 1:421 h (d)   Oct 18 SA 7f ft 1:274 h   Oct 5 SA 5f ft 1:022 h

*Kilijaro

Own.—Fradkof S   **123**

Dk. b. or br. f. 4, by African Sky—Manfilia, by Mandamus

Br.—Irish National Stud Co Ltd (Ire)	1980	11	5	1	2	$241,404
Tr.—Dewieb Olivia	1979	7	0	2	1	$56,181
	Turf	24	7	4	4	$362,413

26Oct80♦3Longchamp:Fra: a7f	1 25⁴sf 2½ 134	① 31½ LquxA	Pr de La Foret.Gr1:	Moorestyle, Crofter, Kilijaro	9
22Sep80♦4MLaffitte:Fra: a6f	1 11¹gd*3-5 131	① 11½ LquuxA	Pr Sein et Ois'e:Gr3:	Kilijaro, Boitron, North Jet	8
7Sep80♦4Longchamp:Fra: a1	1:36⁴gd 6 124	① 1ⁿᵏ Head F	Pr du Moulin(Gr1:	Kilijaro, Nadjar. Katowice	11
28Aug80♦4Deauville·Fra: a1	1:40²fm 11 127	① 13 Head F	Pr Quincey(Gr3:	Kilijaro. Tassmoun. Callio	10
28Aug80♦4Deauville(Fra: a6f	1:11³gd*3-5 120	① 15 LquxA	Pr de Meutry(Gr3:	Kilijaro, Northjet. Standaan	8
1Aug80♦4Deauville a6½f	1:20¹sf 6½ 120	① 3½ LquxA	Pr M Deghesti(Gr2:	Boitron. Moorestyle, Kilijaro	12
29Jun80♦6Longchamp:Fra. a7f	1:24²sf 7½ 124	① 54½ SmniH	Pr Port Maillot(Gr3:	Ya Zaman. Luck of the Draw. Hilal	9
29Jun80—Awarded fourth purse money.					
11Jun80♦5Chantily:Fra: a1	1:37²gd 6½ 120	① 52 LxA	Pr Chmn Defr Dunrd(Gr3:	Rostov, Hilal, Discretion	8
1Jun80♦3Longchamp:Fra: a7f	1.25³gd *2½ 127	① 2³ SmniH	Pr du Palis Royal(Gr3:	Baptism, Kilijaro, Vox Populi	12

paid $1,539. Weeks later Bid for Bucks went favored in a graded U.S. stakes against males.

In all cases, large class differences in overnite races spelled the difference, and the mutuels are big. International racing is hospitable to well-informed handicappers.

To conclude our treatment of stakes and handicaps, handicappers are invited to try their skill with the 1980 running of perhaps the nation's premier turf stakes for fillies and mares. It's Santa Anita's Grade 1 Yellow Ribbon Invitational. Those adhering to this book's guidelines should be able now to identify the very generous winner.

Entries above represent the 1980 Grade 1 Yellow Ribbon Invitational Stakes, for fillies and mares, 3-years-old and up, run at Oak Tree at Santa Anita each fall.

This book recommends limiting play in Grade 1 events to Grade 1 horses. It recommends eliminating the other horses without mercy. With that in mind, try your hand at the Yellow Ribbon. The race illustrates that the method urged here can at times uncover generous winners of the highest grade.

The Grade 1 horses are Bold 'n Determined and Kilijaro. All others can be forgotten. Sisterhood won the Grade 1 Santa Barbara stakes at Santa Anita March 23, but has not impressed since, and has not trained forwardly for the Yellow Ribbon. Both Queen to Conquer and Kahaila placed third under Grade 1 conditions, but that is not good enough. The others are outgunned.

What about Ack's Secret, alone on the probable pace? In Grade 1 races, class laughs at pace.

What of the three-year-old Lady Marion, in peak form and still improving? In Grade 1 races, class overwhelms form.

No, it's Bold 'n Determined versus Kilijaro for this prize, a point arrived at quickly and easily.

Separating the two, however, proved a much sterner task.

Bold 'n Determined had won thirteen of fifteen, finishing second once, and including five Grade 1 stakes, plus $739,543. But she had not won on turf yet and had not defeated older horses of comparable class.

Kilijaro had not won beyond a mile, and had shipped to Santa Anita from France.

After close analysis, Bold 'n Determined's shortcomings remain, but Kilijaro's pale some. Look carefully at this filly's previous five races. To be sure, its latest races have been best, but the pattern reveals much more. August 28 this confirmed sprinter stretched out to a mile under Grade 3 conditions, prompting the Deauville crowd—which had sent her postward at odds-on against the same class eight days ago—to forsake her at 11 to 1. She won breezing; surprise!

Next, having shipped to Longchamp, she repeated the upset, now beating Grade 1 horses at the mile, when ignored at 6 to 1. Perhaps this sprinter had changed colors some? When on October 26 she lost sprinting in a Grade 1 contest, she lost to the continent's premier sprinter Moorestyle, and on soft turf she previously (June 29) disliked. That race set her up nicely for the Yellow Ribbon. Kilijaro had won $362,413 on turf while mainly sprinting. And all of this she accomplished versus males, including older males.

EIGHTH RACE
Santa Anita
NOVEMBER 9, 1980

1 ¼ MILES.(turf). (1.57¾) 4th Running of THE YELLOW RIBBON INVITATIONAL STAKES (Grade I). Purse $200,000. Fillies and mares. 3-year-olds and upward. By invitation with no nomination or starting fees. The winner to receive $120,000, with $40,000 to second, $24,000 to third, $12,000 to fourth and $4,000 to fifth. Weights, 3-year-olds, 119 lbs.; older, 123 lbs. The Oak Tree Racing Association will invite a representative field of fillies and mares to compete. The field will be drawn by the closing times of entries. A trophy will be presented to the owner of the winner. Invitations: Thursday, October 30, 1980. (Weight for age.)
Value of race $200,000, value to winner $120,000, second $40,000, third $24,000, fourth $12,000, fifth $4,000. Mutuel pool $607,522.

Last Raced	Horse	Eqt	A.Wt	PP	¼	½	¾	1	Str	Fin	Jockey	Odds $1
26Oct80 ^{3}Lon^{3}	Kilijaro	b	4 123	10	$5^{1\frac{1}{2}}$	$5^{2\frac{1}{2}}$	$2^{\frac{1}{2}}$	$2^{\frac{1}{2}}$	$2^{1\frac{1}{2}}$	$1^{3\frac{1}{2}}$	Lequeux A	11.30
26Oct80 ^{8}SA^{1}	Ack's Secret	b	4 123	8	1^{4}	1^{5}	1^{5}	$1^{2\frac{1}{2}}$	$1^{\frac{1}{2}}$	$2^{1\frac{1}{4}}$	Valenzuela P A	8.70
26Oct80 ^{8}SA^{4}	Queen to Conquer		4 123	1	10	10	9	8^{7}	$6^{3\frac{1}{2}}$	$3^{\frac{1}{2}}$	Shoemaker W	3.80
25Oct80 ^{7}Kee^{1}	Bold 'n Determined		3 119	2	$2^{\frac{1}{2}}$	2^{hd}	3^{1}	3^{2}	$3^{1\frac{1}{2}}$	4^{2}	Delahoussaye E	1.20
31Aug80 ^{8}Dmr^{5}	Sisterhood	b	5 123	9	$4^{\frac{1}{2}}$	4^{hd}	$4^{1\frac{1}{2}}$	$4^{2\frac{1}{2}}$	4^{2}	$5^{\frac{1}{2}}$	Lipham T	a-17.30
18Oct80 ^{8}BM^{1}	Lady Marion	b	3 119	7	$8^{1\frac{1}{2}}$	9^{3}	8^{4}	7^{3}	5^{1}	6^{8}	Castaneda M	30.40
20Oct80 ^{4}StC^{1}	Benicia		3 119	6	$7^{2\frac{1}{2}}$	6^{hd}	$5^{2\frac{1}{2}}$	5^{hd}	$7^{2\frac{1}{2}}$	$7^{2\frac{3}{4}}$	Gilbert A	26.20
26Oct80 ^{8}SA^{3}	Princess Toby		5 123	4	6^{hd}	7^{hd}	$7^{1\frac{1}{2}}$	6^{hd}	8^{7}	$8^{3\frac{1}{2}}$	Hawley S	23.40
11Oct80 ^{2}Asc^{5}	Kahaila		3 119	5	9^{2}	$8^{1\frac{1}{2}}$	6^{hd}	9	9	9	Pierce D	a-17.30
26Oct80 ^{8}SA^{2}	A Thousand Stars		5 123	3	$3^{\frac{1}{2}}$	3^{1}	—	—	—	—	Pincay L Jr	4.30

A Thousand Stars, Broke down.
a-Coupled: Sisterhood and Kahaila.
OFF AT 4:15 PST. Start good. Won ridden out. Time, :22⅕, :45⅗, 1:09⅘, 1:34¾, 1:59⅕ Course firm.

$2 Mutuel Prices:				
	9-KILIJARO	24.60	11.00	6.40
	8-ACK'S SECRET		8.00	5.20
	2-QUEEN TO CONQUER			4.00

[illegible] 2, Fogelson E E; 3, [illegible] Farm (Lessee); 4, [illegible]
6, Clark D M & D G; 7, Head Mrs A; 8, Breliant W; 9, Summa Stb & Feldman et al; 10, Clore A.

Obviously, this filly deserved high recognition under any circumstances. This she did not receive from the sophisticated Oak Tree crowd. Handicappers who concentrate on Grade 1 horses in Grade 1 races collected a rewarding mutuel this time, as the results chart on the preceding page reminds us.

CHAPTER 5

Classified Allowances

CLASSIFIED ALLOWANCE RACES open to older runners promise the best of handicappers their biggest bonanzas of any season. Aware of this, good handicappers approach classified races with special regard for their conditions of eligibility.

Horses become eligible according to the number, dates, and value of recent winning efforts. Racing secretaries sometimes permit entry of horses that have won repeatedly in recent weeks and for nice purses. Sometimes the secretaries limit entry to horses that have not won one or two races for a time, and these of moderate value. The former kind of classified race can be considered minimally restricted; the latter highly restricted.

Weight allowances vary accordingly. The better recent records, the higher weights. At times other factors, notably distance, are specified. The basic elements of the conditions can combine in so many ways that the fundamental handicapping factors of class, form, distance, and pace, and their several interrelationships, become difficult to understand and interpret. The eligible horseflesh is unusually varied and diverse. Yet out of this considerable variation and diversity comes the classified race's elemental charm.

Fields of classified races reflect the variety of competition engaged by race conditions. The typical array is a mixture of claimers, allowance runners, and stakes horses. Suitable representatives of any class may figure to win. Handicapping must be comprehensive, calling into play all the primary and secondary factors and their interrelations, but the interplay as between class and form often settles the issue best. These brief introductory remarks can be restated for emphasis as three propositions about classified races that underlie successful handicapping:

107

1. More often than do conditions of eligibility for other kinds of races, classified allowance conditions bring together thoroughbreds of diverse quality, varying form, and different preferences as to distance and footing.

2. Though most classified allowance races are won by relatively talented horses, the best horse often loses. Predictably.

3. Consistently effective handicapping depends first and most decidedly on establishing the relationships between the fundamental factors of class and form.

When classified contenders cannot be separated on class and form relationships, preference is given to horses that figure best when class-form relationships are related in turn to (a) distance, (b) footing, (c) early pace, (d) consistency, and (e) well-established routines of contending stables.

Jockeys are secondary now. The best is a jockey who knows the horse well. Few classified horses can be moved up importantly by the conventional jockey switch—from journeyman to leader. The much more interesting (and useful) change is that from leading rider to a journeyman who previously handled the horse best.

Weight assignments, usually incidental to race outcomes, can be influential under classified allowances. Better horses, if these have not raced and won during time intervals specified by the conditions, often run with relatively low weight. This being so, really top-grade horses, sometimes designated "Class A" by racing secretaries, are categorically denied eligibility to classified events. They must compete in stakes. Horses of less class that have been running and winning lately carry higher imposts. The weights may slow them, especially beyond middle distances. As always, handicappers check contenders' demonstrated ability to tote assigned weight over prescribed distances.

Nothing about classified races should be more instrumental to handicappers' calculations than the notion that the best horse often figures to lose. Under classifed allowance conditions, class does not tell the tale. As often as it wins, the best horse loses. An illustration serves the instruction. At Santa Anita, a few years back, I gave a familiar inquisitor a bum steer. I didn't care for the day's feature, a classified allowance sprint on turf, and said so, but the guy persisted, ". . . who do you like?"

"Three of them have earned minor stakes credentials," I noted. "Go with the best sprinter."

The conditions, and the three I had spotted, looked like this:

8th Santa Anita

ABOUT 6 ½ FURLONGS. (TURF). (1.11⅘) CLASSIFIED ALLOWANCE. Purse $20,000. Fillies and mares. 4-year-olds and upward, which are non-winners of $9,000 other than claiming since December 25. Weight, 120 lbs. Non-winners of such a race of $13,000 since October 4 allowed 2 lbs.; of such a race of $11,000 since July 24, 4 lbs.; of such a race of $9,900 since September 13, 6 lbs. Winners preferred.

Giggling Girl

Own.—Fisher Mrs M R **114**

B. m. 5, by Laugh Aloud—Sewing Circle, by Round Table
Br.—Smith M W (Ky)
Tr.—Gregson Edwin

1979	2	0	0	0	$2,025
1978	4	1	2	1	$24,000
Turf	6	2	2	2	$38,100

17Mar79-8GG	1 1/16	:48 1:13 1:46^{1}sl	5¼	117	10^{17} 10^{16} 10^{23} 10^{23}	BltrC^{1}	ⒻGldn Popy H	50	BecmeALrk,DesignerMiss,Innundo	10
23Feb79-8SA	6f	:22^{1} :45^{4} 1:11^{1}m	3¾	115	5^{9} 5^{10} 5^{5½} 4^{8}	Cauthen S^{2}	ⒻAlw	75	Audene, Dianelta, Step in theCircle	6
22Jun78-8Hol	1 1/16 Ⓣ	:47^{3}1:12 1:41^{4}fm	*2-3	114	5^{6½} 5^{2½} 4^{3} 2^{1½}	McHrgDG^{7}	ⒻTypecst	89	GrandeBris,GigglingGirl,GrnjSueno	9
9Jun78-8Hol	1 1/16 Ⓣ	:47^{2}1:11 1:41^{4}fm	*2-3	115	4^{4} 4^{4½} 1^{hd} 1^{3}	McHargue DG^{3}	ⒻAlw	90	Giggling Girl, Prozier, Dina	6
27May78-3Hol	1⅛ Ⓣ	:48 1:13 1:49^{2}fm	2¼	114	5^{4½} 6^{5½} 2^{1½} 2^{nk}	McHargue DG^{2}	ⒻAlw	88	Fairly, Giggling Girl, Formalite	6
10May78-7Hol	1 1/16 Ⓣ	:47^{4}1:11^{4}1:42^{2}fm	*2¼	114	4^{1½} 4^{3} 2^{2} 3^{¾}	McHargue DG^{5}	ⒻAlw	86	Irma, Fairly, Giggling Girl	9
28Aug77-8Dmr	1⅛ Ⓣ	:47^{4}1:11^{3}1:48^{4}fm	3¼	113	7^{8} 4^{2} 4^{3½} 3^{4½}	CrdrAJr^{4}	ⒻDmr Oaks	92	TaisezVous,DramCritic,GigglingGirl	9
14Aug77-6Dmr	7½f Ⓣ	:22^{4} :46^{1}1:29^{3}fm	5¼	120	6^{5} 5^{5} 5^{2} 1^{1½}	McHargue DG^{1}	ⒻAlw	93	Giggling Girl, Lullaby, Taisez Vous	7
3Aug77-7Dmr	1	:46^{2} 1:10^{4} 1:36 ft	2	113	6^{4} 4^{3½} 4^{1½} 1^{1}	McHargue DG^{2}	ⒻAlw	88	GigglingGirl,FiddleMiss,SmckerMc	6
21Jly77-2Hol	6½f	:22 :45^{1} 1:16 ft	5¼	115	8^{3¾} 3^{2½} 1^{3} 1^{5}	Hawley S^{10}	ⒻM20000	90	GigglingGirl,WintrWinnr,ThirdMrs	12

Apr 1 SA 5f ft 1:01^{3} h   Mar 26 SA Ⓣ 4f yl :49^{4} h (d)   Mar 12 SA Ⓣ 7f fm 1:26^{1} h (d)   Mar 7 SA 4f ft :47^{2} h

Stellar Envoy

Own.—Fogelson E E **120**

B. m. 5, by Envoy—Quasar, by Imbros
Br.—Pascoe W T III (Cal)
Tr.—Whittingham Charles

1979	2	0	1	0	$6,000
1978	5	2	2	1	$33,050
Turf	4	1	1	1	$22,750

8Mar79-8SA	6f	:21^{4} :44^{4} 1:09^{2}ft	2¾	121	1^{hd} 2^{1½} 2^{1½} 2^{3}	Shoemaker W^{4}	ⒻAlw	89	Splendid Size, Stellar Envoy, Critic	6
28Feb79-8SA	a6½f Ⓣ	:21 :44 1:15^{1}yl	15	115	6^{5½} 6^{5½} 4^{3} 7^{7½}	PiercD^{1}	ⒻMnrovia H	75	Palmistry, SingBack,PressingDate	10
28Feb79—Run in two divisions, 5th and 8th races.										
2Nov78-8SA	a6½f Ⓣ	:21^{2} :44^{3}1:14^{3}fm	3	118	2½ 3^{1} 1½ 1½	Shoemaker W^{6}	ⒻAlw	86	StellarEnvoy,FairyDnce,CuteSister	8
25Oct78-7SA	a6½f Ⓣ	:21^{2} :44^{1}1:14^{2}fm	*3-5	119	1^{hd} 1½ 1^{hd} 3^{2½}	Shoemaker W^{6}	ⒻAlw	84	Vatican, Dallas Deb, Stellar Envoy	7
5Oct78-5SA	a6½f Ⓣ	:21^{1} :44^{1}1:14^{1}fm	3¼	114	2^{1} 2^{2} 2½ 2^{2}	ShmrW^{1}	ⒻAtm DysH	86	HappyHolme,StellrEnvoy,PetLbel	10
5Oct78—Run in two divisions, 5th and 8th races.										
18Sep78-7Dmr	6f	:22 :44^{4} 1:09^{1}ft	*2-5	114	1^{hd} 1½ 1^{3} 1^{3}	Shoemaker W^{5}	ⒻAlw	92	StellrEnvoy,GentleJzz,MissMrgiMc	7
31Aug78-8Dmr	6f	:21^{4} :44^{4} 1:09^{3}ft	*1e	114	2^{hd} 2½ 2^{1½} 2^{1½}	Shoemaker W^{2}	ⒻAlw	88	AckLikeaLady,StellarEnvoy,Molalla	9
15Apr77-4Hol	6f	:21^{3} :44^{1} 1:09^{3}ft	5¼	119	3^{2} 3^{3½} 2^{2} 1^{¾}	Shoemaker W^{4}	ⒻAlw	91	StellrEnvoy,Fornew,OfferAn'Honor	7
17Mar77-3SA	6f	:22^{1} :46 1:11^{2}sl	2¼	117	1^{1} 1½ 2^{hd} 1^{2½}	ShoemkrW^{3}	ⒻⓈMdn	82	StllrEnvoy,Guggnslockr,StringPullr	7

Mar 31 SA 6f ft 1:15^{3} h   Mar 25 SA 5f ft 1:00^{4} h   Mar 21 SA 3f sl :41 h (d)   Mar 16 SA tr.t 3f ft :39^{1} h

Sisterhood

Own.—Harbor View Farm **118**

B. f. 4, by Exclusive Native—Lost Horizon II, by Court Harwell
Br.—Newstead Farm (Va)
Tr.—Barrera Lazaro S

1979	2	0	0	0	
1978	13	5	0	0	$69,154
Turf	6	4	0	0	$60,319

17Jan79-8SA	1⅛	:48 1:13 1:52^{3}sl	39	115	2^{2} 2^{1½} 7^{3½} 8^{14}	OlrsF^{5}	ⒻSn Grgnio H	54	Via Maris, DramaCritic,DonnaInez	10
6Jan79-8SA	7f	:22 :44^{3} 1:22^{3}sl	43	116	6^{5½} 8^{6½} 9^{12} 8^{11}	OlivaresF^{11}	ⒻLa Brea	79	GretLdyM.,QuenYsn,B.Thoughtful	11
25Oct78-8Aqu	1 1/16 Ⓣ	:49^{1}1:13 1:43^{2}fm	6¼	115	4^{2½} 6^{3½} — —	GnlB^{4}	ⒻLamb Chp H	—	Misgivings, Invision, Terpsichorist	10
25Oct78—Lost rider										
28Sep78-7Med	1 1/16 Ⓣ	:46^{3}1:10^{4}1:41^{2}fm	10	112	3^{3½} 3^{3} 3^{1} 1^{1½}	GnzlB^{2}	ⒻB Springs H	105	Sisterhood,IslandKiss,WhiteStrLine	9
28Sep78—Run in two divisions 6th and 7th races.										
13Sep78-8Bel	1¼ Ⓣ	:48^{2}1:38 2:03^{1}yl	5¾	115	3^{1} 2^{hd} 4^{2½} 6^{8½}	GonzlzB^{6}	ⒻAthenia H	69	Trpsichorist,Consort,BonniBluFlg	12
30Aug78-8Bel	1 1/16 Ⓣ	:46 1:10^{1}1:41^{1}fm	3¼	117	2^{5} 2^{1} 1^{1½} 1^{1¾}	Gonzalez B^{3}	ⒻAlw	90	Sisterhood, Catherine'sBet,Invision	7
21Aug78-7Sar	1 1/16 Ⓣ	:47^{4}1:11^{4}1:42^{3}fm	*3	112	2^{hd} 1^{hd} 1½ 1^{¾}	Gonzalez B^{6}	ⒻAlw	—	Sisterhood, Sue Me Not, MissIvor	12
14Aug78-7Sar	7f	:22^{1} :45 1:23^{1}ft	12	117	2^{hd} 3^{3} 4^{5½} 4^{6½}	Cordero A Jr^{4}	ⒻAlw	83	IvyRod,AfterSchool,Murrumbidgee	7
14Jly78-5Bel	1 Ⓣ	:46^{2}1:10^{4}1:35^{1}fm	14	113	1^{hd} 1^{hd} 1½ 1^{2½}	Cordero A Jr^{2}	ⒻAlw	94	Sistrhood,WorthyMlody,QuidProGl	7
4Jly78-5Bel	1 1/16	:46^{2} 1:11 1:45^{4}sy	13	113	7^{6½} 8^{12} 8^{20} 8^{24}	Cordero A Jr^{6}	ⒻAlw	49	Miss Ivor, Linda Maureen,AcesFull	8

Mar 31 SA 5f ft 1:00^{2} h   Mar 23 SA 5f ft 1:01^{2} h   Mar 14 SA 5f gd 1:01^{4} h   Mar 4 SA 5f ft :58^{4} h

The conditions effectively barred any horse of allowance grade or better that had been racing to advantage within three months, almost seventy-five racing days. California purses allot 55 percent to the winner. "Nonwinners of $9,000 . . ." refers to purses of $16,000, a modest sum for nonclaiming horses stabled at Santa Anita.

Does that mean all decent nonclaiming horses that had been running regularly at Santa Anita 1979 were ineligible for this? Yes, in the practical sense. The racing secretary was offering low grade allowance types a better chance to win.

At least that's the general idea. But other things happen. Clever claiming trainers grab at the softer classified opportunity for their sharp, consistent breadwinners. Other trainers see a chance to warm up good horses returning to training after lengthy layoffs. Still others take this easier spot for horses that have lost successively recently in stakes or tougher classified races.

Knowing all of this, handicappers consider (a) horses that have been performing satisfactorily in recent open stakes, (b) established classified horses that have raced sparingly during the time intervals specified, or (c) any returning stakes performers that look well prepared and well meant. Alternatively, handicappers normally eliminate horses that have raced steadily since the specified dates but remain eligible. They also downgrade unexceptional horses that have been absent from competition for a time prior to the specified dates. The race was not written with them in mind.

The principles underlying this approach are perfectly transportable among all classified allowance conditons. Identify and prefer entrants whose recent records (a) fit the conditions snugly, or (b) outclass the conditions impressively. But sport at the racetrack can get unnerving.

Returning to the past performances of the horses I liked in the eighth at Santa Anita April 5, 1979, the preferred profiles are readily identified. Lightly raced since December 25, and either stakes-placed or a stakes winner in races prior to that specified period, the entrants Giggling Girl, Stellar Envoy, and Sisterhood seemed to fit the conditions very snugly. Stellar Envoy looked clearly best in sprints. Which figured to win? None. As the results chart shows, the three finished second, third, and fourth.

The generous winner looked like this in the past performances:

My Mary — **Ch. f. 4, by Rising Market—Opening Bid, by Windsor Ruler**

Own.—Johnston Mr–Mrs E B & EW **114**

Br.—Elmore Mr–Mrs J J (Cal) — **Tr.—Warren Donald**

1979	2	0	0	1	$3,300
1978	20	1	1	2	$25,800
Turf	10	0	1	0	$9,100

29Mar79-8SA	6½f	:21^4 :44^4 1:17 gd	7¾	114	2^1	1^{hd}	2^{hd}	3^3	McCarron C J^3	ⒻAlw	82	His Squaw, Delphic Oracle, My Mary	8
9Mar79-8SA	6½f	:21^3 :44^1 1:15^{2}ft	36	114	4^{2½}	4^{3½}	6^{4½}	8^{9¾}	McCarron C J^1	ⒻAlw	83	FairyDance, Viking'sJoy, Juanit'sGirl	9
2Nov78-8SA	a6½f	Ⓣ:21^2 :44^{3}1:14^{3}fm	19	116	5^5	5^3	5^3	7^{4¼}	Toro F^1	ⒻAlw	82	StellarEnvoy, FairyDnce, CuteSister	8
25Oct78-7SA	a6½f	Ⓣ:21^2 :44^{1}1:14^{2}fm	23	116	3^{1½}	3^2	3^2	4^{2¾}	Toro F^7	ⒻAlw	84	Vatican, Dallas Deb, Stellar Envoy	7
26Sep78-11Pom	1 1/16	:48 1:12^3 1:44^{4}ft	12	113	4^{1½}	4^4	5^8	6^{14}	ChpmnTM^4	ⒻLsMdsH	74	Pet Label, Catcando, DonnaforSure	7
18Sep78-11Pom	1 1/16	:46^4 1:12 1:45^{3}ft	2¾	119	7^{6½}	7^5	5^8	5^{11}	RslsR^6	ⒻC T B A Mn	73	WestwardSal, DonnforSure, Hot!.oot	8
24Aug78-8Dmr	7½f	Ⓣ:22^3 :46^{1}1:30^{2}fm	*2¾	109	5^5	4^3	5^{2½}	6^{2¾}	Shoemaker W^9	ⒻAlw	86	Habeebti, Pro Tab, Critic	10
13Aug78-9Dmr	1 1/16	Ⓣ:47^{4}1:12^{1}1:44^{1}fm	5¼	111	1^{½}	1^{hd}	1^{hd}	1no†	Shoemaker W^3	ⒻAlw	88	‡MyMry, JessicsGotch, SlideMountin	8
†13Aug78—Disqualified and placed second													
29Jly78-8Dmr	1 1/16	Ⓣ:47^{4}1:12^{3}1:44^{2}fm	17	115	2^{1½}	2^{hd}	3^{½}	5^{2¾}	PiercD^1	ⒻSn Clmnte	84	Joe's Bee, FairyDance, Carrie'sAngel	7
29Jly78—Run in two divisions, 5th and 8th races.													
21Jly78-8Hol	1 1/16	Ⓣ:46^{2}1:11^{1}1:42^{2}fm	14	116	6^5	6^{3½}	4^{3½}	4^{2½}	Pierce D^7	ⒻGlenaris	84	HighPheasant, Agree, JessicasGotch	8

Mar 24 SA 5f ft 1:00 h **Mar 18 SA 7f gd 1:29^2 h** **Mar 7 SA 3f ft :35 h** **Mar 2 SA 6f ft 1:13^2 hg**

Its record characterizes My Mary as an inconsistent, relatively low-level allowance filly equally uncomfortable in sprints and routes. In ten starts, it had failed to win on turf. In its favor, the filly had only two outings since December 25, and the much-improved March 29 sprint hints of a peak effort upcoming. Just the sort of nondescript maverick the racing secretary had in mind, you might say.

Would a truly comprehensive handicapping appraisal expect My Mary to whip Giggling Girl, Stellar Envoy, and Sisterhood under the stated classified conditions? Not in my book. Nor, however, do the three I preferred look "comprehensively" appealing.

Neither Sisterhood nor Giggling Girl can be judged in winning form. Both are more comfortable at middle distances. Stellar Envoy's form looks acceptable, but her class advantage looks marginal, and the probable early pace figured to compromise her chances further. All matters considered, if bets must be placed (which they do not), Stellar Envoy emerges the likeliest of risky investments.

As events proceeded, My Mary's early speed and peaking form combined to withstand repeated challenges by Stellar Envoy throughout the stretch. The $33.40 mutuel might not seem so inexplicable to players attracted by My Mary's small advantage in relation to classified allowance conditions that kept her clear of rough and ready competition.

The lesson is this. As classified allowance conditions become more restrictive, barring many horses from the competition, class advantages of eligible entrants often are nullified by the sharper form of inferior runners. Or, secondarily, by nuances of form in combination with the distance, footing, and pace preferences of contending horses.

Less restrictive classified conditions have an opposite effect. Suppose a classified race of early winter has been carded as follows:

EIGHTH RACE   ALLOWANCE
    PURSE $40,000. FOR CLASSIFIED FOUR-YEAR-OLDS AND UPWARD, WHICH
    ARE NONWINNERS OF $13,000 TWICE AT ONE MILE AND ONE-EIGHTH OR
    OVER SINCE JULY 24 .... 122 lbs.
    Nonwinners of $13,000 twice at one mile or over
            since October 4 allowed .... 3 lbs.
            of such a race since December 25 .... 5 lbs.
            of such a race at one mile and one-eighth or over since July 24 .. 8 lbs.
    (Claiming and starter races not considered)
                                                    ONE MILE AND ONE-EIGHTH

Six months or thereabouts have passed. An early winter race like this intends to bar the cream of the handicap division but still offers a splendid purse to many of the classiest distance runners on the grounds. Handicappers now credit intrinsic class in priority to comparative form. Which horses have been competing under the best eligibility conditions, doing so well, but barely remain eligible today?

Suppose now it's late winter and eligibility conditions look like this:

SEVENTH RACE   ALLOWANCE
    PURSE $30,000. FOR CLASSIFIED FOUR-YEAR-OLDS AND UPWARD,
    WHICH ARE NONWINNERS OF $9,000 OTHER THAN CLAIMING SINCE
    JULY 24 .... 120 lbs.
    Nonwinners of $13,000 at one mile or over since April 9
            allowed .... 3 lbs.
            of such a race in 1978 .... 6 lbs.
    (Races when entered for $45,000 or less not considered in allowances) ONE MILE
                                                          AND ONE-SIXTEENTH

The purse is smaller. The number of permissible victories is zero unless the winner's share drops below $9,000, no great shakes at Santa Anita. No distance restrictions are specified. Winners of claiming races at $50,000 or more will be eligible. The field will be restricted to older runners that haven't done too much for eight months or so. Form often edges class. Among the sharpest contenders, which fits best at the distance, on the footing, with the probable early pace? If a handicap star appears in the entries, it likely has not raced or has raced sparingly since July 24. It might outclass its rivals, but is it in winning form? Suited to the distance? To the footing? To the probable pace? If not, it's probably prepping, and probably will lose. Handicappers should expect that and not be fooled.

The preceding discussion indicates the competition eligible to classified allowance races can be regarded by handicappers as relatively restricted or unrestricted, such that less restriction bows to class and greater restriction bows to form. As racing secretaries attempt to provide fair and favorable opportunities to all kinds of classified horses, the restrictions stated in eligibility conditions are intended variously to favor horses of one kind or another.

Handicappers can move into the secretary's thinking by employing a concept of boundaries, fairly distinguishing less restricted classified races from the highly restricted kind. What kind of borderlines can usefully divide restricted and unrestricted classified events? How many permissible victories? At what winner shares? Over how long a time interval?

The Handicapper's Condition Book recommends classified events be viewed as relatively restricted when the specified restrictions approach or cross these borders: nonwinners for ninety days or longer of a single race at any distance and having a winner's share equal to or lower than the winning share of a nonwinners twice allowance race on the local schedule.

The ninety-day interval exceeds the run of many meetings. Where a meeting does not occur on a continuous circuit, that interval can be replaced by a time interval extending to two-thirds or more of the season.

Boundaries notwithstanding, handicappers everywhere will confront classified races whose conditions contain few clues to the kinds of horses most likely to win.

That being so, a key to success with numerous classified allowances is a fine analysis of each entrant's class in relation to its current form. Remembering that in general less restriction bows to class, and greater restriction to form, handicappers benefit by asking themselves why trainers have chosen particular conditions for their horses.

For example, the classic loser in the highly restricted classified allowance race is the stakes winner returning from a lengthy layoff. In shape, the animal would breeze. But it loses. How come? Smart barns often use classified allowance conditions to warm up their big horses. Rarely do the barns go all out in a hellish try for smaller unimportant purses.

Alternatively, high-priced claimers are often moved from customary selling levels to classified allowances when purses smell good and the eligible competition looks limited. At major tracks where claimers compete while carrying $75,000 claiming tags or such, when classified conditions are highly restricted, a claiming entrant or two actually may be dropping down to a lower purse value. Such horses are discounted only foolishly for their residence in the claiming ranks. Under almost all classified conditions, the racing secretary will have exempted winners of claiming races as incentive for them to try to move up in class. Some have reached peak form, suit the distance and footing nicely, will be favored by the pace, and can handle themselves impressively.

Perpetual classified allowance horses that measure up on other fundamentals are distinguished as to class by sizes of purses they have competed for satisfactorily.

Beyond purse values, handicappers normally need more information than is available to them in past performance tables. They need results charts. These reveal purse sizes, the restrictions specified by conditions, the complete order of finishers, and significant running calls. Charts also reveal fractional times at all points of call and the horses' ages, jockeys, and stable connections.

It's no exaggeration to assert that results charts contain the secrets of many classified allowance propositions. A sharp horse that has just challenged stiffer classified conditions (less restricted) for larger purses and has raced impressively while doing so, finishing ahead of horses of greater quality than those eligible today, several times a season may be sent to the post at unwarranted odds, the better quality of its recent races and finishes having been effectively obscured in the past performances.

The flip side of that situation happens too. Horses go favored under classified conditions at low odds, their recent performances under highly restricted conditions have looked classier in the past performances than they really were. Keepers of charts recognize these and similar situations for what they represent, and may capitalize nicely.

August 9, 1985

7th Saratoga

1 ⅛ MILES. (1.47) ALLOWANCE. Purse $40,000. 3-year-olds and upward, which have not won two races of $12,500 at a mile or over since October 15. Weight, 3-year-olds, 117 lbs., Older, 122 lbs., Non-winners of a race of $15,000 at a mile and a furlong or over since June 1, allowed 3 lbs., Of such a race of $12,500 at a mile or over since January 1, 7 lbs. Maiden, claiming, starter and state-bred races not considered).

Although the purse is the same, the winner of the race above would be fortunate to finish in-the-money in the race below.

The top race bars horses that have accomplished anything of note for the past ten months. Even New York three-year-olds that have won two routes carrying purses of $21,000 or more would be ineligible. The race would be viewed as easy pickings by trainers of nicely developing three-year-olds that have won two nonwinners allowance pots while sprinting and now are ready to stretch out to middle distances.

The race below bars only horses that have won multiple routes in the past two-and-a-half months. Winners of multiple open stakes and close runners-up remain eligible, as long as they won just one of those races since June 15. Nicely developing three-year-olds that have won two or three nonwinners allowance routes are still eligible, as two of those winner shares will be less than $16,500. The likeliest winner will be an open stakes horse.

Classified types moving from the race above to the race below are moving ahead in class considerably, purses notwithstanding. They will be outgunned. Conversely, classified horses that impress in the race below and move to the race above will be dropping in class notably and hold a well-disguised advantage.

Handicappers should watch for classified allowance horses switching from relatively unrestricted conditions to relatively or highly restricted conditions. The class edge can be razor sharp, the odds just as advantageous. For class handicappers, the change represents one of the best opportunities in the game.

August 31, 1985

7th Belmont

1 ¼ MILES. (InnerTurf). (1.40½) ALLOWANCE. Purse $40,000. 3-year-olds and upward, which have not won two races of $16,500 at a mile or over since June 15. Weights, 3-year-olds 117 lbs. Older 122 lbs. Non-winners of a race of $16,500 at a mile or over since August 1 allowed 3 lbs. Of such a race since July 1, 5 lbs. Of two such races since May 1, 7 lbs. (Maiden, Claiming, Starter and State-bred races not considered.)

If handicappers file results charts for no other purpose than their application to classified allowance races, the bother will eventually prove its worth. Maybe a half dozen times a season these handicappers cash tickets on horses that gallop to the wire as overlays, having been misunderstood by the crowd and by handicappers without charts.

In order to deal effectively with classified allowance races, handicappers must appraise effectively the chances of stakes horses entered under these conditions. Two opposing points hound us. Many stakes horses in classified races are not well meant. Many win nonetheless.

In the broad sense, handicappers can approach the problem on these terms.

Graded stakes winners retain little interest in classified allowance races. They use the races to get ready and rarely approach the races seriously.

Ungraded stakes winners care more, but really would rather win another stakes. When these stakes competitors engage classified conditions, handicappers must decide whether they are ready and destined to win. If such horses entered in classified races reveal questionable form *in combination with* any discomfort with the distance or footing, or with a pace that should prove problematic, handicappers should presume the stakes horses will not win today and can shop for horses that fit the race's restrictions.

If graded stakes winners that have been training smartly or racing recently are dropped into classified conditions, handicappers feel a tighter bind. Stakes stars may win classified events in a trot. Their edge depends to some extent on the restrictions specified by the conditions. In this special context, the more restricted the competition, the better the chances of genuinely top horses.

Special considerations aside, the best fit in any classified allowance race is the horse whose recent record most closely matches the restrictions specified by eligibility conditions. If an April race has been restricted to "... nonwinners of $8,800 three times since December 25 ..." an obvious contender is any horse that has won two such races since that date. The higher the winner shares, the better. The fewer the attempts, the better.

Another contender is the horse that has won just one race since December 25, but having a significantly larger winner's share. More so if that horse has finished consistently close for larger purses.

A third contender would be the horse that won several comparable winner shares just prior to December 25, and has raced sparingly or not at all since. The closer to December 25 the winning efforts, the better. The fewer the number of races since, the better.

And a fourth contender would be the horse that had won three or more winner shares since December 25, but at a value below $8,800. The more wins, the better. The closer the winner shares to $8,800, the better.

Similar performance profiles can be related to classified allowance conditions specifying other numbers of permissible victories, having other winner shares, over other time intervals. Four illustrations of this point are discussed at the end of the chapter.

Here, in descending order of preference, are the kinds of past performance profiles suitable to classified allowance conditions. Under minimally restricted conditions, prefer:

1. Graded or open stakes winners in acceptable form, provided the distance and footing are comfortable, and the probable pace is favorable.

Before proceeding, a curt reminder applies. Whenever a Grade 1 or Grade 2 stakes winner looks loaded for the kill, the horse is virtually a shoo-in under any classified allowance conditions.

2. Any entrant whose basic class, as indicated by purse values, restrictions of prior classified conditions, and the quality of horses engaged by its latest best efforts, is superior to today's conditions, provided its form remains in the improvement cycle and it remains eligible today because it has not raced enough recently.

In the absence of the above profiles, prefer:

3. Any entrant whose recent best efforts under classified conditions or better have fallen barely within the races won, money won, and time interval specified by the conditions.

One more win, or a win at slightly better purse value, and the animal would not be eligible. If it wins under today's conditions, a very logical sequence has occurred.

4. Any entrant on the improve and moving from less restricted conditions to more restricted conditions.

The greater the difference between the permissible number of wins, the size of the winner shares, and the specified time intervals, the better an improving horse's present opportunity. The purse will be smaller, but the competition will be weaker.

Under highly restricted conditions, prefer:

1. Currently sharp horses that have been competing for purses of comparable or better value, and are particularly nicely suited to the distance, footing, and probable pace.

Finally, when two or more classified contenders have proved difficult to separate, handicappers generally should prefer the horse that emerges best after a fine analysis of the class and form interaction. In general, less restricted classified competition favors class. More restricted competition favors form.

As major racetracks focus more and more on faster development of younger horses, classified allowance races for older horses have declined. Too, as distance racing and turf racing have expanded, the classified allowance sprint for older runners has practically disappeared.

Nonetheless, properly armed and practiced handicappers still benefit from the challenge of classified allowance races. Unlike the restricted kinds of competition eligible to nonwinner allowance races, classified allowance restrictions actually contribute to widely open, free-swinging contests. When the best horse loses, as so often happens, the best handicappers often win.

Here are four classified conditions that confront handicappers all the time, and the kinds of horses most likely to win.

CLASSIFIED CONDITIONS
Saturday, March 30, 1985

SIXTH RACE   **ALLOWANCE**
  PURSE $25,000. FOR CLASSIFIED FOUR-YEAR-OLDS AND UPWARD, WHICH ARE NONWINNERS OF $14,000 OTHER THAN CLAIMING IN 1984–85 . 121 lbs.
  Nonwinners of a race of $13,000 since December 25 allowed .... 3 lbs.
        of a race of $12,000 since October 4 .... 5 lbs.
        of a race of $11,000 since July 23 .... 7 lbs.
  (Races when entered for $40,000 or less not considered in allowances)
                                            SIX AND ONE-HALF FURLONGS

In this highly restricted event, which bars the best sprinters and even classified horses that have won similar races during the previous 16 months, handicappers prefer:

1. Recent sharp winners of multiple allowance races whose winners shares have been just below $14,000.

2. Stakes and classified allowance sprinters that previous to 1984 won better purses, have raced sparingly in 1984-85, and arrive at this race in sufficiently sharp form to show their previous best.

3. Consistent claiming sprint winners whose winner shares have been equal to or greater than today's share.

Thursday, April 11, 1985

EIGHTH RACE   **ALLOWANCE**
  PURSE $35,000. FOR CLASSIFIED FOUR-YEAR-OLDS AND UPWARD, WHICH HAVE NOT WON $13,000 SINCE JULY 23 .... 122 lbs.
  Nonwinners of $12,000 twice since July 23 allowed .... 3 lbs.
        $11,000 twice since December 25 .... 5 lbs.
        $12,000 since July 23 .... 7 lbs.
  (Claiming and starter races not considered)
                                        ONE MILE AND ONE-SIXTEENTH

In this relatively restricted Hollywood Park event, handicappers prefer:

1. **Stakes horses that have raced consistently well in recent months without winning, provided their form remains sharp or improving.**

2. **Impressive recent winners of multiple nonwinners allowance races, especially such horses that have raced evenly or better in open stakes races.**

3. **Relatively recent winners of classified races whose winner shares were just below $13,000.**

4. **Recent winners of high-priced claiming races having winning shares greater than $13,000.**

September 15, 1984

EIGHTH RACE   ALLOWANCE
PURSE $40,000. FOR CLASSIFIED FOUR-YEAR-OLDS AND UPWARD, WHICH HAVE NOT WON $12,000 THREE TIMES SINCE JUNE 1 .... 122 lbs.
Nonwinners of $14,000 twice since July 23 allowed .... 3 lbs.
     $11,000 three times in 1983–84 .... 5 lbs.
     $13,000 since December 25 .... 7 lbs.
     Such a race since October 4 .... 10 lbs.
(Claiming and starter races not considered)

                                     SIX FURLONGS

This minimally restricted sprint admits multiple open stakes winners of recent races. Handicappers prefer:

1. **Graded or open stakes winners or runnersup of recent races whose winner shares are equal to or greater than today's share.**

2. **Recent impressive winners of two such races.**

3. **Recent winners of one such race having a winner's share greater than $22,000.**

4. **Multiple winners of such races just prior to June 1, provided current form permits a top effort.**

Saturday, February 16, 1985

SEVENTH RACE   ALLOWANCE
PURSE $40,000. FOR CLASSIFIED FOUR-YEAR-OLDS AND UPWARD, WHICH ARE NONWINNERS OF $15,000 TWICE AT ONE MILE OR OVER SINCE APRIL 8.
                       Four-year-olds...121 lbs.   Older...122 lbs.
Nonwinners of such a race of $16,000 since
     December 25 allowed .... 3 lbs.
     of such a race since October 4 .... 5 lbs.
     of such a race since July 23 or such a race of
     $19,000 since June 1 .... 8 lbs.
(Claiming and starter races not considered)
                       ONE MILE AND ONE-SIXTEENTH

In this relatively unrestricted middle-distance race, recent winners of open stakes can drop down in class for a juicy purse, but multiple stakes winners of the past ten months cannot.

The conditions intend to bar only the cream of the handicap-stakes division. Accordingly, handicappers prefer:

1. A recent winner—within three months—of an open stakes, preferably of a graded stakes.

2. Consistent runners-up in open or graded stakes having relatively high values on the schedule of purses.

CHAPTER 6

Claimers

BECAUSE CLAIMING RACES COMPRISE approximately 70 percent of all races carded in the United States, handicappers do not prosper comfortably unless they beat them. Happily, claiming races for horses four and older have long been the expert's bread and butter. But the claiming game has changed. The older claiming horses have lost territory to their younger counterparts.

The two age groups, however comparable their price tags, are worlds apart. Many handicappers have fallen on hard times while trying to stay ahead of claiming races for horses aged three and two. The animals cannot be trusted. They are not nearly as reliable as are older claimers. In consequence, it's harder than ever to stay ahead of the claiming game.

Several other factors have altered traditional practices in the claiming game. A longer season has adversely affected variations in the claimers' form cycles. Now as always, cheaper stock gets overworked. Strain eventually catches up with them all. In the best of situations, where minor or nagging ailments are treated with rest, intermittent layoffs of six to eight weeks can rejuvenate limb and spirit surprisingly well. In the worst cases, where overextension is prolonged, resulting ailments become more pronounced, and the typical layoff serves as little more than a palliative.

In consequence, rises and drops in claiming class have become more frequent and more dramatic than ever. Nearing the midpoint of any major season it is hardly unusual to see a $20,000 plater lowered to $10,000. If eventually given a four-to-six week furlough, it might rise to its former level, perhaps into a higher bracket. After a while, back down it comes. In relatively uneven patterns this kind of cyclical process continues until a more desperate pattern of continuous deterioration sets in.

Too, industrialized breeding centers being erected across the land now churn out a class of thoroughbred whose calling card is cheap speed. Enough merely to struggle through six furlongs or to sputter to the wire at middle distances, perhaps in races restricted to state-breds. As a result, more races are being won by horses that run on or near the early lead. Handicappers that allot extra minutes to their analyses of the probable early pace, intending to identify early speedsters that may stick it out in the stretch, have kept in step with a changing game.

Unabated inflation has lowered the dependability of the claiming tag as the measure of class. Selling prices remain important to handicappers, but not as before. As will be recommended here, handicappers today will be better off to think in terms of claiming brackets, or ranges of selling prices within which horses can be expected to perform effectively.

In southern California, claiming horses moving from a $16,000 claiming race to one where list prices are as high as $25,000 have jumped in class by 55 percent, but no expert on that circuit tosses the animals out at a glance.

At some minor tracks today, a claimer may rise in class by 100 percent, from $2,000 to $4,000, and win handily, depending on other elements in the eligibility conditions.

As a result of inflation too, the $10,000 claimer of just two or three years ago is valued now at $12,500 or more. As claiming price ceilings have risen, lower-priced horses have been phased out at major plants. In the early seventies at Hollywood Park, claiming races were carded regularly for older horses valued at $3,200. The bottom price now is $10,000. Veteran handicappers like to point out that the typical $10,000 claimer of today could hardly knock heads with yesterday's $5,000 horse. It's true, in part because the $5,000 horse is now a $10,000 commodity, in larger part because the quality of claiming competition has seriously declined.

Shipping of claimers has increased, especially throughout the East, and surely during the frigid winter months. When New York claimers ship to Florida or Oaklawn for winter, they may run with $8,000 or $10,000 tags, but no serious New Yorker believes that on return to the big city they will be unable to handle horses there that stayed on and ran with tags of $12,500 or $16,000.

These factors combine to make comparisons of claiming prices trickier than before. Needed as supplements are other indices of claiming class, such as high early speed, adjusted final times, recent consistency, and form advantages.

So lots has gone by the boards in the claiming game. While recognizing that change has occurred, handicappers best approach claiming races by remembering basic facts of claiming life that remain in force at all major plants. The idea is to afford cheaper horses a chance to win by bringing together horses of relatively equal value. That purpose may be harder to achieve in today's game, but it happens far more often than not. Stables that consistently enter $5,000 horses in races for $10,000 stock still get nothing but the monthly bills. And stables that try to sneak a $20,000 horse into that $10,000 race are likely still to come away with a minor winner's share and perhaps the proceeds of a large wager at low odds, but they forfeit a $20,000 value, the horse.

That still being the reality, truly big drops in class among claimers usually result from injury or physical deterioration due to overwork. Once that kind of deterioration sets in, sharp barns drop quickly, knowing the situation will worsen if they wait. To avoid deception involving really big class drops, handicappers need to learn the maneuverings of local claiming barns. Claiming races are won still by horses at the top of the form cycle and suited to the class, distance, and probable early pace. The next sections identify the specific handicapping guidelines, old and new.

BREAD AND BUTTER RACES

Claiming races for horses four-and-older or three-and-older during the core of any major season are the expert's bread and butter. Tom Ainslie coined the phrase. It sticks well. The animals entered in these events already have demonstrated their relative class, distance and pace preferences, speed figures, and variations of their form cycles. Handicappers therefore experience fewer surprises of form, or surprises resulting from rises and drops in class, or surprises of distance and footing changes, or surprises associated with equipment changes and jockey shifts. When the switches do occur, studied handicappers hardly are puzzled by them.

Unless an older plater has been claimed and begins to resemble a new article, handicappers rarely anticipate a dramatic change in performance. While improving three-year-olds that have not tried middle distances or accomplished anything unless allowed to control the early pace may suddenly do both impressively, five-year-old horses or mares that have not done either remain unlikely to do either today. If a six-year-old wins big for a $20,000 price and now has been entered for $32,000, a claiming level it has never negotiated well, handicappers predict confidently it will remain outgunned.

Beyond stability, current form among many older claiming entrants is usually so poor or deteriorating the animals are readily eliminated. The fast eliminations lighten the handicapping load.

Within this framework of relatively stable performance patterns and predictable form cycles, the probability studies of Fred Davis and Bill Quirin have underscored the emergence of three conditions now very prominent in claiming races for older horses.

1. Early speed is more important than ever.

Horses with early speed win more than their fair share and approximately 60 percent of all claiming races. At many plants the percentage is even higher. Smart handicappers take note. An early pace duel may weaken the horses that engage in it, but it does not easily defeat them. The early pace survivor, or the beneficiary that has waited patiently behind the early pace duel, is a likely winner.

Pace analysis should accordingly emphasize the early competition. Which front-runner is likely to survive? Which horse close-up early might inherit an easy lead later on? Pace analysis recognizes that late runners may catch up, but these probably will need (a) a class edge and (b) the benefit of a weakening pace duel.

2. Recent starters are no longer at great advantage.

Davis found that recent starters (within two weeks) win no more than their fair share of claiming races. But claimers away more than three weeks are relatively bad risks.

The exception is the claimer absent for more than three weeks that shows a freshening series of workouts and is returning to a level where it wins consistently or is dropping down to a level where it previously has won impressively.

A particularly successful workout pattern uncovered by Davis is four workouts within twenty days. In a more recent study of contemporary form, William L. Scott found that regardless of time away, horses showing a five-furlong workout within the past fourteen days should not be hastily eliminated.

Handicappers can now be more relaxed about recent racing as the index of current form. They can accept horses that have raced satisfactorily within three weeks. If claimers have been away from three to six weeks, handicappers should demand a series of freshening works. If the works are there, horses qualify.

Now comes the topper from Davis. Although horses that drop 30 percent or more in class represent only 2.8 percent of claiming race starters, they win 10.6 percent of the races. That kind of class drop wins more than 375 percent times its true share. Quite a statistic!

Other statistics show that more than 30 percent of all claming race winners have dropped from their previous best, yet this group represents only 15 percent of the starters. The dropped-down claiming horses win twice their rightful share. Davis has called the statistic representing the drop of 30 percent or more "the strongest probability factor among handicapping characteristics ever discovered scientifically."

Commenting on the findings about dropped-down horses in claiming races, Davis asserts, "A handicapper could do well confining himself to horses of this type—if he could get his price."

Regardless of traditional beliefs and practices, handicappers should find this latest evidence exciting. It gives us the third new guideline:

3. No matter how large or small the drop in claiming price, these entrants win more than their share of claiming races; the greater the drop in class, the stronger the probability of winning; a drop of 30 percent or more in claiming price represents a highly significant class edge.

A reduction in selling price is far from everything, but it is damn important. When contenders that measure up on the several fundamental factors need to be separated, no single indicator will be more favorable to handicapping success than the drop in class.

On separating claiming contenders, the Davis data encourage handicappers to consider the following:

In sprints, if a horse combines a 30 percent or greater class drop with one of the top three speed ratings in the field (average the two highest speed ratings at the distance in the past performances), its chances improve.

In routes, if a horse dropping down in class also has earned the highest speed rating at the distance, it has a better chance.

Consistency, long treasured as a reliable index of class among claimers, is not a reliable method of separating contenders. Inconsistent horses win enough. Yet claimers able to win three of ten starts win double their due. If this kind of selling horse figures, its consistency helps. Recent consistency means even more. Most likely winners are horses that have won two of their latest six.

While claiming class is less a function of form these days, certain form advantages have been more strongly associated with winners than have others. A particularly fascinating advantage is attributed to horses that have been "up close" at every call of their previous race, provided the race did not occur longer than twenty-eight days past and the horses did not lose more than one length from the stretch call to the finish. If a horse is dropping in class, the stretch loss can be disregarded. The up close criterion varies with the distance, as follows:

a. sprints up to 6½ furlongs	within 2¾ lengths
b. races at 7f and 1M	within 3¾ lengths
c. races at 1¹⁄₁₆M or farther	within 4¾ lengths

Horses that won their last claiming race are more likely to repeat if the winning margin were three lengths or more, provided the horses show another plus form factor, such as being up close at every call, an exceptional workout of five furlongs or longer since the win, or a fast return to the races of seven days or less.

At medium class and minor racetracks claiming horses can be considered at advantage on form if they have raced within twenty-one days and since have recorded an exceptional five-furlong workout. To be accepted as exceptionally fast the five-furlong workout must be at least :59 4/5 seconds in the East or Midwest, :58 4/5 in the West.

The form advantages signal handicappers that claiming horses are ready to show their best stuff. In today's sport, a reversal of the past, sharp recent action represents more of an advantage than dull recent action represents disadvantage.

To illustrate the possibilities and complications when combining new and old guidelines, let's look hard at the ninth at Santa Anita Park, January 24, 1985.

9th Santa Anita

6½ FURLONGS. (1.14) CLAIMING. Purse $11,000. 4-year-olds and upward. Weights, 4-year-olds, 121 lbs.; older, 122 lbs. Non-winners of two races since November 6 allowed 3 lbs.; a race since Decmeber 25, 5 lbs.; since November 6, 8 lbs. Claiming price $10,000. (Races when entered for $8,500 or less not considered).

Coupled—Lucky Scam and True Promise.

Luderic — B. h. 5, by Cornish Prince—Dols Jaminque, by Kennedy Road
Br.—Akin P & W (Ky)
Own.—Givaudan L — 114 — Tr.—Russell John W — $10,000

Lifetime	10	1	3	0	$27,872	
1984	3	0	0	0	$700	
1983	5	1	2	0	$21,471	
Turf	8	1	3	0	$26,372	

30Dec84-5SA	6f :22 :45² 1:11³sl	30 116	3²½ 5⁶ 11¹⁶ 11¹³	McHargue DG¹⁰	25000	67-33	LuckyBddy,BoldPldg,OvrlndJorny	12
12Dec84-7Hol	6f :23¹ :46³ 1:11⁴gd	15 116	4¹¼ 3¹½ 3⁶ 5¹²¾	Olivares F⁷	Aw28000	77-18	FlngIrshmn,Mr.Unblvbl,Dctr'sOrdrs	8
12Nov84-5Hol	1⅛Ⓣ:48 1:12¹ 1:48³fm	9 117	4¹¾ 3½ 11²⁰ 11¹⁸¼	Pincay L Jr⁷	Aw22000	69-12	Mngione,Mirmelindo,FbuluxPrinc	11
12Nov84—Bumped start								
4Aug83♦3Deauville(Fra) a1¼	2:06 gd	9 123	Ⓣ 8⁶¾	LequuxA	PxVille deTrville		Mille Balles, Piermont,PortSaigon	10
2Jly83♦5Evry(Fra) a1⅛	1:59²gd	10 128	Ⓣ 2nk	SamniH	Pr Daphnis(Gr3)		Glenstal, Luderic, Redmead	7
12Jun83♦2Chantilly(Fra) a1	1:40¹gd	6½ 123	Ⓣ 4¹	LquuxA	Pr de Pontarme		Rodwell, Anne Stuart, Un Monsieur	9
13May83♦2StCloud(Fra) a1	1:52¹sf	*1-5 123	Ⓣ 1²½	LquuxA	Pr Opott(Mdn)		Luderic, Soliloquy,NaskraDrummer	8
19Apr83♦7StCloud(Fra) a1	1:46⁴sf	*2½ 126	Ⓣ 2½	LquxA	Pr Auriban(Mdn)		Mrgouzed,Luderic,TwoMinuts4ro	20
4Nov82♦2StCloud(Fra) a1	1:44¹sf	9 123	Ⓣ 2²½	LquxA	Pr As d'Atout(Mdn)		Jeu de Paille, Luderic, ValDanseur	10

Jan 16 SA 5f ft 1:01² h Jan 9 SA 5f ft 1:03⁴ h Dec 24 SA 6f ft 1:17 h Dec 2 Hol 6f ft 1:14 h

Tilt the Balance *

B. g. 10, by Balance of Power—Mulembra, by Mr Mustard
Own.—K & L Stable 114
Br.—Bennett & Strugar (Wash)
Tr.—Stute Warren $10,000
1984 1 0 0 0
1983 7 1 1 1 $14,750
Lifetime 51 12 9 7 $255,545
Turf 6 1 2 0 $25,465

30Dec84-7BM 6f :22^{1} :45^{3} 1:10^{1}ft 31 114 7 7½ 9 9 10^{16} 10 20¾ Loseth C^{10} 25000 67-24 FlyingJgur,LongGylnd,SirPortRulr 10
18Dec83-6BM 6f :23^{1} :47^{3} 1:14^{1}sl 19 114 54½ 79¾ 811 818½ Davidson JR^{3} Aw20000 50-40 MxmGorky,HllowdEnvoy,StupdPlsr 8
26Aug83-9Lga 6½f :22^{2} :45^{4} 1:17 ft 2½ 122 33 32 512 511¾ Stevens G L^{2} Aw10000 72-23 Chip o' Lark, Che, Musical Boy 5
4Jly83-9Lga 1$\frac{1}{16}$:46^{4} 1:11^{3} 1:43^{1}ft 14 117 66½ 89¾ — — StnsGL^{10} Indep Day H — — Moonlately,‡WnderKind,E-thquck 10
4Jly83—Eased
12Jun83-9Lga 1 :46 1:10^{2} 1:35^{4}ft 12 118 1¾ 11½ 13 43¾ StnsGL^{6} Spc Needle H 86-22 Moonlately, Earthquack,BigCougar 9
28May83-9Lga 6f :21^{4} :44^{2} 1:09^{2}ft *3-4 113 42½ 44 35 1¾ Stevens G L^{6} Aw10000 89-21 Tilt The Balance, Che, Chip o' Lark 8
15May83-9Lga 6f :22 :45 1:09^{1}m 3 118 53½ 53½ 56 35½ Stevens GL^{5} Renton H 84-22 FoolishOwners,Moonltly,TiltThBlnc 7
1May83-9Lga 5½f :22 :45 1:03^{1}ft 6½ 118 21½ 1hd 2hd 21½ StsGL^{8} [S]Lws & ClrkH 94-16 FoolishOwners,TiltThBlnc,Moonltly 8
25Nov82-8BM 1$\frac{1}{16}$:47^{3} 1:12^{3} 1:44^{4}gd 30 114 2hd 31½ 11^{16} 13^{15}½ MhornyW^{5} Thksgvg H 60-37 ClsscGoGo,HllowdEnvoy,SrstnlGy 13
9Nov82-6BM 1 :46^{1} 1:11^{3} 1:37 sy *9-5 117 36 3½ 22 38 Davidson JR^{1} Aw15000 76-23 Josher, Head Hawk, TilttheBalance 6
Jan 23 SA 3f ft :35^{3} h Jan 18 SA 6f ft 1:16^{3} h Jan 13 SA 6f ft 1:14 h Dec 14 BM 5f ft 1:01 h

Golden Minstrel

Ch. h. 5, by Golden Eagle II—Tudor Flame, by Tudor Minstrel
Own.—Orange Tree Stable 117
Br.—Palmer Mr-Mrs W B (Cal)
Tr.—Bernstein David $10,000
1985 2 0 1 1 $3,850
1984 25 4 0 1 $29,775
Lifetime 58 7 8 11 $86,851

10Jan85-2SA 6½f :21^{4} :44^{3} 1:17^{1}ft 5½ 122 53½ 43½ 31 2½ Stevens G L^{9} 10000 83-20 Svour,GoldenMinstrel,BoldMessge 12
3Jan85-1SA 6f :21^{4} :45 1:10^{1}ft 11 122 63½ 45 46½ 34½ Stevens G L^{7} [S] 12500 83-15 Chris'sLd,ShstFleet,GolderMinstrl 12
21Dec84-1Hol 6f :22^{3} :45^{4} 1:10^{4}m 6½ 122 32½ 34 36 57¾ Stevens G L^{5} 12500 87-11 Senior Senator, Chris's Lad,Savour 8
15Dec84-1Hol 7f :21^{4} :44^{2} 1:23^{2}ft 12 117 2½ 2hd 22 87½ Stevens G L^{3} 16000 82-06 PapaToo,SparAround,NevadaSage 10
30Nov84-5Hol 6f :22^{2} :46 1:11^{1}ft 15 117 5¾ 45 54½104¾ Stevens G L^{10} 16000 88-11 Mingash,Negotiate,Marnie'sDncer 11
14Nov84-1Hol 6f :22^{2} :46^{3} 1:12^{3}ft 9½ 122 21 2hd 2hd 11 Stevens G L^{1} [S] 12500 — — GoldenMinstrl,Chris'sLd,PrfctCovr 8
31Oct84-9LA 6f :21^{4} :44^{4} 1:10^{2}ft 3¾ 114 44 44½ 31 11½ Stevens G L^{4} 12500 93-11 GoldnMinstrl,RulingPositon,AcKng 8
26Oct84-10LA 6½f :21^{1} :46^{2} 1:17^{4}ft 6½ 109^{5} 75¾ 74½ 44 45 Proctor L^{2} 10000 83-16 JonnyJumpUp,Urgold,PrivteRoom 10
30Sep84-8Pom 6f :21^{4} :45^{2} 1:11^{4}ft 4½ 116 44 31 54 51¾ Noguez A M^{4} 12500 83-17 RulingPosition,PerfctCovr PrBook 6
30Sep84—Clipped heels, stumbled final turn
20Sep84-10Pom 6f :21^{4} :45^{3} 1:11^{4}ft 19 116 56 54½ 32 11¾ Delgadillo C^{4} 8000 85-19 GoldenMinstrel,ImAnAce,DepotBay 8
Jan 18 SA 3f ft :35^{4} h Dec 10 Hol 4f gd :51^{2} h Nov 24 Hol 4f ft :49^{2} h

Lucky Scam

Ro. g. 6, by Lucky Break—Willow Chic, by Count Chic
Own.—Baze J-JW-Beverly 109^{5}
Br.—Scamahorn M C (Wash)
Tr.—Baze Joseph W $10,000
1985 1 0 0 1 $1,650
1984 17 4 1 3 $18,082
Lifetime 35 6 2 5 $26,412

9Jan85-1SA 6½f :21^{4} :45 1:17 ft 4½ 116 41¾ 31 31 31½ Hawley S^{9} 10000 83-19 Zapallar, Echo Place, Lucky Scam 11
9Jan85—Checked, altered course at 1/16
30Dec84-1SA 6f :22^{3} :46^{1} 1:13^{3}sl 12 116 47 48 49½ 49½ Tatro J^{7} 12500 60-33 Attack, Ismael, Reckless Pleasure 7
30Dec84—Broke against bit
15Dec84-3Hol 7f :22^{1} :45 1:23^{3}ft 21 117 11 11 1½ 31¾ Tatro J^{9} 10000 87-06 The Bagel Kid, Jimsel,LuckyScam 12
2Dec84-2Hol 6f :22^{2} :46 1:10^{1}ft 8¾ 117 1½ 1½ 2^{4} 45½ Tatro J^{2} 10000 92-05 HerbieQuyl,EchoPlc,RulingPosition 8
24Nov84-4Hol 6f :22 :46 1:12^{2}sy 22 117 32½ 43½ 42½ 23½ Tatro J^{7} 12500 83-07 SprAround,LuckyScm,RcklssPlsur 10
24Nov84—Wide throughout
11Nov84-1Hol 7f :22^{4} :46^{1} 1:23^{3}ft 13 117 21½ 31½ 69 711¾ Tatro J^{6} 10000 — — HerbieQuyl,ExclusivKid,PrivtRoom 8
31Oct84-1SA 6f :21^{3} :44^{2} 1:10^{2}ft 21 116 44 54½ 55 32½ Stevens G L^{6} 10000 84-19 RecklessPlsur,Chris'sLd,LuckyScm 9
31Oct84—Wide into stretch
18Oct84-7SA 6½f :22 :45^{1} 1:17^{3}ft 36 116 31 32½ 57 55½ Steiner J J^{6} 10000 76-20 EchoPlce,RecklessPlesur,PrbiQuyl 12
13Oct84-11Fno 5f :22 :45 :57^{1}ft 11 115 61¾ 74½ 32 31½ HollngsworthR^{2} 10000 90-16 Po Don't, Washoe Lea,LuckyScam 10
20Sep84-10Pom 6f :21^{4} :45^{3} 1:11^{4}ft 11 116 31 44 66½ 55 Hollingsworth R^{5} 8000 80-19 GoldenMinstrel,ImAnAce,DepotBay 8
20Sep84—Lugged out 1st turn
Jan 28 SA 5f ft :59^{2} h

Savour

Dk. b. or br. h. 5, by Bold Forbes—Relish, by Traffic Judge
Own.—Barrera-Hancock III-Shwab 119
Br.—Hancock III & Shwab (Ky)
Tr.—Barrera Larry S $10,000
1985 2 1 0 0 $6,050
1984 9 0 0 1 $2,700
Lifetime 17 2 1 2 $26,180

10Jan85-2SA 6½f :21^{4} :44^{3} 1:17^{1}ft 8½ 116 32 33 43 1½ Sibille R^{12} 10000 84-20 Svour,GoldenMinstrel,BoldMessge 12
5Jan85-1SA 6f :21^{2} :44^{1} 1:10 ft 16 116 73¾ 75½ 86½ 85 Haire D^{5} 12500 83-12 OneEyedRomo,ExclusivKid,EsyEsy 9
29Dec84-2SA 6f :22^{2} :46^{2} 1:12^{3}gd 6½ 116 64 46 45½ 46 Haire D^{5} 16000 69-33 The Bagel Kid, Hackney, Mingash 9
29Dec84—Steadied at 5 1/2
21Dec84-1Hol 6f :22^{3} :45^{4} 1:10^{4}m 16 117 44½ 46 46½ 33¾ Haire D^{1} 12500 91-11 Senior Senator, Chris's Lad,Savour 8
25Aug84-9Dmr 1$\frac{1}{16}$:46^{1} 1:11^{1} 1:43^{2}ft 21 116 52½11^{11}2 11^{23} 11^{25}½ Sibille R^{1} 20000 58-18 Eagle'sBek,BeOnTime,ScurePlese 11
25Aug84—Bumped start; lugged out, wide 7/8 turn
17Aug84-7Dmr 6f :22^{2} :45^{3} 1:09^{2}ft 47 116 62¾ 66 7^{10} 69½ Drexler H^{4} 25000 81-18 RedyRb,AMomntInTim,GoodbyJ.Y. 7
17Aug84—Broke in tangle, bumped off stride start
1Aug84-6Dmr 6f :22^{3} :45^{4} 1:10^{4}ft 7 116 41¾ 66¾ 79¾ 79¾ Meza R Q^{8} 25000 74-18 Meteorite,FrenchMjesty,WhitCloud 8
22Jly84-4Hol 6½f :21^{4} :44^{3} 1:16^{4}ft 17 116 2½ 31 65 72¾ Meza R Q^{6} 32000 83-15 BlueSeas,SeniorSenator,Calabonga 7
12Jly84-7Hol 6f :22 :44^{4} 1:09^{4}ft 24 116 65½ 77 711 711¼ Lipham T^{5} 40000 77-20 ToghEnvoy,Jojohnck,HndsomPckg 7
6Jly84-9Hol 7f :22 :44^{3} 1:21^{3}ft 21 116 1hd 21½ 815 816½ Lipham T^{1} 62500 72-15 Embolden, Laughing Boy, 'ceCaper 8
6Jly84—Steadied at 1/4
Dec 14 Hol 5f ft 1:01 h Dec 7 Hol 6f ft 1:15^{1} hg Nov 29 SA 5f sl 1:01^{4} h

***Dakar II**
Ch. h. 7, by Schleswig—Diabolica II, by Yonder
Br.—Haras Matancilla (Chile) 1984 15 2 0 2 $18,975
Own.—Garman & Yanez 114 Tr.—Free Robert N $10,000 1983 5 1 2 1 $3,354
Lifetime 40 7 5 4 $47,703 Turf 23 5 5 2 $28,537
5Nov84-9SA 1 1/16 :463 1:113 1:443ft 12 116 43 22 2½ 1hd Simpson D W1 10000 78-18 Dakar II, Ice It, Private Room 12
31Oct84-1SA 6f :213 :442 1:102ft 10 118 811 811 78 45¼ Simpson D W2 10000 81-19 RecklessPlsur,Chris'sLd,LuckyScm 9
14Oct84-1SA 7f :222 :451 1:24 ft 9¼ 118 1011 1116 1018 1013½ Sibille R12 12500 66-18 NevadaSage,Sunol'sStr,Stingingly 12
11Aug84-2Dmr 6½f :221 :451 1:161ft 10 116 1114 1011 69¾ 57¼ Sibille R5 c16000 — — Restge,WickedHitter,LVrn'sBigMc 11
11Aug84—Bumped hard, pinched back start
4Aug84-1Dmr 6f :22 :452 1:11 ft 12 115 811 77¼ 32 11¾ Sibille R9 c10500 83-16 DakrII,RogerGummo,NewStrdegy 10
23Jly84-2Hol 6f :222 :454 1:112ft 26 116 911 98¾ 79¼ 55¾ Fernandez A L3 12500 74-18 Major Bill, PreBook,RogerGummo 10
23Jly84—Bumped, took up start
16Jun84-2Hol 6f :22 :444 1:102ft 22 115 116¾ 810 711 69 Guerra W A2 c12500 76-16 TheBgelKid,LongLivethKirg,Rstg 12
6Jun84-2Hol 7f :22 :452 1:232ft 7½ 115 85 78 33 33¼ Fell J1 10000 77-20 Incursion, Herbie Quayie, Dakar II 11
2Jun84-1Hol 6f :221 :453 1:112ft 18 115 812 87½ 86 54½ Fell J2 12500 75-16 Roger Gummo, Pre Book, Eruptive 8
23May84-1Hol 7f :222 :453 1:224ft 35 116 2½ 21½ 99¾ 912¼ Fell J7 20000 71-19 Major Bill, Jam Man, Neutron 9
Jan 18 SA 4f ft :52 h Jan 6 SA 4f ft :51 h Dec 16 SA 3f ft :383 h

Exclusive Kid
Ch. g. 7, by Exclusive Native—Hasten On, by Fleet Nasrullah
Br.—Spendthrift Farm (Ky) 1985 3 0 2 0 $5,200
Own.—Hall G 114 Tr.—Hall Taylor $10,000 1984 11 3 1 2 $24,325
Lifetime 42 7 9 7 $101,128 Turf 12 1 2 3 $27,683
17Jan85-1SA 6½f :214 :45 1:171ft *3 116 1hd 2hd 3nk 68¼ Ortega L E2 12500 76-18 HerbieQuyle,AMomentInTim,Krln 12
11Jan85-5SA 6f :214 :442 1:101ft 7 114 53 32½ 33½ 2½ Ortega L E2 14000 86-15 SeniorSentor,ExclusivKid,Chris'sLd 9
5Jan85-1SA 6f :212 :441 1:10 ft 20 116 3½ 31½ 21 22 Ortega L E2 12500 86-12 OneEyedRomo,ExclusivKid,EsyEsy 9
29Dec84-2SA 6f :222 :462 1:123gd 10 114 43½ 813 714 716½ Ortega L E9 14000 59-33 The Bagel Kid, Hackney, Mingash 9
29Dec84—Veered in, bumped start
30Nov84-5Hol 6f :222 :46 1:111ft 16 117 2½ 55½ 64¼ 84¾ Ortega L E2 16000 88-11 Mingash Negotiate,Marnie'sDncer 11
24Nov84-4Hol 6f :22 :46 1:122sy *9-5 119 21 32 3½ 45¼ Maffeo C9 c12500 82-07 SprAround,LuckyScm,RcklssPlsur 10
11Nov84-1Hol 7f :224 :461 1:233ft *3-2 119 11½ 11½ 2hd 21¾ Guce J1 10000 — — HerbieQuyl,ExclusivKid,PrivtRoom 8
11Nov84—Lugged out stretch
11Oct84-3SA 6½f :22 :45 1:162ft 20 114 42½ 2½ 2hd 32¾ Guce J8 14000 85-18 TheBgelKid,Eruptive,ExclusiveKid 12
23Sep84-12Pom 6f :212 :452 1:104ft *2¾ 119 21 1½ 11 1½ Guce J2 12500 90-18 Exclusive Kid, Pre Book, SwiftReb 8
27Aug84-1Dmr 6f :221 :451 1:101ft 4¼ 118 43 34½ 34½ 66½ Guce J4 12500 88-19 Trxton'sDbl,W.C.Shcky,OnEydRm 11
Dec 8 Hol 4f sy :49 h

Le Smirk
B. h. 6, by Olden Times—Hot Rumor, by Swift Ruler
Br.—Farish W S III (Ky) 1985 1 0 0 0
Own.—Ten Star Stable 114 Tr.—Lewis Craig $10,000 1984 5 1 1 0 $1,648
Lifetime 24 4 4 2 $46,873
10Jan85-2SA 6½f :214 :443 1:171ft 18 118 2hd 2hd 2½ 74¾ McHargue D G5 10000 79-20 Svour,GoldenMinstrel,BoldMessge 12
30Dec84-1SA 6f :223 :461 1:133sl 12 1115 1hd 2½ 22½ 59¾ Dominguez R L5 12500 60-33 Attack, Ismael, Reckless Pleasure 7
15Dec84-1Hol 7f :214 :442 1:232ft 5½e 119 1½ 1hd 1017 — Guerra W A2 16000 — — PapaToo,SparAround,NevadaSage 10
15Dec84—Eased
24Nov84-4Hol 6f :22 :46 1:122sy 4½ 119 11 11 2½ 109¼ Black K4 c12500 78-07 SprAround,LuckyScm,RcklssPlsur 10
3Nov84-10SJD 4½f :52 ft *3-5 122 4 2hd 1hd 33¾ Timm R V8 Aw1675 — — ‡CoolMac,Trextothestars,LeSmirk 10
3Nov84—Placed second through disqualification
27Oct84-11SJD 4½f :54 ft *2 119 5 21 11 1½ Timm R V7 Aw1675 — — LeSmirk,StarArrival,PecefulCreek 10
24Oct83-9LA 6f :214 :451 1:102ft *3-2 118 1hd 32 613 619¾ Black K6 25000 73-14 Cintolove, Proud Duke, The Rizzuli 7
27Sep83-11Pom 5½f :202 :434 1:03 ft 8¾ 117 21½ 34 411 720 Black K6 Aprisa H 82-13 CoolFrnchy,GminiDrmr,PtrickMcFg 7
18Sep83-10Pom 5½f :214 :451 1:04 ft *4-5 117 11½ 14 12½ 12¾ Black K3 Aw13000 97-18 LeSmirk,AckAckEnergy,Hanoverin 7
3Sep83-5Dmr 6f :222 :451 1:094ft 25 118 12½ 11½ 35½ 715 Lamance C8 Aw17000 74-16 PcMni,PrinceOfAsturis,SndDigger 10
Dec 23 Hol 3f gd :372 h Nov 30 Hol 6f ft 1:144 h

Kerlan
Ro. g. 6, by Roan Drone—Song of Hari, by Make Money
Br.—Proctor J & W L (Tex) 1985 2 0 0 1 $1,800
Own.—Brown R 114 Tr.—Kooba Paul $10,000 1984 5 0 0 0 $525
Lifetime 18 4 1 4 $66,125 Turf 6 2 1 1 $34,800
17Jan85-1SA 6½f :214 :45 1:171ft 3 116 2hd 1hd 2hd 35 Hawley S5 12500 79-18 HerbieQuyle,AMomentInTim,Krln 12
6Jan85-2SA 6f :212 :441 1:09 ft 7¾ 114 21 22½ 46 78¾ Hawley S7 18000 84-10 Mingash, Menderes, Goodtye J. Y. 9
30Dec84-5SA 6f :22 :452 1:113sl 23 1115 53 1213 1219 1218 Lozoya D A2 25000 62-33 LuckyBddy,BoldPldg,OvrlndJorny 12
30Dec84—Crowded, steadied, broke stride at 3/8
2Dec84-5Hol 6f :221 :45 1:103ft 28 1125 21½ 33 34½ 53 Lozoya D A3 25000 93-05 NghtCommnd,LckyBddy,WorldRlr 11
23Nov84-6Hol 6f :224 :463 1:122ft 14 1125 31½ 56½ 75¾ 76 Lozoya D A5 32000 81-19 Meteorite,GallantSpecial,Menderes 9
27Oct84-6SA 6½f :214 :442 1:162ft 80 116 51¾ 76 1215 1219½ Garcia J A4 50000 68-13 UnbknownsttM,StndPt,Dggr'sPnt 12
22Jly84-9AC 6f :22 :44 1:081ft 9-5 113 22 21 2½ 53½ Ruiz F2 Aw5000 94-12 Givemeaclue,SwiftReb,Yukon'sStar 5
22Jly84—Steadied at 3/8
13Mar83-5SA a6½f Ⓣ:204 :43 1:133fm 13 114 64¾ 78 64 75¼ Hawley S2 Aw26000 86-15 Ski Racer, Beldale Lustre,Berengo 12
11Nov82-8BM 1 1/16 :471 1:111 1:423m 3¾ 115 53½ 56½ 612 617¼ Lamance C1 L Stnfrd 69-26 InevitblLdr,PwtrGry,NightCommnd 8
30Oct82-8BM 1 1/16 Ⓣ:481 1:14 1:473yl 2½ 116 43 53½ 79¾ 811½ Baze R A7 Ascot H 58-30 Pt'sDd,TrvllngVctor,NghtCommnd 9
Dec 23 Hol 4f gd :48 h

Daring Jerry

Own.—Landry G   **114**

Gr. g. 5, by Terester—Daring Thoughts, by Daring Knight
Br.—Dutton J (Idaho)   1984 7 1 0 1 $6,230
Tr.—Holt Burlin C $10,000   1983 2 M 0 0
Lifetime 10 1 0 1 $6,230

9Dec84-2Hol	1 :454 1:104 1:373gd	67 116	121512231231112641	Drexler H3	12500 61-10	CelticWrrior,SilingWest,LcstCrek	12
24Nov84-4Hol	6f :22 :46 1:122sy	49 119	641 911 991 971	Barrera G8	12500 79-07	SprAround,LuckyScm,RcklssPlsur	10
31Oct84-9LA	6f :214 :444 1:102ft	22 1125	55 581 610 581	Braswell J M3	12500 84-11	GoldnMinstrl,RulingPositon,AcKng	8
23Sep84-12Pom	6f :212 :452 1:104ft	11 1115	771 561 581 5101	Braswell J M3	12500 80-18	Exclusive Kid, Pre Book, SwiftReb	8
19Sep84-7Pom	6f :214 :454 1:121ft	81 1135	521 41 1hd 111	Braswell J M4	M32000 83-19	Daring Jerry, Jestabird, Fastic	8
17Aug84-7Stk	6f :223 :463 1:112ft	41 120	631 663 66 691	Winick D7	M10000 83-10	ProperKin,TheosCn,SecretDyment	10
18Jun84-5Fno	51f :22 :452 1:034ft	15 120	411 351 331 321	Bazan J6	Mdn 89-14	Mrquemrkette,FrshFrnk,DringJrry	10
15Apr83-4SA	61f :22 :45 1:181ft	117 115	1061111 16 917 912	Meza R Q9	M28000 67-18	My Dear Falcon, Recind,Contrivor	12
17Mar83-3SA	6f :22 :452 1:122ft	22 118	781 1018101910191	ValenzuelPA10	M32000 56-20	OnTheFly,BombayBrtender,Recind	10
17Mar83—Lugged in down backstretch, eased in stretch							
29Sep82-4SA	6f :213 :451 1:113gd	77 118	1110111710181022	Valenzuela P A5	Mdn 58-22	Glem Mchine,NoFlk,RightOnCentr	12
29Sep82—Bumped at start							
Jan 6 SA 5f ft 1:002 h							

Perfect Cover

Own.—Mari-mar Stables   **114**

B. g. 5, by Envoy—Round Alibi, by Round Table
Br.—Pascoe W T III (Cal)   1985 1 0 0 0 $825
Tr.—Lassiter Harlee W $10,000   1984 26 0 3 5 $19,208
Lifetime 36 2 5 6 $39,433

10Jan85-2SA	61f :214 :443 1:171ft	27 116	851 68 541 421	Maffeo C4	10000 82-20	Svour,GoldenMinstrel,BoldMessge	12
24Dec84-1Hol	7f :22 :453 1:24 ft	14 117	641 621 351 341	Maffeo C1	10000 82-11	EchoPlce,Alshurouk,PerfectCover	11
9Dec84-2Hol	1 :454 1:104 1:373gd	26 116	871 710 714 613	Maffeo C4	12500 75-10	CelticWrrior,SilingWest,LostCrek	12
25Nov84-1Hol	6f :231 :463 1:111gd	41 117	23 231 25 241	Maffeo C6	10000 86-08	Chris's Lad, Perfect Cover, Daisky	6
14Nov84-1Hol	6f :222 :463 1:123ft	33 116	871 610 541 34	Maffeo C8	Ⓢ 12500 — —	GoldenMinstrl,Chris'sLd,PrfctCovr	8
14Nov84—Swerved to avoid fallen horse at 3/8							
5Nov84-9SA	11 :463 1:113 1:443ft	34 116	321 341 710 7131	Maffeo C9	10000 64-18	Dakar II, Ice It, Private Rcom	12
5Nov84—Wide							
26Oct84-10LA	61f :211 :462 1:174ft	11 1095	1071 1081 771 67	Dominguez R L1	10000 81-16	JonnyJumpUp,Urgold,PrivteRoom	10
8Oct84-1SA	6f :22 :444 1:091ft	15 116	67 69 513 514	Maffeo C7	Ⓢ 10000 78-16	LuckyBuddy,DncngRbot,GlncAbout	7
30Sep84-8Pom	6f :214 :452 1:114ft	23 116	58 65 641 2no	Maffeo C3	12500 85-17	RulingPosition,PerfctCovr,PrBook	6
30Sep84—Very wide stretch							
17Sep84-10Pom	11 :513 1:191 1:54hy	18 116	411 614 616 5181	Maffeo C4	10000 — —	Preservtive,BoldN'Bettr,Alshurouk	8
Jan 20 Hol 3f ft :381 h		Dec 22 SA 3f ft :36 h		Dec 5 SA tr.t 4f ft :49 h			

Snakebite Medicine

Own.—Reed T L   **114**

Dk. b. or br. g. 5, by Out of the East—So Khal, by Khalex
Br.—Sears D (Wash)   1985 1 0 1 0 $1,102
Tr.—Valenzuela Martin $10,000   1984 12 1 2 2 $7,900
Lifetime 29 4 4 4 $23,882

13Jan85-7AC	6f :223 :452 1:093ft	71 114	21 2hd 2hd 2hd	Razo A2	12500 91-13	LightBlubrry,SnkbitMdicin,SwiftRb	8
15Dec84-9AC	1 :46 1:104 1:37 gd	31 119	331 31 11 11	† Razo A1	12500 88-19	‡SnkebiteMedicine,SwiftRh,Avndro	5
15Dec84—Disqualified and placed second							
18Nov84-7AC	1 :463 1:112 1:37 m	*2 115	12 12 11 11	Razo A1	8500 88-17	SnkebiteMedicin,Avndro,Oscr'sPrid	8
3Nov84-7AC	6f :454 1:10 1:36 ft	5 116	421 531 31 35	Razo A1	12500 88-14	RisingHope,HfAdi,Snkebite Medicin	6
28Oct84-7AC	6f :223 :451 1:103ft	31 115	641 631 411 21	Razo A6	8500 85-16	HafAdi,SnkebiteMedicine,PlckRolls	7
13Oct84-8AC	6f :222 :45 1:10 ft	91 113	541 621 521 43	Peniche J R2	12500 86-15	Swift Reb, Rising Hope,FlintImage	7
30Sep84-5AC	6f :223 :45 1:09 ft	7 113	731 621 65 571	Peniche J R6	8500 87-13	Echo Place, Spar Around, Agent X	7
10Mar84-8AC	6f :223 :441 1:084ft	61 114	521 651 421 55	Castanon A2	10000 90-13	B.K.'sWindyIsle,MxElPro,Tlmnchus	9
26Feb84-7AC	6f :222 :45 1:09 ft	21 116	77 76 651 561	Mercado V V2	8000 87-10	ClGurd,AnotherSnowJob,DrkMster	7
17Feb84-9SA	11 :462 1:112 1:442ft	41 115	731 651 771 791	Fernandez A L1	10000 70-17	Alabado,KingoftheRanch,TheBigT.	11
17Feb84—Broke slowly							
● Jan 21 AC 4f ft :464 h		Jan 7 AC 6f ft 1:13 h		Dec 3 AC 5f gd 1:034 h			

Also Eligible (Not in Post Position Order):

True Promise

Own.—Bongarts & Stewart   **1095**

B. g. 5, by Valid Appeal—Dindy's Girl, by Twist the Axe
Br.—Double Diamond Fms Inc (Fla)   1985 1 0 0 0
Tr.—Baze Joseph W $10,000   1984 14 1 1 0 $7,675
Lifetime 33 5 3 3 $43,395

17Jan85-1SA	61f :214 :45 1:171ft	32 116	541 1013121412 18	Lipham T8	12500 66-18	HerbieQuyle,AMomentInTim,Krln	12
29Jly84-5Lga	6f :22 :452 1:101ft	*31 116	951 771 661 431	Frazier B8	16000 81-17	DcptionDcison,HIsAJk,ShonO'Shy	11
18Jly84-8Lga	6f :22 :451 1:094ft	12 116	731 511 1hd 141	Frazier B10	10000 87-25	TruPromis,King'sTurbin,TrorIndgr	12
4Jly84-7Lga	6f :214 :442 1:094ft	71 116	861 941 661 651	Baze D3	12500 81-19	NghtTmMk,JllyAndBrv,DtrmndFr	10
17Jun84-5Lga	6f :22 :444 1:162ft	3 116	971 77 11131181	Baze D4	16000 78-16	Nuncio, Clear Logic, Flag Master	12
17Jun84—Broke slowly							
6Jun84-7Lga	6f :22 :452 1:102ft	81 116	651 751 56 211	Baze D4	16000 82-26	SteelPrince,TruPromis,Mr.SrSpirit	11
26May84-9Lga	6f :22 :45 1:093gd	51 116	60 671 68 771	Baze D3	20000 80-27	JustTrnLft,CopprDrm,JonnyJmpUp	8
10May84-8Lga	6f :221 :452 1:094ft	61e 116	311 21 341 44	Baze D3	20000 83-18	FrethGold,CopprDrum,ShortSocks	12
10May84—Clipped heels, checked near 1/4							
21Mar84-1SA	61f :214 :444 1:162ft	24 118	631 661 58 771	Drexler H1	16000 80-15	RisABoy,Goldy'sCommndr,PrBook	12
21Mar84—Broke slowly							
17Mar84-1SA	6f :213 :444 1:11 ft	81 118	741 65 681 431	Lipham T4	12500 79-17	NevadaSge,TurningWheels,Grciolic	9
17Mar84—Veered in, bumped at start, wide final 3/8							
Jan 11 SA 6f ft 1:132 hg		Jan 5 SA 6f ft 1:14 h		Dec 22 Hol 4f gd :484 h		Dec 15 Hol 3f ft :383 h	

Luderic. Awful recent form on "off" tracks. More importantly, this five-year-old has obviously soured since competing well against much better in France at age three. Trainer Russell is dropping the horse to the bottom of the barrel, hoping for a claim much more than expecting a win. No play.

Tilt the Balance. Another one-time classy animal that has just about bottomed out at major tracks, this ten-year-old plunges in class today, but without any signs the drop signifies expected improvement—no early speed, awful form, last-place finishes. Out.

Golden Minstrel. A 20 percent drop last out resulted in a solid second-place finish, the kind that often signals impending victory. Class range from $8,000 to $12,500, the horse is perfectly spotted at $10,000. No form advantages—not up close at first two calls January 10—but horse figures in thick of things. Contender.

Savour. Winner at this level last out, but not by three (the telltale) lengths; barely. Picked up three-and-one-half lengths in stretch run. Modern handicappers have been rightly advised not to get carried away by strong stretch gains; they are overrated. Dropdown off fast $12,500 helped set up victory. Close enough at each call. Figures strong again today. Contender.

Dakar II. Unraced since November 5 win at middle distance. Short, irregular workouts since; unacceptable form.

Exclusive Kid. Combines good early speed, 20 percent drop in class, and a form advantage—up close every call except finish seven days ago. Returning in seven days. Deeper look is not as promising. Declining performance last out, despite drop in class. Could be attributed to pace duel with better. Closer look at adjusted final times and pace figures indicates this seven-year-old has been deteriorating since early January efforts. May bounce back to earlier figures against slightly cheaper, but not likely. Handicappers need adjusted final times and figures on these kinds. Otherwise, they are very apt to be misled. No play.

Kerlan. Another that combines the appealing early speed, drop in class, and improving form factors in claiming races. Qualifies for form advantage—up close at each call except last while dropping down today. Returning in seven days—a second form advantage. Second successive drop in class, having moved down about 38 percent last out. Figures and finishes improving with drops. May have early speed advantage here. Contender.

Daring Jerry. Unimpressive in four successive starts versus winners. Unacceptable form today. Out.

Perfect Cover. Poor early speed, same class today, zero for twenty-seven during last two seasons. Favorable jockey change to Darrel McHargue, but very unlikely winner at Santa Anita. Out.

Snakebite Medicine. Shippers from Caliente sometimes win at Santa Anita, but not often, and rarely when exiting exclusively claiming competition at the Mexican track. Besides, this 5-year-old has a kind of early speed better suited to routes, and belongs to a low-percentage trainer. Not today, its sharp form notwithstanding.

True Promise. No excuses last out. This Longacres horse might fit well with $10,000 horses at Santa Anita eventually but not until it shows some signs of life. No early speed, even when in tiptop shape. Out.

The contention boils down to Golden Minstrel, Savour, and Kerlan. Conventional handicapping wisdom might suspect Kerlan will be burned out in an early pace duel with Exclusive Kid, but the probabilities are quite different. Horses that engage in early speed duels may be weakened by the fights, but they are not defeated enough to be totally discounted. When one such horse has declining figures, as does Exclusive Kid, and the other improving figures, as does Kerlan, the improving horse can often steal the spotlight from wire to wire.

Golden Minstrel might win, but could not be backed as the 5-to-2 favorite.

Savour had slower adjusted times last out than did Kerlan and did not satisfy the repeat-win form standards. If Kerlan continued to improve with today's 20 percent dropdown, it might just take this lackluster field all the way. After all, it combines early speed, a drop in class, and improving form, the main mix of the claiming race winners.

That's exactly what happened in this case, and the price was right to boot (see next page).

Earlier *The Handicapper's Condition Book* pointed to class as the handicapping factor most fundamentally saluted by eligibility conditions. In claiming races the conditions fulfill this purpose by specifying the selling prices. As experienced players appreciate, horses entered for the same selling price can differ from one another markedly. To be more precise, one claiming race can differ markedly from another having the same claiming values.

To reach for the ludicrous example, a three-year-old maiden filly entered in a sprint for a claiming price of $25,000 cannot get within a furlong of a consistent five-year-old gelding that wins open claiming

NINTH RACE
Santa Anita
JANUARY 24, 1985

6 ½ FURLONGS. (1.14) CLAIMING. Purse $11,000. 4-year-olds and upward. Weights, 4-year-olds, 121 lbs.; older, 122 lbs. Non-winners of two races since November 6 allowed 3 lbs.; a race since Decmeber 25, 5 lbs.; since November 6, 8 lbs. Claiming price $10,000. (Races when entered for $8,500 or less not considered).

Value of race $11,000; value to winner $6,050; second $2,200; third $1,650; fourth $825; fifth $275. Mutuel pool $200,642. Exacta Pool $352,847.

Last Raced	Horse	Eqt.A.Wt	PP	St	¼	½	Str	Fin	Jockey	Cl'g Pr	Odds $1
17Jan85 $^{1}SA^{3}$	Kerlan	b 6 114	7	3	$1^{1\frac{1}{2}}$	$1^{1\frac{1}{2}}$	1^{2}	1^{2}	Hawley S	10000	6.00
10Jan85 $^{2}SA^{1}$	Savour	b 5 119	4	5	$3^{1\frac{1}{2}}$	$2^{\frac{1}{2}}$	$3^{2\frac{1}{2}}$	2^{nk}	Sibille R	10000	5.30
10Jan85 $^{2}SA^{2}$	Golden Minstrel	b 5 117	3	6	4^{hd}	$3^{2\frac{1}{2}}$	2^{hd}	$3^{1\frac{1}{4}}$	Stevens G L	10000	2.50
5Nov84 $^{9}SA^{1}$	Dakar II	7 118	5	10	11	9^{2}	$5^{2\frac{1}{2}}$	$4^{\frac{1}{2}}$	Simpsoq D W	10000	12.00
30Dec84 $^{5}SA^{11}$	Luderic	5 114	1	11	$9^{2\frac{1}{2}}$	4^{hd}	4^{3}	5^{4}	Olivares F	10000	26.60
17Jan85 $^{1}SA^{12}$	True Promise	5 109	11	1	$8^{\frac{1}{2}}$	8^{1}	7^{2}	6^{hd}	Lozoya D A^{5}	10000	23.10
17Jan85 $^{1}SA^{6}$	Exclusive Kid	7 114	6	2	5^{hd}	7^{1}	6^{hd}	$7^{1\frac{1}{2}}$	Ortega L E	10000	5.90
9Dec84 $^{2}Hol^{11}$	Daring Jerry	b 5 115	8	8	$10^{1\frac{1}{2}}$	11	11	$8^{\frac{1}{2}}$	McGurn C	10000	99.20
10Jan85 $^{2}SA^{4}$	Perfect Cover	b 5 115	9	7	$6^{2\frac{1}{2}}$	5^{2}	$8^{2\frac{1}{2}}$	9^{2}	McHargue D G	10000	8.00
13Jan85 $^{7}AC^{2}$	Snakebite Medicine	b 5 114	10	9	7^{hd}	$10^{\frac{1}{2}}$	$9^{\frac{1}{2}}$	$10^{8\frac{1}{2}}$	Fernandez A L	10000	9.50
30Dec84 $^{7}BM^{10}$	Tilt the Balance	10 114	2	4	2^{hd}	6^{hd}	$10^{1\frac{1}{2}}$	11	Pedroza M A	10000	10.30

OFF AT 4:44 Start good. Won driving. Time, :21⅘, :44⅘, 1:09⅖, 1:16⅕ Track fast.

$2 Mutuel Prices:				
	7-KERLAN	14.00	7.60	3.60
	4-SAVOUR		7.20	3.20
	3-GOLDEN MINSTREL			2.80

$5 EXACTA 7–4 PAID $148.50.

Ro. g, by Roan Drone—Song of Hari, by Make Money. Trainer Kooba Paul. Bred by Proctor J & W L (Tex).

KERLAN established a clear lead in the opening quarter, was rated on the pace, then responded in the final drive and held SAVOUR safe. The latter, in contention from the outset, could gain little in the final furlong. GOLDEN MINSTREL, forwardly placed throughout, responded in the drive but also could gain little. DAKAR II passed mostly tired horses in the stretch, as did LUDERIC. EXCLUSIVE KID showed little. SNAKEBITE MEDICINE was wide. TILT THE BALANCE tired badly after a half.

sprints at the same price. The former race is limited to a tub of early washouts; the latter is open to the most impressive $25,000 sprinters on the grounds.

Similarly, two contenders in a race with $6,500 tags may come together from poles far apart. One may be dropping down after a second-place finish in an $8,000 race that had been won by a horse that last time out finished a gaining third when entered for $9,000 in a $10,000 to $9,000 race in which the first two finishers were entered for $10,000. Suppose the winner had itself dropped down from a $12,500 race. The other contender may have lost a close decision in a $5,000 race that barred multiple winners to a horse entered for $4,500. Suppose the winner that was entered for $4,500 had moved up from $3,500.

The two are not $6,500 horses of a kind. The former should trounce the latter, and any like it.

To consider a slightly different situation with the same claiming price, the $6,500 race may bar horses that have won two or more races this season. But it may exempt horses that won races in which the top claiming price had been $5,000 or less. A consistent $5,000 winner has every right to step up and defeat chronic nonwinners at the slightly loftier level. This happens at minor tracks every day.

But a horse with one recent win at the $8,000 level may drop down and humble the consistent $5,000 kind.

Variations on the numbers and situations described are absolutely basic to the writing of eligibility conditions in claiming races. Handicappers have no alternative but to study and use eligibility conditions effectively. It prevents the embarrassment of betting on a horse worth approximately $3,500, as in the first example, when another horse in the same race is worth approximately $12,500.

Handicappers should understand that conditioned claiming races offer more frequent advantages to players who collect results charts or record in a notebook the conditions of the claiming races carded on the local circuit. The crowd sees only the latest claiming tags, but experts know more.

In major league racing the conditioned claiming races offer opportunities similar to the ones just discussed but more often will relate claiming prices to other factors, such as distance. Consider the conditions at Santa Anita season after season.

9th Santa Anita

1 ¹⁄₁₆ MILES. (1.40½) CLAIMING. Purse $14,000. 4-year-olds and upward, non-winners of two races at one mile or over since December 25. Weight, 121 lbs. Non-winners of such a race since December 25, allowed 3 lbs.; of such a race since November 5, 5 lbs.; Claiming price $20,000; if for $18,000, allowed 2 lbs. (Claiming and starter races for $16,000 or less not considered.)

The racing secretary has juggled the competition near the $20,000 claiming level in three ways. First, he bars the consistent route winners.

Second, by granting exemptions to horses running in claiming and starter races at $16,000 and less, he invites horses at those levels to move up in class.

Third, he invites the $20,000 sprinters to try to stretch out under more favorable conditions.

Under these conditions, alert handicappers would accept as contenders any $20,000 sprinter that has left clues it might route effectively. Since the better routers tend to run near the lead, and these have been barred, sprinters may find themselves unmolested on the early pace. They might relax and win, the late-comers so far in arrears they cannot catch up.

When analyzing conditioned claiming routes that bar multiple winners, handicappers should prefer, in descending order of their relative likelihood:

1. Any horse, valued at the top specified price or better, that has

won once (or once less than the number of permissible victories) since the specified date.

The higher its claiming price when it won, the better. The fewer its attempts since the specified date, the better.

2. A consistent router at the top exemption price, provided it remains in sharp or improving form.

3. A hard-knocking sprinter, valued at today's top claiming price or better, that figures to stretch out effectively, provided it can control or survive the early pace.

In reference to the top profile, if a horse that normally runs well at today's top claiming price has not won but remains eligible merely because it has not been active lately, handicappers respect the animal's past credentials. It may win breezing.

Another kind of conditioned claiming race is normally inferior to claiming events open to all comers. To honor horses bred in the home state with frequent opportunities to win, racing secretaries write races restricted to state-breds. Unless your track sits in Kentucky or Florida, the state-bred race is likely to rank below the overall quality of open races. Handicappers that collect charts are advised to find out what else was in the previous field.

So handicappers with seasoning in their play confront claiming races from the perspective that similar claiming prices often cover a variety of possibilities. In the search for sharp horses suited to the class, distance, footing, and early pace, such handicappers explore all the possibilities diligently. They are seldom fooled.

In capsule form, the relative quality of various claiming races having the same selling prices can be listed from least to most as follows:

1. For maiden fillies and mares.

2. For maiden males.

3. For nonwinners of two.

4. For nonwinners of three.

5. For nonwinners since a specified date or during the season.

6. For nonwinners of two or more similar races since a specified date. (The more the permissible number of victories and the shorter the specified time interval, the better the race.)

7. For nonwinners of two or more at a specified distance since a specified date.

8. Open to all comers.

At any level of competition, finally, the open race is usually superior to the state-bred kind.

CLAIMING RACES FOR THREE-YEAR-OLDS

To benefit at all from the preceding discussion, handicappers absolutely must appreciate the differences between older claiming horses and their three-year-old counterpart. The five-year-old entered at a $32,000 claiming price normally belongs there or thereabouts. The three-year-old so entered may be worth less than half that amount.

This essential distinction comes increasingly into focus as the season progresses and three-year-olds compete against older horses throughout the second half. It's evident too early next season, when the three-year-olds turn four. In both cases three-year-olds that have been racing regularly against their own kind will need a drop in selling price to get the job done. To cement the point, the three-year-old that competes successfully against its own kind at $40,000 during April would need the proverbial wings and prayers if entered against $40,000 older claimers at that time.

To understand the situation at a fundamental level, handicappers first appreciate that three-year-olds typically enter the claiming ranks at inflated prices. The selling prices may be much too high. This is done to protect owners from the surprises of sudden or late development. The three-year-old is a young racer. Eventually it may get going and soar. If another stable would chance that possibility, the owner figures that stable should be willing to pay a premium price. So many three-year-olds are tagged at unrealistically high values. Once they lose a few times miserably, and no claim occurs, the selling prices may be lowered.

In the usual case, the three-year-old entered for too high a claim is lowered successively until the level at which the thing can compete effectively is found. Handicappers notice the class drops all right, but they recognize the traditional shopping spree. Handicappers ignore the animals until they show satisfactory form. If another drop follows an improved performance, handicappers at last may have spotted a bet.

At whatever level, once young claimers begin to win or to run impressively, cycles of improvement are very possible. Not the kind of tremendous improvement characteristic of better, nonclaiming three-year-olds. Gradual improvement. Should three-year-olds return from claiming races to nonwinners allowances, for example, they had better arrive there with a newborn spirit. There they meet the better horses of the division, horses on the way up. Their own cheap speed is not enough.

The three-year-old claiming horse's gradual kind of improvement is normally consistent with its physical development and the seasoning it achieves in competition. For many three-year-olds the growing and seasoning processes continue throughout spring and summer and begin to level off during fall. During these periods, handicappers credit any improved performance by three-year-old claimers but permit step-ups that are realistic. When confronted by an uncommon rise, handicappers hesitate. Is this claiming horse changing its colors? Where has it been? What has it done? Where can it go?

If a big jump has been premature and results in a shellacking, handicappers become even more guarded. The three-year-old claimers may have trouble readjusting to their recent winning level. A furious licking dampens the spirits of young racehorses. Few enjoy running to exhaustion under a stinging whip to no avail. They resent the treatment. They sulk. They resist. They tail off, maybe for weeks or months.

Some three-year-olds are entered in claiming races immediately following the maiden win. Management sees little or no likelihood of development. The early entry for a claim, however realistic the assessment, is a negative sign and the price is probably too steep. Handicappers wait to see.

Opportunities in three-year-old claiming races do occur. Handicappers remain on alert as soon as any three-year-old runs a much improved race. The win is just around a corner. The stable knows it. The next spot, up or down, should be its best assessment as to where the animal should win. Wanting the win badly, at this point an eager stable may play it extra safe. The stable drops the horse even lower on the claiming scale. If the class drop subsequent to the improved performance is accompanied by a favorable jockey switch or by a change to a more comfortable distance, handicappers have found a potential play among the cheaper three-year-olds.

Of more appeal still is the three-year-old that demonstrated its improved performance under nonwinners allowances and then is dropped into a claimer. If the allowance race were an even effort or better, this ready three-year-old may hold a razor's edge in the claiming race.

Otherwise, claiming races for three-year-olds are best handicapped in a straightforward way. After a three-year-old has won a claiming race, handicappers note its rises and drops in class. The handicapping emphasizes speed figures, form and unusual signs of improvement or deterioration. What kind of move does the evidence support?

Following the next brief chapter on starter races, this book returns to the mysteries of three-year-olds. With so many of them on the scene, it's high time that handicappers brush up on the eligibility conditions that rule their races.

CLAIMING BRACKETS AND RISES AND DROPS

During the Oak Tree meeting at Santa Anita several seasons ago, a seven-year-old named Eagle in Flight was haltered for ten grand. Within weeks it had won for $16,000, again for $20,000, again for $40,000. Next it finished a rallying third in a turf stakes, beaten two disappearing heads. In fall 1984, a front-running four-year-old Ice capade colt named Fatih was claimed for $80,000. Six months later, at age five, Fatih had won six nonclaiming races, including two Grade 2 stakes, and no less than $326,220, plus a potential career at stud.

In his *Encyclopedia of Thoroughbred Handicapping,* Tom Ainslie reports that in recent times claiming and allowance grade animals won more frequently and raced more impressively than ever in New York stakes and handicaps.

Racing indeed has moved deeply into a time of change. What's the handicapper to do? Recognize how the game is changing.

Ordinarily a contemporary claimer's rise in class will not be so terrific as was Eagle in Flight's. Yet claiming horses now move up effectively at greater percentages than before. Handicappers benefit if they replace the notion of claiming prices with that of claiming brackets. A bracket can be seen as a range of claiming prices within which a horse figures to run well.

Winning claiming horses can be expected as a matter of course to move up and down easily within familiar brackets, less easily outside those brackets.

The handicapping experience and close observation of the local circuit suggests the appropriate number and kinds of brackets.

On the southern California circuit at this writing claiming horses move up and down more readily within these price brackets:

$ 8,000–$12,500
$12,500–$16,000
$16,000–$25,000
$25,000–$30,000
$32,000–$40,000
$40,000–$50,000
$50,000–$62,500
$62,500–$80,000
Above $80,000

I hope handicappers will not mind the overlaps. They are dealt with sensibly. A top animal within the $8,000 to $12,500 bracket may succeed in the $12,500 to $16,000 bracket also but would look marginal alongside a top animal there.

An $8,000 winner that runs at $12,500 has jumped up by 55 percent.

At a medium level, the $16,000 winner that repeats for $25,000 has won while moving ahead by 56 percent. In general, the move up from $22,500 to $30,000 is just 33 percent, but is decidedly more difficult.

The southern California brackets suggest horses there can move up in selling price approximately 30 percent to 56 percent. The old benchmarks of 20 to 25 percent have risen sharply. And the higher percentage rise within customary brackets is more easily accomplished than the smaller rises outside of comfortable brackets.

By taking time to identify claiming price brackets that are customary at local tracks, handicappers can determine more reliably whether percentage rises and drops are normal and acceptable.

Price brackets not only provide new order to the claiming ranks, they also set up class barriers regular players can exploit.

In southern California, to illustrate, a four-year-old claimer moving down from $32,000 to $25,000 drops 22 percent, but it has entered a lower order of competition and may figure to pickle its rivals. Yet the horse moving down the 20 percent from $40,000 to $32,000 may be no bargain whatsoever, the order of competition having remained virtually unchanged. Variations on the theme can be multitudinous and intriguing to handicappers wanting every edge.

Regarding class moves between brackets, older claimers most likely to succeed are horses that have been there before. Eagle in Flight won stakes at three. If the claiming horse has "back class," it someday may begin feeling its former self. Handicappers can tolerate the return to former heights. Especially if a new barn has taken charge and appears to have rejuvenated both limbs and spirit.

To sum up, five guideposts will help handicappers relate claiming price brackets to rises and drops in class. When in shape, and suited to the distance, footing, and probable pace:

1. Percentage rises and drops are not as important as changes in the order of competition to which the claimer has become accustomed.

2. A claiming horse can be expected to move about within its customary price bracket with relative ease, but outside its brackets only with relative difficulty.

3. Dramatic rises in class of two or more brackets can be negotiated best by horses that have been there before, or by relatively young or lightly raced animals that suddenly show improved form.

4. No claimer should be expected to move up outside its brackets effectively after a win in which it was all out, or in which it lost ground in the stretch while tiring.

An exception, of course, is the tiring finish that foreshadows improvement in the normal form cycle.

5. Class drops of a bracket or more represent significant changes in the quality of competition and can usually be expected to help a claiming horse win, provided the horse has been running evenly or better in the higher bracket.

Handicapping fanatics may wish to take the idea of claiming price brackets and apply it to individual horses. The completed project is represented by a file containing the price bracket history of every claiming horse on the grounds. An invaluable tool!

CLAIMING RACES AT MINOR TRACKS

Where claiming horses are valued below $8,000, any discussion of price brackets and attendant considerations of class rises and class drops slams into the dense impenetrable barriers that prevent those maneuverings with slow, reluctant horses. At minor tracks class barriers stand firmly erect and remain rather severe. The same is so at many major tracks near the bottom of the claiming scale.

Handicappers should understand the cheapest of claiming horses constitute a special subclass. They tend to be older. They race repeatedly, without extensive layoffs. All are sore and jaded. When rested periodically, they are rushed to return as soon as possible. It is hardly uncommon for the horses to race twenty to thirty times a season. Cheap horses earn small monies. They must therefore race continually to pay their barn bills.

As a result, the cheapest horses tend to settle at specific claiming levels, where they can best earn their way, and to stay there. So the $2,500 claiming horse competes with $2,500 selling tags every couple of weeks. Class rises between levels are not typical. When they do occur, step-ups are not as successful as they routinely are at higher price levels. Class drops occur more frequently but not often among the most consistent stock. The $5,000 breadwinner that drops to $4,-000 is very likely to win, all right, but even more likely to be claimed. Small-time owners do not cherish losing cheap horses that earn good dollars. Neither do their trainers.

To combat the tendency of better low-priced claimers to beat the others repeatedly, racing secretaries at minor tracks use restrictive clauses to write the claiming conditions. Thus, while between-level class maneuvers are discouraged, within-level rises and drops are greatly encouraged and facilitated. Handicappers should anticipate numerous gradations of class at the same low-selling prices. They must rely on results charts or personal notebooks to spot the opportunities.

From most to least restricted, the restrictions at the typical $2,500 claiming level might look like this:

- Nonwinners twice (three times) lifetime
- Nonwinners during this year and last
- Nonwinners during the current year
- Nonwinners twice (three times) during the current year
- Nonwinners since the starting date of the meeting
- Nonwinners twice (three times) since the starting date of the meeting
- Nonwinners since a specified date; nonwinners twice (three times) since a specified date
- Nonwinners at a mile or over since a specified date; nonwinners twice (three times) at a mile or over since a specified date
- Open to all comers

The sequence represents a nine-level hierarchy at the $2,500 class level. In general, horses moving from a less restricted race to a more restricted race are dropping in class, perhaps substantially. Cheap horses that impress in claiming races open to all comers are usually dropping big when entered in any restricted race at the same price level. A change from one kind of restricted race to another can represent a real change in the order of competition as well, as from nonwinners since a specified date to nonwinners during the year or for the past two years. The first kind of race may contain several winners, but the second kind will not. It is likely instead to be filled with chronic losers (see following pages).

Years ago, handicapping author Steve Davidowitz illustrated this type of claiming class hierarchy for $1,500 horses at Waterford Park in West Virginia. Davidowitz urged handicappers to exploit the class-within-a-class hierarchies commonplace at minor tracks. He flatly asserted these maneuvers afforded the bettors some of their juiciest class opportunities anywhere.

The assertion is well taken. It's normally easier for horses to jump from $2,500 races that are open to $3,000 races that are open than for horses at the lower levels of the $2,500 hierarchy to advance to the upper levels at $2,500. Step-ups within hierarchies prove too difficult for numerous horses. They remain trapped at the bottom levels for long periods. For this reason dropdowns from open races can enter fields that are virtually at their mercy. For this reason, too, cheaper maiden winners can often enter against winners at the lowest levels of the claiming price hierarchy and win consecutively.

Similarly, when claiming-race conditions bar multiple-route winners, the repetitive nonwinners at the route become easy prey for winning sprinters. The restricted conditions invite the sprinters to stretch out, and statistics persuade us they can do it successfully.

Claiming class barriers being as thick as they are at minor tracks, whenever a clever dropdown has been engineered, handicappers on the alert do find splendid betting opportunities. During the 1984 World Series of Handicapping at Penn National Racetrack, no less than eleven of the thirty races in the contest were written for $2,500 claimers. But those races differed from one another markedly. One offered handicappers who understand class restrictions a well-disguised jewel of a wagering opportunity. Below are six of the twelve starters. Try to find the class stickout and easy winner.

The heavy favorite was Sinnalot. Dropping off a solid front-running effort against open $3,000 horses October 5, the filly obviously figured against $2,500 runners that had not won two races since April 27, six months ago.

But Sinnalot hardly figured to handle an authentic $5,000 horse and precisely that kind had been cleverly maneuvered into this restricted $2,500 field. The class standout is the four-year-old filly Forever There. Let's examine its record in detail.

Most bettors at Penn National saw a middle-distance grass horse

10 PENN NATIONAL

6 FURLONGS
PENN NATIONAL

6 FURLONGS. (1.08⅘) CLAIMING. Purse $2,400. Fillies and Mares, 3-year-old and upward, which have not won two races since April 27, weights, 3-year-olds, 119 lbs. Older, 122 lbs. Non-winners of a race since September 27, allowed 3 lbs. A race since August 27. 6 lbs. Claiming price $2,500.

Party Punch — B. m. 5, by Parade of Stars—Pelouse Party, by Pelouse — $2,500 — Br.—Flying I Ranch (Ky) — Tr.—Beattie Thomas — 116
Own.—Dulcadare Stable
Lifetime 31 1 1 6 $7,556 — 1984 7 0 1 1 $890 — 1983 18 1 0 4 $5,727 — Turf 1 0 0 0

5Oct84- 9Pen fst 1 :48 1:13⅗ 1:41 3↑Ⓕ Clm 2500 7 7 711 1024 930 929¼ Tillotta N b 116 27.30 47-23 Morning Glad 1126¾ Oddity 1168½ Miss Chevette 1184½ Outrun 10
26Sep84- 3Pen fst 1 :48⅗ 1:14⅖ 1:42⅕ 3↑Ⓕ Clm 2500 5 5 65 64¾ 79 712½ Tillotta N b 116 8.30 58-21 Wind N' Willow 1092 Concordia 1161 Oddity 116hd No factor 8
7Sep84- 9Pen fst 1 :48 1:14 1:41⅖ 3↑Ⓕ Clm 2500 6 5 52½ 43½ 4¾ 23¾ Rozell R M b 116 8.60 70-17 La DuchesseEnVol1143¾PartyPunch116¾FriendlyFour116½ Rallied 8
29Aug84- 2Pen fst 6f :22⅘ :46⅗ 1:12⅗ 3↑Ⓕ Clm 5000 5 7 89½ 811 68¾ 614½ Surrency M b 116 12.40 67-19 Hbbrd'sGpbord1226½OnNntyWtlng116hdCptnsJtSt1123 NO factor 8
19Aug84- 5Pen fst 6f :22⅘ :46⅖ 1:14 3↑Ⓕ Clm 3000 10 5 42½ 42½ 53½ 65¾ Rozell R M b 113 18.80 68-18 Limosano 1162¾ Re Arranged 113nk Chapel Princess 116no Wide 11
25Jly84- 2Pen fst 6f :23⅖ :47⅗ 1:14⅕ 3↑Ⓕ Clm 3000 6 8 5¾ 55½ 75¾ 36½ Rozell R M b 113 11.30 66-21 Charlo Wish 1163 Bluffer's Baby 1163½PartyPunch113½ Mild gain 10
11Jly84- 5Pen gd 6f :23 :46⅖ 1:13 3↑Ⓕ Clm 2500 6 8 88½ 88½ 85½ 85 Tillotta N b 116 44.50 74-18 Damarullah 122hd Abloom 119hd Leaving Lucille 1192½ Outrun 9
9Nov83- 1Pen fst 6f :23 :47⅕ 1:13⅗ 3↑Ⓕ Clm 3000 3 7 78½ 58½ 612 712¾ Seefeldt A J b 113 19.40 63-27 Poppi's Fanci 1167¾ Val's Now 116¾ Silver Dove 1131½ Outrun 9

Forever There — Ch. f. 4, by Vent du Nord—Sassy Cynthia, by Native Roman — $2,500 — Br.—Stavola M J (Fla) — Tr.—Benetto Mario — 116
Own.—Arenel Farms
Lifetime 23 2 3 1 $11,635 — 1984 12 1 1 0 $4,785 — 1983 10 1 2 1 $6,850 — Turf 11 1 2 0 $6,655

21Oct84-10Pen fm 1 Ⓣ 1:36⅖ 3↑ Clm 5000 8 1 1½ 3nk 76 912¼ Boileau J L b 110 50.60 72-20 Sirius A. B. 109nk Smoke Rise 1142¾ Koboko 113hd Bumped 11
7Oct84-10Pen fm 1⁷⁰ Ⓣ 1:41⅕ 3↑ Clm 5000 11 6 84¾ 97¼ 1115 1116¾ Boileau J L b 115 22.80 63-21 BankOnJohn113noLaGrandeRogue113nkSmokeRise113nk Fell back 12
30Sep84- 8Pen fm 1⅟₁₆ Ⓣ 1:43⅘ 3↑Ⓕ Hcp 5000s 5 5 43½ 1½ 2hd 54½ Boileau J L b 108 13.90 66-23 April's Frosty Miz 1122 R. K.'s Issue 122nkRoyalTanya1101½ Tired 9
23Sep84- 5Pen fm 1⅟₁₆ Ⓣ 1:42⅗ 3↑ Clm 5000 2 3 34 32½ 44 55½ Colton R E b 116 8.90 71-15 ⒹSky Gun 114¾ Sam Batt 1132½ Hillside Ruler 1191½ Tired 12
9Sep84- 2Pen fm 1⅟₁₆ Ⓣ 1:42⅘ 3↑ Clm 8000 2 2 23½ 24½ 48 714½ Colton R E b 112 4.50 61-17 Smokum Scout 1135½ Bank On John 1162½ Czar'sGold1092½ Tired 8
25Aug84- 1Pen fm 1⅟₁₆ Ⓣ 1:43 3↑Ⓕ Clm 5000 7 1 13 13 13½ 12 Colton R E b 113 5.40 75-21 ForeverTher1132BonitoWind1131¾ⒹBrigtownLss1131½ Ridden out 12
3Jly84- 3Mth fst 6f :22⅕ :45⅘ 1:12 3↑Ⓕ Clm 7500 5 7 67 711 712 710½ Melendez J D b 114 9.80 69-17 Devil Dance 1161½ Puff Away 1141½ Queen Biretta 115½ Outrun 7
21Jun84- 6Mth fm 1⅟₁₆ Ⓣ :48⅖ 1:12⅖ 1:44⅖ 3↑Ⓕ Clm 20000 1 1 12 55½ 913 1017¼ Antley C W b 112 3.20e 72-06 Lovin' Letter 116½ Laura Mac 1163 Time Well Spent 1163 Tired 10
LATEST WORKOUTS Sep 18 Pen 5f fst 1:04 b

Sinnalot — B. f. 4, by Dr Joseph—Nocturnal Sin, by Nocturnal Baker — $2,500 — Br.—Beckstead D (Utah) — Tr.—Wolfe Bob — 116
Own.—Hogentogier E F & G & R
Lifetime 17 3 1 4 $10,278 — 1984 17 3 1 4 $10,278 — 1983 0 M 0 0 — Turf 2 0 0 1 $649

5Oct84- 5Pen fst 6f :22⅗ :46⅖ 1:13⅗ 3↑Ⓕ Clm 3000 8 2 1½ 21 12 2hd Burton J E 116 5.00 77-23 Bubbly Jane 112hd Sinnalot 116¾MogulPrincesses1121 Just failed 11
19Sep84- 9Pen fst 6f :22⅘ :46⅕ 1:12⅘ 3↑Ⓕ Clm 3500 5 5 1½ 11 14 11¾ Burton J E 116 *2.60 80-19 Sinnalot 1161¾ Round Tuit 109½ I'm A Pro 1163¾ Driving 12
27Aug84- 4Pen fst 5f :22⅕ :46⅘ :59⅖ 3↑Ⓕ Clm 4000 2 4 34 35 34 31 Slysz M A 113 9.30 86-17 Dela G. 114nk Ikenobo's Lady 114¾ Sinnalot 1131½ Evenly 6
17Aug84- 1Pen fst 5½f :22⅘ :46 1:06⅘ 3↑Ⓕ Clm 4000 7 4 53½ 54½ 41¾ 42½ Slysz M A 114 10.50 79-19 Ikenobo'sLdy108hdGllntToo114¾SometimeTomorrow1131½ Evenly 8
27Jly84- 6Pen fst 6f :22⅘ :46 1:12⅕ 3↑Ⓕ Clm 6250 5 3 1hd 22½ 56½ 59½ Slysz M A 115 11.40 74-21 Littleorphanyankee1152½Tuesdy'sFlsh1192Snelly'sImp1193¾ Tired 6
14Jly84- 3Pen fst 6f :22 :45⅖ 1:12⅕ 3↑ Clm c-5000 3 3 21 21 35 48 Hansen N J 114 4.50 75-16 Debby's Brass 116hd Michael's Will 1166 Mad Scientist1162 Tired 6
4Jly84-10Pen fm 5f Ⓣ :59 3↑ Clm 10000 7 8 65 65¾ 67½ 88 Hansen N J 114 17.90 77-31 October Wind 1132½ Sicilian Jet 114hd Kalathi 1142½ No factor 11
23Jun84- 1Pen fm 5f Ⓣ :58⅗ Ⓕ Clm 10000 2 9 53 32 43 31½ Hansen N J 119 28.60 86-22 Rosy Sky 1151 Queen Of Gold 114nk Sinnalot 119hd Evenly 11

Ronnie's Renigade — Ch. m. 6, by Gaelic Christian—Sudden Glory, by Quick Wink
Own.—Folk Robert P — $2,500 — Br.—Meador A J (Tex) — Tr.—Beattie Dennis M — 116
Lifetime 74 5 15 14 $32,521 — 1984 14 0 5 3 $5,087 — 1983 22 3 3 3 $15,447 — Turf 2 0 1 0 $980

8Oct84- 9Pen fst 170 :47⅘ 1:14⅕ 1:47 3+ⒻClm 2500 3 3 31½ 33 35 46¼ Deibler C E III b 116 7.20 59-25 GrapeDelight1144SssyButSweet1191½BrigtownLss1131 Weakened 10
29Sep84- 3Pen fst 6f :22⅘ :47 1:13⅕ 3+ⒻClm 2500 4 5 22½ 31 23 22½ Smith D D b 116 6.30 75-24 NgHggenbed1162½Ronnie'sRenigde1162½MistyMxine1092¾ Rallied 6
12Sep84- 8Pen fst 6f :22⅘ :46⅗ 1:12⅖ 3+ⒻClm 2500 7 8 913 79½ 710 67½ Smith L S5 b 111 5.40 74-20 Delta Dear 1161½ Best Event 109¾ NagHaggenbed1161¼ No threat 9
31Aug84- 2Pen fst 170 :48 1:14⅕ 1:47⅕ 3+ⒻClm 2500 5 4 53¾ 68¾ 77¾ 79¾ Randolph J L b 114 3.00 54-21 Sassy But Sweet 1132 Anahauc 113hd Radiant Rosie 1192½ Tired 8
25Aug84- 1Pen fm 1116 Ⓣ 1:43 3+ⒻClm 5000 4 4 47½ 55 711 1016¾ Randolph J L b 113 5.20 58-21 Forever There 1132 Bonito Wind1131½ⒹBrigtownLass1131¼ Tired 12
15Aug84- 7Pen fst 6f :22⅖ :46⅖ 1:12⅗ 3+ⒻClm 5000 5 7 85¾ 53½ 44½ 32¼ Randolph J L b 113 15.20 79-22 Gladascanbe 1161¼ Abloom 1141 Ronnie's Renigade 113hd Rallied 9
4Aug84- 1Pen fm 170 Ⓣ 1:42⅘ 3+ⒻClm 5000 10 7 65 52½ 2hd 2nk Randolph J L b 113 27.10 72-25 RoseyPierre114nkRonnie'sRenigde1131½BrigtownLss1062½ Gamely 11
30Jly84- 1Pen fst 6f :22⅗ :46⅖ 1:13⅗ 3+ⒻClm c-2500 2 4 56½ 55 53½ 2½ Salvaggio M P7 b 109 2.20 75-18 MogulPrincesses116½Ronnie'sRenigde109nkDivinDncr1162 Rallied 7

Range In Color — Ch. m. 5, by Larum's Irish—Whisper Sweet, by Great Jimminy
Own.—Mayer P — $2,500 — Br.—Butts Bros (Tex) — Tr.—DeMario Charles A — 116
Lifetime 41 4 5 6 $19,958 — 1984 17 1 1 4 $4,600 — 1983 3 0 0 0 $168 — Turf 3 0 0 0 $234

9Jly84- 7Pen fst 5½f :22⅖ :46⅖ 1:06 3+ⒻClm 2500 7 4 55 54½ 35½ 45¾ Rozell R M b 119 7.20 80-15 Belle de Troder 1193¾ What A Friend 1141½ War Life 109½ Outrun 7
29Jun84- 3Pen fst 5½f :22⅖ :46 1:06 3+ⒻClm 2500 6 1 64½ 4¾ 1½ 11½ Rozell R M b 113 6.90 86-13 Range InColor1131½MoneyAhead116¾SundaySunday1132¾ Driving 7
20Jun84- 4Pen fst 5½f :22⅗ :46⅖ 1:06⅗ 3+ⒻClm 2500 6 3 43 45 47 36½ Seefeldt A J b 113 8.70 77-20 BelledeTroder1145BeautifulSilence1131½RngeInColor113¾ Rallied 6
8Jun84- 1Pen fst 6f :22⅘ :46⅖ 1:12⅕ 3+ⒻClm 2500 6 3 44 33 34 34¾ Rozell R M5 b 117 5.50 78-17 Abloom 1222½ Ronnie's Renigade1222½RangeInColor1171½ Evenly 8
26May84- 8Pen fst 6f :22⅘ :47 1:13⅖ ⒻClm 2500 7 2 65¾ 63¾ 54¾ 45¼ Seefeldt A J b 116 11.40 72-24 Grape Delight 1162BelleTina1121MogulPrincesses1162¼ No threat 8
18May84- 2Pen fst 6f :23⅕ :47⅕ 1:12⅘ ⒻClm 2500 5 4 2hd 11½ 21½ 56¼ Seefeldt A J b 116 6.10 73-21 Missmissy 1164½ Toys to Toddle116nkHereComesAlice117nk Tired 9
9May84- 5Pen fst 6f :23 :47⅕ 1:14⅘ ⒻClm 2500 8 1 41 31½ 42½ 52¾ Seefeldt A J b 116 4.80 67-28 Sea Suspicion 116nk SweetVelvet109hdMaggiesGal1161 Weakened 11
27Apr84- 1Pen fst 5½f :23 :47⅖ 1:06⅗ ⒻClm 2500 4 3 78½ 65½ 45½ 33 Seefeldt A J 113 8.00 80-21 Rostraver Mary 1192 Miss Naf 1131 Range In Color 1131½ Rallied 9

Nag Haggenbed — B. m. 8, by Crobeau—Lady Clay, by Law and Order
Own.—Harner & Wames — $2,500 — Br.—Stahlin J L (W.Va.) — Tr.—Wames John — 122
Lifetime 95 10 15 10 $43,639 — 1984 10 1 3 2 $3,826 — 1983 17 2 1 5 $6,310 — Turf 1 0 0 0

8Oct84- 4Pen fst 6f :23⅖ :46⅗ 1:14 3+ⒻClm 2500 2 8 53¾ 33 32½ 31¾ Barton S E 122 4.30 72-25 DHⒹGldnDrtr1101½DHWhtAFrnd1161½NHnbd1222½ *Bumped start 10
8Oct84-Placed second through disqualification
29Sep84- 3Pen fst 6f :22⅘ :47 1:13⅕ 3+ⒻClm 2500 2 3 33 1½ 13 12½ Appleby D L Jr 116 *1.30 78-24 NgHggenbed1162½Ronnie'sRenigde1162½MistyMxine1092¾ Driving 6
12Sep84- 8Pen fst 6f :22⅘ :46⅗ 1:12⅖ 3+ⒻClm 2500 5 9 88½ 54½ 33½ 32¼ Boileau J L 116 2.70 80-20 Della Dear 1161½ Best Event 109¾ Nag Haggenbed 1161¼ Rallied 9
3Sep84-10Pen fst 6f :22⅘ :46⅖ 1:12⅗ 3+ⒻClm 2500 5 5 54¼ 54½ 33 22 Baker C J 116 7.40 79-23 No More Sugar 1222 NagHaggenbed1162StylishMiss1071½ Rallied 10
8Aug84- 1Pen fst 6f :22⅘ :46⅘ 1:13⅖ 3+ⒻClm 2500 4 5 42½ 43½ 33 51¾ Baker C J 116 3.30 75-17 MogulPrincesss1221½MistyMxin109noFrindlyFour116hd Weakened 8
21Jly84- 3Pen fst 6f :22⅗ :46⅕ 1:11⅗ 3+ⒻClm 2500 6 4 33 35 38 29½ Baker C J 116 5.10 76-23 Abloom1199½NgHggenbed1161½MogulPrincesses1165½ Gained 2nd 6
2Jly84- 7Pen sly 6f :23 :46⅗ 1:13 3+ⒻClm 2500 6 5 86½ 79½ 79 68 Aviles R B 116 6.30 71-19 CaptainsBeuty119½Abloom1221½MogulPrincesses1163¾ No factor 9
22Jun84- 9Pen fst 6f :22⅗ :46⅖ 1:12⅗ 3+ⒻClm 2500 4 6 31½ 2hd 1hd 32½ Baker C J 116 6.80 78-18 Damarullah116hdCaptainsBeuty1222½NgHggenbed116½ Weakened 10

LATEST WORKOUTS Sep 1 Pen 4f fst :51 b

dropping a suspicious 50 percent following two recent awful finishes. Class experts saw much more.

Six days ago this filly flashed speed for six furlongs against $5,000 turf routers. The horses were males. The class translation from $5,000 males to $2,500 females is tremendous, at least half again as great as 100 percent. When Forever There last faced $5,000 fillies and mares August 25, it romped. Besides, Penn National's leading trainer Mario Beneito was switching today from jockey J. L. Boileau to leading rider Robert Colton.

Now the filly can be seen as a dropdown of a different color. This is a fancy class drop-jockey switch-distance change maneuver, engineered by a leading trainer who brings his horse back in six days. In the recesses of class handicappers' minds they might rightly have wondered whether the filly could show adequate sprint speed at six furlongs. Changes from routes to sprints are known to be significantly less successful than the converse. But Forever There's six-furlong speed October 21 should have been reassuring on the point at least.

When the gates opened, favored Sinnalot dashed to the lead as expected, but Forever There just as quickly secured the second spot, at which point class handicappers could feel quite relaxed about the eventual outcome. The single question mark had concerned the filly's early speed. The dropping horse romped, by six uncontested lengths. It paid a handsome $11.40; keyed an easy Exacta as well.

Handicappers who emphasize class evaluations in their proceedings have no cause to shy from minor tracks. Class distinctions count at all racetracks, however large or small. To be sure, when they go to small-time ovals, handicappers need the results charts. They need to differentiate the restricted claiming races from the open kind, and the various restrictions of the races at the same selling prices. In that way they will find betting bonanzas far beyond the awareness of the crowd. At any racetrack that is the name of the game.

CHAPTER 7

Starters

THE NEW RACING SECRETARY at Hollywood Park does not card starter races, long a popular item there. He displeases many owners of consistent claiming horses, their maneuvering trainers, and at least as many handicappers. Starter races are fascinating. Owners and trainers compete for higher purses while protecting claiming horses at lower selling prices than they otherwise would run for. Handicappers win mutuels of relatively low risk, and consistently.

Yet the secretary merely has kept abreast of the changing game. His barns fill with more two- and three-year-old stock than ever. He must write races for them. Starter races too have lost out to the faster development of younger horses.

Handicapping opportunities in these specialties still exist, so starter races deserve recognition here.

Starter races are open to certain horses that have "started" for a specified claiming price or less within the past season or two. Horses entered are not subject to claim. Purses excel those of open claiming races at similar selling prices.

That being so, starter races invariably become hideouts for consistent claiming horses that could earn their keep and more at higher but open claiming prices. Which owner or trainer would not prefer to see the stable's consistent $20,000 meal ticket safely exempted from the claiming box, yet eligible to a series of races restricted to horses that have started for $12,500 or less within the past two seasons?

The starter game becomes one of eligibility. The horseman's purpose is to obtain eligibility for better horses than the kind invited by starting prices. More stables than ever seem inclined and capable of performing this eligibility trick, thereby assuring handicappers that half or more of starter fields will be horses competing below their true value by 20 to 50 percent. Still, multiple races in any starter series are likely to be won by the same horse. That is, the horse that really belongs in a claiming race whose selling prices are farthest removed from the starting prices. That is the horse that outclasses the specified starting competition the most.

To correct for potentially great imbalances in the competition, the conditions of eligibility of each race in the series will likely contain one or more restrictive clauses. The racing secretary may limit eligibility to horses that not only have started for a certain claiming price, but since that time have not (a) won a race other than maiden or claiming races, (b) won a starter or open claiming race at a price exceeding the starting price, (c) won two or more starter races at the specified price, or (d) won two or more races at a specified distance.

To reduce further the possibility that a single horse may outclass its rivals repeatedly, the racing secretary may card one or two races in the series under handicap conditions, and assign punishing weights to repeat winners. The secretary, moreover, can favor the differing preferences of eligible horses by altering the distance or footing.

The rules of racing also do their part. Notwithstanding current eligibility, following a claim, horses lose their eligibility until they race at the starting price or lower for the new owners. Private sales normally are exempt.

None of this does much to defeat the slick maneuverings of trainers. If the trainer possesses a classy, relatively versatile claiming horse, he does whatever he can to get the thing eligible. The trainer may ship it miles and enter it cheaply at a sister track. He even may smuggle it out of state, and enter at a track far off the beaten trail. He may wrap its fronts legs in long tendon bandages, then drop it $20,000 in price. He may dull its form in unsuitable races at unsuitable distances, then drop big. He may lay it off for weeks, stop the normal training pattern, then make the drop.

The sudden, suspicious drop in class is part and parcel of gaining eligibility. The maneuvers often are completed early in the season, when many horses are returning from vacations. Current form remains more of a guessing game.

Years ago, toward the latter part of the southern California season, the marvelously clever Robert Frankel claimed a plater named Tregilick for $16,000. Frankel wrapped up the horse for six weeks, then entered it in a $10,000 claiming race. No one wanted the claim. Tregilick pounded the $10,000 competition by ten lengths. It then won five or six starter races at the lower prices, until it went sour. Confident, aware handicappers collected the mutuel each time. Among $10,000 starters, Tregilick was a class standout, precisely the kind that finds its way into these affairs and that handicappers look to find.

The key to starter races is class. Among those eligible, handicappers want to know which could be winning at the loftiest level of claiming competition. If one entrant has superior class credentials, and it likes the distance and footing, a potential sweet bet has loomed up quickly.

To illustrate, we turn to a starter race for better claimers, run under allowance conditions February 19, 1979, at Santa Anita. Read the conditions. Review the past performances. Can you spot the predictable winner?

9th Santa Anita

1 ⅛ MILES. (1.46⅕) STARTER ALLOWANCE. Purse $15,000. 4-year-olds and upward, which are non-winners of two races at one mile and one-eighth or over since December 25, which have started for $25,000 or less in 1978–79 and since have not won a race other than maiden or claiming, or starter, or a claiming or starter race exceeding $25,000. Weights, 4-year-olds, 120 lbs.; older 121 lbs. Non-winners of such a race since then allowed 3 lbs.; of a race at one mile or over since then, 5 lbs.; of such a race since November 5, 7 lbs. (Claiming and starter races for $20,000 or less not considered.)

***Campodonico *** — **114**

Ch. h. 6, by Atlas—Snow Night, by Snow Cat
Br.—Marmol & Troica (Arg)
Own.—Hirsch C L **Tr.—Stute Warren**

1979	3	0	1	0	$3,900
1978	16	1	0	2	$16,750
Turf	6	0	0	1	$2,900

2Feb79-8SA	1¼ :492 1:41 2:083sy	21	115	1119	108¾	56	56¾	Mena F5	H25000	46	Jayston,BackdoorMn,OfftoMonte	11
19Jan79-7SA	1¼ :483 1:401 2:054hy	11	115	89	54½	56½	58½	Cauthen S5	A25000	58	Grvenhgue,BckdoorMn,TotlReson	11
5Jan79-4SA	1⅛ :47 1:11 1:503sy	2¾	114	514	53	41½	21	Mena F2	A25000	77	ExtrStrong,Cmpodonico,Postscript	6
18Nov78-7BM	1⅛ Ⓣ:464 1:12 1:502fm	7½	119	922	1017	99½	31	Pincay L Jr6	A25000	—	SpanishSilver,Jyston,Cmpodonico	12
29Oct78-9SA	1 1/16 :464 1:112 1:43 ft	8½	117	711	54½	31½	1nk	Mena F3	25000	86	Campodonico, Postscript, Gollete	8
19Oct78-5SA	7f :213 :441 1:22 ft	36	117	811	911	913	64¼	Noguez A11	25000	89	Qulifiction,EgleinFlight,ProperKid	12
23Aug78-9Dmr	1 1/16 :452 1:10 1:422ft	34	116	88½	97¼	78¼	74½	Encinas R5	25000	83	ChumChum,GrahmHegney,Dbghin	12
13Aug78-7Dmr	1 1/16 :46 1:103 1:413ft	36	116	56	31½	46	411	Encinas R10	25000	81	Chiloquin,Dabaghian,GrhmHegney	11
24Jly78-5Hol	1 1/16 Ⓣ:471 1:112 1:421fm	37	114	2½	42½	73	87½	McCarron C J5	Alw	80	AsdeCops,BootsColonro,ElMorgon	9
16Jly78-3Hol	1 :46 1:101 1:35 ft	19	114	64½	58	46	57½	Mena F6	Alw	83	Nantequos, LetsGotoEdwards,Seep	7

Feb 14 SA 4f sl :51 h **Feb 9 SA 6f ft 1:132 h** **Jan 27 SA 6f ft 1:133 h** **Jan 17 SA 4f m :532 h (d)**

***Gravenhague** — **120**

B. c. 4, by Bold Lad—Scotia's Girl, by Star Gazer
Br.—Sangster R (Fra)
Own.—Siegel Jan **Tr.—Gregson Edwin**

1979	3	1	0	0	$9,925
1978	8	1	1	2	$12,910
Turf	11	4	1	1	$15,400

2Feb79-8SA	1¼ :492 1:41 2:083sy	*3¼	120	34	55	1011	916	McHargueDG9	H25000	37	Jayston,BackdoorMn,OfftoMonte	11
19Jan79-7SA	1¼ :483 1:401 2:054hy	8	114	52	32	1hd	11½	McHargueDG9	A25000	67	Grvenhgue,BckdoorMn,TotlReson	11
5Jan79-4SA	1⅛ :47 1:11 1:503sy	*2½	114	2½	1hd	21	44¼	McHargueDG4	A25000	74	ExtrStrong,Cmpodonico,Postscript	6
20Dec78-9Crc	a1 1/16 Ⓣ 1:45 fm	8¼	114	21	2½	2½	2nk	Thornburg B10	50000	90	Noholme'sStr,Grvenhgue,TllowMn	10
9Dec78-9Crc	1 1/16 Ⓣ:462 1:102 1:421fm	20e	108	1217	1215	1012	88¾	MillsBL6	Gld Coast H	85	FleetGar,PrinceMisko,RymondErl	12
13Oct78-8Med	1 1/16 Ⓣ:464 1:112 1:431fm	*3¼	116	42½	2hd	11	14	Thomas D B9	25000	96	Gravenhague,Savoury,FbledPrince	11
16Sep78-7Med	170 :462 1:112 1:414sy	11	112	48	46	55½	59	Gomez M A2	Alw	83	QllonDggr,Mrsh'sRomo,NwMrktAx	9
2Sep78-8Mth	1 :47 1:122 1:382gd	18	111	39	36	45¼	39	Gomez M A1	Alw	72	RzzleDzzleRey,WildrnssBy,Grvnhgu	7
23Aug78-8Mth	5f Ⓣ:21 :442 :564fm	8½	112	76½	612	54½	76	MacBeth D6	Alw	93	RglAndRoyl,FrstAmbssdor,Pokbrry	8
28Jly78-8Mth	6f :221 :46 1:114m	4¼	112	57½	56	57	49½	MacBeth D2	Alw	71	SeeTheU.S.A.,Sig'sSecrt,HickoryCp	5

Feb 17 SA 3f ft :353 h **Feb 11 SA 6f ft 1:143 h** **Jan 28 SA 5f ft 1:032 h** **Jan 14 SA 5f ft 1:01 h**

Jayston — B. g. 5, by Le Fabuleux—Banja Luka, by Double Jay
Br.—Keck H B (Ky) — 1979 2 1 0 0 $12,200
Own.—Bradley & Whittingham C **121** Tr.—Whittingham Michael — 1978 11 1 3 3 $23,800
Turf 6 0 2 2 $9,525

2Feb79-8SA	1¼ :492 1:41 2:083sy	5	116	11	12½	12	13½	Olivares F1	H25000	53	Jayston,BackdoorMn,OfftoMonte	11
19Jan79-7SA	1¼ :483 1:401 2:054hy	17	115	41½	11½	32	46½	Olivares F10	A25000	60	Grvenhgue,BckdoorMn,TotlReson	11
18Nov78-7BM	1⅛ Ⓣ:4641:12 1:502fm	18	115	34	41½	3½	2¾	Toro F2	A25000	—	SpanishSilver,Jyston,Cmpodonico	12
13Oct78-8SA	1⅛ Ⓣ:48 1:12 1:492fm	15	115	44½	66½	79	712	Olivares F1	A25000	68	Latrobe, GrahamHeagney,T.K.O.Joe	7
19Aug78-9Dmr	1⅛ Ⓣ:4741:12 1:50 fm	3e	115	87	54	66½	36	Baltazar C5	H25000	85	Latrobe, El Tarta, Jayston	10
6Aug78-9Dmr	1⅛ Ⓣ:4721:1221:51 fm	*8-5e	117	47	42	64	54½	Olivares F4	H25000	81	DeepBlueWater,WinnerCrest,ElTrt	10
10Jun78-4Hol	1⅛ Ⓣ:4721:1141:484fm	3½	114	65	64¼	43½	31¾	Olivares F6	A25000	89	ForgetThShowrs,MistySton,Jyston	6
17May78-9Hol	1⅜ Ⓣ:4841:3832:16 fm	5½	118	42	2hd	11½	21	Olivares F3	H25000	74	Trond Sang, Jayston, CloseToNoon	9
19Apr78-5Hol	1⅛ :462 1:11 1:492ft	4½	119	22	22	34	32¾	Olivares F4	A25000	82	ForgtThShowrs,LughingRivr,Jyston	9
31Mar78-7SA	1¼ :472 1:361 2:014gd	18	117	2½	2½	21	2nk	Olivares F6	A25000	87	Serafino, Jayston, Trond Sang	6

Feb 15 SA 5f ft :591 h Feb 9 SA 3f ft :36 b Jan 30 SA tr.t 4f ft :493 h Jan 25 SA 3f ft :371 b

Taste Tempter * — Dk. b. or br. c. 4, by Ambehaving—Pecans And Peaches, by Top Singer
Br.—Meadowbrook Farm Inc (Fla) — 1979 1 0 0 0 $1,050
Own.—Long-Martin-Pavlovich **1085** Tr.—Early Don — 1978 9 0 0 1 $3,750

11Feb79-9SA	1 :46 1:102 1:362ft	16	1105	1013	97¼	83¾	44	Chiang R6	25000	83	Rise N Reform, Right Me Up,Shiv	10
27Sep78-11Pom	1⅛ :454 1:11 1:504ft	44	114	915	914	913	79¾	Rankin A5	Pom Dby	80	Gallantly,SoftMarket,Baker'sBelief	9
20Sep78-11Pom	1 1/16 :464 1:11 1:442ft	33	114	711	613	612	49	Rankin A1	Dby Trl	81	Effortlessly, IowaFlash,SoftMarket	9
4Sep78-5Dmr	1 1/16 :443 1:102 1:44 ft	25	1095	1120	1014	68½	52	Chiang R8	35000	78	ProudRulr,‡Gvmshout,GoodInFrnc	11
24Aug78-9Dmr	1 :452 1:102 1:363ft	41	1095	814	712	55	31 ♦	Chiang R2	25000	84	Triggeroy,Givemeshout,TsteTemptr	9

♦24Aug78—Dead heat

26Jly78-7Dmr	6f :221 :444 1:101ft	66	1095	79½	713	77	55¾	Chiang R2	Alw	81	Cala Guard, Stand Pat, RightonTop	9
3Jun78-2Hol	6½f :214 :443 1:164ft	61	114	911	109	109¾	98¾	Culberson R1	Alw	77	Sea Ride, Bendowin, Liquor Law	10
20May78-5Hol	6f :22 :451 1:101ft	47	114	99	84	76½	57¾	Culberson R1	Alw	78	Hail Ribot,SaliSands,PashanatReb	10
4Feb78-1SA	6f :214 :442 1:091ft	80	114	77½	710	79	710	Culberson R6	Alw	83	CourtinSession,SpottdChrgr,HotOil	8
11Jan78-5SA	6f :214 :452 1:112sl	4	116	87¼	86¾	54½	66½	Cauthen S1	c20000	75	Instant Policy,Son'sSon,Reb'sMark	9

●Feb 6 SA 1 ft 1:394 h Jan 30 Pom 6f ft 1:194 h Jan 25 Pom 6f ft 1:183 h Jan 20 Pom 6f sl 1:231 h

Extra Strong * — Dk. b. or br. g. 5, by Hillary—Fleet Jill, by Fleet Nasrullah
Br.—Old English Rancho (Cal) — 1979 3 1 0 0 $9,750
Own.—Westerly Stud Farms **121** Tr.—Dunn Joe S — 1978 13 1 3 4 $23,555
Turf 1 0 0 0

2Feb79-8SA	1¼ :492 1:41 2:083sy	20	116	68	33	44	46¼	Hawley S4	H25000	47	Jayston,BackdoorMn,OfftoMonte	11
19Jan79-7SA	1¼ :483 1:401 2:054hy	8½	119	1113	1113	1122	1137	Pincay L Jr7	A25000	30	Grvenhgue,BckdoorMn,TotlReson	11
5Jan79-4SA	1⅛ :47 1:11 1:503sy	4½	114	413	31	11	11	ShoemakerW6	A25000	78	ExtrStrong,Cmpodonico,Postscript	6
22Dec78-6BM	1 :46 1:112 1:363ft	*3¼	114	1011	88	53	2nk	McHargue D G9	Alw	86	GoodPersonlity,ExtrStrong,YLittl	10
1Dec78-7BM	1 1/16 :47 1:121 1:45 gd	5½	113	52½	56	712	917	Mercado V V1	Alw	57	Guayo, Ackcelisor, Crabner	12
18Nov78-6BM	1 1/16 :46 1:11 1:433ft	8½	114	1011	95¼	2½	21½	Mercado V V3	Alw	79	BiminiCptin,ExtrStrong,FleetStvn	11
5Nov78-9SA	1 1/16 :471 1:12 1:432ft	12	117	59	53¼	54½	55¾	Mena F6	20000	78	MisterDan,Chum-Chum,ErlyCotton	8
15Oct78-9SA	1 1/16 :463 1:11 1:424ft	32	117	108½	87	55	45½	Chapman T M1	20000	81	Marathon, Prices Run, Anticuado	12
5Oct78-9SA	1 1/16 :462 1:104 1:424ft	33	117	65½	65½	88½	89	Chapman T M5	25000	78	Marathon,WinnerCrest,WindyDncer	8
28Apr78-5Hol	1 1/16 Ⓣ:4711:1111:421fm	6¾	117	86	85	97¼	108¾	Pierce D7	Alw	79	RisingArc,FoxyGrampa,AsdeCopas	12

Feb 16 SA 5f ft 1:021 h Jan 26 SA 4f ft :481 h Jan 12 SA 4f ft :481 h Jan 1 SA 4f ft :484 h

***Newburg II** — B. g. 7, by Lord Gayle—Fishfinger, by Golden Cloud
Br.—Finnegan M A (Eng) — 1978 12 2 1 2 $24,400
Own.—Legare & Mizin **114** Tr.—Nelson Kathleen S — 1977 17 4 1 2 $35,775
Turf 35 9 3 4 $56,225

18Nov78-7BM	1⅛ Ⓣ:4641:12 1:502fm	9¼	117	1125	916	1010	72½	Chapman TM7	A25000	—	SpanishSilver,Jyston,Cmpodonico	12
4Nov78-5SA	1⅛ Ⓣ:47 1:1041:47 fm	62	114	820	821	821	822	Chapman T M5	Alw	70	Bywayofchicago,Latrobe,‡Semillon	8
13Oct78-8SA	1⅛ Ⓣ:48 1:12 1:492fm	9½	120	713	78½	66½	47	Chapman TM2	A25000	73	Latrobe, GrahamHeagney,T.K.O.Joe	7
10Sep78-9Dmr	1 1/16 Ⓣ:4641:1041:442fm	3	116	816	45	2½	12	Chapman T M3	25000	87	Newburg II, Gollete,LaughingRiver	8
2Sep78-5Dmr	1⅛ Ⓣ:4641:11 1:50 fm	30	114	1027	1024	1022	1020	Baltazar C2	Alw	71	BlckSlphr,AbsntMndd,HmblHowrd	10
19Aug78-5Dmr	1⅛ Ⓣ:4921:1341:50 fm	16	119	54½	58	33	24	Chapman T M8	Alw	87	Zor, Newburg II, Northern Drive	9
30Jly78-6Dmr	1 1/16 Ⓣ:4921:1341:434fm	16	119	44½	44	46½	49	Chapman T M2	Alw	81	Bywyofchcgo,BlckSulphr,Dr.Rddck	6
16Jly78-5Hol	1⅜ Ⓣ:4841:3812:153fm	13	1095	714	711	76¼	54	Chapman T M7	Alw	73	Fashion Lad, Black Sulphur, Paris	8
3Jly78-5Hol	1⅛ Ⓣ:4721:1141:483fm	4¼	1155	711	67	56	33	Chapman T M5	Alw	89	BlckSulphur,BootsColonro,NwbrgII	8
18Jun78-5Hol	1⅛ Ⓣ:47 1:1121:484fm	9	120	1113	117¼	74½	72½	Castaneda M8	Alw	88	FshonLd,BootsColonro,HowCuros	12

Feb 16 Hol 4f ft :511 h Feb 10 Hol 1 ft 1:452 h Feb 5 Hol 6f ft 1:184 h Jan 29 Hol 5f ft 1:021 h

Latrobe — B. g. 6, by Bold Bidder—Dedicated To Me, by Dedicate
Br.—Walnut Hill Farm (Ky) — 1979 1 0 0 0
Own.—Ferrari B **114** Tr.—Winick Randy — 1978 16 2 3 2 $34,825
Turf 33 6 8 3 $76,709

5Jan79-7SA	1⅛ :464 1:111 1:501sy	*3-2	1145	22	21½	11	3¾ †	Sorenson D2	A25000	79	El Provincial, OfftoMonte,‡Latrobe	7

† 5Jan79—Disqualified and placed seventh

4Nov78-5SA	1⅛ Ⓣ:47 1:1041:47 fm	29	1095	11	1hd	2hd	2hd	Sorenson D8	Alw	92	Bywayofchicago,Latrobe,‡Semillon	8
28Oct78-8SA	1⅛ Ⓣ:4611:10 1:464fm	14	112	32½	86½	89½	86½	Mena F7	H P Rsl H	86	Cheraw,AlwaysGallnt,SonnyCollins	8

28Oct78—Run in two divisions, 5th and 8th races.

13Oct78-8SA	1⅛ Ⓣ:48 1:12 1:492fm	*1	118	13	1½	11	11¾	Pincay L Jr7	A25000	80	Latrobe, GrahamHeagney,T.K.O.Joe	7
19Aug78-9Dmr	1⅛ Ⓣ:4741:12 1:50 fm	*1	121	21	11	12	11	ShoemakerW6	H25000	91	Latrobe, El Tarta, Jayston	10
5Aug78-7Dmr	1⅛ Ⓣ:5021:1441:514fm	9	116	42	41	2½	3nk	Castaneda M6	50000	82	No Saint, Approval, Latrobe	7
24Jly78-7Hol	1 Ⓣ:4611:1021:344fm	10	116	45	32½	2½	21½	Castaneda M5	50000	94	Approval, Latrobe, Concussion	8
3Jly78-7Hol	1⅛ Ⓣ:4631:1131:49 fm	*9-5	114	510	42	2½	3nk	Castaneda M6	A25000	90	Mr. Irv M., As de Copas, Latrobe	7
18Jun78-9Hol	1 1/16 Ⓣ:4721:1141:423fm	14	114	94¾	52½	51¾	2hd	Castaneda M6	22500	86	As de Copas, Latrobe, Postscript	9
6May78-10GP	1 1/16 Ⓣ:4811:1141:431fm	7	116	86¾	76¾	63¼	62¼	Silva C H4	25000	83	ComncheChief,Wllspokn,SwnFlight	8

Feb 17 SA 3f ft :363 b Feb 12 SA 5f ft 1:003 h ●Feb 5 SA 4f ft :46 h Jan 28 SA 1 ft 1:41 h

Trond Sang
Ch. g. 7, by Trondheim—Constant Song, by Mr Consistency
Br.—Shahan E H (Cal) 1979 3 0 0 0 $375
Own.—Headley & Qvale 114 Tr.—Headley Bruce 1978 10 1 4 3 $39,625
Turf 13 2 3 1 $44,875

2Feb79-8SA 1¼ :492 1:41 2:083sy 34 116 45½ 66 9101017 Toro F6 H25000 36 Jayston,BackdoorMn,OfftoMonte 11
19Jan79-7SA 1¼ :483 1:401 2:054hy 21 115 1011 97 912 823 Toro F8 A25000 44 Grvenhgue,BckdoorMn,TotlReson 11
5Jan79-7SA 1⅛ :464 1:111 1:501sy 9½ 116 412 714 77 67½ Toro F7 A25000 73 El Provincial, OfftoMonte,‡Latrobe 7
5Jan79—Placed fifth through disqualification
19Aug78-9Dmr 1⅛Ⓣ:4741:12 1:50 fm 14 117 1013 97½ 56 56½ Galarsa R3 H25000 85 Latrobe, El Tarta, Jayston 10
17May78-9Hol 1⅜Ⓣ:4841:3832:16 fm 2½ 116 95½ 74½ 42 11 Toro F9 H25000 75 Trond Sang, Jayston, CloseToNoon 9
29Apr78-8GG 1⅜Ⓣ:4641:37 2:15 fm 54 108 910 86½ 2½ 2½ GalrsR7 Roilng Grn H 98 TarSienpre,TrondSng,BoldImpulse 10
19Apr78-5Hol 1⅛ :462 1:11 1:492ft 9 114 814 78 78½ 78 McCarron CJ6 A25000 77 ForgtThShowrs,LughingRivr,Jyston 9
31Mar78-7SA 1¼ :472 1:361 2:014gd 4½ 115 54½ 52½ 52½ 32½ Toro F3 A25000 85 Serafino, Jayston, Trond Sang 6
16Mar78-6SA 1⅛ :47 1:111 1:50 ft 4½ 115 56 56 35½ 35 Toro F4 A25000 77 Lalo II, Close To Noon, TrondSang 7
12Feb78-4SA 1⅛ :47 1:11 1:502ft 2 115 59 38½ 37½ 24 Toro F3 A25000 76 Repurchase, TrondSang,BigDestiny 6
Feb 17 SA 4f ft :49 h Feb 11 SA 5f ft 1:004 h Feb 2 SA tr.t 3f m :393 h Jan 28 SA 6f ft 1:141 h

Backdoor Man ✻
Ch. c. 4, by High Tribute—Lismara, by No Robbery
Br.—Talbot Brothers & Dawson (Ky) 1979 3 0 2 1 $9,450
Own.—Purple MtEsts-HalfHorseFm 113 Tr.—Jones Gary 1978 17 4 1 3 $34,749
Turf 10 3 0 2 $22,149

2Feb79-8SA 1¼ :492 1:41 2:083sy 5½ 117 56 22½ 22 23½ McCarronCJ11 H25000 49 Jayston,BackdoorMn,OfftoMonte 11
19Jan79-7SA 1¼ :483 1:401 2:054hy 5½ 113 2½ 21½ 2hd 21½ McCarron CJ1 A25000 65 Grvenhgue,BckdoorMn,TotlReson 11
5Jan79-7SA 1⅛ :464 1:111 1:501sy 2½ 112 33½ 33½ 21 42½ McCarron CJ6 A25000 78 El Provincial, OfftoMonte,‡Latrobe 7
5Jan79—Placed third through disqualification
1Oct78-8SA 1⅛Ⓣ:48 1:12 1:492fm 3½ 117 33 43 44½ 58 McCarron CJ6 A25000 72 Latrobe, GrahamHeagney,T.K.O.Joe 7
5Oct78-2SA 1 1/16 :461 1:10 1:42 ft 4½ 117 41½ 31½ 2½ 21 Toro F3 Alw 90 GenuineGuy,BckdoorMn,SiSiMjsty 11
4Sep78-9Dmr 1 1/16Ⓣ:4841:13 1:444fm 6½ 111 75 63½ 42 31 McCarron C J2 Alw 84 MontMonnaie,Sebert,BackdoorMn 11
23Aug78-7Dmr 1⅛ :45 1:094 1:483ft 2½ 122 711 64½ 66½ 65½ McCarron CJ7 H25000 82 CourtMssngr,ProudRulr,R.U.Lstnng 7
14Aug78-9Dmr 1⅛Ⓣ:48 1:1311:504fm *2 124 54½ 63½ 65½ 45 McCarron CJ6 H25000 82 T.K.O. Joe, Smoky Isle, Mr. Agent 8
23Jly78-8Hol 1⅛Ⓣ:4621:1021:472fm 28 113 96½12101215 1225 Olivares F2 Cinema H 73 Kamehameha,ElFantastico,Smgulr 12
14Jly78-9Hol 1⅛Ⓣ:48 1:13 1:491fm *1 122 32 1hd 12 16 McCarron CJ4 A25000 89 BckdoorMn,OrkneyIsle,FutureofPc 8
Feb 15 SA 4f ft :484 h Jan 2 SA 4f ft :48 h Dec 21 SA 6f ft 1:133 h

Off to Monte ✻
Dk. b. or br. g. 4, by Run of Luck—Gentlewoman, by Sisters Prince
Br.—Rowan L R (Cal) 1979 2 0 1 1 $6,000
Own.—Dante-Dante-Dante 117 Tr.—Moreno Henry 1978 18 2 5 1 $28,175
Turf 2 0 0 0

2Feb79-8SA 1¼ :492 1:41 2:083sy 6 116 1016 86½ 33½ 34½ Pierce D8 H25000 49 Jayston,BackdoorMn,OfftoMonte 11
5Jan79-7SA 1⅛ :464 1:111 1:501sy 6½ 115 718 511 64 2½ Pierce D5 A25000 79 El Provincial, OfftoMonte,‡Latrobe 7
26Dec78-9SA 1 1/16 :463 1:112 1:431ft 9½ 115 109½ 94½ 45 1½ Pierce D10 25000 85 OfftoMonte,ErlyCotton,Postscript 12
5Nov78-5SA 1⅛Ⓣ:4631:1031:481fm 9 115 11161111108½105½ Pierce D3 Alw 80 T.K.O. Joe, Kia Mata, Equa 12
26Oct78-9SA 1 1/16 :46 1:103 1:422ft 7 117 1010 95½ 64½ 41 Pierce D9 30000 88 AnotherToast,PirteFleet,GyRipple 11
6Oct78-1SA 6f :212 :441 1:092ft 73 117 12191215 67½ 21½ Pierce D5 25000 90 SpottdChrgr,OfftoMont,Wndy'sDk 12
30Jun78-5Hol 1⅛Ⓣ:4711:12 1:493fm 15 116 910 97 86½ 78½ Pierce D1 A25000 78 BckdoorMn,CourtMessngr,T.K.O.Jo 9
16Jun78-6Hol 1 1/16 :46 1:114 1:452ft *9-5 118 915 74½ 3½ 12½ Pierce D6 M25000 68 Off to Monte,Lobsang,PirateFleet 12
17May78-6Hol 1⅛ :462 1:111 1:504ft 6 118 914 65½ 25 24 Pierce D5 M30000 74 PssngLgnd,OfftoMont,ProntoSnor 10
11May78-6Hol 6f :214 :442 1:092ft *2½ 118 109½1112 68½ 711 Pincay L Jr7 M30000 79 PashanatReb,BrndyRoyl,Chowchll 12
Feb 13 SA 7f ft 1:284 h Feb 8 SA 4f ft :531 h Jan 31 SA tr.t 4f m :504 h Jan 26 SA 1 ft 1:42 h

Si Si Majesty
Ch. c. 4, by His Majesty—Waltz Si Si, by Bold Lad
Br.—Winchell V H Jr (Ky) 1979 3 1 0 0 $9,850
Own.—Chism W A 117 Tr.—Palma Hector O 1978 21 3 1 6 $28,810
Turf 2 0 0 0

8Feb79-7SA 1 :452 1:101 1:354ft 4½ 113 31 3½ 54 58½ Hawley S3 20000 81 TurrMurr,RignngNtv,SwngThHrbor 6
28Jan79-9SA 1 1/16 :471 1:111 1:43 sl 15 115 1½ 13 14 13½ McCarron C J9 25000 86 SiSiMajesty,Mr.Agent,TripleStkes 11
14Jan79-9SA 1 1/16 :46 1:102 1:434m 14 115 21½ 22 33 59½ McCarron C J1 25000 72 Total Reason, Gallantly, Mr. Agent 9
28Dec78-5SA 1 1/16 :454 1:101 1:423ft 13 115 65½11121216 1229 Toro F5 Alw 59 RichCrem,Blondi'sDncr,KingGoGo 12
2Nov78-4SA 1 1/16 :47 1:112 1:433ft *9-5 117 58½ 42½ 3½ 1no Castaneda M6 c20000 83 Si Si Majesty,FastFist,TrustRobert 6
26Oct78-9SA 1 1/16 :46 1:103 1:422ft 3½ 117 52½ 62½ 1081 1010 Hawley S4 30000 79 AnotherToast,PirteFleet,GyRipple 11
15Oct78-7SA 1 1/16 :462 1:103 1:422ft 2½ 112 32½ 32 42½ 69½ Shoemaker W2 Alw 79 Parse, Soft Market, As deEspadas 10
5Oct78-2SA 1 1/16 :461 1:10 1:42 ft 14 117 73½ 75 42 31 Pierce D2 Alw 90 GenuineGuy,BckdoorMn,SiSiMjsty 11
4Sep78-5Dmr 1 1/16 :443 1:102 1:44 ft 7½ 114 710 912 57 41½ McCarron C J3 35000 78 ProudRulr,‡Gymshout,GoodInFrnc 11
24Aug78-3Dmr 1 :443 1:094 1:352ft 8 117 59½ 33½ 35 24 Pincay L Jr5 35000 87 ForeverGllnt,SiSiMjesty,Foyt'sAck 7
Feb 15 SA 4f ft :47 h Feb 4 SA 4f sl :473 h Jan 23 SA 4f ft :47 h Jan 11 SA 4f ft :47 h

On the alert for horses that have been dropped down to starter race prices from previous claiming price highs, handicappers settle on Latrobe. The consistent versatile six-year-old has raced effectively for $50,000 at Hollywood Park and Del Mar and November 4 almost measured the multiple stakes winner Bywayofchicago in fast time on turf under classified allowance conditions, when overlooked at 29 to 1. Following that narrow loss, Latrobe remained eligible for Santa Anita's $25,000 starter series.

The gelding is practically the prototype of the handicapper's starter play. Already two for four in the series, it has never been beaten by even a length. A jockey switch to Shoemaker added insurance today, Latrobe having been poorly handled January 5 by apprentice Danny Sorenson. The result chart suggested Latrobe might have won that one too.

Without Latrobe in the field, importantly, six or seven horses appear relatively equal. The race would have been unplayable. To be sure, the entrant Gravenhague had started for $50,000 at Calder, blasted the field October 13 at the Meadowlands while qualifying, and recently won a $25,000 starter race at Santa Anita. Its Calder price, however, translates to $40,000 at Santa Anita. Latrobe remains the previous highest-priced claiming horse.

In textbook manner, Gravenhague finished second to easy win-

9th Race Santa Anita Feb. 19, 1979

1 ⅛ MILES. (1.46⅕) 4-Year-Olds and Up. Starter Allowance. Purse $15,000. — which are non-winners of two races at one mile and one-eighth or over since December 25, which have started for $25,000 or less in 1978-79 and since have not won a race other than maiden or claiming, or starter, or a claiming or starter race exceeding $25,000. — Value of race $15,000, value to winner $8,250, second $3,000, third $2,250, fourth $1,125, fifth $375. Mutuel pool $234,937. Exacta Pool $527,595.

Last Raced	Horse	Wt.	PP.	½	Str	Fin	Odds $1
5Jan79 $^{7}SA^{7}$	Latrobe	114	7	2^{2}	1^{3}	1^{4}	2.20
2Feb79 $^{8}SA^{9}$	Gravenhague	120	2	4^{3}	$3^{1\frac{1}{2}}$	2^{2}	11.30
2Feb79 $^{8}SA^{2}$	Backdoor Man	113	9	5^{4}	4^{2}	$3^{1\frac{1}{2}}$	3.10
2Feb79 $^{8}SA^{5}$	Campodonico	117	1	7^{2}	$6\frac{1}{2}$	$4\frac{3}{4}$	12.10
2Feb79 $^{8}SA^{10}$	Trond Sang	114	8	$8\frac{1}{2}$	$7\frac{1}{2}$	5^{1}	78.00
2Feb79 $^{8}SA^{3}$	Off to Monte	117	10	11	9^{4}	6^{hd}	4.30
2Feb79 $^{8}SA^{1}$	Jayston	121	3	$3\frac{1}{2}$	$5\frac{1}{2}$	$7^{3\frac{1}{2}}$	9.80
11Feb79 $^{9}SA^{4}$	Taste Tempter	108	4	6^{1}	$8^{1\frac{1}{2}}$	8^{hd}	18.40
8Feb79 $^{7}SA^{5}$	Si Si Majesty	117	11	1^{1}	$2\frac{1}{2}$	9^{7}	9.70
2Feb79 $^{8}SA^{4}$	Extra Strong	121	5	9^{1}	10^{6}	10^{8}	30.20
18Nov78 $^{7}BM^{7}$	Newburg II	116	6	$10\frac{1}{2}$	11	11	61.00

Time, :23, :46⅘, 1:11, 1:35⅘, 1:48⅘ Track fast.

OFF AT 5:29 PST.

7-LATROBE	6.40	4.40	2.80
2-GRAVENHAGUE		10.20	6.40
9-BACKDOOR MAN			2.80

$5 EXACTA 7-2 PAID $163.00.

B. g, by Bold Bidder—Dedicated To Me, by Dedicate. Trainer Winick Randy. Bred by Walnut Hill Farm (Ky).

Jockeys— 1, Shoemaker W; 2, McHargue D G; 3, Hawley S; 4, Pincay L Jr; 5, Castaneda M; 6, Pierce D; 7, Olivares F; 8, Chiang R[5]; 9, McCarron C J; 10, Cordero A Jr; 11, Toro F.

Owners— 1, Ferrari B; 2, Siegel Jan; 3, Purple Mt Ests-Half Horse Fm; 4, Hirsch C L; 5, Headley & Qvale; 6, Dante-Dante-Dante; 7, Bradley & Whittingham C; 8, Long-Martin-Pavlovich; 9, Chism W A; 10, Westerly Stud Farms; 11, Legare & Mizin.

ner Latrobe. As the chart reveals, the gelding tracked the early pace in hand, and drew out in the stretch. The Exacta paid $163.

Because class drops from previous claiming highs can be so dominant a factor in starter races, a perfectly legitimate play in any series is the horse that already has won a race in the series. The *Form* past performances may not contain the race by which the horse became eligible, but so what? Handicappers know what has transpired. If the starter win was convincing, it probably can be repeated. At Santa Anita 1979, Latrobe could have beaten the $25,000 starter horses successively, but its management pursued purses of classified allowance events and even tried Latrobe in an open stakes.

When analyzing starter allowances or starter handicaps, handicappers should prefer:

1. Horses that have won or run close previously at the highest open claiming price.

2. Any horse in the field that has won a race in the series.

If nothing in the field qualifies, handicappers best examine the recent races of any horse that became eligible to the series last time out. Where class drops were big, and previous races against better were even or better, the horses may enjoy an edge.

3. Any horse that became eligible last time out, provided its recent races against better were even or better.

Handicappers will uncover overlays by adhering to this guideline. The maneuver looks like this:

9th Golden Gate

1 ¼ MILES. (1.58⅘) STARTER ALLOWANCE. Purse $6,000. 4–year–olds and upward. Non–winners of two starter races since March 1, which have started for a claiming price of $4,000 or less in 1984–85 and since that start have not won a race other than maiden, starter or claiming, or a claiming or starter race exceeding $4,000. Weight, 120 lbs. Non–winners of one such race since May 1 allowed 3 lbs.; one such race since April 1, 5 lbs.; one such race since March 1, 7 lbs. (Maiden, starter and claiming races for $3,500 or less not considered).

Innocent Age — **LAMANCE C** — **113**
Own.—Frank J R
B. g. 4, by Judger—Happy Spirit, by Native Charger
Br.—Mabee Mr–Mrs J C (Ky) — **1985 1 0 1 0 $721**
Tr.—Jenda Charles J — **1984 7 2 1 2 $16,300**
Lifetime 14 2 3 2 $18,781

3May85-12Fno	1	:46	1:11^{3}	1:37^{3}ft	*2½	117	6$^{9\frac{1}{4}}$	6$^{4\frac{3}{4}}$	1^{hd}	2no	Sanchez R A^{3}	4000	83-17	JohnJmes,InnocntAg,TrdrSt.John	10
23May84-9GG	1$\frac{1}{16}$	:47^{1}	1:11^{1}	1:44^{1}ft	*9-5	114	4^{10}	3^{6}	2^{4}	3^{5}	Lamance C^{9}	12500	77-19	FunnyFichte,DressRich,InnocntAg	10
11May84-6GG	1$\frac{1}{16}$	:48^{2}	1:12^{1}	1:44^{1}ft	*6-5	114	2^{1}	2$^{1\frac{1}{2}}$	2$^{1\frac{1}{2}}$	3^{4}	Lamance C^{5}	16000	78-23	DevintDncer,GntlPrsudr,InnocntAg	7
17Apr84-1GG	1$\frac{1}{16}$	:45^{4}	1:10^{3}	1:43^{3}ft	11	114	4^{9}	1^{hd}	2$^{1\frac{1}{2}}$	4$^{3\frac{1}{4}}$	Lamance C^{6}	25000	82-14	Gallant Oak,EasternJo,Intelligencer	7
16Mar84-7GG	1$\frac{1}{16}$	:48	1:13	1:46 gd	3½	114	5^{6}	3$^{3\frac{1}{2}}$	2^{4}	2^{8}	Lamance C^{2}	20000	65-28	CrdicBowl,InnocentAge,Intelligncr	8
29Feb84-7GG	1$\frac{1}{16}$	:46^{4}	1:11^{2}	1:43^{3}ft	9½	112	7$^{7\frac{3}{4}}$	7$^{6\frac{1}{2}}$	6$^{5\frac{3}{4}}$	4$^{8\frac{1}{4}}$	Lamance C^{9}	28000	77-19	LittleMatador,Literki,ElCminoJohn	9
25Jan84-1BM	1$\frac{1}{16}$	:49^{1}	1:14	1:47 ft	4½	114	5^{4}	2^{1}	1^{1}	1^{1}	Lamance C^{3}	16000	64-25	InnocentAge,FirstAmour,BillyBlwit	7
25Jan84—Bumped break															
4Jan84-3BM	1$\frac{1}{16}$	:48	1:14^{3}	1:49^{1}ft	12	118	8$^{9\frac{1}{4}}$	4^{6}	1^{hd}	1$^{1\frac{1}{2}}$	Lamance C^{6}	M20000	53-36	InnocentAge,Intelligencr,DrssRich	12
21Dec83-1BM	1$\frac{1}{16}$	:49	1:15^{1}	1:49^{3}gd	8	118	4^{5}	2$^{\frac{1}{2}}$	1^{hd}	5$^{2\frac{3}{4}}$	Baze R A^{6}	M10000	48-33	NorthernFlme,WyMker,RichPrinc	12
1Dec83-1BM	6f	:23^{3}	:48	1:15^{2}gd	5½	118	8$^{5\frac{1}{2}}$	9$^{7\frac{3}{4}}$	9$^{9\frac{1}{4}}$	7^{6}	Baze R A^{1}	M12500	57-32	Brddock,WinningTri,UnonJuncton	12

May 19 GG 4f ft :49 hg   Apr 27 Pln 6f ft 1:14^{2} h   Apr 22 Pln 7f ft 1:30 h   Apr 16 Pln 6f ft 1:15 h

As an interesting postscript, horses moving from starter races to open claiming races at prices equal to or less than the starting price actually are dropping in class, perhaps by 50 to 100 percent. If such horses move to open races at higher claiming prices, but the new prices are higher than the starting price by 25 percent or less, a nicely hidden drop in class may have been engineered. The odds may be absolutely delightful.

THE HANDICAPPER'S CONDITION BOOK TRAINER PROFILE

Robert Frankel of Southern California

Working almost exclusively with claiming horses, southern California trainer Robert Frankel during the 1970s dispensed a performance perhaps unmatched in the annals of the sport. During the first half of the decade a Frankel horse in the entries absolutely grabbed the attention not only of handicappers in attendance but also of horseplayers of whatever description, sending thousands of them to the windows with greater expectation of catching a winner. Frankel did not disappoint for long. For the decade his winning pace was 22 percent. No one else in major racing was close. New York's Frank Martin and California's Charles Whittingham finished nearest at .17. Lazaro Barrera and Woody Stephens scored at a .14 clip. Others hovered there or thereabouts.

Some particular Frankel feats leap to mind, as still does his claim in the late sixties in New York of Barometer for $15,000 and later winning the Grade 1 Suburban Handicap with him. At Hollywood Park 1972, Frankel sent out 180 horses, and won with 60 of them, an incredible win rate of .33. In 1978, Frankel by October 1 had earned more than one million in purses, and this without having even a single stakes winner. Five times during the decade Frankel ranked among the top ten trainers in money won, and this without once taking charge of a line of nicely bred two- and three-year-olds from a leading breeder. With the genuinely top horses he did get hold of, usually indirectly—Linda's Chief, Life Cycle, Zanthe, and Johnny's Image—Frankel won major titles and major money, and with two he set track time records. And at least twice during the decade Frankel used personal funds to reclaim elderly geldings which had done exceptionally well for him, and turned them out to pasture, a dignified retirement.

So mystical seemed Frankel's charms with racehorses, soon after his arrival there the southern California racing officialdom set out to discover what made Bobby's horses run. Frankel was called in, questioned, watched, charted, tested, and interrogated again. Officially hounded is a fair enough phrase. In a transposition of the rules of justice, the man was badgered more or less until cleared by the surmounting lack of evidence. Suspicion was based on all those winners he sent out.

Robert Frankel won with 22 percent of 4,792 starters during the 1970s, a remarkable achievement. He now splits the top ten standings in money won with stakes and allowance horses that win big races—on both coasts.

He is pictured here in the Hollywood Park walking ring with jockey Ruben Hernandez.

What racing officials learned ace handicappers knew all along. Frankel plays a fast game with horses, but he plays it straight arrow. His weapons are comprehensive care, conditioning, nutrition, and proper placement. Frankel tends to horses closely and completely, corrects problems and deficiencies, and enters them in races they have a fighting chance to win. In the paddock and walking ring Frankel horses glow with the health and alertness of properly-cared-for, well-trained animals. They rarely break out in a lather, let alone break down in races. They are mounted by leading jockeys. Win or not, they run their race. Normally they hold contending form for lengthy periods.

Concerning our topic, Frankel works with the condition book like a master, which he is. He wins claiming races, allowances, or stakes. Class rises or class drops he wins with equal frequency. Short or long, the same. Dirt or turf, the same. He matches a rider to horse expertly. Best of all, he matches horses to races. Frankel actually exploits the condition book, sometimes planning ahead by weeks. With few exceptions, Frankel horses are entered to win, a point the trainer himself has stressed in public forums since his early days. Frankel himself sees little mystery to his winning ways. It's a matter of fundamentals, he might say, alluding once more to the cumulative benefits of good care, the best feed, top conditioning, effective teaching, leading jockeys, and proper placement.

The following is Robert Frankel's training record, 1970–79.

Year	Starts	1st	2nd	3rd	Win Pct.	Money Won	Rank
1970	418	73	71	54	.17	$ 597,717	21
71	409	84	84	61	.20	645,374	20
72	447	112	79	68	.25	853,830	12
73	509	143	83	53	.28	1,344,670	7
74	451	101	76	61	.22	979,662	14
75	506	124	86	53	.24	1,242,128	9
76	439	93	71	46	.21	974,313	20
77	528	116	89	74	.22	1,147,130	10
78	563	105	103	81	.19	1,392,215	8
1979	521	113	87	83	.22	1,733,644	7
10-Yr.	4792	1064			.22	$10,910,683	

Frankel's ten-year record can be compared tellingly with that of Frank Martin, of New York, who during the decade claimed horses at will for the late Sigmund Sommer and who has won more money in the claiming game than any trainer in history. During 1970–79 Martin won $16,288,093, never ranked lower than eighth in money won, and outdistanced Frankel in that definitive category each season. Yet Martin started 7,466 horses, won with 20 percent of them just once (1974), and actually averaged $95 less per starter than did Frankel.

Indeed, Frankel of 1970–79 compares favorably with all-time great Frank Martin:

Records 1970–79	Frankel	Martin
Starts	4,792	7,466
Winners	1,064	1,244
Win Pct.	.22	.17
Money Won	$10,910,683	$16,288,093
Average Earnings per start	$2,275	$2,180

A man of immensely independent mind and murky personality, Robert Frankel keeps his own counsel, goes his own way, and generally steers clear of established offices and people he feels do not understand or accept him. Horsemen put off by his ways or manner are quick to salute his talent. No wonder.

During the 1980s Frankel has changed course completely. He no longer claims horses, his specialty. He concentrates on the stakes and allowances. Matters are proceeding swimmingly. Frankel ranked as high as thirteenth on the list of 1984 stakes-winning trainers, despite starting a low seventy-seven horses in the added-money events. In 1985, he ranked higher. The numbers looked like so:

	Sts	1	2	3	Pct.	Money Won	Rank
Frankel, Robert	77	14	21	8	.182	$1,941,766	13

In a surprising development of 1983, Frankel managed firm connections with leading international breeder Bertrom Firestone, who today sends the trainer a string of older runners having stakes potential. Some regard the tandem as racing's odd couple. But it's working. Frankel wins with the better horses as well, under all conditions, and is fully capable of handing Firestone a champion. If that happens, Frankel will be immediately contacted by other breeders and buyers of distinction in the sport. Frankel has opened an eastern division and is prepared for the future.

Yet a familiar cloud hangs over Frankel still. His ability to win early with younger developing horses remains undocumented. Statistics representing the past six seasons show that Frankel remains approximately a five percent trainer with maidens. Handicappers on the beam know to toss out the Frankel first-starters unblinkingly. If the truly important horses and goals will be met, Frankel must improve significantly in this vital arena. He must learn to take well-bred yearlings off the farms and develop them to their full potential at the racetrack. It's not easy, demanding of trainers a fine-tuned blend of patience, knowhow, technique, and assertiveness.

In these adventures, if I may tender a personal judgment, Frankel will be sustained. The man's talent is basic, and it is enormous. That kind of ability transfers nicely to all kinds of horses. Mistakes made in the beginning will give way to fundamental competence, and soon. And once again, in the interest of handicappers, Frankel will display a wizardry with the condition book, now placing developing horses in races perfectly suited to their recent records, physical maturity, and competitive seasoning. The horses will win, and win again.

Tom Ainslie once mused in print that if the American horseplayer has a best friend, it might be Frankel. By all means. By watching where he runs his horses, then reflecting on the matter, handicappers can also learn from Frankel much about condition books.

PART 2

ELIGIBILITY CONDITIONS AND DEVELOPING HORSES

CHAPTER 8

Nonclaiming
Three-Year-Olds

As a group, nonclaiming three-year-olds present handicapping problems peculiar to them, and eligibility conditions designed to facilitate their development represent both part of the problem and its likeliest solution. An unlikely solution is reliance on class-consistency handicapping, speed handicapping, or other methods that depend for their effectiveness on identifying accurate and stable indicators of true performance. The past performances of nonclaiming three-year-olds generally provide neither.

The reasons for this should be understandable. Three-year-olds are developing horses. Until they mature and settle, handicappers know less about them than they do about older horses. Class levels remain comparatively uncertain; form cycles uneven; distance, footing, and pace preferences inconclusive. Potentially outstanding three-year-olds can remain virtual mysteries for a long time, even to their owners and trainers. For handicappers, the problem is predictability. How to predict the results of races featuring developing horses? In this chapter, The Handicapper's Condition Book offers the best approach, one neither commonly understood nor practiced. The approach is analytical and interpretive, and is not easily translated into numbers or ratings.

Concerning predictability, three conditions conspire to conceal three-year-old class.

First, physique affects performance. The maturation of young thoroughbreds evolves dramatically during their second season, but that evolution can proceed rapidly, gradually, or slowly from horse to horse, depending on contributions from genetics, nurturing, and training.

Second, seasoning affects performance. The experiences young horses encounter in competition enhance or depress their racing abilities, and these experiences vary in kind and degree within weeks or months, contributing to effects on performance that also vary in kind and degree.

Third, the conditions of eligibility under which three-year-olds develop in physique and experience are themselves evolving, and in ways that alter the quality of the opposition and other crucial factors, particularly distance, from the less to the more demanding. Even as they grow and learn, three-year-olds compete under conditions that bring together increasingly fast and competitive horses.

The three circumstances are entirely interlocking, each influencing the others by degrees not entirely reflected by recent races or best efforts. In consequence, handicappers are less sustained by methods of analysis perfectly suited to well-established patterns of performance. Big wins by three-year-olds are not repeated. Dull efforts turn golden next time out. The upsets of one kind or another can be considered characteristic of nonclaiming horses that are still finding their way.

What to do?

While owners and trainers indulge the luxury of finding out about their most promising three-year-olds, handicappers must predict the outcomes of their races with satisfactory consistency and profit. In these efforts, absolutely the key to working effectively with races for nonclaiming three-year-olds is a shrewd, comprehensive understanding of the eligibility conditions under which their careers progress. In effect, the quality of performance typically demanded by today's conditions becomes the standard by which past performance tables are best analyzed and evaluated. Where past performance patterns indicate the typical class demands of today's conditions will be met, handicappers can accept three-year-olds as contenders. If not, horses can be eliminated.

Ultimately, contenders can be separated by handicapping procedures that honor the developing nature of three-year-olds and are designed to establish which horse is best suited to today's conditions. Some three-year-olds fit nonclaiming conditions nicely; others excel them. Many are outright frauds. Which profile fits best?

To answer that question, handicappers need to consider (a) typical patterns of development among three-year-olds, as reflected by the kinds of races they enter, (b) typical demands of class associated with each kind of race, and (c) the three-year-old record of each entrant.

By examining the kinds of races individual three-year-olds have entered, handicappers can relate particular patterns of development to stereotypical patterns, and better predict the kinds of races in which developing horses are more likely to succeed.

By comprehending the qualities of class demonstrated under previously contested conditions, handicappers can relate current and potential class to normal class demands of various eligibility conditions, and decide how well horses fit specific conditions.

These considerations inform handicappers as to which three-year-olds are suited to the conditions of the race, and which are not. The next sections provide the specific handicapping guidelines.

PATTERNS OF DEVELOPMENT

Early races selected by its management provide handicappers with first indications of a three-year-old's potential. The horse's performances confirm or disconfirm original expectations and influence selection of the next spot. For example, three-year-olds that show owners and trainers they can run fast and hard do not get entered early in claiming races, unless serious infirmities should soon surface.

When analyzing nonclaiming races for three-year-olds, handicappers benefit if they attend to the sequence of conditions under which the horses have so far competed. Developing horses proceed into the mainstream of competition in stereotypical ways. Depending on abilities exhibited early on, they follow one of four basic patterns:

Class A

Maiden, nonclaiming
Allowance, nonwinners other than maiden or claiming
Allowance, nonwinners twice other than maiden or claiming
Allowance, nonwinners three times other than maiden or claiming, or
Conditioned stakes
Allowance, nonwinners four times other than maiden or claiming, or
Open stakes, listed or lower grade
Grade 1 and Grade 2 stakes

Class B

Maiden, nonclaiming
Allowance, nonwinners other than maiden or claiming
Allowance, nonwinners twice other than maiden or claiming
Allowance, nonwinners three times other than maiden or claiming, or
Conditioned stakes, or open unlisted stakes
Claiming races, at relatively high price brackets, or
Allowance, nonwinners three times other than maiden or claiming
Claiming races, at high to moderate price brackets, or
Classified allowances, or
Minor stakes

Class C

Maiden, nonclaiming
Allowance, nonwinners other than maiden or claiming
Allowance, nonwinners twice other than maiden or claiming, or
Claiming races, at relatively high price brackets
Claiming races, at high to moderate price brackets, or
Allowances, nonwinners once or twice (if eligible)
Claiming races, at moderate to low price brackets

Class D

Maiden claiming
Claiming races, at moderate to high price brackets, or
Allowance, nonwinners other than maiden or claiming
Claiming races, at moderate to lower price brackets
Claiming races, at relatively low price brackets

The classifications overlap, the sequences vary. Class A three-year-olds of April, competing then in conditioned stakes or under nonwinners three time allowances, may be struggling against Class C claiming horses by September. An occasional maiden claiming horse, typed Class D by its first start, may get going temporarily and win one or two allowance races, after which it might be tested in a conditioned stakes.

Regardless of variations in horses' records, handicappers prosper once they recognize the basic pattern of development most characteristic of each three-year-old. Usually, the sequence of best performances, however embedded in the total record, tells which basic pattern represents the animal's future.

Class A three-year-olds, by far the smallest group, usually complete nonwinners allowance conditions with ease. Then they trounce horses eligible to restricted stakes. They treat open but minor stakes competition with almost the same nonchalance. Variations in their patterns might include a loss or two, perhaps due to unfamiliar distances or footing, or merely on a day they disliked the rider's handling and refused to respond.

Handicappers notice Class A division leaders more by their manner of victory than by the victories themselves, which after all have been accomplished against preliminary competition. Regardless of final times or winning lengths, Class A horses reveal reserves of speed and power as they roar through maiden and nonwinners allowance conditions. The same when they enter restricted stakes. Only when they face other Class A horses do small differences between them count.

No matter the conditions completed, all other three-year-olds can be expected to stumble a number of times as they progress to true levels of performance. The progression of eligibility conditions recognizes reality. It provides for lots of restricted competition where horses can demonstrate basic abilities and preferences as to distance, footing, and pace. While finding out which conditions suit them best, the horses lose. Handicappers need not stumble so much. If they honor eligibility conditions by refusing to bet on three-year-olds that do not meet the stricter demands at each higher step, handicappers avoid the biggest obstacles to success in these races.

Here are customary class demands at each step, and the most suitable past performance profiles:

MAIDENS

Unexceptional three-year-olds can win maiden races for that age by combining moderate speed and basic competitiveness. The two qualities permit horses to race near the early pace, and to challenge for the advantage while rounding the far turn or in the stretch. When facing fields low on talent, that's enough.

Even three-year-olds lacking noticeable competitive spirit, but having enough early speed to set the pace, will break maiden ranks, eventually, when speed sends them to the front unthreatened and sustains them there unchallenged.

As revealed in Part 1 of this book, handicappers can predict the outcomes of maiden races with better-than-average frequency. Fred Davis's discoveries that second-place finishers in races for older maidens win more than 250 percent their rightful share, while first-time starters win less than 50 percent their rightful share, apply to maiden races limited to three-year-olds. They apply more reliably as the calender year progresses.

Careful handicappers protect themselves from talented first starters, particularly during the first months of the year, by invoking minimum speed standards. In sprints, second-place finishers must have earned speed ratings of eighty-six or better. To win now, first starters must finish within two-and-one-half seconds of the track distance record, a tough proposition.

The significance of the second-place finish last out in maiden races for three-year-olds reflects something fundamental about developing horses. They are likelier to shine once they can combine basic talents with physical maturity, effective schooling, and competitive seasoning.

Handicappers realize the hard truth of that when maiden winners move to allowance races restricted to three-year-olds that have not won a specified number of nonclaiming races.

PRELIMINARY NONWINNER ALLOWANCES

Until three-year-olds have won two allowance races, they compete under preliminary conditions. Class demands typically remain less than severe and prolonged. That being the case, decent horses can be expected to survive these conditions in time, and good horses often breeze through the conditions, even when not particularly familiar or comfortable with the distance, footing, or pace.

NONWINNERS OTHER THAN MAIDEN
OR CLAIMING

Allowance races for nonwinners other than maiden or claiming races normally demand more than moderate speed and basic competitiveness. These races demand stronger combinations of speed and competitiveness, plus other racing attributes. The conditions and their class demands:

Allowance, nonwinners other than maiden or claiming	Moderate-to-high early speed; moderate competitiveness; late drive; moderate determination; at the route, add stamina

A brief digression is appropriate, to comment on the several qualities of thoroughbred class, as listed here and throughout the remainder of the chapter.

Racing attributes are essentially relative and qualitative, and best understood in those terms, particularly when combined to various degrees. Definitions of the above qualities and other attributes of class are presented in an accompanying chart. The definitions attempt to translate abstract terms into abilities observable in races. If handicappers become familiar with the definitions now, subsequent discussion will gain more common meaning and interpretation.

Speed handicappers might employ final times, fractional times, par times, and pace ratings to define suitable performance standards under various conditions of eligibility, but this book does not recommend that approach, especially for appraising developing three-year-olds. Speed figures translate poorly between different classes of nonclaiming competition, as from maiden conditions to nonwinners allowances, or allowances to stakes, and they do not apply when distances change.

More important, speed figures too often obscure the combinations of attributes they intend to reflect. Worse, they can mislead handicappers into believing the numbers reflect qualities they actually do not. Classy horses are usually fast, but many fast horses are none too classy. Misinterpretations of this kind, attributing to horses qualities they do not possess, are far too prevalent in relation to developing three-year-olds. Accurate time figures help, by all

DEFINITIONS OF RACING ATTRIBUTES

High early speed	Able to set or attend a relatively rapid early pace.
Basic competitiveness	Notwithstanding ability, demonstrates desire to run faster than other horses.
Late drive	Able to sustain approximate rate of speed in final quarter mile of race, even while tiring.
Readiness	Extent to which horse has mastered the mechanics and basic techniques of racing; adequate experience in competition.
Determination	Digs in when challenged; tries harder when pressured.
Willingness	Readily attempts to overcome obstacles or mishaps encountered during the running of races. Responds eagerly to challenge.
Relaxed stride	Running under smooth, easy control of rider; responsive to handling.
Stamina	Capable of competing at middle distances without tiring.
Endurance	Keeps to task, despite running problems or relatively continuous pressure from other horses. Can compete at longer and classic distances.
Courage	Demonstrates unusual combinations of speed, endurance, determination, and willingness, usually under prolonged periods of pressure or repeated challenge.

means. But when eligibility conditions toughen, ratings obtained under cheaper conditions absolutely must be adjusted to account for effects of faster competition. Few handicappers possess the time, energy, and know-how to calculate accurate figures, in the first instance, and to make proper adjustments when eligibility conditions change.

End of digression.

The following past performance profiles qualify under nonwinners once allowances:

1. **Horses that have registered successively faster and more competitive efforts under similar conditions, and have not failed to beat those conditions more than six times.**

2. **Handy maiden winners that set or attended a relatively rapid early pace before passing horses or drawing clear, and earning a speed rating of eighty-seven or better.**

3. **Horses that finished in-the-money or ran close under similar conditions last out, after challenging for the lead at some point during the final stages of the race.**

At the route, also prefer:

4. **Horses that have shown significant improvement and finished competitively when first tested at middle distances.**

5. **Regardless of final times, horses that have set or attended the pace before drawing away to win by two lengths or more versus maidens.**

Regarding maiden graduates last out, the qualifying performances must have been accomplished without tiring noticeably.

Impressive maiden winners at the route are invariably a threat to repeat when entered under nonwinners once allowances at the same or related routes. The horses prefer the distance, a fundamental advantage.

Numerous entries of nonwinners once allowance races for nonclaiming three-year-olds will show maiden victories and allowance attempts of dubious character. Handicappers avoid confusion by eliminating horses whose records do not reflect *all* the qualities normally needed to defeat nonwinners once contenders. Without a certain measure of determination, for example, horses will usually fall back when hard pressed. If the past performances do not reflect a determined effort, eliminate the horses.

Certain eliminations are run-of-the-mill:

1. Horses that have lost more than six similar races, unless the most recent race or two show significantly improved performance.

When confronted by the much-improved performance, among several mediocre ones, handicappers should search for corroborating evidence that a real change has occurred, such as improved workout times or a favorable jockey switch.

2. Horses moving into allowances from claiming conditions, unless only a single claiming race shows and that resulted in an impressive victory characterized by a fast clocking.

3. Horses that must survive a much faster early pace than previously encountered, unless they are lightly raced and completed

the maiden win with obviously ample reserves of speed and energy.

4. Speed horses that cannot be rated efficiently and are stretching out to distances longer by a quarter mile or more.

In general, where qualifications remain dubious, three-year-olds are better eliminated. Regarding three-year-old racing, handicappers prosper by accentuating the positive, and distrusting all else. It pays to limit investment to horses well suited to the conditions, and to concentrate on three-year-olds whose previous performances give promise they can excel what is typical of today's conditions.

NONWINNERS TWICE OTHER THAN MAIDEN OR CLAIMING

Most likely under nonwinners twice allowance conditions are three-year-olds that recently scored impressively under nonwinners once allowances. Most unlikely are horses that struggled under nonwinners once conditions, winning barely or unremarkably in ordinary time and manner. Unlikely too are horses that once scored impressively under nonwinners once conditions, but have failed repeatedly to complete this next step. It is not a giant step, to be sure.

Almost invariably, contenders for nonwinners twice purses must defeat horses that have already won an allowance race impressively. And the persuasive allowance win usually reflects the qualities of class typically demanded at the nonwinners twice level. These are:

Allowance, nonwinners twice other than maiden or claiming	High speed; moderately strong competitiveness; late drive; moderate-to-high determination; willingness; at the route, stamina and moderate endurance

At this point, the extent to which three-year-olds can combine the several qualities of class begins to make the difference. High speed but low competitiveness does not go far. The concept of potential class, as reflected by the horses' entire pattern of three-year-old performance, enters the handicapper's analysis, and often supersedes the details of recent races or best efforts.

Yet, and because the overall quality of three-year-old competition has so declined in major racing, nonwinners twice allowance conditions many times are not much stiffer than those at the previous step. At times exceptional performance may be required, but only sometimes. Nonwinners twice races bring together horses rather more alike than dissimilar from those that win nonwinners once races.

The speed quotient goes up to high. A more sustained late drive is demanded. The competitive qualities of willingness and determination come into play more, but not forcefully.

While remembering that three-year-olds capable of winning nonwinners once allowance races in ordinary time and style will also beat nonwinners twice conditions eventually, and in like manner, handicappers concerned with profits generally restrict play to horses sporting more distinguished profiles:

1. Horses that recently completed nonwinners once conditions handily, with notable reserves of speed and power at their command.

2. Horses whose nonwinners once win last out looked decidedly more impressive than the maiden win.

3. Horses whose few losses under nonwinners twice allowance conditions were consistently strong efforts in fast time.

The horses have demonstrated a touch of class, enough to qualify under preliminary allowance conditions. A nontiring close finish in par time qualifies. So does a finish within six lengths of the winner, where a blazing early pace took its toll.

If the early pace of the most recent losing race under nonwinners twice conditions were faster than today's probable fractions, and this kind of contender figures to grab the lead easily, it will likely hold the advantage, even if challenged by similar horses in the latter stages.

Three-year-olds en route to better races win nonwinners twice allowance races so nonchalantly that handicappers hardly should bother with horses unable to qualify with one of the above profiles. Over a season, strict eliminations in nonwinners twice races cut losses appreciably.

Alternatively, many handicappers accept marginal horses in these races, arguing the conditions are preliminary and permit laxity. No doubt handicappers win a few at decent odds this way, but I submit their seasonal results would improve if they passed on the following:

1. Any unexceptional tiring win under nonwinners once allowances.

2. A pair of uncontested front-running victories under maiden and nonwinners once conditions, interspersed with losses when challenged early.

3. Significantly poorer performances under nonwinners twice conditions than in races under prior conditions.

4. More than six losses under nonwinners twice conditions.

5. Successive losses in ordinary time under nonwinners twice conditions, following prolonged stretch battles in which the horses finished all-out in fast time.

6. Broke maiden conditions under maiden claiming conditions.

7. Any come-from-behinder whose nonwinners once score resulted from an early pace duel that weakened other contenders unusually, and not from the winner's particular stretch power.

At this point, some potentially outstanding three-year-olds are taught to control their natural speed and release it late, at the rider's discretion. That's different. Charles Whittingham resorts to this tactic every season in southern California. His talented horses lose until they learn how to deliver the late blows. Finally, they romp under preliminary nonwinners allowances. If three-year-olds can ease into contention from far back on the far turn, then unleash a late drive of twenty-four seconds or less, they are contenders in nonwinners twice allowance fields.

8. Horses whose recent efforts indicate dulling or deteriorating form, and whose stables do not fare well with developing horses.

9. Horses that defeated maidens after pressing or tracking a fast early pace, but could not handle nonwinners once contenders after challenging comparable fractional times.

10. While winning, horses that raced sufficiently "green" to warrant chart comment.

Strict adherence to elimination rules gets handicappers to the guts of nonwinners twice allowance races, events written for better three-year-olds on the path to greater accomplishments.

NONWINNERS TWICE ALLOWANCES: THE DIVIDING LINE

Nonwinners twice allowance conditions serve handicappers as the dividing line. Beyond that point, the quality of competition increases intensely. Horses eligible to win must combine the several qualities of class in impressively strong degrees.

Moreover, these classier three-year-olds must now satisfy appropriate standards of form and distance too. They must be comfortable with the footing. They must indicate they can survive the probable pace. And whatever basic advantages horses might enjoy, these must not be nullified by the probable effects of jockey, weight, and post position.

In sum, contenders must not only equal the class demands of eligibility conditions, they must also check out impressively on the fundamental factors of handicapping.

Notwithstanding all of this, handicapping by the conditions is guided by an overriding concern about class. To qualify as contenders under nonwinners three times allowance conditions or better, three-year-olds' past performances must show the horses possess the several qualities of class combined to considerable extent. Big winners under nonwinners twice allowance conditions do not immediately qualify for nonwinners three times conditions, although moving just a step ahead in class. That step regularly confronts horses that soon will win stakes races.

Other fundamentals of handicapping now become correspondingly more important, lest these factors nullify class advantages or render them inoperative. Concerning the appropriate standards of form and distance for nonclaiming three-year-olds under testing eligibility conditions, handicappers prosper if they eliminate horses in accordance with the following considerations and guidelines:

Form

When analyzing the form of older horses, handicappers depend upon recent competitive experiences as accurate predictors of form cycles that improve and deteriorate in relatively normal and predictable patterns. Problems of form analysis generally relate to indicators of soundness and fitness.

With nonclaiming three-year-olds, form analysis involves different considerations and problems. If not absolutely so, most three-year-olds enjoy states of relative soundness and fitness. These horses are young, sturdy, energetic. Aside from checking the past performances to decide whether recent races and workouts signal acceptable fitness, the handicapper's problem with three-year-olds can be reduced to apprehending the youngsters' readiness.

Developing horses cannot do their best unless they receive effective schooling and adequate seasoning. Those are the concerns of handicappers. Effective schooling. Adequate seasoning. Is the three-year-old ready?

Advancing three-year-olds should demonstrate readiness not only to race correctly and without fear or hesitation, but also to cope with the physical and temperamental stresses of competing against successively punishing opposition.

Depending on the carefulness and business of their trainers, schooling of three-year-olds includes techniques of galloping, standing in and breaking from the starting gate, familiarity with the paddock and walking ring, experiments with equipment and shoes, sensitivity to the jockey's hand signals, running around turns and into straightaways, where lead changes should occur, running alongside the rail, and running behind, in front of, and alongside other moving horses.

Not many three-year-olds benefit from this kind of schooling prior to entering their first races. They learn even as they race. If they do not master the subject matter before they progress beyond nonwinners twice allowances, chances are bad habits will hold them back unduly, or maybe doom them thereafter.

A common occurrence upsetting to handicappers involves impressive speed horses that respond to a kind of handling by jockeys, but not to another kind. A powerful win might follow a dull effort in which the rider applied early restraint, but the colt resisted or sulked, simply refusing to extend itself or emptying its energies in a tug-of-war prior to the stretch drive. Next time, urged to run free and loose from the start, the colt wins in a breeze. What will happen next? Who knows?

Or, the rider's early restraint might follow a triumphant romp in which a colt was permitted to run on its own, and that splendid performance is followed now by a puzzling losing performance. The tight early hold on its fighting spirit might continue for a numbr of races, resulting in successive losses of energy and races. Suddenly, the colt explodes again, winning by half a furlong at 8 to 1. The colt has learned finally to respond to the jockey's restraint with relaxed stride and effort, and to take off strongly when roused.

Numerous like patterns contribute to the schooling and seasoning of three-year-olds, concurrent with the losses of aggravated handicappers. As this book intends to emphasize, the surest of remedies involves supplementing the study of past performances with a scheduled observation of horses in their formative races. Sophisticated trip handicapping is the key to numerous three-year-old races.

Before accepting nonclaiming three-year-olds on form, when entered against horses that won two or more races of allowance grade or better, handicappers should insist the horses:

1. Break from the gate alertly and smoothly, not sluggishly or badly.

Gate problems become obvious to most handicappers, and though rarely overlooked, often are misinterpreted. Too many handicappers use the incidents to excuse performances. It's far safer to relate the incidents to improper or incomplete schooling, and demand evidence, such as sharp workouts from the gate, that the bad habits have been corrected.

2. Secure early position calmly and efficiently, and respond to the rider's rating and hand signals cooperatively.

So many talented three-year-olds lose nonwinners allowance races due to poor rapport with their jockeys that handicappers cut losses appreciably once they pay attention to the predicaments. Handicappers look for a tight or pulling hold against a thrusting stride. The jockey's hold will usually be short on the reins, tense, and nearer to the neck, not loose or long or relaxed, and near to his own body. Horse and jockey may not fight, but each will struggle against the other's force. On close observation, the struggles are despairingly evident. In truly desperate circumstances, more readily observed, horses will climb or toss their head wildly, trying to get release.

3. Demonstrate appropriate racing habits; respond to typical situations instinctively and coolly.

Expressed positively, the guideline is a catchall. It includes taking the turns, changing leads, maneuvering between horses, moving out and around, reacting to the whip without bearing in or lugging out, settling in behind other horses, running with relaxed gait (crucially important in routes), and continuing to exert its energies when a horse gets to the front.

Handicappers can agree that better young horses will suffer one or more deficits of readiness but win still. If the bad habits persist or worsen, however, handicappers had better eliminate the horses, and certainly so when they arrive at eligibility conditions that invite multiple allowance race winners.

4. Have not received a shellacking last time out, when entered prematurely against seasoned horses under conditions for which they have not been adequately prepared.

A situation badly misunderstood by horsemen and handicappers alike involves the seasoning three-year-olds have received, in contrast to that of the opposition. Unready three-year-olds can suffer greatly from hasty or aggressive entry against competition they cannot yet handle.

The classic blunders find solid prospects in stakes races for which they have not been sufficiently prepared. Either the horses have not yet developed the combinations of speed, endurance, and determination demanded by stakes conditions, or they have yet to experience anything comparable to the exhaustive stretch responses often required to win those events.

If nicely developing three-year-olds suddenly lose miserably after all-out responses versus advanced competition, handicappers must decide whether the frustrated exertions will deaden the form or enthusiasm. If a veritable shellacking has occurred, handicappers can fairly anticipate a setback, and should require a respite and more appropriate conditions of eligibility before expecting three-year-olds will snap back to previous form.

To a lesser extent the problem can arise whenever three-year-olds bypass the next appropriate step as they move through non-claiming eligibility conditions.

Winners of allowance races, for nonwinners other than maiden or claiming, next tackle allowances for nonwinners three times other than maiden or claiming, at a longer distance. Worse, the horses enter conditioned stakes that coincidentally have been scheduled in tune with their racing schedules.

Or, winners of allowance races for nonwinners twice other than maiden or claiming start next in open stakes, before experiencing the less rugged conditioned kind that typically bar the highly seasoned, farthest advanced three-year-olds in training.

Or, multiple allowance winners or minor stakes winners are asked to defeat a genuine Grade 1 article in that kind of event.

In situations of that kind chances for the proverbial shellacking improve, and so do chances for the resulting deterioration of form.

Handicappers should expect three-year-olds to proceed to eligibility conditions for which the manner of performance in their latest races qualifies them. If they venture too far too soon, anticipate a temporary regression.

To be sure, the cream of the Class A group, those few three-year-olds that combine the several qualities of class in maximum degrees, can move along quickly and smartly under all circumstances. But all other grades of three-year-olds might end in trouble of varying kinds and degrees. The better the grade of horse, and the closer the race demands to present preparations, the likelier form will survive.

Distance

By spring the past performances of most regularly running three-year-olds reveal the horses that have competed at six furlongs, at six-and-one-half furlongs, at a mile, at a mile and one-sixteenth, and probably farther than that. Those starting in summer will reveal similar patterns by fall. A few races likely will have occurred on turf.

Of the complicating issues inherent in the handicapping of three-year-olds, nothing could be more conspicuous than their repeated entrance in races at distances they have not yet traveled. Is the three-year-old suited to today's distance? While stables indulge the luxury of finding out, handicappers must anticipate their discoveries.

To do so consistently, handicappers cannot rely exclusively on distance principles, as those apply to older runners. Too often the past performances do not contain a race at the exact distance. Even when they do, the lines and charts often contain insufficient and therefore unreliable evidence of the horses' preferences.

Instead, handicappers must often make judgments about three-year-olds' comfort at new distances from (a) performances at related distances, (b) demonstrated class and form, and (c) established developmental patterns of stables. This information is best interpreted in a context that considers the class and readiness demands of eligibility conditions.

An improving colt of good connections might be acceptable while moving from sprint to route under allowances for nonwinners twice other than maiden or claiming. The same colt and move would not be accepted under allowances for nonwinners three times other than maiden or claiming. Not only has the distance changed importantly, so has the quality of the competition.

Unavailable or inconclusive performances at exact distances notwithstanding, and regardless of eligibility conditions, nonclaiming three-year-olds can usually be evaluated on distance rather surely. That is because distance considerations for better three-year-olds are solidly rooted in performances at related distances.

Related distances can be grouped as (a) sprints, or races around one turn, (b) middle distances, or races of one mile to one mile and three-sixteenths, and (c) classic distances, or races of one-and-one-quarter miles and farther.

By applying the concept of related distances wisely and confidently, handicappers can judge the majority of situations involving better three-year-olds and distance. Two basic guidelines point the way:

1. At exact or related distances, accept horses that have won, finished second, or finished within three lengths of the winner.

2. At new or unfamiliar distances, credit horses that have won, finished second, or finished within three lengths at distances *both* shorter and longer by a furlong or farther.

The second guideline emerges—again—from the probability studies of Fred Davis. It gets good mileage with nonclaiming three-year-olds. It helps especially with the challenging and more-frequently-than-ever-carded distances of six-and-a-half furlongs, seven furlongs, and one mile.

Of the classic situation among developing three-year-olds, that of first stretching out from sprints to middle distances, handicappers absolutely must ponder beforehand the bases upon which horses will be acceptable, or will not. The circumstance is routine. In major racing it can be taken for granted that three-year-olds demonstrating even traces of ability will sooner rather than later be tested at longer distances.

Knowledge of eligibility conditions helps handicappers predict which three-year-olds can pass muster. In maiden races, or in allowance races for nonwinners once or twice other than maiden and claiming, three-year-olds stretching out for the first time often can be accepted at face value. Accept horses whose records reflect:

a. Brilliant speed, of the kind that pronounces the horse an unmistakable leader of the division.

b. A definitive win at the preceding step, of the kind that indicates ample reserves of speed and power.

A horse is able to set or to attend the early pace, then draw away strongly in the final quarter mile, leaving the others easily and finishing without tiring.

c. An even effort or better until the prestretch call, then a final quarter completed in twenty-four seconds or less while gaining on the leaders.

If stretching out of this kind is accompanied by a favorable jockey switch, and the maneuvers are carried out by stables with reputations for distance racing, handicappers can award extra credit, particularly if none of the other contenders give indications that they prefer the distance.

Concerning the top two circumstances, the kind of towering performances referred to rarely end at the finish of six furlongs. They stretch out, especially under preliminary conditions of eligibility which so many three-year-olds use to develop their distance talents.

Under more advanced allowance conditions, or in stakes races, handicappers benefit by remaining strict about three-year-olds and distance. If stretching out from sprint to route for the first time, only horses that have logged exceptional performances in nonwinners twice sprints, flashing strong combinations of late speed and endurance, can be expected to survive.

Not sensitive enough to demands of advanced eligibility conditions, many handicappers accept three-year-olds switching to routes under any conditions as long as they have completed the final quarters of their latest sprints in twenty-four seconds or less. A bit more discrimination pays better, especially in races open to multiple allowance winners. If they finish strongly, without tiring, such horses might be accepted occasionally, but only when all of the following criteria are also satisfied:

a. Regardless of its fast finishes, the three-year-old must possess enough early speed to gain a favorable position within five lengths of the early pace of routes.

Three-year-olds so devoid of speed that they bring up the rear of route races rarely win first attempts at middle distances, no matter what happens up front. As plodders, these need not only added ground but more experience before they understand the idea is to advance to the front. Late-running sprinters do not ordinarily stretch out effectively. The extra ground relieves them of the late punch they retain at six furlongs.

b. The horse must retain top form, or at least show sharply improving form.

c. The horse must not have run rank or green in sprints, or have given signs it cannot be rated efficiently at the slower pace of the longer distances.

Since its publication in 1981, Steve Roman's research on dosage, the ratio of speed to stamina in a Thoroughbred's immediate four-generation pedigree, has illuminated as never before the most prestigious races carded in this country for the very best of three-year-olds. The dosage evidence contributes the third guideline on three-year-olds and distance:

3. At classic distances under Grade 1 or Grade 2 stakes conditions, prefer three-year-olds having a dosage index of 4.00 or less.

The point can hardly be overstated. Relying on dosage indexes to separate the cream of the three-year-old crop at one mile and one-quarter or farther has worked with astonishing reliability. Since

1940, no less, no horse having a dosage index above 4.00 has won the Kentucky Derby, and just two have won the Belmont Stakes.

Now that near-unanimous 1985 pre-Derby favorite Chief's Crown (DI 5.00) has struggled in third, unable even to hold place in the long Kentucky Derby stretch, handicappers feeding on dosage figures to get bonanza payoffs at Louisville will probably see the next years' prices fall. No matter. Dosage applies to the Jersey Derby, the Belmont, the Travers, the Super Derby, the Breeders' Cup Classic, and the several fall handicaps in which the three-year-olds challenge their elders.

Handicappers will benefit importantly once they begin evaluating three-year-olds' chances at new or unfamiliar routes by considering the fundamental factors of class and distance in combination. Once again, knowledge of eligibility conditions helps. Because three-year-olds develop as they do, and conditions of eligibility progress as they do, many three-year-olds move forward in distance and class at the same time.

The combined challenges of longer, unfamiliar distances and better, unfamiliar opponents usually mean defeat for unexceptional three-year-olds.

Handicappers can rule out three-year-olds if they have looked unexceptional and attempt to combine any of the following class-distance moves:

Class Jumps	Distance Changes
From a maiden claiming race to non-winners once allowances	From a sprint to a middle distance
From nonwinner twice allowances to nonwinner three times allowances or a conditioned stakes	From a mile to a mile and one-eighth or farther
From any nonwinner allowances to an open stakes	From any middle distance to a mile and one-quarter
From a claiming race to a nonwinners twice allowance	From any shorter distance to a mile and one-half
From any lower grade stakes to the Grade 1 kind	

In each instance, while calling into play the qualities of stamina and endurance required over longer distances, three-year-olds must simultaneously tap whatever reserves of speed, willingness, and determination are needed to overcome better horses. Few three-year-olds can summon all of this at once.

Under certain circumstances, finally, and regardless of eligibility conditions, when nonclaiming three-year-olds below Class A switch to longer distances, handicappers know enough not to accept the risks. Do not accept three-year-olds at new or unfamiliar longer distances when:

1. The distance is a mile or a mile and one-sixteenth; the post position is ten, eleven, or twelve; and the horses must be gunned to gain early position into the clubhouse turn.

2. Form is less than peaked, weight exceeds 120, and the horses have not won handily at shorter distances under weight within five pounds.

3. The horses cannot be rated kindly.

4. The jockeys are not familiar with the horses, are not local or national leaders, and have not won with at least 15 percent (12 percent in New York or southern California) of their mounts.

5. The horses are front-runners and the probable early pace figures rugged and fast.

6. The past performances reveal patterns of alternating sprints and routes, none too successful.

The last circumstance is deadly. Back and forth the three-year-olds go. A race or two might have been on turf. The patterns suggest (a) indecisive handling or (b) inability to get any distance comfortably.

ADVANCED NONWINNERS ALLOWANCES

Once nonclaiming three-year-olds proceed to races for previous winners of two races of allowance grade or better, whatever talents, qualities, and preferences they combine must surface in impressive degrees. Class demands rise noticeably. Handicappers limit play to horses that qualify in full measure. Either that or their chances for profits diminish. Handicappers should not forget that winners of these races are ticketed for action in stakes.

NONWINNERS THREE TIMES OTHER
THAN MAIDEN OR CLAIMING

Advanced allowances almost invariably demand the several qualities of class, combined to impressive degrees. The conditions alert handicappers to insist on creditable class:

Allowance, nonwinners three times other than maiden or claiming	High speed; late drive; endurance; readiness; willingness, determination; all of the above combined in relatively large measure; at the route, also suitability to exact or related distances, relaxed stride, and high stamina

Beyond that classy combination of attributes, contenders must have served notice they can cope with the footing and probable pace. At middle distances or farther, exceptions should be restricted to horses whose earlier wins imply large supplies of speed and power in reserve, or to sufficiently competitive horses of high early speed that figure to control the early pace without overexertion.

Handicappers sensitive to the superior class demands of nonwinners three times allowances do not err often if they eliminate three-year-olds that have:

1. Finished all-out or driving in ordinary time under nonwinners twice allowance conditions, even if won.

2. Lost three consecutive races under nonwinners three times allowances, unless each effort has reflected relatively superior ability and competitiveness.

3. Displayed increasingly dull form while losing two or more consecutive nonwinners three times races.

4. Started for a claiming price at any time subsequent to the first satisfactory three-year-old performance.

5. Won two allowance races impressively but were humiliated in stakes competition.

6. Have a front-running style, are switching from sprint to route, and figure to contend with a rapid, rugged early pace.

The eliminations honor the class factor, especially in relation to form, distance, and pace, fundamentals all. Handicappers should not practice leniency.

The next step is simple to announce, difficult to complete. Find the classiest of the remaining contenders. If nothing about the probable pace or the assigned jockey, weight, and post position threatens to nullify its advantages, the class of the field gets the play. A mere edge can be enough. Handicappers are encouraged to favor the following performance profiles:

1. Recent races reveal a decisive nonwinners twice allowance score, followed by an even effort or stronger in an open stakes.

Potentially elite three-year-olds often follow a second allowance win with entry in stakes. An acceptable performance under open stakes conditions deserves extra favor, a logical position supported strongly by probability studies.

2. The horse is lightly raced and strongly on the upgrade, as indicated by stylishly impressive wins versus maidens and under preliminary nonwinners allowance conditions.

The above profiles remind handicappers that advanced nonwinners allowances are written for developing horses markedly on the rise. Contenders should sport performance patterns closely tied to the purposes of eligibility conditions. Under these conditions and immediately beyond, Ainslie's classic portrait of the nicely bred, lightly raced, improving three-year-olds from good barns that have accomplished everything asked in high style and merely are moving along to the next stop in the competition is absolutely the kind on which handicappers fasten their attention. Because these comers reveal class of a higher order than allowance grade, they are legitimately the best selections of the day or week.

When solid handicappers spot these contenders in allowance fields, they suspend calculations, except to check the odds and ponder the size of the bet.

NONWINNERS FOUR TIMES OTHER THAN MAIDEN OR CLAIMING

Although top three-year-olds at major tracks normally proceed to stakes before they bother to win four allowance races, nonwinners four times allowances remain attractive conditions, and even stakes winners still eligible will return to claim these juicy winner shares.

Handicappers have every right to expect contenders for these monies to have competed well in open stakes competition, or to have won a conditioned stakes already. In fact, they might insist on it. The stakes caliber of potential winners is so common, handicappers are rightly encouraged to discard three-year-olds that have already tried conditioned stakes but lost in any display of ordinariness. If the conditioned event were won by a potential star of the division, the horses should have finished second or third.

More automatic eliminations apply to three-year-olds that have revealed themselves to be of allowance potential only. Handicappers can eliminate:

1. Horses that have won three allowance races handily but have been slaughtered when entered in stakes competition.

2. Horses that struggled with nonwinners three times conditions for a time, before winning in ordinary style.

3. Horses entered to be claimed at any time.

4. Horses that won a third allowance event a time ago, but since that time have not won and have never been entered in a stakes.

In their efforts to separate contenders by finding the classiest horse, handicappers look for:

1. Any lightly raced three-year-old from a leading barn that is dropping back to allowances after recently contesting the final parts of Grade 1 or Grade 2 stakes.

2. Horses that finished in-the-money or within three lengths of the winner in an open stakes having a relatively large value on the local purse schedule.

3. Horses that have won a conditioned stakes, provided the time or manner of victory has been genuinely impressive.

4. Horses that have won three allowance races in short order and, despite not having an acceptable stakes performance to their credit, have revealed the several qualities of thoroughbred class, combined in greater degree than those allowance conditions required.

The last profile merely reminds handicappers to prefer horses of better than allowance grade, which is solely what should interest them when confronting these most advanced conditions of the nonwinners allowance series.

STAKES FOR THREE-YEAR-OLDS

Better nonclaiming three-year-olds eventually sort themselves out in a program of stakes designed to accomplish the sorting. The races assume well-calculated positions in a hierarchy. At the base are conditioned stakes; at the pinnacle, Grade 1 events. In between are lower-grade, listed, and ungraded unlisted open stakes, which welcome all comers. Of these, Grade 2 stakes offer sizeable purses to three-year-olds that cannot defeat the handfuls of top-grade standouts, yet deserve high recognition and distinction.

Although similar in structure to stakes schedules for older horses, three-year-old stakes programs differ in purpose and programming, and horses of each age group proceed to appropriate stakes conditions in different ways. Older horses move almost directly to races intended for their established class. Stakes series for specific classes of horses tend to be clustered within closer time frames, and older horses do not often enter stakes not appropriate for their class, whether lower or higher. To comprehend the relative quality of older stakes competition, handicappers need understand little more than which horses generally run well for what kind of purses.

Stakes schedules for three-year-olds intend rather a more assorted, more graduated array of possibilities, so that developing horses can proceed to true levels of performance and the parties concerned might come to understand the true value of their horses over reliable time spans and after numerous races.

To comprehend stakes conditions for three-year-olds, handicappers must entertain several considerations that are relevant. Purse comparisons are necessary but insufficient. Developing horses proceed to major objectives more slowly, more gradually, more deliberately. They enter more preliminaries. A potential Grade 1 standout may reach that pinnacle by contesting conditioned stakes, ungraded stakes, and lower-grade stakes, losing a few times along its path.

Also, leading stables combine racing objectives and breeding purposes. A score in a graded stakes may be more valuable to the stable, though its purse is smaller than that of an ungraded opportunity. A Grade 2 stakes winner, purse of $75,000, may therefore rate higher in class than three-year-olds that have annexed purses of $100,000 or more in ungraded competition. The graded-race field might be considerably more talented. Again, the full record and manner of performance supplement isolated races, and complement them reliably.

Stakes for three-year-olds below Grade 2 are fairly distinguished by purse size. Even as three-year-olds develop, stake possibilities have become numerous, and bigger purses attract better horses.

Purses aside, conditioned stakes winners joining open fields are moving up. Grade 1 winners and close runners-up are moving down. Grade 2 winners are usually moving down, especially horses that also have pushed emerging Grade 1 stars toward their upper limits.

Unless the field allows speed horses to steal off by themselves, stakes conditions of any kind almost invariably demand that three-year-olds call upon the several qualities of class, combined to varying degrees depending on the quality of the field.

Handicappers get best results by examining entire records, seeking to determine which horses have proven they can combine speed, stamina, and competitive spirit to the necessary limits, or beyond.

By asking how strongly each three-year-old acceptable on form, distance, and pace has overpowered its prior conditions, handicappers can more effectively judge where each belongs in the stakes program. Extending a process begun once three-year-olds enter advanced nonwinners allowance races, as horses advance to more demanding stakes conditions they must combine the several qualities of class to increasingly high degree. The pattern is a logical progression:

Stakes Conditions	*Class Demands*
Conditioned stakes, for nonwinners of stakes or nonwinners of specified amounts	The several qualities of class, combined in moderate degree
Open, listed, or lower grade stakes	The several qualities of class combined in relatively high degree, consistent with purse values
Grade 2 stakes	The several qualities of class, combined in outstanding degree
Grade 1 stakes	The several qualities of class, combined in maximum degree

As handicappers proceed to determine how well three-year-olds are suited to stakes conditions at particular points in their development, they are guided well by four guidelines:

1. Conditioned stakes serve mainly as stepping-stones to larger events.

Because these stakes bar former stakes winners or previous winners of relatively big purses, ordinary three-year-olds sometimes win conditioned stakes.

Because three-year-olds are developing horses, potential Grade 1 champions can tally under conditioned stakes conditions merely by stopping there along their way.

Handicappers thus can appreciate that conditioned stakes for three-year-olds often remain open to horses of greatly diverse quality, even as do nonwinners allowance races. Three-year-olds that have won only a single allowance race sometimes take the prize. Horses collecting two allowance wins regularly try their luck. And horses having three allowance wins in the bank might already have defeated a field superior to the three-year-olds entered in conditioned stakes.

What to do?

Consider the full record. The nonwinners once allowance graduate must have looked tremendous. But the nonwinners twice graduate may qualify merely by looking impressive. And the nonwinners three times graduate automatically qualifies. Each might beg further study. Which combines demonstrated class with the greatest potential?

2. Grade 1 stakes for three-year-olds generally belong to those few horses that mark themselves indelibly early on, with repeated sensational outpourings of class.

Class demons of the seventies—Secretariat, Seattle Slew, Affirmed, Alydar, Spectacular Bid—unleashed their extraordinary power immediately, under allowances or in stepping-stones stakes. Recent national division leaders Swale and Spend A Buck ranked a cut below these champions and did not secure their status until winning the three-year-old classics.

To less obvious extent, local division leaders generally excel their three-year-old contemporaries by wide enough margins so that regular handicappers can scarcely fail to note the differences. In conditioned, ungraded, or lower-grade stakes, handicappers do not often trifle with the chances of these genuinely classy three-year-olds.

3. Grade 2 stakes for three-year-olds generally are taken by Grade 1 horses en route to glory.

This happens more frequently the first part of the season, when Grade 1 horses themselves are moving through basic conditions. Later, horses a cut or so below top-grade can earn these fat, prestigious purses, as Grade 1 three-year-olds prepare to battle their counterparts in the older divisions.

4. Open stakes below Grade 2 usually are won by various three-year-olds belonging to the better half of the division, depending on how well these combine the several qualities of class with current form and preferences for the distance, footing, and probable pace.

Class edges count most, but not decisively if deficits on other fundamentals can be spotted. Relating eligibility conditions and class, handicappers should require open stakes contenders to have compiled multiple impressive performances under nonwinners allowances or in conditioned stakes. Strong showings in Grade 3 or listed stakes deserve extra credit. In these races, purse values provide useful but inconclusive distinctions.

If three-year-olds entered in open stakes have not progressed beyond preliminary nonwinners allowance conditions, handicappers should demand the nonwinners twice win look particularly powerful, and that other evidence in the past performances supports a case for high potential. Regardless of potential class, throw out horses lacking in seasoning, unfamiliar with the distance or footing, untested by the probable pace, or disadvantaged by any combinations of jockey, weight, and post position.

Handicappers should rightly applaud the proliferation of stakes in three-year-old racing, even louder the grading of stakes in terms of competitive quality. By tracking the quality of performance rendered by better members of the three-year-old division in each of their earlier races, handicappers earn the edge they need to match three-year-olds and stakes conditions.

The handicapping procedures presented next have been found by the author to be particularly effective for relating past performance patterns to the demands of eligibility conditions in races for nonclaiming three-year-olds. Because they reveal *how well* each contender fits specific conditions, they are especially useful for separating the genuine contenders.

CHAPTER 9

To Separate Contenders: Total Performance Handicapping

THE HANDICAPPING PROCEDURES explained and illustrated here derive from the persuasion of hard experience, that nonclaiming three-year-olds are best evaluated when submitted to analyses that take into account *their entire three-year-old record. The Handicapper's Condition Book* refers to its method, if you please, as total performance handicapping. Because it reveals how strongly a race's contenders fit eligibility conditions, the method is particularly useful for separating horses that already have qualified as suited to the conditions.

The method's logic is explained quickly.

When analyzing older horses, handicappers concentrate on recent races and best efforts, and rightly, as these contain relatively stable and accurate indicators of current form and true class, fundamental factors that influence one another importantly. As developing horses, in contrast, nonclaiming three-year-olds are changing continually in ways so basic they alter basic abilities and preferences. And even as they mature and learn the game, nonclaiming three-year-olds compete under conditions of eligibility so various they can camouflage a sensational performance and sensationalize a common one. Recent races and best efforts are indicative, all right, but they are not enough. In a context of eligibility conditions, moreover, recent races and best efforts can even become frustratingly misleading.

Is the lackluster performance of the latest outing due to lack of ability or lack of seasoning? If lack of seasoning, what factors played a part, and next time will the experiences be repeated or corrected? Do dull recent races relate to inability or to unfamiliarity? With the distance? With the footing? With the toughness of the competition? What will happen when the unfamiliarity rubs off?

Alternately, what accounts for that easy victory or big win in dazzling time last out? Is that the stuff of a potential champ? Or merely the easy competition of restricted nonwinners eligibility conditions? Did victory result from an uncontested early pace? Or was it the consequence of track conditions? When the early pace or track conditions change, or when competition stiffens, what will happen then?

To settle these matters and their like, and to avoid the upsets that regularly besiege owners and trainers of three-year-old hopefuls, handicappers are encouraged to supplement study of recent races and best efforts with total performance handicapping procedures. These engage handicappers in systematic review of a three-year-old's entire pattern of development. That kind of study reveals to what extent performances under conditions so far completed should lead to success under today's conditions.

Total performance handicapping involves a qualitative analysis and works as follows:

After reading the conditions of eligibility, and calling into mind the qualities of class typically demanded of winners under those conditions, handicappers identify the conditions of recent races and determine whether present form under those conditions can be regarded as relatively strong or weak. Even efforts or better are accepted, unless the races themselves look dismal. In tough contests, accept performances that beat half the field, or include high early speed that lasts until the quarter pole or later. As long as latest races and workouts are recent and satisfactory, handicappers analyzing form can remain relatively lenient about actual performances of nonclaiming three-year-olds in recent races. This becomes notably the case where apparently poor performances actually resulted from poor trips. This happens more frequently with developing three-year-olds whose handling can be far more complicated for jockeys.

The next step begins the more critical assessment, that of class. Find the latest winning race, and identify its eligibility conditions. What qualities of class were exhibited there? Consider what that kind of performance projects for the near future, then analyze the next performances and assess to what extent the latest win and its aftermath reveal a performance pattern that is positive and consistent, or uneven and inconsistent. Credit horses with a specific measure of class and potential, as revealed by analysis of the latest win and its aftermath.

Equipped now with first indications of potential class and present form, handicappers gain best understanding of nonclaiming three-year-olds by returning to their earliest races at three and tracing the pattern of development that has led to the present. What kind of racehorse are you looking at? Relate each horse's performance pattern to the stereotypical patterns presented in Chapter 8. Where is the horse headed? For what eligibility conditions has it qualified? Stakes? Classified allowances? Nonwinners allowances? Claiming races?

Earliest races become most useful when connections between recent races and best efforts appear dubious, inconsistent, or contradictory. First efforts display not only the three-year-old's first combinations of speed and competitiveness but also what management thought of its future at the outset. Was it entered under maiden claiming conditions? At the route? Was a top rider employed? How low were the odds? How well did it perform?

The handicapping process might be said to involve three stages of analysis or review of three component parts of the record: present performance, power performances, and pattern of performance. The three contribute to a total performance profile.

As handicappers proceed through past performances from first to last, the pattern of development illuminates overall potential, explains apparent inconsistencies and contradictions, and projects to conditions of eligibility for which nonclaiming three-year-olds are ready and best suited. Handicappers continually relate past performances to the demands of conditions. When judging a five-length romp under nonwinners once allowances, they do not scorn the winner by saying it beat nothing. Knowing handicappers consider manner of victory as much as victory itself.

Moving carefully from race to race, they identify not only the qualities and degrees of class and form exhibited so far but also best indications of distance preferences, pace preferences, and footing preferences. When these several abilities and preferences are related to the typical demands of today's conditions, handicappers can judge how well horses are suited to those conditions. Which is best suited? That horse represents a potential play.

Naturally, as the season progresses and nonclaiming three-year-olds accumulate more lines in their past performance tables, the method's reliability is enhanced. Yet total performance handicapping works effectively with lightly raced horses as well, a circumstance characteristic of many notable three-year-olds at any point in the season. When the 1983 Eclipse filly Heartlight No. 1 annexed that season's Hollywood Oaks, a Grade 1 event, she was merely a maiden graduate last out. The maneuver by trainer Pedro Marti startled owner Burt Bacharach, who had been awaiting a nonwinners of two allowance race to fill, but handicappers who understand the special charms of developing three-year-olds got a chance at a good thing. Heartlight No. 1 had already shown unmistakable brilliance in her short career. Marti knew it, and he also understood that the others in the Grade 1 field had looked lackluster. Heartlight No. 1 won by twelve lengths; paid $8.80.

For that reason, too, total performance handicapping is neither too complicating nor too time-consuming and handicappers in a hurry often can use the method efficiently.

To illustrate how total performance handicapping might be applied advantageously, let's examine a typical nonclaiming middle-distance event limited to three-year-olds, a field of six entered. I chose the race because I believe it highlights distinctions the method can achieve. I believe conventional speed handicappers, or class-consistency handicappers, or even comprehensive handicappers surely would land on the mistaken favorites. Total performance handicapping identifies another contender, and by comparison of total performance profiles in preference to recency alone, favors the less obvious.

Examine the conditions, and recall the class demands typically associated with them.

Restricted stakes normally demand the several qualities of class—speed, endurance, competitiveness, willingness—combined to moderate extent. A horse that combines those qualities strongly can win in a breeze. A horse that possesses speed but lacks competitive spirit is very likely to lose. Restricted stakes conditions will attract winners of one or two allowance races and perhaps runners-up in open stakes. The handicapping is difficult. It depends on a real grasp not only of the horses' recent victories but also of the manner of performance in those races.

What do handicappers know so far about the horses entered in the Bradbury Stakes at Santa Anita, March 20, 1985?

Protect Yourself. Its present performance includes a decent third under preliminary allowance conditions, for nonwinners twice other than maiden or claiming, and a narrow win when favored February 10 versus nonwinners once other than maiden or claiming. It faced no allowance winners that day.

8th Santa Anita

1⅛ MILES. (1.45⅘) 12th Running of THE BRADBURY STAKES. $60,000 added. 3-year-olds which have never won *$17,000. (Allowance) By subscription of $50 each to accompany the nomination, $600 additional to start, with $60,000 added, of which $12,000 to second, $9,000 to third, $4,500 to fourth and $1,500 to fifth. Weight, 118 lbs. Non-winners other than maiden or claiming at one mile or over allowed 4 lbs. Starters to be named through the entry box by the closing time of entries. A trophy will be presented to the owner of the winner. Closed Wednesday, March 13, 1985 with 17 nominations. *A race worth $17,000 to the winner.

Protect Yourself

Own.—Hooper F W **118**

Dk. b. or br. c. 3, by Lord Rebeau—Fleeting Maid, by Crozier
Br.—Hooper F W (Fla)
Tr.—Fenstermaker L R
Lifetime 12 2 1 4 $52,975

1985	4	1	1	1	$26,575
1984	8	1	0	3	$26,400
Turf	2	0	0	1	$5,250

6Mar85-4SA 1⅛ Ⓣ:474 1:123 1:49 fm *8-5 118 510 34½ 47 36¾ Hawley S1 Aw30000 75-19 Young Beau,Induit,ProtectYourself 6
10Feb85-4SA 1 :453 1:102 1:363ft 8-5 118 46½ 32 1hd 1hd Hawley S4 Aw28000 85-15 ProtctYorslf,Ascnson,KnghthoodII 7
10Feb85—Veered in, bumped after start
30Jan85-9SA 1 1/16 :473 1:114 1:433ft 3½ 118 64 54 43¼ 43 McCarronCJ3 Aw25000 80-17 RoylOlympi,RelunchATun,Turkomn 7
6Jan85-4SA 1 :452 1:101 1:36 ft 8½ 118 56½ 23 22½ 2¾ Hansen R D6 Aw24000 87-10 Tnk'sProspct,ProtctYourslf,FtrFbl 6
24Dec84-7Hol 1 :46 1:103 1:362ft 7 115 910 86¼ 64¼ 34 HansenRD5 Ⓡ Kndy Rd 89-11 FstAccount,AirAlert,ProtectYourslf 9
15Dec84-7Hol 1 Ⓣ:474 1:12 1:372fm 13 118 129½ 1212 96¼ 53½ Hansen R D12 Aw30000 77-18 SvnnhDncr,BoldrThnBold,RdDusty 12
21Nov84-7Hol 1 :461 1:114 1:381gd 4¾ 120 77½ 57 34 3¾ Hansen R D4 Aw24000 83-16 JustTheFcts,Dr.Riv,ProtectYourself 7
7Nov84-6Hol 1 :46 1:114 1:373ft 3¾ 118 75½ 55 3½ 11 Hansen R D2 Mdn — — ProtctYorslf,ByShorDrv,FstAccont 8
28Oct84-2SA 1 :461 1:112 1:381ft 48 117 65¾ 53¼ 22 3hd Hansen R D5 Mdn 77-17 LittlMissouri,Dynmt,ProtctYourslf 10
28Oct84—Lugged out 7/8
11Oct84-6SA 6f :221 :451 1:104ft 26 118 54½ 512 611 58 Sibille R1 M50000 76-18 Mi Dicha, Two Hearts, Bronzino 7
11Oct84—Bore out at 5/16

Mar 14 SA 1 ft 1:40 h Mar 5 SA 3f ft :363 h Feb 24 SA 1 ft 1:413 h Feb 8 SA 5f ft 1:04 h

Reckoner

Own.—Hibbert R E **114**

Ch. c. 3, by Inverness Drive—Reckoning, by Olden Times
Br.—Hibbert R E (Ky)
Tr.—Manzi Joseph
Lifetime 3 1 1 1 $20,600

1985	3	1	1	1	$20,600
1984	0	M	0	0	

10Mar85-4SA 1 1/16 :463 1:112 1:431ft *4-5 117 32½ 41½ 2½ 21 Pincay L Jr1 Aw26000 84-15 Cosmotron, Reckoner, Fiesty Fouts 5
24Feb85-6SA 7f :224 :454 1:231ft *1-2 118 54 42½ 32½ 1½ Pincay L Jr4 Mdn 84-16 Reckonr,JusttoStisfyYou,GoSwiftly 7
9Feb85-6SA 6½f :221 :452 1:172gd *6-5 118 97¼ 86¼ 45 3nk Pincay L Jr5 Mdn 83-20 Rich Earth, Equilibre, Reckoner 11
9Feb85—Lugged in

Mar 17 SA 4f ft :493 h ●Mar 4 SA 7f ft 1:251 h Feb 18 SA 6f ft 1:123 h Feb 7 SA 4f ft :473 hg

Fleet Majesty

Own.—Dollase-Grutman-Lucian **114**

Dk. b. or br. c. 3, by His Majesty—Born for Fun, by Fleet Nasrullah
Br.—Cahan & Gillespie (Ill)
Tr.—Dollase Wallace
Lifetime 2 1 0 0 $13,225

1985	2	1	0	0	$13,225
1984	0	M	0	0	

3Mar85-3SA 1 1/16 :463 1:112 1:432ft 4½ 118 1½ 12½ 12 15 Stevens G L1 Mdn 84-14 FleetMajesty,Bonham,BernieLittle 11
17Feb85-6SA 1 1/16 :461 1:103 1:434ft 8 118 811 610 56 55½ Stevens G L4 Mdn 76-13 ChfRunRun,Lord'nRulr,AcdmyRod 11

Mar 18 SA 4f ft :494 b Mar 9 SA 6f ft 1:12 h Feb 24 SA 5f ft 1:002 h Feb 11 SA 1 ft 1:391 h

Bolder Than Bold

Own.—Bradley-Chndler-Whittinghm **118**

B. c. 3, by Plum Bold—Fact, by Dancing Moss
Br.—Bradly-Whttnghm-Chndlr (Ky)
Tr.—Whittingham Charles
Lifetime 12 2 2 2 $67,632

1985	3	1	0	1	$26,200
1984	9	1	2	1	$41,432
Turf	3	0	1	0	$17,500

3Mar85-6SA 1 1/16 :461 1:102 1:432ft 3 118 88½ 54¾ 2½ 1no ShoemkerW4 Aw28000 84-14 BolderThnBold,Ascension,Turkomn 9
3Mar85—Fanned wide into stretch
6Feb85-8SA 1 1/16 :463 1:104 1:423ft 3¼e 114 98½ 75¼ 66¾ 33 ShmkrW7 Ⓡ Sta Ctina 85-15 FlotngRsrv,BrcnsChrg,BldrThnBld 11
6Feb85—Broke slowly
13Jan85-4SA 1 1/16 :462 1:112 1:42 ft 3½ 118 74 54¼ 55½ 49 Pincay L Jr4 Aw24000 82-13 Skywalker,Turkoman,Roya'Olympia 7
13Jan85—Lugged in stretch
15Dec84-7Hol 1 Ⓣ:474 1.12 1:372fm *7-5 118 84½ 41½ 1hd 2¾ McCrronCJ11 Aw30000 80-18 SvnnhDncr,BoldrThnBold,RdDusty 12
23Nov84-8Hol 1 1/16 Ⓣ:462 1:101 1:414fm 11 117 911 99¼ 77¼ 42¾ PincyLJr4 Hst The Flg 87-13 Overtrump, Right Con, Herat 11
11Nov84-4Hol 1 Ⓣ:461 1:10 1:343fm 10 115 911 811 811 64½ Shoemaker W6 Bckpsr 90-08 Herat, Sapient, Private Jungle 9
11Nov84—Run in divisions
27Oct84-8SA 1 1/16 :463 1:104 1:422ft 8¾ 118 52 42¾ 47½ 511¾ PincayLJr5 Norfolk 77-13 Chief'sCrown,MtthewT.Prkr,VivMxi 6
27Oct84—Grade I; Bumped at 1/8
17Oct84-6SA 1 1/16 :463 1:114 1:451ft *3-5 117 21½ 2hd 11 11¾ McCarron C J4 Mdn 75-18 BolderThanBold,VivaMaxi,Klystron 6
7Oct84-2SA 1 :461 1:104 1:37 ft *7-5e 117 52½ 52¾ 32 2nk McCarron C J9 Mdn 83-12 SmrtenUp,BolderThnBold,Rvlrout 10
7Oct84—Fanned wide late
12Sep84-6Dmr 1 :462 1:113 1:38 ft 4¾ 116 86¾ 63½ 33 31½ Shoemaker W10 Mdn 76-17 Sapient,SmrtenUp,BolderThnBold 10
12Sep84 Fanned wide turn

Mar 15 SA 6f ft 1:151 h Mar 10 SA 3f ft :384 h Feb 28 SA 4f ft :462 hg Feb 23 SA Ⓣ 5f fm 1:02 h (d)

Pacific Mail
B. g. 3, by Arts and Letters—Polynesian Charm, by What a Pleasure
Br.—Eaton Farms Inc&RedBullStb (Ky) 1985 1 0 0 0
Own.—Sheikh Al Maktoum 114 Tr.—Drysdale Neil 1984 4 2 0 1 $8,959
Lifetime 5 2 0 1 $8,959 Turf 5 2 0 1 $8,959
13Mar85-8SA a6½f Ⓣ:214 :4411:144fm 5¼ 116 813 812 712 77 DelhoussyeE8 Baldwin 78-20 KnighthoodII,FullHonor,Infntrymn 8
17Sep84◆2Goodwood(Eng) 1 1:431gd 5¼ 131 Ⓣ 34½ PggttL Westhampnett St. Hilarion, Great Reef,PacificMail 7
25Aug84◆2Newmarket(Eng) 1 1:432gd *6-5 130 Ⓣ 54 CuthnS Denepak Bacon Reach. SoldatBleu, NorthernPride 5
11Jly84◆2Newmarket(Eng) 7f 1:274gd *2¼ 123 Ⓣ 1½ PgttL BernardVanCutsem Pacific Mail, MrJayZee, Zaizafon 7
4Jly84◆3Yarmouth(Eng) 7f 1:254fm*6-5 123 Ⓣ 14 Piggott L Bradwell PacificMail,BntuWrrior,DwnJustice 6
Mar 9 SA 6f ft 1:143 h Mar 4 SA Ⓣ 7f fm 1:312 h (d) Feb 27 SA 6f ft 1:144 h Feb 22 SA 4f ft :492 h

Creekarosa
B. c. 3, by Darby Creek Road—Miss Nijinsky, by Nijinsky II
Br.—Northwest Farms (Ky) 1985 3 1 0 0 $11,075
Own.—Carrillo F 114 Tr.—Spawr William 1984 2 1 0 1 $13,357
Lifetime 5 2 0 1 $24,432
27Feb85-4SA 1 :464 1:114 1:37 ft 7¼ 117 54½ 43 54¼ 43¼ Stevens G L5 62500 80-17 Young Beau, Beau's Bafti,Cacnuma 7
14Feb85-9SA 1⅛ :472 1:121 1:444ft *2½ 116 63½ 87¼ 811 810½ ValenzuelaPA3 c50000 67-19 Young Beau, Cachuma, Jet Royale 9
14Feb85 Bumped in rear quarters, knocked off stride after start
1Feb85-2SA 7f :221 :441 1:231ft 6 116 68¾ 611 23 11½ Stevens G L9 c32000 84-15 Creekarosa,KingOfCalifornia,Singlet 9
30Sep84-9Lga 1⅛ :451 1:103 1:433ft 8¾ 122 913 85¾ 69¼ 33¼ Moore K D5 Lga Lads 77-16 Aegean's Kin, MyLyon,Creekarosa 13
14Sep84-3Lga 6½f :22 :452 1:18 ft 3¾ 120 1110 78 55¾ 2½ Moore K D9 M20000 78-16 ‡Bold Horn,Creekarosa,SuperBear 12
14Sep84 - Placed first through disqualification
Mar 16 SA 6f ft 1:161 h Feb 8 SA 4f ft :473 h Jan 29 SA 6f ft 1:133 h Jan 23 SA 6f ft 1:133 hg

Cosmotron
Ch. g. 3, by Prove Out—Conciliacion, by Tale of Two Cities
Br.—Fredericks F L (Ky) 1985 5 2 1 0 $32,100
Own.—Pulliam C N 118 Tr.—Pulliam Vivian M 1984 5 M 0 1 $4,325
Lifetime 10 2 1 1 $36,425
10Mar85-4SA 1⅛ :463 1:112 1:431ft 6 120 42¾ 3½ 1½ 11 Stevens G L3 Aw26000 85-15 Cosmotron, Reckoner, Fiesty Fouts 5
3Mar85-6SA 1⅛ :461 1:102 1:432ft 7 118 31 65¼ 711 814 Meza R Q7 Aw28000 70-14 BolderThnBold,Ascension,Turkomn 9
6Feb85-8SA 1⅛ :463 1:104 1:423ft 19 117 75½ 53½ 44½ 55 OrtegaLE1 Ⓡ Sta Ctlina 83-15 FlotngRsrv,BrcnsChrg,BldrThnBld 11
6Feb85—Taken up at 3/16
27Jan85-6SA 1⅛ :471 1:113 1:432ft 3½ 118 11 1½ 13 15 Ortega L E7 Mdn 84-12 Cosmotron,FiestyFouts,AcdmyRod 8
27Jan85—Bumped hard start; lugged out 7/8 turn
13Jan85-6SA 1⅛ :472 1:121 1:444ft 12 118 1hd 1hd 2hd 22½ Ortega L E4 Mdn 75-13 Gold Knight, Cosmotron, Dynamite 7
30Dec84-6SA 1⅛ :491 1:142 1:471sl 14 118 61½ 88¾ 817 816½ Ortega L E1 Mdn 48-33 BeAHawaiian,ByShoreDrive,Bonhm 9
30Dec84—Steadied at 3/8
16Dec84-3Hol 1 :452 1:113 1:373gd 32 118 66¼ 44 43½ 31¼ Ortega L E8 Mdn 86-07 ExclsvDrlng,ByShorDrv,Cosmotron 8
16Dec84—Bumped start
23Nov84-3Hol 1 :462 1:121 1:383ft 17 116 52¾ 54¾ 48 517 Pedroza M A4 M45000 65-19 Ascension,TwoHearts,Chucklecator 8
23Nov84—Veered in, bumped start, 1/8, lugged in
14Nov84-7Hol 6f :223 :462 1:123ft 47 116 97¾ 611 68½ 55¼ Pedroza M A1 M45000 — — Conteal, Petrov, Infantryman 11
14Nov84—Veered in start
1Nov84-4SA 6f :22 :451 1:104ft 57 118 78¼ 912 912 913½ Lamance C9 M40000 70-16 FbulosPrtndr,SmlTody,IsanEmpror 9
Feb 24 SA 7f ft 1:262 h Feb 19 SA 6f ft 1:124 h Feb 14 SA 4f ft :492 h Jan 22 SA 4f ft :482 h

Fiesty Fouts
Ch. c. 3, by Northern Jove—Just One More Time, by Raise a Native
Br.—Spendthrift Farm (Ky) 1985 5 1 1 1 $24,625
Own.—Klein Mr-Mrs E V 114 Tr.—Lukas D Wayne 1984 0 M 0 0
Lifetime 5 1 1 1 $24,625
10Mar85-4SA 1⅛ :463 1:112 1:431ft 3½ 120 55¼ 52 42 34½ ValenzuelPA4 Aw26000 80-15 Cosmotron, Reckoner, Fiesty Fouts 5
10Mar85—Wide
3Mar85-6SA 1⅛ :461 1:102 1:432ft 15 118 53½ 32 31 44½ ValenzuelPA5 Aw28000 80-14 BolderThnBold,Ascension,Turkomn 9
3Mar85—Crowded, checked at 1/8
10Feb85-6SA 1⅛ :48 1:122 1:443ft 3½ 118 31 3½ 1hd 1hd Velasquez J7 Mdn 78-15 Fiesty Fouts, Witan, Bonham 8
10Feb85—3-wide
27Jan85-6SA 1⅛ :471 1:113 1:432ft *9-5 118 34 2½ 23 25 Valenzuela P A6 Mdn 79-12 Cosmotron,FiestyFouts,AcdmyRod 8
27Jan85—Broke slowly, fanned wide 7/8 turn
13Jan85-6SA 1⅛ :472 1:121 1:444ft 11 118 76¼ 68¼ 56 45 Valenzuela P A5 Mdn 72-13 Gold Knight, Cosmotron, Dynamite 7
13Jan85—Broke slowly, wide into stretch
Feb 26 SA 4f ft :483 h Feb 20 SA 4f ft :481 h Feb 5 SA 5f ft 1:01 h Jan 21 SA 5f ft 1:01 h

The power performance is the nonwinners once allowance win, where it survived a long stretch duel, but in ordinary time. Nothing about the power performance signals better things to come.

The full record likewise supports a case for mediocrity. Entered to be claimed first out October 11, the horse later handled non-claiming maidens and proceeded to the customary allowance conditions. Six races later it broke the allowance barrier. The pattern indicates nice efforts but small talents. Protect Yourself will struggle as before to win another allowance race, let alone a restricted stakes.

Reckoner. This nicely bred colt is prototypical of three-year-olds that regularly lose restricted stakes at low odds. Odds-on to break allowance conditions first try March 10, Reckoner instead lost after challenging at the eighth pole. It previously graduated from the maiden ranks in ordinary time and manner, at 1 to 2.

Now the colt is skipping its preliminary allowance conditions to try restricted stakes competition, usually a mistake. To repeat, top prospects can handle this jump readily. All others normally lose. Nothing in Reckoner's record suggests it is anything more than a decent prospect; maybe.

The crowd forgives the loss at the route, arguing it represents a first try and the horse should improve. Okay. But under stakes conditions the horse must improve at the distance while jumping up in class. It's tough. This is not an easy game for horses any more than for horseplayers. When Reckoner was bet down in the Bradbury, handicappers should have been prepared to look for the probable winner elsewhere.

Fleet Majesty. A powerful maiden win on the lead two weeks ago persuaded this well-bred colt's managers that it might be any kind and the Bradbury an appropriate next spot. The colt is also attractive to speed handicappers, as there should not be much keen early lick in this restricted stakes. Won't Fleet Majesty simply dart to the front and lead all the way?

It's unlikely. Three-year-olds often show unexpected speed. The important question is what Fleet Majesty will likely do if contested early by other allowance winners. Who knows? The running time March 3 was ordinary at each call. The colt has not been tested yet by allowance winners. Will it respond and draw out; or capitulate and fall back? At 2 to 1, handicappers should wait to see.

Bolder Than Bold. Present performance shows a nose victory against nonwinners once allowance horses following a wide trip around the far turn. The longer distance today and win after a wide trip March 3 was enough to make the colt favored in the Bradbury, especially after it got third in the restricted Santa Catalina stakes February 6 while breaking slowly.

The power performance would be the Santa Catalina third. What qualities of class were demonstrated there? Willingness, perhaps, but not much speed and no late drive. The come-home time was approximately :31 2/5 seconds for five-sixteenths, no great shakes. It suggests the colt will beat preliminary nonwinners allowance conditions, but says little about its prospects in future stakes.

What about the full record?

Bolder Than Bold broke maiden ranks on the third try October 17 when odds-on to do so, in dismally slow time. It was then entered in graded and open stakes, but was humiliated in the Norfolk, just beaten off in the two open encounters. Bolder Than Bold showed more on the turf.

When returned to nonwinners allowance conditions, it lost a long turf drive at 7 to 5 December 15, again in ordinary time and manner. A good horse would have won.

It finally won its first allowance race three months later, which brings us to the present. The pattern of performance indicates a late-running horse of quite ordinary dimensions. It might show more in the Bradbury, but no one should bet on that, especially at odds of 9 to 5. The colt looks like an also-ran under stakes conditions. Nothing about the recent past is significantly more impressive than the not-so-recent past. This colt will struggle to win its second allowance race, and does not figure in the Bradbury.

Creekarosa. A weak trainer jumps a recently claimed young horse that lost its last under claiming conditions to a restricted stakes? It did not even beat half the field in the selling race. When young developing three-year-olds move from claiming races to allowance races, they had better bring with them a newborn maturity, seasoning, speed, and competitiveness. This happens. But this is hardly a case in point. The pattern of performance suggests Creekarosa is a claiming horse tried-and-true. It is badly outgunned in the Bradbury, and handicappers should recognize that for sure.

Cosmotron. Let's take a long studied look at this colt's record. It's instructive, and these kinds can be the source of generous mutuels in the three-year-old division season after season.

Present performance shows a one-length win against nonwinners once allowance competition. The time is satisfactory but uninspiring, notably to permit a double-jump rise to a restricted stakes.

The allowance win followed an awful performance March 3, which followed a dismal stakes effort, which followed an easy maiden romp. This kind of unevenness is commonplace among developing three-year-olds. Handicappers need all the evidence they can muster.

Check the power performance, which in this case is well hidden. In the Santa Catalina stakes February 6, Cosmotron had made a strong charge along the inside entering the stretch, before taking up in trouble, as the *Form* trouble line notes. The bold move suggested Cosmotron would soon handle nonwinners allowance conditions and would be competitive in restricted or minor open stakes.

At this point the entire pattern of development tells the tale, as it so often does.

Its management did not think much of Costmotron early on, entering it with claiming tags as a maiden. It ran as expected; badly. Suddenly it improved, and following a second-place finish in slow time versus straight maidens January 13, it walloped similar maidens in sharp time January 27. Next came the strong charge before taking up in the stretch of the restricted stakes February 6. A pattern of continual improvement is telltale. Handicappers should always seek out the improving three-year-olds.

Next came the awful allowance race and unexpected win a week later. These two races hold the key. Whenever a nicely developing three-year-old tosses in a dull one but follows that immediately with a ringing performance, throw out the bad race. Young horses will do that; they're inconsistent. Trainers know that. Many of them will wheel their rising three-year-olds right back, anticipating a return to normal. If the comeback succeeds, credit the comeback and forget the dull race. It remains inexplicable, so why worry?

On March 10 Cosmotron handled odds-on favorite Reckoner easily. It returned to a pattern which had begun to reveal it as a nicely bred, nicely developing, improving three-year-old, the kind that handicappers should want to accompany on the way up. A restricted stakes is an inviting stop along the way. When the odds beckon, and the rest of the field begs for more, make the plays.

In the running of the Bradbury, Cosmotron sped to the front alongside Fleet Majesty, which quit before the two had rounded the clubhouse turn. Speed handicappers, to be sure, were quite surprised by that. But it happens. Not much class. At this point Cosmotron assumed command, slowed the pace, and drew out in the stretch. It was just that easy, and often is. Class tells in races for developing three-year-olds. Handicappers who learn how to spot the differences will be leaps ahead of the crowd and will earn substantial profits in the three-year-old division every year.

EIGHTH RACE

Santa Anita

MARCH 20, 1985

1 ⅛ MILES. (1.45%) 12th Running of THE BRADBURY STAKES. $60,000 added. 3-year-olds which have never won *$17,000. (Allowance) By subscription of $50 each to accompany the nomination, $600 additional to start, with $60,000 added, of which $12,000 to second, $9,000 to third, $4,500 to fourth and $1,500 to fifth. Weight, 118 lbs. Non-winners other than maiden or claiming at one mile or over allowed 4 lbs. Starters to be named through the entry box by the closing time of entries. A trophy will be presented to the owner of the winner. Closed Wednesday, March 13, 1985 with 17 nominations. *A race worth $17,000 to the winner.

Value of race $64,450; value to winner $37,450; second $12,000; third $9,000; fourth $4,500; fifth $1,500. Mutuel pool $264,545. Exacta Pool $233,872.

Last Raced	Horse	Eqt.A.Wt PP St	¼	½	¾	Str	Fin	Jockey	Odds $1
10Mar85 4SA1	Cosmotron	3 118 6 1	2$1\frac{1}{2}$	1^2	$11\frac{1}{2}$	$13\frac{1}{2}$	1^4	McCarron C J	3.90
6Mar85 4SA3	Protect Yourself	3 118 1 2	$51\frac{1}{2}$	5^2	$5\frac{1}{2}$	3^{hd}	2no	McHargue D G	5.60
10Mar85 4SA2	Reckoner	3 117 2 4	3^5	$32\frac{1}{2}$	3^1	$22\frac{1}{2}$	3^4	Pincay L Jr	4.70
27Feb85 4SA4	Creekarosa	3 115 5 5	6	6	6	6	4^{nk}	Toro F	34.50
3Mar85 6SA1	Bolder Than Bold	b 3 118 4 6	$4\frac{1}{2}$	4^1	$42\frac{1}{2}$	$52\frac{1}{2}$	$51\frac{1}{2}$	Shoemaker W	1.90
3Mar85 3SA1	Fleet Majesty	3 114 3 3	1^{hd}	2^1	$2\frac{1}{2}$	4^1	6	Stevens G L	2.40

OFF AT 4:52. Start good. Won easily. Time, :23⅗, :47⅕, 1:12, 1:37, 1:49⅗ Track fast.

$2 Mutuel Prices:				
7-COSMOTRON		9.80	5.00	3.80
1-PROTECT YOURSELF			6.20	4.80
2-RECKONER				4.80

$5 EXACTA 7-1 PAID $126.00

Ch. g, by Prove Out—Conciliacion, by Tale of Two Cities. Trainer Pulliam Vivian M. Bred by Fredericks F L (Ky).

COSMOTRON, rated on the early pace, drew off quickly when given reign entering the stretch and won in hand. PROTECT YOURSELF, unhurried for six furlongs, rallied outside horses thereafter and finished strongly. RECKONER, reserved off the early pace, stayed outside the leaders to the stretch, responded in the drive but could not menace the winner. CREEKAROSA was never a factor. BOLDER THAN BOLD showed little. FLEET MAJESTY engaged for the lead briefly after the start, took back off the winner's early pace but offered little when roused for the drive and tired badly in the stretch. PACIFIC MAIL (5) WAS WITHDRAWN. ALL WAGERS ON HIM IN THE REGULAR AND EXACTA POOLS WERE ORDERED REFUNDED AND ALL OF HIS PICK SIX SELECTIONS SWITCHED TO THE FAVORITE, BOLDER THAN BOLD (4).

Owners— 1, Pulliam C N; 2, Hooper F W; 3, Hibbert R E; 4, Carrillo F; 5, Bradley-Chandler-Whittingham; 6, Dollase-Grutman-Lucian.

Trainers— 1, Pulliam Vivian M; 2, Fenstermaker L R; 3, Manzi Joseph; 4, Spawr William; 5, Whittingham Charles; 6, Dollase Wallace.

Overweight: Reckoner 3 pounds; Creekarosa 1.

Scratched—Pacific Mail (13Mar85 8SA7); Fiesty Fouts (10Mar85 4SA3).

While Cosmotron was no fluke under the restricted circumstances of the race, three conditions were absolutely vital to successful handicapping:

First, in opposition to a concentration on recent races only, or on handicapping factors (early speed, final time, consistency) which obtain less reliability when analyzing the performances of developing horses, a commitment to total performance handicapping, a systematic procedure which entails evaluation of the *entire three-year-old record*.

Second, the use of results charts. With nonclaiming three-year-olds, handicappers need to supplement what was done with descriptions of how it was done.

Third, close personal observation of the qualities of class and form exhibited by the contenders in their races.

Handicappers who had watched Cosmotron and Hail Bold King in their recent races should have recognized the acceleration and improving performances of the former, the rather even and ordinary late run of the latter. Only in this complete a context, and with odds at amusing variance with real chances, can handicappers opt for Cosmotron.

I know of no sounder approach to analyzing past performances of nonclaiming three-year-olds with persistent effectiveness. Because the conditions under which they race vary so, while the horses themselves continue to grow and gain experience, the functions of speed handicapping or class-consistency handicapping have but limited application. If concentrated on races in which three-year-olds were not well suited to the conditions, or were gaining seasoning, or were being schooled, these methods could easily misinterpret matters. By apprehending total performance profiles, alternatively, handicappers avoid the three-year-old traps.

Handicappers interested in applying total performance handicapping procedures to nonclaiming three-year-olds' past performances will find the following guidelines useful for separating relatively like contenders:

1. When comparing two contenders whose performance profiles fit the conditions of eligibility with relatively equal force, emphasize the qualities of class and racing preferences exhibited by the power performances.

If further evaluation is necessary, rely on pace analysis. Pay stricter attention to the probable effects of early pace as that applies to horses running nearer to the lead.

2. If a sudden positive reversal of form follows a succession of dull or deficient races, relate the happy reversal to early signs of high potential (impressive races or workouts; low odds; the presence of the leading rider; fashionable breeding). If signs of high potential can be evidenced, presume the three-year-old will begin to approach that potential.

A few times each season at every major track a young potential star gets the blues and refuses to demonstrate its true abilities. The horses go favored and lose, maybe consistently. Suddenly, the telltale reversal of form. If handicappers can relate form reverses to early indicators of high potential, they might set themselves for a serious wager and a juicy payoff. Still eligible for piddling conditions, the horses can run big, and now they act as if they want to do it.

3. If a three-year-old has been entered in two or more consecutive claiming races, and today's race is another claiming event, total performance handicapping bows to the close analysis of recent races.

Elsewhere, the player's book deals extensively with the handicapping of three-year-olds in claiming races.

The continual presence in claiming races suggests the three-year-old's potential has become limited, at least so far as its management has been persuaded. The surest barometer of what a claiming horse might accomplish now is its performances in its latest races, particularly as these reveal current form. Procedures associated with possibly grand but hidden potential do not apply.

4. In cases where a three-year-old's maiden victory proved a while in the making, recognize the point of departure for total performance handicapping as the maiden win or the first satisfactory performance under maiden conditions.

It makes little sense to penalize a young horse for lackluster performance when fear or the inability to adapt to an alien game has thrown it into an entirely reluctant state. Discount the awful races.

The same applies to any well-established three-year-old that wanders inexplicably "off form." More so if the youngster has shipped to an unfamiliar track. During Santa Anita 1979 the top New York three-year-old Instrument Landing ran pitiably poor in a series of stakes races. Many locals, in a torrent of incredulous logic, concluded the New Yorker's races proved the relative superiority of southern California three-year-olds.

The Eastern horse had not competed, for whatever reasons, and could not be evaluated fairly. When returned to New York, to home, Instrument Landing immediately annexed the Grade 1 Wood Memorial at Aqueduct.

5. Use the factors of jockey, weight, and post position negatively, or in combination with one or more of the fundamentals.

Three-year-olds typically carry unfamiliar jockeys and weights, and they exit from the various posts. Standing alone, the factors contribute little to handicapping analysis. Many players, nonetheless, become jittery if the jockey, weight, and post position do not please their appetites. If nerves persist, the best solution treats the factors negatively. If you do not like the jockey, pass the race. Weight and post position, the same.

When unfavorable jockeys, weights, or post positions combine with questionable class, form, or distance-footing-pace preferences, that's another issue. Three-year-olds typically will need extra dimensions on the other fundamentals (class especially) to overcome the likely disadvantges in the running. Most can be eliminated.

6. If a three-year-old relinquished its maiden status under maiden claiming conditions, and now is moving from claiming con-

ditions to allowances, total performance handicapping must uncover the qualities of class typically demanded by today's conditions.

Check the power performances carefully. What qualities of class were exhibited there? Obviously, the recent claiming race should feature a win, or at least a powerfully close finish while gaining in the stretch.

Maiden claiming graduates do not often earn a living in nonclaiming races. If these horses have been showing better speed while moving ahead in claiming class, the start at the maiden claiming level probably signals a physical problem that will surface eventually under repeated racing.

The reverse of the pattern happens more commonly. Once a maiden claiming winner exhibits deteriorating form, handicappers can interpret the present by having high regard for the lowly beginnings.

Whenever a maiden claiming winner returns to the claiming ranks—usually immediately after the maiden win—its expected class level can be estimated by cutting the selling price of the maiden race by 50 percent. The horse should level off there or thereabouts.

7. Beware of three-year-old maidens entered under nonwinners once allowances on turf.

This maneuver occurs more frequently on circuits where few routes on turf are carded for maidens. If maidens belong to successful turf parents, that footing should move them up. That is precisely why stables enter against previous winners. Because the horses remain maidens, the odds will be higher. If fields of previous winners, but nonwinners in allowance races, look lackluster, possibilities for exploitation increase.

Pursuing this line, if a three-year-old's obvious power performance is also its first and single race on the grass, award the horse extra credit next time on grass, even if moving ahead in class by two steps. It likes turf and will likely repeat its powerful performance.

8. Be careful not to overestimate or underestimate the two-year-old record.

Top horses aside, two-year-old records often do not translate reliably to three-year-old performance. These horses are maturing greatly, changing dynamically. The very best of thoroughbreds at two will normally develop nicely at three. All others become suspect. Handicappers should be particularly suspicious of stakes winnings and placings that occurred in the juvenile dashes. If the horses have been acting more like claiming animals at three, mark the early performances down.

Alternatively, the same maturation and change that turns two-year-old speedsters into washouts at three can transform juvenile tabbies into tigers next year. If races at two look miserable, but recent races sharp, count on continued improvement for three-year-olds and forget the lowly beginnings.

On the next pages are fourteen carefully selected past performance tables. Labels are omitted, but total peformance handicapping has been applied, and it reveals whether the horses are suited to the conditions of eligibility specified.

6th Belmont

1 MILE. (1.33) MAIDEN SPECIAL WEIGHT. Purse $23,000. 3-year-olds and upward. Weights, 3-year-olds 113 lbs. Older 124 lbs.

If I Had A Hammer
Dk. b. or br. c. 3, by Cox's Ridge—Calyptra, by Le Fabuleux
Br.—King Ranch (Ky)
Own.—Keller M   113   Tr.—Ribaudo Robert
1985 2 M 0 1 $3,180
1984 0 M 0 0
Lifetime 2 0 0 1 $3,180

20May85-3Bel	1¹⁄₁₆:47 1:12 1:43³ft	*2½ 113	1¹ 3½ 42½ 49½	McCarron G⁴	Mdn 74-22 BhGrnd,Trn'nTogthr,BnnyThGrftr 10
21Apr85-3Aqu	6f :22³ :46¹ 1:11 ft	5½ 112	3¹ 2½ 2½ 32½	Santagata N⁶	M75000 83-21 AreRug,LuckyBelief,IfIHdAHmmer 7

May 9 Bel ⓣ 5f fm 1:00² h (d)   ● Apr 18 Bel 4f ft :47¹ hg   Apr 12 Bel tr.t 4f ft :52 b   Apr 6 Hia 5f ft 1:01² bg

Mamluk
B. c. 3, by Le Fabuleux—Sunny Dame, by Damascus
Br.—Live Oak Stud (Fla)
Own.—Live Oak Plantation   113   Tr.—Kelly Patrick J
1985 3 M 1 2 $7,640
1984 0 M 0 0
Lifetime 3 0 1 2 $7,640

17May85-5Bel	7f :23¹ :46¹ 1:24²ft	*2½ 113	7⁶ 55½ 33½ 23½	Cordero A Jr⁴	Mdn 76-19 Lucky Belief, Mamluk, Lychey 9
16Feb85-2GP	7f :22³ :45² 1:24⁴ft	3½ 122	97¾ 65¾ 43½ 3ⁿᵏ	Solomone M⁹	Mdn 80-21 AswnHigh,Cormornt'sPrty,Mmluk 11
4Feb85-6GP	6f :22 :45² 1:10²ft	8½ 122	10¹⁵ 6¹³ 59½ 37½	Solomone M⁵	Mdn 79-18 FirstGuess,SomethingCool Mmluk 11

May 24 Bel 4f ft :49² b   May 13 Bel 4f ft :48 hg   May 10 Bel 5f ft 1:01⁴ h   May 6 Bel 5f ft 1:01² h

Which of the above best fits the maiden conditions at Belmont Park?

It's Mamluk, the colt that finished second last out, an excellent predictor of impending victory in maiden races for three-year-olds.

Would the horse below figure to beat both of the above?

Same Conditions, Same Race, Another Horse

Dancing Secret
B. f. 3, by Nijinsky II—Secret Beauy, by Raise A Native
Br.—Oxford Stable (Ky)
Own.—Oxford Stable   114   Tr.—Hirsch William J Jr
1980 0 M 0 0
1979 0 M 0 0

Jun 5 Bel 4f ft :46⁴ h   Jun 2 Bel 6f ft 1:15 b   May 29 Bel 4f ft :46³ hg   ● May 24 Bel 6f ft 1:11⁴ b

With blazing workouts and royal breeding, this kind is tempting under maiden conditions, but handicappers had better resign themselves to the facts—these kinds are bad bets. It's June 8 and statistics tell us first-time-starting older maidens lose more than 50 percent their rightful share of these races. Inexperience defeats them. Dancing Secret is not acceptable until it shows itself to advantage in actual competition.

9 MONMOUTH 6 FURLONGS

6 FURLONGS. (1.08) 38th Running. THE SELECT HANDICAP. $40,000 Added. (The Owner of the Winner to Receive a Trophy). 3-year-olds. By subscription of $25 each which should accompany the nomination, $150 to pass the entry box, $250 to start with $40,000 added of which 60% of all monies to winner; 20% to second; 11% to third; 6% to fourth; and 3% to fifth. Weights 5 p.m., Monday, May 20, 1985. Starters to be named through the entry box by the usual time of closing. Closed Monday, May 13, 1985 with 35 nominations.

Geiger Counter B. c. 3, by Mr Prospector—Thong, by Nantallah
Own.—Brant P M Br.—Claiborne Farm & Gamely Corp (Ky) Tr.—Jolley Leroy
115 Lifetime 4 2 2 0 $26,930 1985 4 2 2 0 $26,930 1984 0 M 0 0

24Apr85- 5Aqu	fst	6f	:22 3/5	:45 3/5	1:10	3↑Alw 22000	5	3	1hd	1 4	1 4	1 3 1/4	Vasquez J	112	*1.00	91-23	Geiger Counter 112 3/4 Nordico 121 8 BroadwayRisk113 1/2	Riddenout	10
6Mar85- 6GP	fst	1 1/16	:48	1:12 3/5	1:45	Alw 17800	2	1	1 1 1/2	1 2 1/2	1 3 1/2	2nk	Vasquez J	117	*.80	76-20	Super Baron 119nk Geiger Counter117 4 1/2 ClockTower117 4 1/2	Gamely	8
9Feb85-11GP	fst	1 1/16	:46 4/5	1:11 4/5	1:45	Alw 15000	1	1	1 1	1 2 1/2	1 3	2 1 1/2	Guerra W A	119	*.80	74-18	BlockPrty122 1 1/2 GeigerCounter119 1 UptownSwll122no	Unruly early,	9
26Jan85- 3GP	fst	6f	:21 4/5	:45 3/5	1:11 2/5	Md Sp Wt	2	3	1 1 1/2	1 2	1 3	1 4 1/2	Guerra W A	122	*.80	82-19	Geiger Counter 122 4 1/2 Our Colors 122 5 1/2 Beveled 122 1	Handily	12

LATEST WORKOUTS ●May 20 Bel 5f fst :59 3/5 h ●May 13 Bel 3f fst :34 3/5 h May 6 Bel 6f fst 1:13 2/5 b Apr 21 Bel 5f fst :59 3/5 h

Handicappers probably lose more money on this kind of young horse than any other. Everything looks right. This beautifully bred colt has just romped at Aqueduct under nonwinners once allowance conditions, completing the final quarter of today's distance in a splendid :24 2/5 seconds, its best time by far. The adjusted time is sensational. The colt has been odds-on since its debut. It is now shipping to Monmouth Park, a lower-class track than Aqueduct. The trainer is Leroy Jolley. Isn't this precisely the nicely bred, lightly raced, improving three-year-old from a leading barn that handicappers prefer?

Perhaps, but not today. Geiger Counter is not moving from nonwinners once to nonwinners twice allowances, or even to a restricted stakes, but from nonwinners once allowances to an open stakes. The pace will be quicker, more hotly contested, and the finish more exhausting. This is a speed horse moving ahead too quickly in class. The colt has shown brilliance, all right, but never has shown either endurance or competitiveness. In fact, it lost easy route leads under preliminary nonwinners allowance conditions. How good is the colt? Nobody knows.

If today's stakes were the conditioned kind, restricted to horses that had never won a stakes or a specified amount of first money since a time ago, Geiger Counter might look tempting. But not in an open stakes such as the Select. At a puny price, Geiger Counter will meet other, more seasoned stakes horses, and has every right to run

hard and lose. It happens all the time. Later on, maybe; not today—too much too soon.

5 PIMLICO 1 1-16 MILES PIMLICO ▲Start ▲Finish

1 $\frac{1}{16}$ MILES. (1.40⅘) ALLOWANCE. Purse $11,500. Fillies. 3-year-olds which have never won a race other than Maiden or Claiming. Weight 120 lbs. Non-winners of a race other than Claiming at one mile or over since April 22 allowed 3 lbs.; such a race since March 22, 5 lbs.; such a race since February 22, 8 lbs.

Cando Sue — **B. f. 3, by Kamehameha—Do's Ninkster, by Snow Twist**
Br.—Newmarket Stables (Va)
Own.—New Market Stable — **Tr.—Tuminelli Joseph M**
112 — Lifetime 15 3 0 3 $17,235 — 1985 9 3 0 2 $16,080 — 1984 6 M 0 1 $1,155

11May85- 6Pim	fst	$1\frac{1}{16}$	:48 1/5	1:12 1/5	1:44 3/5		ⒻAlw 11500	7	2	2^{hd}	$3^{1\frac{1}{2}}$	2^{2}	$3^{3\frac{1}{4}}$	Kupfer T J		112	3.90	78-15	Escanaba $115^{2\frac{1}{4}}$ B. O. One 115^{1} Cando Sue 112^{7}	Weakened	7
20Apr85- 1Pim	fst	$1\frac{1}{16}$	:47	1:12 1/5	1:46 2/5		ⒻClm 14500	3	3	$4^{2\frac{1}{2}}$	3^{2}	$1^{1\frac{1}{2}}$	$1^{3\frac{1}{2}}$	Kupfer T J		114	*2.70	72-12	Cando Sue $114^{3\frac{1}{2}}$ Northwitch 114no Lotatan 115^{2}	Drew clear	8
9Apr85- 6Pim	fst	$1\frac{1}{16}$	:47 2/5	1:13 1/5	1:47	3↑	ⒻClm 11500	5	5	$4^{5\frac{1}{2}}$	$5^{2\frac{3}{4}}$	2^{hd}	1^{3}	Kupfer T J		114	14.00	69-21	Cando Sue 114^{3} One Step Further 112^{4} Our Kathy114^{nk}	Drew off	7
28Mar85- 5Pim	fst	6f	:23 1/5	:46 2/5	1:12 4/5		ⒻClm 11500	7	7	7^{18}	7^{18}	6^{17}	$6^{15\frac{1}{4}}$	Kupfer T J		114	21.30	67-20	No No Nicky $109^{4\frac{3}{4}}$ Nutbush Queen 109^{1}Susan'sGold$114^{3\frac{1}{4}}$	Outrun	7
19Mar85- 3Pim	fst	6f	:23 3/5	:47 1/5	1:13 1/5		ⒻClm 13500	3	2	$6^{2\frac{1}{4}}$	6^{8}	$5^{5\frac{3}{4}}$	$5^{8\frac{3}{4}}$	Kupfer T J	b	112	14.70	71-19	Miss Bedford $114^{\frac{3}{4}}$ Vicky's Reason$114^{4\frac{1}{2}}$RunToPappa109^{no}	Outrun	6
15Feb85- 4Lrl	fst	6f	:23	:47	1:12 4/5		ⒻClm 14500	4	3	4^{3}	5^{8}	$6^{7\frac{3}{4}}$	$6^{8\frac{1}{2}}$	Kupfer T J		119	4.70	70-23	LetsShre$114^{3\frac{1}{2}}$Bbyneedsnewshos$114^{\frac{3}{4}}$Anthony'sGirl$115^{1\frac{1}{4}}$	Fell back	6
2Feb85- 2Lrl	sly	$6\frac{1}{2}$f	:23 2/5	:48 2/5	1:23 2/5		ⒻClm 14500	2	4	$4^{2\frac{1}{4}}$	$4^{4\frac{1}{4}}$	3^{4}	$3^{\frac{3}{4}}$	Kupfer T J		119	14.20	— —	Janet's Devotion $117^{\frac{3}{4}}$ Princess ofIola117^{no}CandoSue119^{4}	Rallied	8
19Jan85- 1Bow	fst	6f	:23 1/5	:47 3/5	1:14 3/5		ⒻMd 14500	7	1	$4^{5\frac{1}{2}}$	$4^{4\frac{1}{2}}$	$2^{1\frac{1}{2}}$	$1^{1\frac{1}{2}}$	Miller D A Jr		122	3.60	67-29	Cando Sue $122^{1\frac{1}{2}}$ Shutter Happy $117^{5\frac{1}{2}}$ JudexLady122^{1}	Drew clear	12
9Jan85- 9Bow	fst	$6\frac{1}{2}$f	:22 3/5	:45 4/5	1:19		ⒻMd 14500	5	1	5^{4}	8^{12}	6^{5}	$5^{1\frac{3}{4}}$	Jones S R5		117	9.70	90-08	Jnet'sDevotion122^{no}ShutterHppy122^{no}FrozenSection$120^{\frac{3}{4}}$	Evenly	12
19Nov84- 9Lrl	sly	6f	:23 1/5	:47 4/5	1:14 4/5		ⒻMd 16000	7	4	2^{2}	3^{5}	3^{6}	$4^{2\frac{1}{4}}$	Jones S R5		112	20.50	67-26	Vicky'sReason$112^{\frac{3}{4}}$BrillintQueen117^{nk}PointSetter$114^{1\frac{1}{4}}$	Weakened	12

LATEST WORKOUTS May 2 Pim 5f fst 1:03 1/5 b — Mar 23 Pim 3f sly :37 h

Typical of three-year-olds, Cando Sue has shown marked improvement of late, probably relishing the change to distance racing. Does it figure to break the allowance barriers as well?

The full record indicates the answer is probably no. Cando Sue has competed since the beginning against low-level types exclusively, breaking its maiden against the cheaper claimers. The wins April 9 and April 20, while rising in class, signal more than anything else another jump in claiming class. The change to nonwinners allowance races instead is typical of trainers, who prefer allowance horses to claiming horses. But this maneuver asks too much of claiming winners below $20,000. Cando Sue actually ran well in the allowance race May 11, her best effort yet, and may do so again, but that's the point. The filly's best effort is probably something short of allowance caliber.

When three-year-olds begin to improve, handicappers permit step-ups that are realistic and reasonable. They remain acutely aware of horsemen's tendencies with young horses—to move too fast. They therefore remain prudent, knowing full well that cheaper claiming race winners do not easily join the allowance ranks successfully.

7 CALDER

6 ½ FURLONGS. (1.17) ALLOWANCE. Purse $13,000 (Plus $1,600 FOA). 3-year-olds and upward which have never won three races other than Maiden or Claiming. Weights, 3-year-olds, 115 lbs. Older, 124 lbs. Non-winners of $12,000 in 1985 allowed, 2 lbs. $10,000 since January 15, 4 lbs. (Races where entered for $25,000 or less not considered in allowances.)

Coupled—Green Cedars and The Minster.

Mr. Introienne — **B. c. 3, by Introienne—Miss Hilarious, by Hilarious**
Own.—Hilltop Stable & Grossman — **Br.—Powers J C Jr & Sandra D (Fla)** — **Tr.—Stutts Charles R** — **111**

Lifetime							
21 5 3 3	1985	9	1	0	0	$12,764
$52.599	1984	12	4	3	3	$39,835
	Turf	3	0	0	0	$1,807

9May85- 7Crc	fst	6f	:21⅘	:45⅕	1:12⅕	3↑ Alw 13400	2	6	$3^{3½}$	$2^{½}$	2^{hd}	$1^{¾}$	Vergara O	b	114	4.10	90-13	Mr Introienne114¾PublicFinnce120²Slwmobil115½	Bumped,driving 9
4May85- 9Crc	fm	1 1/16 Ⓣ	:48	1:11	1:41⅕	Needles	5	9	$7^{4½}$	5^{4}	6^{10}	6^{14}	Vergara O	b	114	52.30	85-01	Foundation Plan 123½ Verification 123^{11} Crovero 115½	No factor 13
10Apr85- 9Hia	fst	6f	:22	:45⅗	1:08⅘	Ⓡ Biscayne Bay	3	2	$2^{2½}$	2^{4}	$5^{6½}$	$4^{7½}$	Solis A	b	115	31.90	89-16	Damascus Sam 117^{4} Concert 115½ Cameo King 119^{3}	Weakened 6
20Mar85- 9Hia	fst	7f	:22⅖	:44⅗	1:23	Ⓢ J M Ofarrell	5	7	$6^{6½}$	5^{7}	5^{8}	$5^{8½}$	Solomone M	b	119	38.70	80-19	Sir Leon 119¾ Cherokee Fast 119^{nk} Cameo King 119^{1½}	No factor 8
21Feb85- 5GP	fst	6f	:21⅘	:45	1:10⅖	Alw 16000	2	7	$7^{4½}$	$7^{6½}$	5^{7}	$5^{9½}$	Velez J A Jr	b	117	23.20	78-24	HonestCut122½FelterOnTheQuay117^{6}ColderThana119^{2½}	No factor 8
11Feb85- 8GP	fm	1 Ⓣ	:48⅕	1:11⅖	1:35⅕	Gldn Grass	9	7	$6^{3½}$	$5^{6½}$	5^{9}	$5^{9¾}$	Fires E	b	113	16.50	84-07	Ⓓ FoundtonPln119^{nk}CovrtOprton119^{3½}Mr.Hppy113^{3}	Wide 1st turn 13
11Feb85-Run in divisions																			
31Jan85- 8GP	fm	*1 Ⓣ			1:37⅖	Alw 18000	11	2	$1^{1½}$	$1^{1½}$	3^{nk}	$5^{4¾}$	Velez J A Jr		117	30.80	88-11	DH Stack 117½ DH Silver Rich 119¾ Lautaro 117^{1½}	Tired 11
23Jan85- 7GP	fst	7f	:22	:45	1:24⅖	Alw 16200	10	6	$4^{7½}$	$4^{2½}$	4^{1}	$5^{4½}$	Velez J A Jr	b	117	11.10	78-22	Sir Leon 117^{3½} Colder Thana 122^{nk} Bowladrome 122½	Evenly 12
8Jan85- 9GP	fst	6f	:21⅖	:44⅗	1:10⅖	Spect'lr Bid	9	10	$8^{8½}$	11^{9}	$10^{9¾}$	$7^{5½}$	Velez J A Jr	b	112	51.30	81-16	Cherokee Fast 112½ Vindaloo 112^{1} SecretaryGeneral112^{1½}	Outrun 11
10Oct84- 9Crc	fst	1^{70}	:48⅕	1:13⅘	1:45⅘	Alw 20800	2	1	$1^{2½}$	2^{hd}	2^{3}	$2^{13½}$	Velez J A Jr	b	112	1.70	67-23	Alfred 112^{13½} Mr Introienne 112^{1} HopalongJustice112^{11}	2nd best 5

LATEST WORKOUTS May 18 Crc 5f fst 1:03 b   May 1 Crc Ⓣ 7f fm 1:30⅘ b (d)   Apr 25 Crc 1 fst 1:43 b (d)   Apr 20 Crc 6f fst 1:17⅗ b (d)

When stakes efforts look dull but allowance races competitive, handicappers should draw the line at two allowance victories. The change from nonwinners twice other than maiden or claiming to nonwinners three times other than maiden or claiming is from preliminary allowances to advanced allowances and one of the stiffest for young horses to negotiate. Eliminate Mr. Introienne and its like as probably outclassed by the conditions, which, after all, invite horses that have stakes races in their future.

Whether it wins or not, White Flannel is perfectly suited to nonwinners twice allowance conditions on turf. Its single poor race was on dirt. Otherwise, it has improved with racing while advancing in class. Do not be misled by the slow times. The variants are large. The turf April 11 was "yielding." These kinds may be difficult to evaluate, but they are not easy to eliminate.

7th Belmont

WIDENER TURF COURSE

1 MILE. (Turf). (1.33) ALLOWANCE. Purse $26,000. 3-year-olds which have never won two races other than Maiden, Claiming or Starter. Weights, 122 lbs. Non-winners of a race other than Maiden or Claiming at a mile or over since May 1 allowed 3 lbs. Of such a race since April 15, 5 lbs.

White Flannel — **Ch. c. 3, by Snow Knight—Tricot, by The Axe II**
Own.—Walker Mrs J Jr — **117** — **Br.—Walker Mrs J Jr (Pa)** — **Tr.—Penna Angel Jr**

Lifetime 6 2 0 2 $19,680	1985	3	2	0	1	$17,400
	1984	3	M	0	1	$2,280
	Turf	5	2	0	2	$19,680

11Apr85-9Hia	a1⅛ Ⓣ	1:51^{1}yl	*2¼	122	11^{7}	$9^{7½}$	$3^{½}$	$3^{1½}$	Santos J A^{4}	Aw15000	74-28	HectorJ.,SenorVerde,WhiteFlnnel	12
15Mar85-7Hia	a1⅛ Ⓣ	1:51^{2}fm	2¾	120	10^{10}	7^{6}	3^{4}	1^{hd}	Santos J A^{2}	Aw11500	74-24	WhitFlnnl,OurDiplomt,SportingFr	10
15Mar85—Bore in, drvg													
19Feb85-4GP	a1 1/16 Ⓣ	1:47 fm	*2¾	122	8^{12}	$7^{5¾}$	$4^{1¾}$	$1^{½}$	Santos J A^{6}	Mdn	71-26	WhiteFlnnel,ProfitPlus,RoundRidg	9
8Nov84-6Aqu	1⅛ :49^{4} 1:15^{2}	1:54^{3}ft	3¾	113^{5}	$7^{5½}$	$4^{1½}$	5^{15}	$5^{23¼}$	Ward W A^{8}	Mdn	39-26	Stack, Dancin On Pins, Olajuwon	8
22Oct84-6Bel	1 1/16 Ⓣ:47^{1} 1:11	1:43^{3}fm	3¼	118	$6^{4½}$	$5^{4½}$	2^{5}	5^{5}	Cordero A Jr^{6}	Mdn	73-18	SpceRider,LordAshley,RoundRidg	11
8Oct84-6Bel	1 1/16 Ⓣ:48 1:12^{2}	1:43^{3}fm	7	118	9^{6}	$7^{3¾}$	3^{6}	$3^{7½}$	Cordero A Jr^{11}	Mdn	70-22	Dnger'sHour,SpceRider,WhitFlnnl	12

May 14 Bel 4f ft :48^{3} h   May 8 Bel 6f ft 1:14^{3} h   May 2 Bel 5f gd 1:00^{1} h   Apr 27 Bel 6f ft 1:16 b

7th Hollywood

TURF COURSE
1 1-16 MILES
HOLLYWOOD PARK
START
FINISH

1 1/16 MILES. (Turf). (1.39⅘) 45th Running of WILL ROGERS HANDICAP (Grade III). (Stretch start.) $60,000 added. 3-year-olds. By subscription of $100 each, which shall accompany the nomination, $600 additional to start, with $60,000 added, of which $12,000 to second, $9,000 to third, $4,500 to fourth and $1,500 to fifth. Weights, Monday, May 20. Starters to be named through the entry box by closing time of entries. A trophy will be presented to the owner of the winner. Closed Wednesday, May 15, 1985, with 17 nominations.

Rich Earth
HAWLEY S **119**
Own.—Elmendorf Farm Inc
B. c. 3, by Transworld—Pout, by Rash Prince
Br.—Elmendorf Farm (Ky) **1985 6 3 1 0 $67,100**
Tr.—McAnally Ronald **Turf 2 2 0 0 $43,700**
Lifetime 6 3 1 0 $67,100

10May85-8Hol 1 1/16 Ⓣ:4641:11 1:412fm 9½ 119 85 74½ 2hd 12½ Hawley S2 Ⓡ Caucasus 92-08 RichEarth,Emperdori,PintedCnyon 8
20Apr85-8GG 1⅛ :474 1:112 1:483ft 25 115 87 85½ 66½ 66¾ ChpnTM7 Cal Dby 83-13 Hjji'sTresur,Turkomn,Nostlgi'sStr 10
20Apr85—Grade II; Bobbled break
6Apr85-5SA 1⅛ Ⓣ:4721:1231:494fm*8-5 114 24 22½ 11½ 11½ McCarronCJ8 Aw30000 78-17 Rich Earth, Julie'sMark,Ascension 10
24Mar85-5SA 1 1/16 :453 1:101 1:423ft 14 114 23½ 22 1hd 21½ Hawley S7 Aw28000 86-12 Don'tSyHlo,RichErth,LuckyNGreen 9
3Mar85-6SA 1 1/16 :461 1:102 1:432ft 6¾ 117 1½ 1hd 1½ 54¾ Pincay L Jr2 Aw28000 79-14 BolderThnBold,Ascension,Turkomn 9
9Feb85-6SA 6½f :221 :452 1:172gd 3½ 118 31 1hd 2hd 1hd Hawley S7 Mdn 83-20 Rich Earth, Equilibre, Reckoner 11
May 19 Hol 4f ft :481 h May 5 Hol 6f ft 1:16 h Apr 15 SA 3f ft :354 h Apr 1 SA 4f ft :472 h

Matthew T. Parker
DELAHOUSSAYE E **114**
Own.—Moss Mr-Mrs J S
Dk. b. or br. g. 3, by Rock Talk—Dee's Might, by Might
Br.—Lege F M III (Md) **1985 3 0 0 0 $9,950**
Tr.—Frankel Robert **1984 8 2 3 0 $125,970**
Lifetime 11 2 3 0 $135,920 **Turf 1 0 0 0 $1,200**

10May85-8Hol 1 1/16 Ⓣ:4641:11 1:412fm 11 117 31 31½ 3nk 54½ PincyLJr6 Ⓡ Caucasus 87-08 RichEarth,Emperdori,PintedCnyon 8
23Feb85-8SA 1 :454 1:101 1:361ft 25 118 42 811 816 916½ McHrgDG9 Sn Rfael 71-13 SmartenUp,FstAccount,Stn'sBower 9
23Feb85—Grade II
3Feb85-8BM 1 1/16 :453 1:093 1:41 ft 18 120 11½ 2hd 53 56 StnsGL5 Cmn Rl Dby 81-13 Tnk'sProspect,RightCon,‡Skywlker 9
3Feb85—Grade III
16Dec84-8Hol 1 1/16 :453 1:103 1:432gd 14 121 76¼ 96 914 912 DlhossyE1 Hol Fut — — Stphn'sOdyssy,FrstNormn,RghtCn 13
16Dec84—Grade I
5Dec84-8Hol 7f :213 :442 1:221ft 3-2 119 44½ 45 47 49½ DelhoussyE2 Hol Prvu 86-07 FirstNormn,TeddyNturlly,Dn'sDiblo 6
27Oct84-8SA 1 1/16 :463 1:104 1:422ft 9¼ 118 1½ 2hd 2hd 21½ Black K2 Norfolk 87-13 Chief'sCrown,MtthewT.Prkr,VivMxi 6
27Oct84—Grade I
17Oct84-8SA 7f :224 :453 1:234ft 7¼ 117 52¼ 52¼ 31½ 11 DlhossyE2 Snny Slpe 81-18 MtthwT.Prkr,PrivtJungl,Dn'sDiblo 11
17Oct84—Grade III
5Sep84-8Dmr 6f :221 :452 1:114ft 13 117 93¼ 74¼ 65¾ 2no DlhossyE4 Ⓡ Rcho Sfe 79-21 KerbrCo.,MtthwT.Prkr,Mtronomic 11
5Sep84—Fanned wide, lugged in
11Aug84-9Mth 6f :221 :451 1:102ft 18 122 66 68 616 820½ BrccileVJr7 Sapling 67-12 DoublyClear,Tiltalting,DoItAginDn 10
11Aug84—Grade II
27Jly84-4Mth 5½f :224 :46 1:052sy 7 118 2½ 2hd 2hd 12 Melendez J D7 Mdn 88-21 MtthewT.Prker,FutureRelity,Woltn 9
May 19 Hol 5f ft 1:00 h May 7 Hol 6f ft 1:143 h May 1 Hol Ⓣ 6f fm 1:142 h (d) Apr 26 Hol 5f ft 1:01 h

Don't Say Halo
MCHARGUE D **118**
Own.—Buckland Farm
Dk. b. or br. c. 3, by Halo—Never Babble, by Advocator
Br.—Evans T M (Va) **1985 5 3 1 0 $74,500**
Tr.—Speckert Christopher **1984 4 M 1 0 $5,040**
Lifetime 9 3 2 0 $79,540 **Turf 1 1 0 0 $41,800**

27Apr85-7Hol 1 Ⓣ:4541:0921:341fm 5¼ 115 56 33 1hd 11 McHargueDG2 Sptlght 92-08 Don'tSayHlo,WellReltd,HuddleUp 9
6Apr85-8SA 1⅛ :463 1:103 1:482ft 9 122 62¼ 63¼ 912 810¾ McHrDG8 S A Dby 76-10 Skywalker,FstAccount,Nostlgi'sStr 9
6Apr85—Grade I; Wide early
24Mar85-5SA 1 1/16 :453 1:101 1:423ft 4¼ 115 49 45½ 32 11½ McHrgueDG4 Aw28000 88-12 Don'tSyHlo,RichErth,LuckyNGreen 9
24Mar85—Lugged in late
2Mar85-4SA 6f :221 :46 1:11 ft *4-5 120 55¾ 43½ 46 24 ShoemkerW2 Aw26000 79-18 Infantryman,Don'tSayHlo,PineBelt 6
2Mar85—Veered in, bumped at start, again shortly after
16Feb85-6SA 6f :212 :443 1:092ft 9-5 118 55 3½ 1hd 13 Shoemaker W2 Mdn 91-16 Don'tSyHlo,ExclsvCpd,Alln'sPrspct 7
26Aug84-8Sar 6½f :214 :444 1:16 ft 58 122 44½ 64 88¼ 814¼ MiglioreR4 Hopeful 78-15 Chif'sCrown,TiffnyIc,Mugzy'sRullh 9
26Aug84—Grade I
11Aug84-4Sar 6f :23 :47 1:114ft *2 118 65 21 22 23 Maple E7 Mdn 78-15 MedivlMyhm,Don'tSyHlo,FuturFbl 11
26Jly84-6Bel 6f :223 :461 1:113ft *9-5 118 64 44½ 35½ 46 Cruguet J5 Mdn 78-17 SalemDrive,Anconeus,Haberdsher 10
28Jun84-8Bel 5½f :222 :462 1:053ft 3½e 113 88 88½ 77½ 68½ Velasquez J10 Juvenile 78-18 SkyCommnd,MnPrspctr,DItAgnDn 10
May 21 SA 5f ft 1:013 h May 16 SA 1 ft 1:382 h May 11 SA 6f ft 1:14 h Apr 21 SA 6f ft 1:133 h

Which of the three-year-olds above, if any, are suited to the Will Rogers, a Grade 3 stakes?

Rich Earth and Don't Say Halo are well suited, but Matthew T. Parker is not. The unsuited horse won the Grade 2 Sunny Slope at Santa Anita at age two, and placed in the Grade 1 Norfolk to boot, but has not followed up very impressively at three. Its three starts have been disappointing, and the lost ground in the stretch of the restricted Caucasus stakes last out does not translate readily into Grade 3 credentials next time.

Handicappers must be prepared to discount the two-year-old record of horses that cannot repeat the feats at three. Distrust the early performances until proven wrong.

Rich Earth and Don't Say Halo have looked impressive lately, except when entered in Grade 2 and Grade 1 races, respectively. Rich Earth last out won a restricted stakes impressively enough to qualify in open, listed, and Grade 3 races, but not Grade 2. Don't Say Halo last out won an open stakes, and likewise fits with open, listed, and Grade 3 company. This one may eventually move up to Grade 2, but that possibility is undetermined now.

These analyses are tough and close. Handicappers need information about manner of previous performances as well as the results.

8th Belmont

1⅛ MILES. (1.45⅘) 32nd Running THE PETER PAN (Grade I). Purse $75,000 Added. (Plus $25,000 Breeders' Cup Premium Awards). 3-year-olds. By subscription of $150 each, which should accompany the nomination; $1,200 to pass the entry box, with $75,000 added. The added money and all fees to be divided 60% to the winner, 22% to second, 12% to third and 6% to fourth. 126 lbs. Non-winners of a race of $75,000 at a mile or over allowed 3 lbs.; of a race of $25,000 at any distance, 6 lbs. of three races other than maiden or claiming, 9 lbs. Of two races other than maiden or claiming, 12 lbs. Starters to be named at the closing time of entries. A trophy will be presented to the winning owner. Closed Wednesday, May 8, 1985 with 39 nominations.

Salem Drive — **B. c. 3, by Darby Creek Road—Northern Sunset, by Northfields**

Own.—Payson Virginia **114** **Br.—Payson Virginia Kraft (Ky)** 1985 5 1 1 2 $20,590

Tr.—Lundy Richard J 1984 2 1 0 0 $10,800

Lifetime 7 2 1 2 $31,390

28Apr85-5Aqu	1	$:46^{3}$	$1:11^{1}$	$1:36^{2}$ft	*8-5	122	6^{6}	$3^{3\frac{1}{2}}$	$3^{3\frac{1}{2}}$	$3^{1\frac{1}{4}}$	Ward W A^{2}	Aw24000	83-21	Summitry,CutlassReality,SlemDrive	8
9Apr85-5Aqu	1⅛	$:48^{4}$	$1:13^{4}$	$1:50^{4}$ft	3½	117	3^{2}	$3^{2\frac{1}{2}}$	$1^{2\frac{1}{2}}$	$1^{6\frac{1}{2}}$	Ward W A^{7}	Aw23000	81-25	SlemDrive,PerfectPrde,Crystllcbrg	7
16Mar85-7Hia	7f	:23	$:45^{2}$	$1:23^{4}$ft	7	115	$5^{3\frac{1}{2}}$	$7^{5\frac{1}{4}}$	$4^{1\frac{1}{2}}$	$3^{2\frac{1}{2}}$	Maple E^{3}	Aw12500	81-13	Travaux, My Shane, Salem Drive	12
9Feb85-8GP	6f	$:22^{1}$	$:45^{4}$	1:11 ft	4½	117	11^{11}	11^{12}	$11^{6\frac{1}{2}}$	$8^{6\frac{1}{2}}$	Guerra W A^{5}	Aw14800	77-18	HonstCut,WrriorCountry,LibrtyRx	12
26Jan85-5GP	6f	$:22^{3}$	:47	$1:12^{4}$ft	4	117	$4^{2\frac{1}{2}}$	3^{2}	1^{hd}	2½	Maple E^{2}	Aw14000	74-19	Avey'sBrother,SlemDrive,Pichinch	11
26Jly84-6Bel	6f	$:22^{3}$	$:46^{1}$	$1:11^{3}$ft	17	118	1^{2}	1^{3}	$1^{2\frac{1}{2}}$	1¾	Maple E^{3}	Mdn	84-17	SalemDrive,Anconeus,Haberdsher	10
5Jly84-6Bel	5½f	$:22^{2}$	$:45^{4}$	$1:04^{2}$ft	7	118	$4^{3\frac{1}{2}}$	4^{5}	4^{7}	$5^{11\frac{1}{4}}$	Cordero A Jr^{1}	Mdn	82-15	Chief'sCrown,DesertWr,TigerBiddr	9

May 23 Bel 5f ft $1:01^{4}$ b ●May 18 Bel 1 gd $1:39^{1}$ h May 13 Bel 6f ft $1:16^{2}$ b ●Apr 23 Bel 5f ft $:59^{4}$ h

Clean Machine — **B. c. 3, by Alleged—Azeez, by Nashua**

Own.—Singer C B **114** **Br.—Jones W L Jr (Ky)** 1985 3 2 0 0 $22,800

Tr.—Tesher Howard M 1984 1 M 1 0 $4,620

Lifetime 4 2 1 0 $27,420 Turf 3 1 1 0 $12,420

20May85-4Bel	1¼ Ⓣ	$:47^{3}$	$1:36^{1}$	$2:01^{1}$fm	3¾	113	$6^{3\frac{1}{2}}$	11^{13}	10^{15}	$11^{18\frac{3}{4}}$	Migliore R^{10}	Aw26000	69-15	WlcomSuitor,ColdFtII,Pigwidgon	11
8May85-3Bel	1$\frac{1}{16}$	$:48^{1}$	$1:12^{4}$	$1:44^{2}$ft	4½	112	$5^{1\frac{3}{4}}$	4^{4}	$2^{1\frac{1}{2}}$	$1^{1\frac{1}{2}}$	Migliore R^{3}	Aw25000	80-18	ClenMchine,CoyoteDncer,Hberdshr	7
28Mar85-7Hia	a1⅛ Ⓣ			1:53 fm	*6-5	119	$3^{5\frac{1}{2}}$	3^{4}	$2^{2\frac{1}{2}}$	1½	Cruguet J^{5}	Mdn	66-28	Clean Machine, Passenger, Le Wild	9
19Nov84-6Aqu	1$\frac{1}{16}$ Ⓣ	:50	$1:16^{2}$	$1:51^{4}$sf	*2	118	$7^{2\frac{3}{4}}$	$6^{4\frac{3}{4}}$	$4^{5\frac{1}{2}}$	2^{2}	Migliore R^{2}	Mdn	44-46	Olajuwon,CleanMachine,ProAppeal	8

May 16 Bel Ⓣ 6f fm $1:13^{4}$ h (d) May 5 Aqu 5f ft $1:00^{3}$ h Apr 29 Aqu 3f ft :37 b ●Apr 23 Aqu 6f gd $1:14^{2}$ h

When unseasoned three-year-olds are ceremoniously moved from the nonwinners allowance series to Grade 1 competition, they are practically by definition outclassed and should be unceremoniously eliminated by handicappers. Trainers get carried away by promising young horses, but handicappers need not.

What about the following horse in the same race?

```
Concert                                  B. c. 3, by Naskra—Hail to the Fleet, by Hail to Reason
                                         Br.—Postell A J (Wash)              1985  3 0 2 1   $21,843
Own.—Dumas R                       120   Tr.—Derein David B                  1984  5 4 0 0   $28,665
                                      Lifetime   8 4 2 1   $50,508
8May85-8Bel   1  :46   1:11^1 1:36^3ft   40f 126  5^3¼ 6^5 5^2½ 3^3     McCrrnG^1    Withers  79-18 El Basco, Another Reef, Concert  12
    8May85—Grade II; Altered course
28Apr85-9Rkm  6f :21^4 :45   1:10^4ft   *2-3 120  6^7 4^5½ 3^6 2^7      GafflioneS^4 Pine Echo 83-26 MedivlScrt,Concrt,ClssicCompnion 9
10Apr85-9Hia  6f :22   :45^3 1:08^4ft    4  115  6^7½ 5^6¾ 4^6¼ 2^4     StsJA^1 [R]BiscayneBay 93-16 DamascusSam,Concert,CameoKing 6
1Dec84-8Aqu   1  :47   1:12^2 1:38^1ft   11  114  10^3 10^12 10^14 9^16½ BrnrhffD^3  Nashua   58-28 Stone White, BannerBob,OldMain 12
    1Dec84—Grade III
12Nov84-9Suf  1^70 :46^3 1:12^2 1:44^3m *7-5 117  4^5 2^1½ 1^2 1^2¾    BrnrhffD^6 M Standish 77-24 Concert, Artie Baby, Damas Sham 10
    12Nov84—Steadied, drvng
28Oct84-7Rkm  6f :22   :45^3 1:12 gd    3  115  7^2¾ 3^1 1^2½ 1^3½     BrnrhffD^5 Blues Alley 84-24 Concert,Bowladrome,Sm'sPlesure 11
16Oct84-5Rkm  6f :22^1 :45^3 1:12^1ft  *9-5 120  6^6 3^6 2^3 1^1       Brinkerhoff D^5 Aw7500 83-23 Concert,Sam'sPleasure,Bowldrome 7
5Oct84-6Suf   6f :22^4 :46^4 1:13^3ft   3½ 118  5^3½ 3^1 2^hd 1^4      Brinkerhoff D^6  Mdn   73-29 Concert,Starstuff,BackBayBanquet 6
   May 19 Rkm 5f sy 1:03^3 b     Apr 26 Rkm 3f ft :37^2 h     ●Apr 21 Rkm 5f ft 1:02 h     ●Mar 28 GP 6f ft 1:13^2 hg
```

Concert has just finished third after altering course in the stretch of the Grade 2 Withers Stakes. Does the colt fit in the Grade 1 field? It might. It depends on the corroborating evidence, the total pattern of performance.

Unfortunately, Concert's efforts in the restricted Biscayne Bay stakes and open Pine Echo stakes, the latter a minor affair at Rockingham Park, do not support the leap to Grade 1 conditions.

Similarly, the two-year-old record at Suffolk and Rockingham might be entirely misleading, as the dismal drubbing of Concert in New York's Grade 2 Nashua Stakes portends. Concert may be a stakes horse after all, but it will not be a Grade 1 stakes horse; a minor stakes horse.

7th Santa Anita

1 MILE. (1.33%) ALLOWANCE. Purse $40,000. 3-year-olds and upward, which have not won two races of $13,750 at one mile or over since April 7. Weights, 3-year-olds, 116 lbs.; older, 120 lbs. Non-winners of $13,750 since July 21 allowed 2 lbs.; since June 1, 4 lbs.; since April 7, 6 lbs. (Races when entered for $40,000 or less not considered.)

```
Back'n Time                              Dk. b. or br. c. 3, by First Back—Exigency, by Prize Host
                                         Br.—Post Time Stables (Cal)          1980  5 3 0 1   $24,825
Own.—Post Time Stables             110   Tr.—McAnally Ronald                  1979  0 M 0 0
21Sep80-10DMF 6f :21^2 :43^4 1:07^4ft  *1-2 113  1^hd 1^4 1^7 1^8      Valenzuela P A^1   Alw  99 Bck'nTime,VoomVoom,AmnBrothr 9
8Sep80-7Dmr  6f :21^2 :44   1:08^2ft  *1-2 118  1½ 1^3½ 1^4 1^4½     Pincay L Jr^6      Alw  96 Back'nTime,StatelyNtive,BronzeStr 7
22Aug80-6Dmr 6f :22   :44^1 1:08^1ft  *9-5 117  1^1½ 1^5 1^6 1^10     Pincay L Jr^3    [S]Mdn 97 Back'n Time,TrammelLuck,Donald 11
10May80-2Hol 6f :21^4 :44^4 1:10^1ft   5¼ 118  4^2¼ 3^1½ 3^2½ 3^2¼    McHargueDG^5    M50000 84 Olympd'sSon,WtrfrdBlly,Bck'nTm 11
5Jan80-3SA   6f :21^3 :45   1:10^3ft   13  118  5^2¼ 6^3¼ 8^3¾ 5^9¾    McHargueDG^9    [S]Mdn 76 WoodlndLd,SgcosStory,FortClgry 12
   Oct 28 SA 1 ft 1:43^2 h     ●Oct 15 SA 7f ft 1:25^1 h     Oct 8 SA 6f ft 1:14^2 b     Oct 1 SA 4f ft :50^4 b
```

This classified mile admitting three-year-olds during Oak Tree at Santa Anita 1980 provides an instructive note on which to end this chapter.

To recall, classified conditions of fall can often favor late-developing three-year-olds that project a higher class under non-winners conditions. The colt Back'n Time certainly fits that description. Moreover, six months of the core season have elapsed since April 7, the specified date of the classified restrictions. Any horse that has won two or more routes of classified or stakes quality has effectively been barred from the competition, the usual layups excepted. The conditions are thus relatively restrictive. So much more in favor of developing three-year-olds.

Does Back'n Time figure to win in a breeze? Not according to total performance handicapping procedures, which are enlightening in this instance, as is so often the case.

Having won a maiden race and two allowance races, Back'n Time can be credited with having proceeded to advanced nonwinners allowances. Its power performance September 21 at Del Mar surely indicates Back'n Time will be a monster sprinting under NW3 conditions if not pressed hard on the front. What that victory says about future races under classified or stakes conditions at longer distances or on turf is far more speculative, much more risky.

The total record is similarly of concern. After a hapless performance January 5, the colt was not favored in a maiden claiming sprint four months later, which it lost. No one wanted the claim. Next came the rejuvenating workouts and the devastating maiden and preliminary nonwinners races at Del Mar. Back'n Time might have an exceptional future, after all.

But the time to bet on it was not the Oak Tree classified mile. Not only was the fast colt attempting a distance of two turns for the first time, but also it was jumping greatly in class. Do the Del Mar races support the combined moves? They do not. Anyone who watched those Del Mar romps saw a fast but free-running colt, and ability to get middle distances had to be of concern. With classier horses running at it, that concern should have mounted. At low odds, handicappers prefer to pass rather than risk good money.

Back'n Time weakened in the final sixteenth of the Oak Tree mile and lost the decision to a middling classified miler of no previous distinction. Had better horses been eligible, Back'n Time would have lost more persuasively, notwithstanding its strong betting favoritism. As events proceeded, a nondescript animal proved good enough to handle this developing three-year-old. But the race was written for just that kind of nondescript classified maverick. I hope handicappers who begin paying stricter attention to racing conditions will stop betting on young colts that are not favored by the conditions, and therefore do not figure to win.

CHAPTER 10

Three-Year-Olds and Up

ACCELERATED DEVELOPMENT of young stock means in part that three-year-olds now race earlier and more frequently against older horses.

On Sunday, July 7, 1985, practically the season's midpoint, every race open to older horses at Belmont Park, Arlington Park, Hollywood Park, and Monmouth Park invited three-year-olds as well. The invitations had been standard fare since spring. At Hollywood Park three-year-olds remain eligible to every stakes event on the calendar, which begins in April.

On that July 7, of interest to handicappers, three-year-olds at Belmont, Arlington, Hollywood, and Monmouth had a legitimate right to win any nonclaiming race that they entered. Several statistical compilations persuade us that they did, even at the route.

If doubt persists, consider the early July speed disadvantages common to three-year-olds, in relation to older horses, as uncovered by William Quirin's computer analyses of final times typical of three-year-olds vis-à-vis those of older horses:

6f +1

(**Translation**: Three-year-old races at six furlongs in July are typically slower than similar races open to older horses by one length.)

6½f	+2
7f	+2
1m	+3
1-1/16m	+3
1⅛m	+4

Although older horses generally run faster than three-year-olds, the time differences decrease as the season progresses. The implications of this should be of fascinating importance to handicappers. The one-length disadvantage at six furlongs in July suggests typical three-year-olds actually will enjoy speed advantages at this frequently run distance in the fall. This they do in nonclaiming sprints by wide margin, beginning November 1. Consider the seasonal speed differences at common distances, as identified by Quirin's comprehensive study and presented in Table 1, below.

Their three- to four-length speed disadvantages at middle distances in July means only the better three-year-olds in each class-distance category deserve support against older horses at that time. Because they run faster than what is typical of three-year-olds, this better group overcompensates for normal time disadvantages. And so it goes, for example, that when nonclaiming three-year-olds that have been doing well against better drop down in July to class-distance categories of lower status and encounter older horses, statistics indicate they run at no standard time disadvantage, and have a perfect right to win.

Considering the mythologies that endure in these matters among even highly experienced handicappers, it's reassuring to learn from science that three-year-olds win their appropriate shares of maiden, allowance, and stakes races when confronting four-year-olds and up. And it's exciting to know the standard speed disadvantages three-year-olds in various class-distance categories need to overcome at each succeeding month of the season.

To realize furthermore that all speed disadvantages beyond one length disappear at distances up to one and one-sixteenth miles by October 15 permits handicappers to approach the fall races for mixed ages completely at ease about the statistical chances of three-year-olds.

Nonetheless, two barriers to the effective handicapping of races for three-year-olds and up remain firmly erect. First, allowance and added-money races are carded in multiple form. Within broad confines, handicappers need to understand which particular conditions inviting three-year-olds and up afford three-year-olds a better or worse chance. Some allowances and stakes are decidedly more hospitable to three-year-olds than others.

Table 1
Time Differences of Races Open to Older Horses vs. Races
Restricted to Three-Year Olds

Do older horses run faster than three-year-olds? In general, they do. But the full answer is related to distance and to time of the season. An orderly pattern exists, with early-season speed advantages of older horses at all typical distances decreasing as the season progresses. Handicappers will benefit if they spend a few minutes reviewing the time differences of races for the two age groups.

The table below shows those differences in fifths of a second, and the dates on which the differences change. The differences appear in the left and right margins, the dates in the body of the table.

	6F	6½F	7F	1M–1^{40}M	1^{70}M–1¹⁄₁₆M	1⅛M	
+9						Jan.1	+9
+8						Feb. 1	+8
+7					Jan.1	Mar.15	+7
+6					Feb. 15	May 1	+6
+5				Jan. 1	Apr. 15	June 1	+5
+4		Jan. 1	Jan. 1	Apr. 15	June 1	July 1	+4
+3	Jan. 1	Feb. 1	Mar. 15	June 1	July 1	Aug. 1	+3
+2	Apr. 15	June 1	June 15	July 15	Aug. 15	Sept. 15	+2
+1	July 1	Aug. 1	Aug. 15	Sept. 15	Oct.15	Dec. 1	+1
0	Nov. 1	Dec. 1	Dec. 15	——	——	——	0

Winning at the Races, Computer Discoveries in Thoroughbred Handicapping,
by William L. Quirin, Ph.D., William Morrow & Company, Inc., New York, 1979,
p. 159.

Thus, on January 1, older horses finish faster by three lengths at six furlongs, by nine lengths at one and one-eighth miles.

By July 1, the six furlong advantage of older horses is one length, the middle distance advantages three to four lengths.

By November 1, all six furlong advantage has disappeared. The advantage of older horses at one and one-eighth miles holds at two lengths.

Second, to specify seasonal speed disadvantages belonging to groups of horses that represent age-distance levels is a basic kind of help, but that information specifies nothing about the current status of a single horse's class, form, or distance-footing-pace preferences. Statistical data can be terribly mismanaged. To assume a three-year-old will outrun a four-year-old at six furlongs in November because its age-distance category holds a speed advantage at that time gets handicappers a head start on upset. To assume a five-year-old can outkick a three-year-old at one and one-eighth miles in June, when its age-distance category holds a five-length speed advantage, achieves only a similar fate.

What if the June route is an allowance race of the kind that limits eligibility to horses that have never won an allowance race? Now do handicappers prefer five-year-olds?

Statistical study and computer generation identify new and significant generalities about handicapping and thus provide handicappers with directions and applications formerly unknown or only intuitively sensed, but neither supplants the fundamentals of handicapping. Cold-blooded numbers should help shape better handicapping judgments, but they had better not substitute for them.

A race at Hollywood Park as far back as 1979 can reside here as an illustration of several matters jointly considered. Not only does the race showcase the greater oppportunities for three-year-olds in races open to older horses, it illuminates (a) the importance of eligibility conditions, (b) the mythology still surrounding three-year-olds and up, and (c) the ultimate importance of comprehensive handicapping.

Those who favor the kind of handicapping analysis guided by an understanding of eligibility conditions will more likely identify the likeliest winner than those who do not.

When analyzing nonwinners three times allowances, such handicappers will remain on the alert for something younger rather than older; for something lightly raced and still improving rather than hard-raced and settled in the allowances; for something demonstrating a touch of class beyond nonwinners allowance races. Handicappers practiced in this approach begin instinctively by calling into mind the qualities of class associated with advanced nonwinners allowances or better, and then shop the past performances for the most suitable profiles.

Whether handicappers attend in that way to eligibility conditions or not, absolutely the key to working effectively with the Hollywood sprint and its like is the attitude held toward the chances of any three-year-olds that have been entered.

Handicappers who found the three-year-old Infusive a kind of class article under these conditions share a point of view and attitude not yet widely distributed among regular racegoers.

For example, and notwithstanding logistical constraints that hamper their selection procedures, public selectors for *Daily Racing Form* did not very much value the differences of class attributed

4th Hollywood

7 FURLONGS. (1.19%) ALLOWANCE. Purse $18,000. 3-year-olds and upward which have not won $2,500 three times other than maiden, claiming or starter. Weights, 3-year-olds, 116 lbs.; older, 123 lbs. Non-winners of two such races since April 24, allowed 2 lbs.; two such races since March 19, 4 lbs.

Laurel's Raider *

Own.—Moss J S — 119

Dk. b. or br. c. 4, by Sadair—Laurel Mae, by Crafty Admiral
Br.—Diamante Stables (Fla)
Tr.—Frankel Robert

1979 13 4 2 2 $71,275
1978 7 2 1 0 $19,150
Turf 4 0 1 0 $5,500

29Jun79-6Hol 6f :213 :441 1:083ft 2¼ 117 65½ 75 51¼ 1hd Pincay L Jr5 50000 94 Laurel's Raider, SeaRide,Nola'sGuy 7
22Jun79-6Hol 6f :221 :444 1:084ft *1 117 33 3½ 21 31¾ Pincay L Jr6 60000 91 Under Tack,SeaRide,Laurel'sRaider 6
10May79-8Hol 6f :214 :441 1:08 ft 7 117 1hd 2½ 34½ 59¾ Pincay L Jr5 Alw 87 Syncopate, Foyt's Ack, Maheras 8
3May79-8Hol 6f :221 :451 1:091ft 4½ 115 3hd 42 54½ 78 Hawley S5 Alw 83 Little Reb, No No, B. W. Turner 7
21Apr79-7Hol 7f :221 :443 1:212ft *8-5 116 — — — — Hawley S3 Alw — Pleasure Shack, Stand Pat, Don F. 6
21Apr79—Lost rider
1Apr79-6SA 7f :222 :451 1:221ft 9-5 116 21 21 1½ 1½ Hawley S8 60000 92 Laurel'sRaider,CrashProgrm,SldSm 7
21Mar79-5SA 1 :452 1:102 1:344gd *2½ 116 21 1½ 2hd 37 McHargue DG2 60000 88 Rex, Legendario III, Laurel'sRaider 7
11Mar79-5SA a6½f ⓣ:211 :4341:132fm 7 114 52 2hd 1½ 2hd McHargue D G4 Alw 92 Smoggy, Laurel'sRaider,Postmark 11
2Mar79-8SA 6½f :213 :44 1:151ft 4½ 114 1hd 31½ 43½ 43¾ Hawley S4 Alw 90 WhiteRammer,Maheras,BackByBet 6
10Feb79-5SA a6½f ⓣ:214 :4441:154sf *2½ 113 62½ 31½ 51½ 42½ Hawley S3 Alw 77 He's Dewan, Sea Ride, Nola's Guy 10

● Jun 15 Hol 5f ft :582 h Jun 10 Hol 5f ft 1:00 h ● Jun 5 Hol 4f ft :471 h May 20 Hol 4f ft :48 b

Crimson Commander

Own.—Greliness-King-Victor — 119

Ch. h. 5, by Crimson Satan—Merry Command, by Bold Commander
Br.—Braugh Ranches (Ky)
Tr.—King Hal

1979 10 3 4 1 $42,400
1977 9 2 2 0 $17,500
Turf 2 0 1 0 $3,400

13Jun79-7Hol 7f :22 :442 1:213ft *2-3 115 54 42½ 31 1hd Pierce D4 Alw 91 CrimsonCommnder,Lm,RisingEcho 6
20May79-6Hol 1⅛ :454 1:092 1:474ft *1 114 2hd 11 2½ 2nk Hawley S3 Alw 93 TkthBlnc,CrmsnCmmndr,Kndnsky 11
13May79-5Hol 7f :214 :434 1:202ft *8-5 117 1hd 11½ 15 15 Pincay L Jr2 c32000 97 CrimsonCommander,Kaskee,Mrcho 8
3May79-5Hol 7f :22 :442 1:213ft 4½ 116 71½ 2hd 1hd 13½ DelhoussyE10 c25000 91 CrmsnCmmndr,PtmcPrd,AndrFny 10
1Apr79-6SA 7f :222 :451 1:221ft 14 116 11 11 2½ 45½ Baltazar C4 60000 86 Laurel'sRaider,CrashProgrm,SldSm 7
8Mar79-5SA 1⅛ ⓣ:4711:1121:484fm 17 114 11 1½ 1½ 2½ Castaneda M1 A25000 82 KAccnt,CrmsnCmmndr,DncD'Espr 12
4Mar79-9SA 6½f :214 :442 1:154ft 3½ 116 52 34 23 22½ McHargue DG4 40000 88 Shckls,CrimsonCommndr,Strwood 10
10Feb79-4SA 7f :22 :444 1:22 ft 4½ 116 42 31 2hd 2¾ McHargue DG7 32000 92 Crorate,CrimsonCommander,NoBis 7
21Jan79-5SA 6f :22 :45 1:09 ft 9½ 116 52 31½ 33 34½ McHargue DG8 25000 89 ChiefArtist,Lrky,CrimsonCommndr 9
7Jan79-1SA 6f :213 :443 1:10 ft 12 116 64½ 63 64½ 711 McHargue DG7 25000 78 ChiefArtist,SeniorDirctor,Rkindld 11

Jly 5 Hol 4f ft :51 h Jun 28 Hol 5f ft 1:021 h Jun 21 Hol 5f ft 1:00 h Jun 10 Hol 5f ft 1:04 h

Don F.

Own.—Frazee T & L — 119

B. c. 4, by Don B—Flessie Betty, by Doc Scott J
Br.—Frazee & Frazee (Cal)
Tr.—Brooks L J

1979 10 0 1 3 $18,600
1978 7 1 0 1 $19,325
Turf 3 0 0 0 $1,500

23May79-7Hol 6f :221 :443 1:09 ft 8 116 81¾ 76½ 89¾ 810 Olivares F3 Alw 82 Sea Ride, Nola'sGuy,Someonenoble 9
6May79-7Hol 1⅛ ⓣ:4641:1111:472fm 8 115 56½ 32 42¾ 62¾ Delahoussaye E5 Alw 95 DoubleWin,Mary'sPolicy,JzzSinger 8
21Apr79-7Hol 7f :221 :443 1:212ft 5 116 55 46½ 34 33 Delahoussaye E1 Alw 89 Pleasure Shack, Stand Pat, Don F. 6
11Apr79-7Hol 6f :223 :454 1:094ft 4¾ 116 43¾ 33½ 21 2½ Delahoussaye E3 Alw 87 Se Le Te, Don F., Hot Property 7
25Mar79-7SA 1 :453 1:091 1:341ft 7¾ 117 32 43½ 44 46¾ Pincay L Jr9 Alw 91 Chief Artist, Addison, Stand Pat 9
11Mar79-5SA a6½f ⓣ:211 :4341:132fm 16 114 63½ 54½ 62½ 4nk Olivares F3 Alw 92 Smoggy, Laurel'sRaider,Postmark 11
4Mar79-6SA 7f :22 :441 1:212ft 11 114 44½ 48 36 36¾ Olivares F2 Alw 89 Windy's Duke, No No, Don F. 7
4Feb79-7SA 7f :22 :451 1:223gd 7¾ 114 65½ 68½ 69 513 Ramirez R4 Alw 77 Hrry'sLove,CrshProgrm,LittleJoker 9
27Jan79-6SA 6½f :214 :441 1:153ft 10 114 78¾ 77½ 53½ 31½ Ramirez R3 Alw 90 Reb'sGoldenAle,Lurel'sRider,DonF. 8
14Jan79-6SA 6f :212 :44 1:093m 12 114 32½ 43½ 56½ 44½ Ramirez R3 Alw 86 Syntarial,PleasureBent,SpanishWy 8

Jly 3 Hol 7f ft 1:292 h Jun 27 Hol 6f ft 1:113 h Jun 21 Hol 5f ft :594 h Jun 15 Hol 5f ft 1:022 h

Infusive

Own.—Hooper F W — 112

Dk. b. or br. c. 3, by Noholme II—Fuzier, by Crozier
Br.—Hooper F W (Fla)
Tr.—Fenstermaker L R

1979 9 1 1 2 $49,250
1978 10 2 2 1 $21,390
Turf 2 0 1 0 $4,000

23Jun79-6Hol 1¹⁄₁₆ :454 1:094 1:413ft 9 1085 12 14 21½ 37¾ Rodriguez W3 Alw 79 Valdez, Shamgo, Infusive 6
16May79-8Hol 1 ⓣ:4621:1041:352fm 4½e 116 34½ 32 67½ 710 Toro F2 Sptlght H 83 CrestoftheWve,Beu'sEgle,PintKing 9
6May79-3Hol 1 ⓣ:4621:1021:343fm 4 1095 1½ 11 11 27 Rodriguez W1 Alw 90 Ibacache, Infusive, Share a Lark 6
28Apr79-8Hol 1 :453 1:10 1:353ft 78 113 41¾ 41½ 41½ 54 RodrgzW3 El Drdo H 84 DbonrRogr,SwtchPrtnrs,KnghtsChc 7
18Apr79-8Hol 6f :221 :45 1:084ft 9e 122 51½ 3½ 56½ 68½ Hawley S8 Debonair 85 ToB.orNot,CrestoftheWve,Mlscott 10
1Mar79-7SA 6½f :213 :434 1:153sl 15 1175 42 63½ 612 622 Rodriguez W1 Alw 70 KnightsChoice,Eloqunt,AmnBrothr 6
7Feb79-8SA 7f :22 :442 1:211ft 3½e 122 1hd 1½ 22 37¼ McCrrnCJ3 SnVicent 90 Flying Paster,OatsandCorn,Infusive 5
24Jan79-8SA 6f :212 :441 1:09 ft *6-5e 120 52 51½ 42½ 44¼ McCrrnCJ7 SnMiguel 90 CrstofthWv,RomnOblisk,I'mSmokn 7
10Jan79-8SA 6f :213 :443 1:102ft 9½ 120 31½ 32 32 1no RodriguzW2 Los Feliz 87 Infusive, Swiss Chief, Striding Out 8
28Dec78-6SA 6f :214 :444 1:10 ft 5½ 1155 33 3½ 11 13¼ Rodriguez W8 Alw 89 Infusive,SprtnEndurnc,Empror'sKy 8

Jly 3 Hol 6f ft 1:133 h Jun 16 Hol 7f ft 1:312 h Jun 10 Hol 5f ft 1:002 h May 27 Hol 1 ft 1:401 h

Stand Pat *

Own.—Ferguson Mrs J K — 119

Dk. b. or br. g. 4, by Run of Luck—Good Thought, by On-and-On
Br.—Rowan L (Cal)
Tr.—Richardson Thomas F

1979 12 1 2 2 $32,250
1978 22 4 8 1 $56,425
Turf 8 0 1 0 $4.125

8Jun79-7Hol	6f	:221 :454 1:101ft	8	116	54 21½ 4¾ 21¾	Cespedes R6	Alw	84	Someonenoble,StandPat,Nola'sGuy	6
27May79-7Hol	7f	:213 :434 1:201ft	18	115	51¾ 52¾ 811 816	Hawley S3	Alw	82	WhiteRmmer,FleetTwist,PlesurBnt	8
12May79-7Hol	7f	:221 :45 1:21 ft	11	116	52 41 2hd 34	Hawley S8	Alw	90	Fleet Twist, Shackles, Stand Pat	8
29Apr79-6Hol	1	Ⓣ:463 1:103 1:351fm	15	116	85¼ 73¼ 72¼ 84	Hawley S10	Alw	90	PlesurBnt,Mry'sPolicy,ThArgylKid	10
21Apr79-7Hol	7f	:221 :443 1:212ft	14	116	32¼ 33½ 21 21	McCarron C J2	Alw	91	Pleasure Shack, Stand Pat, Don F.	6
11Apr79-7Hol	6f	:223 :454 1:094ft	3	116	64¾ 55 42 45	McCarron C J1	Alw	83	Se Le Te, Don F., Hot Property	7
31Mar79-7SA	6½f	:221 :45 1:151ft	8½	117	2hd 2½ 3½ 45¾	McHargue D G1	Alw	89	Hawkin'sSpecil,PlesureBent,SeRide	6
25Mar79-7SA	1	:453 1:091 1:341ft	11	114	42 33 32½ 36	Barraza J8	Alw	92	Chief Artist, Addison, Stand Pat	9
16Mar79-7SA	6f	:213 :443 1:101m	14	116	75½ 74¾ 44 12½	Barraza J7	50000	88	StandPat,CrashProgram,IowaFlash	9
11Mar79-5SA	a6½f	Ⓣ:211 :434 1:132fm	38	121	31½ 75¾ 117 118¾	Grant H10	Alw	84	Smoggy, Laurel'sRaider,Postmark	11

Jun 30 Hol 5f ft 1:002 h   Jun 24 Hol 5f ft 1:012 h   Jun 17 Hol 5f ft 1:03 h   Jun 4 Hol 4f ft :512 h

Yack Yack

B. h. 5, by Ack Ack—She's Beautiful, by On-and-On
Own.—Bradley Mary **1145** **Br.—Jones Mary F (Ky)** **Tr.—Whittingham Charles**

1979	3	0	0	0	$450
1978	5	1	3	1	$26,450
Turf	7	0	2	0	$10,175

6Jun79-7Hol	1 1/16	Ⓣ:463 1:11 1:421fm	8½	115	1hd 2hd 88½ 816	Delahoussaye E5	Alw	72	Saros, Ardiente, Sharpen Your Eye	9
23May79-7Hol	6f	:221 :443 1:09 ft	8	116	6½ 52½ 63¾ 52¾	Shoemaker W9	Alw	89	Sea Ride, Nola'sGuy,Someonenoble	9
12May79-7Hol	7f	:221 :45 1:21 ft	12	116	72¾ 62½ 76¾ 814	Shoemaker W2	Alw	80	Fleet Twist, Shackles, Stand Pat	8
10May78-7Hol	6f	:221 :444 1:092ft	3-2	118	41 22 32½ 34½	Shoemaker W6	Alw	86	Fingal, Prince Of Saron, YackYack	6
22Apr78-5Hol	1	:46 1:104 1:364ft	*2½	114	2hd 1hd 2½ 21	Shoemaker W7	Alw	81	TequilSunrise,YckYck,AshfordCstle	8
9Apr78-7SA	7f	:223 :452 1:221ft	2½	114	51½ 31 2hd 11	Shoemaker W4	Alw	92	Yack Yack,PassN'Run,MinstrelGrey	7
25Mar78-5SA	7f	:222 :45 1:22 ft	2¾	114	52 2hd 2½ 21½	Shoemaker W2	Alw	91	Kaskee, Yack Yack, Crew of Ocala	9
15Mar78-2SA	a6½f	Ⓣ:21 :433 1:134fm	3½	114	76 53 1hd 24	Shoemaker W3	Alw	86	AshfordCastle,YackYck,Chiloquin	12
27Oct77-8SA	1⅛	Ⓣ:472 1:114 1:48 fm	7¾	114	31 42 56 57	Moreno H E5	Alw	80	Mr. Redoy, CentennialPride,Laredo	8
20Oct77-7SA	a6½f	Ⓣ:214 :443 1:142fm	5½	117	52½ 44 55 55½	Shoemaker W3	Alw	81	CurrentConcept,Replnt,MinstrelGry	5

Jly 1 Hol 5f ft :584 h   ● Jun 25 Hol 6f ft 1:111 h   Jun 17 Hol 5f ft :591 h   ● Jun 4 Hol 3f ft :34 h

Shackles

B. c. 4, by Ack Ack—Flutter Away, by Double Jay
Own.—Fidler-Gallagher-Porter **119** **Br.—Gay A B (Ky)** **Tr.—Rettele Loren**

1979	13	4	2	2	$56,275
1978	9	1	0	0	$5,760

8Jun79-7Hol	6f	:221 :454 1:101ft	*8-5	120	66 54¾ 52¾ 54¼	Delahoussaye E2	Alw	82	Someonenoble,StandPat,Nola'sGuy	6
23May79-7Hol	6f	:221 :443 1:09 ft	*6-5	120	4nk 42 53¼ 4¾	Delahoussaye E7	Alw	91	Sea Ride, Nola'sGuy,Someonenoble	9
12May79-7Hol	7f	:221 :45 1:21 ft	3½	122	2½ 2hd 3½ 23	Delahoussaye E3	Alw	91	Fleet Twist, Shackles, Stand Pat	8
28Apr79-9Hol	7f	:214 :44 1:204ft	3½	119	31 31½ 1hd 1¾	DelahoussyeE5	50000	95	Shackles, Sea Ride, Foyt's Ack	8
14Apr79-4Hol	6f	:221 :451 1:092ft	3	121	41½ 33 31 1hd	Delahoussaye E1	Alw	90	Shackles, TeteaTete,Someonenoble	6
25Mar79-5SA	6½f	:213 :442 1:152ft	*6-5	120	31½ 41¾ 43 45½	Pincay L Jr1	Alw	87	MchoHombre,Somonnobl,BrtsBob	12
16Mar79-5SA	6½f	:22 :45 1:161ft	*3	120	62½ 51¾ 22½ 24	Pincay L Jr9	Alw	85	Foreign Power, Shackles, Sponge	11
4Mar79-9SA	6½f	:214 :442 1:154ft	*8-5	120	2½ 11½ 13 12½	Pincay L Jr9	40000	91	Shckls,CrimsonCommndr,Strwood	10
25Feb79-9SA	6½f	:214 :442 1:151ft	4	117	31 11½ 12 11	Pincay L Jr6	Alw	94	Shackles,Ackcelisor,DropndWiggle	9
16Feb79-5SA	1	:444 1:093 1:352ft	8	113	31 1½ 3½ 43	Olivares F8	Alw	89	MickeyMoch,FtherDuffy,Ackcelisor	8

Jly 5 Hol 3f ft :36 h   Jun 29 Hol 4f ft :47 h   Jun 22 Hol 5f ft :581 h   Jun 4 Hol 4f ft :473 h

here to the three-year-old. Not one felt sufficient three-year-old leanings to include Infusive among his top three selections.

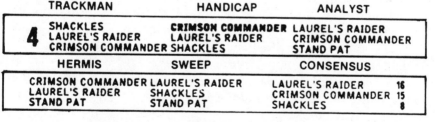

	TRACKMAN	HANDICAP	ANALYST
4	SHACKLES	CRIMSON COMMANDER	LAUREL'S RAIDER
	LAUREL'S RAIDER	LAUREL'S RAIDER	CRIMSON COMMANDER
	CRIMSON COMMANDER	SHACKLES	STAND PAT

HERMIS	SWEEP	CONSENSUS	
CRIMSON COMMANDER	LAUREL'S RAIDER	LAUREL'S RAIDER	16
LAUREL'S RAIDER	SHACKLES	CRIMSON COMMANDER	15
STAND PAT	STAND PAT	SHACKLES	8

SWEEP

FOURTH RACE ***Probable Post, 3:30***

7 FURLONGS. 3-Year-Olds and Up. Allowance. Purse $18,000.

1	LAUREL'S RAIDER	Pincay L Jr	119	Boasts touch of quality	2-1
7	SHACKLES	Delahoussaye E	119	Draws cozy post	4-1
5	STAND PAT	Hawley S	119	Comes off game bid	9-2
2	CRIMSON COMMANDER	PircD	119	Take some catching	3-1
4	INFUSIVE	Rodriguez W	112	Shorter trip helps	8-1
6	YACK YACK	Valenzuela P A	5114	Toss out turf router	10-1
3	DON F.	Olivares F	119	Non-winner this year	15-1

The *Form*'s oddsmaker *Sweep* and the track's official morning line handicapper both judged the three-year-old among the relatively undeserving.

FOURTH RACE

Purse $18,000. Three year olds and upward which have not won $2,500 three times other than maiden, claiming or starter. Three-year-olds 116 lbs. Older 123 lbs. Non-winners of two such races since April 24 allowed 2 lbs. Two such races since March 19, 4 lbs.

Track Record—TRIPLE BEND (4) (123) May 6, 1972 1:19 4/5

MAKE SELECTIONS BY NUMBER		PROBABLE ODDS
OWNER	TRAINER	JOCKEY
J.S. Moss	Robert Frankel	**2**
Light blue and black checks, light blue "MMM" on back, black sleeves and cap		Laffit
1 LAUREL'S RAIDER 119		Pincay, Jr.
Br.c. '75, Sadair—Laurel Mae, by Crafty Admiral		
Craig, Grollnek & Victor	Hal King	**5/2**
White, maroon basketball net on back, maroon check trim, white and maroon cap		Donald
2 CRIMSON COMMANDER 119		Pierce
Ch.g. '74, Crimson Satan—Merry Command		
Terry & Logan Frazee	L.J. Brooks	**12**
Black, green shamrock in gold horseshoe on back, gold cap		Frank
3 DON F. 119		Olivares
B.c. '75, Don B.—Flossie Betty, by Doc Scott J		
Fred W. Hooper	L.R. Fenstermaker	**8**
Blue, white circle "H", white shoulder straps, red sleeves, blue and red cap		William
4 INFUSIVE 112		Rodriguez
B.c. '76, Noholme 2nd—Fuzier, by Crozier		
Mrs. J.K. Ferguson	T.F. Richardson	**5**
Orange, triple white sash, orange cap		Sandy
5 STAND PAT 119		Hawley
Br.g '75, Run of Luck—Good Thought		
Mary Jones Bradley	Charles Whittingham	**15**
Red, white tie, red cap		Patrick
6 YACK YACK *114		Valenzuela
B.h '74, Ack Ack—She's Beautiful, by On-and-On		
Crockett, Fidler, Gallagher & Porter	Loren Rettele	**3**
White, green dots		Eddie
7 SHACKLES 119		Delahoussaye
B.c '75, Ack Ack—Flutter Away		

HOLLYWOOD PARK'S MORNING LINE

Regular handicappers who like to scoff at the picks of public selectors will not rejoice at the findings of an informal survey taken among their own kind. Of the regulars I spotted and quizzed about the race, not one preferred the younger Infusive.

"He's a three-year-old," remarked one, in a tone intended to straighten me up about something obvious.

"It's too early in the year for three-year-olds," advised another, on the matter of three-year-olds versus older in early July.

And so it went.

I recall the incidents not to engage in cheap shots at valued colleagues, but because they beg review. Misguided attitudes regarding three-year-olds and up remain intact across the land. It's precisely because public selectors and regular racegoers rank among the best of handicappers that their disregard for a three-year-old that actually stood out under nonwinners allowances demands examination.

Insufficient regard for eligibility conditions played a part, I believe, but outstandingly the confusion resulted from enduring myths that abound when three-year-olds challenge their elders. Those familiar with southern California racing who did not dismiss Infusive prematurely because of age noticed its previous eight races had been contested against eight open stakes winners. Several performances had been impressive.

Those who completed a version of total performance handicapping related Infusive's competitive finish at the route June 23 versus the graded stakes winner Valdez to its power performance May 8 against the graded stakes star Ibacache. They next found the consecutive sprint victories of December–January, when Infusive, still a two-year-old, annexed the Los Feliz Stakes, a sprint.

To handicappers who penetrated it that far, Infusive's total performance profile persuaded them the horse remained eligible for nonwinners three times allowances only because it had followed the spring stakes score with races against other stakes horses it could not handle, occasionally at distances at which it felt overextended. Although Infusive did not model so well Ainslie's nicely bred, lightly raced, improving three-year-old profile that classically wins this type of allowance race, the colt did remain lightly raced *under nonwinners allowance conditions*. So the improved workout following the June 23 route versus Valdez, plus the return to its favored distance, plus a switch to conditions more hospitable to better three-year-olds, combined to afford handicappers an opportunity to bet on a colt of substantial promise.

Against this portfolio of relatively high sprint class, exactly what recommends the older contestants?

Laurel's Raider had won many sprints, but not even three of allowance grade, and it had never even tiptoed into the handicap division. It made money primarily at the expense of better claiming sprinters. These cannot handle an Infusive.

A cheaper claimer still, Crimson Commander, while in outstanding form, had survived cheaper nonwinners allowances by a head. A class move ahead seemed unlikely.

Don F. over two seasons had won one of seventeen races.

After thirty-six races versus nonwinners allowance sprinters, Stand Pat remained eligible for this. It last won in the mud, March 18, beating claimers.

Yack Yack remained lightly raced and it likes seven furlongs, but its basic class appeared low-grade and its form remained on the short side.

Shackles almost replicated the profile of the rail horse, with a touch less intrinsic ability.

Only prejudices held toward three-year-olds versus older horses in July could entice practiced handicappers to pick among these middling allowance sprinters against a colt of Infusive's standing. In response to the latest scientific evidence, and to the improving status of three-year-olds in major racing, it's high time that the prejudices cease.

Despite the scenario just elaborated, horse racing's habit of turning well-laid tables upside down spoiled a golden occasion for handicappers. Infusive was sent off at 5 to 1, but to no avail.

The early pace had proved hard to anticipate and too quick for Infusive to survive. Infusive figured to relax behind the early fractions, then challenge while rounding the far turn, eventually to draw clear. Instead, and through no mishap by the jockey, the three-year-old became engaged in a deadly pace duel, the early fractions blazing. Able to withstand that and to draw away briefly into the stretch, the three-year-old could not withstand the late and unlikely surge of Stand Pat.

Pace nullified a three-year-old's basic class advantages against older sprinters at Hollywood July 9. Were the suicidal pace and the resulting upset predictable beforehand? Not easily. Yet this unhappy result serves usefully to remind all that, eligibility conditions and the age factor aside, the final decrees of comprehensive handicapping preside.

FOURTH RACE
Hollywood
JULY 9, 1979

7 FURLONGS. (1.19⅗) ALLOWANCE. Purse $18,000. 3-year-olds and upward which have not won $2,500 three times other than maiden, claiming or starter. Weights, 3-year-olds, 116 lbs.; older, 123 lbs. Non-winners of two such races since April 24, allowed 2 lbs.; two such races since March 19, 4 lbs.

Value of race $18,000, value to winner $9,900, second $3,600, third $2,700, fourth $1,350, fifth $450. Mutuel pool $258,537. Quinella Pool $430,535.

Last Raced	Horse	Eqt.	A.	Wt	PP	St	¼	½	Str	Fin	Jockey	Odds $1
8Jun79 ^{7}Hol^{2}	Stand Pat	b	4	119	5	6	5^{1}	4^{1}	2^{hd}	1^{2}	Hawley S	11.20
23Jun79 ^{6}Hol^{3}	Infusive	b	3	112	4	3	2^{hd}	1^{hd}	$1^{1\frac{1}{2}}$	$2^{1\frac{1}{2}}$	Rodriguez W	5.00
29Jun79 ^{6}Hol^{1}	Laurel's Raider		4	119	1	7	7	6^{3}	6^{5}	3no	Pincay L Jr	2.20
13Jun79 ^{7}Hol^{1}	Crimson Commander	b	5	119	2	5	4^{hd}	$5^{2\frac{1}{2}}$	5^{hd}	4no	Pierce D	3.40
8Jun79 ^{7}Hol^{5}	Shackles	b	4	119	7	2	1^{1}	3^{3}	3^{3}	$5^{5\frac{1}{2}}$	Delahoussaye E	2.40
6Jun79 ^{7}Hol^{8}	Yack Yack		5	114	6	1	$3^{2\frac{1}{2}}$	2^{hd}	4^{hd}	$6^{\frac{1}{2}}$	Valenzuela P A^{5}	12.40
23May79 ^{7}Hol^{8}	Don F.	b	4	119	3	4	$6^{1\frac{1}{2}}$	7	7	7	Olivares F	20.60

OFF AT 3:32 PDT. Start good. Won driving. Time, :21⅗, :43⅗, 1:08⅘, 1:21 Track fast.

$2 Mutuel Prices:				
	5–STAND PAT	24.40	10.60	5.20
	4–INFUSIVE		7.60	4.40
	1–LAUREL'S RAIDER			3.20

$5 QUINELLA 4–5 PAID $156.50.

dk b or br. g, by Run of Luck—Good Thought, by On-and-On. Trainer Richardson Thomas F. Bred by Rowan L (Cal).

STAND PAT lacked early speed, rallied strongly outside the leaders when set down in the drive, gained command and drew clear in the final sixteenth. **INFUSIVE** got the lead inside of rivals on the stretch turn, drew clear but weakened in the final sixteenth. **LAUREL'S RAIDER** had to be checked when he swerved toward the inside leaving the chute, swung wide rallying into the stretch but finished willingly. **CRIMSON COMMANDER** rallied just inside LAUREL'S RAIDER in the drive but could not menace. SHACKLES tired in the upper stretch. YACK YACK was finished after a half.

Owners— 1, Ferguson Mrs J K; 2, Hooper F W; 3, Moss J S; 4, Craig-Grollnek-Victor; 5, Crkt-Fdler-Galghr-Prtr; 6, Bradley Mary; 7, Frazee T & L.

Nonetheless, eligibility conditions do count, and often count big.

When the three-year-olds of spring, summer, and fall are entered against older horses, having discarded any generalized prejudices against them, handicappers benefit greatly by apprehending the conditions of eligibility under which each age group enjoys real substantive advantages.

Here's the laundry list at this writing, with annotation:

Maidens, three-years-old and up	Advantage threes

Whether for males or females, homebreds or not, at the sprint or route, on dirt or turf, in the spring, summer, or fall, three-year-olds hold a decided advantage. Excepting the nicely bred, lightly raced kind from the better stables, thoroughbred maidens four or older do not figure to win now. These carry heavy weights and light hopes. Handicappers should not trust too much the lickety-split workouts.

Allowances, for nonwinners other than maiden or claiming	Advantage threes
Allowances, for nonwinners two times other than maiden or claiming	Advantage threes

Older horses that have not yet managed to win an allowance race or two do not often shine under these preliminary allowance conditions. During the first four months of the year sparsely raced four-year-olds fill the bill admirably. After that, three-year-olds deserve the benefit of the doubt, and increasingly so with every passing day. Handicappers should examine closely the past performances and commentary in the box below.

Late in the season, three-year-olds that have started at midseason or later press an even greater advantage against older horses that remain eligible.

Allowances, for nonwinners three times other than maiden or claiming	Advantage, better threes

A little more basic quality goes far in these competitive races. Cheap speed and no quality gets nothing. Older claiming horses do not ordinarily belong. In practice, three-year-olds figure to win, but handicappers might insist they belong to the upper crust of their division. When better three-year-olds are absent, an unusual situation, older horses of various stripes get the nod. Handicappers sometimes emphasize previous performance and consistency in high-priced claiming races whose purses are comparable to the allowance offer.

Allowances, for nonwinners four times other than maiden or claiming	Advantage, top threes

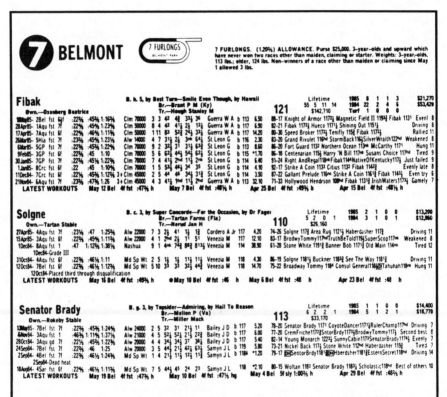

This illustrative race took place May 24, 1985, late spring, and represents a steady source of financial loss even among practiced handicappers. Which of the three horses above figures to win?

Halfway through the betting the New York crowd had Fibak backed down to 3 to 2, and the five-year-old eventually went off at 2.90 to 1, second choice in the field of eight. Presumably, the New York handicappers did not have much respect for the conditions of eligibility.

Why would handicappers bet money on a five-year-old that had won five of *fifty-five races*, $142,710, and was *still eligible* to an allowance race that barred any horse that had won *two races* other than maiden, claiming, or starter? Fibak—and horses like it—hardly fits the conditions. Lightly raced three-year-olds should be expected to whip heavily raced five-year-olds under preliminary nonwinners allowance conditions, and they do.

Whether Solgne will beat Senator Brady or vice versa is a difficult question to settle, but either horse figures to manhandle Fibak—and any horse like it. I implore handicappers to understand the point and stop wasting money on horses so obviously unsuited to allowance conditions, notably at short odds. Nicely bred, lightly raced, from outstanding barns, the three-year-olds Solgne and Senator Brady are practically the prototypes of the racehorses for which preliminary allowance conditions are written. If Fibak were allowance grade material, it would have become ineligible for this kind of race two seasons ago.

The handicapping illogic used to support the case for Fibak holds that the horse has beaten high-priced claiming winners, while Solgne and Senator Brady have so far handled only maidens and nondescript younger horses. Forget it. Fibak is a claiming horse inside-out, and does not figure to survive under eligibility conditions written strictly with younger nonclaiming horses in mind. The argument for Fibak applies only during the first three months of the season, in preliminary allowance races restricted to four-year-olds and up, and then only when no impressive lightly raced fours from good barns appear in the allowance line-ups.

SEVENTH RACE
Belmont
MAY 24, 1985

7 FURLONGS. (1.20⅘) ALLOWANCE. Purse $25,000. 3-year-olds and upward which have never won two races other than maiden, claiming or starter. Weights: 3-year-olds, 113 lbs.; older, 124 lbs. Non-winners of a race other than maiden or claiming since May 1 allowed 3 lbs.

Value of race $25,000; value to winner $15,000; second $5,500; third $3,000; fourth $1,500. Mutuel pool $99,697, OTB pool $136,444. Exacta Pool $148,715; OTB Exacta Pool $179,721.

Last Raced	Horse	Eqt.	A.	Wt	PP	St	¼	½	Str	Fin	Jockey	Odds $1
13May85 7Bel1	Senator Brady	b	3	113	7	4	$2^{1\frac{1}{2}}$	1^{1}	$1^{2\frac{1}{2}}$	$1^{1\frac{1}{4}}$	Bailey J D	1.70
27Apr85 4Aqu1	Solgne		3	112	5	1	3^{hd}	$4^{1\frac{1}{2}}$	2^{2}	$2^{3\frac{1}{4}}$	Cordero A Jr	2.90
4Jly84 7Bel	Romantic Tradition	b	4	121	4	5	$4^{1\frac{1}{2}}$	$5^{2\frac{1}{2}}$	$3^{\frac{1}{2}}$	$3^{2\frac{1}{2}}$	Maple E	11.50
8May85 1Bel1	First Conquest	b	3	113	1	3	$6^{1\frac{1}{2}}$	6^{7}	5^{3}	4^{1}	Migliore R	5.00
15May85 2Bel3	Fibak	b	5	121	3	6	5^{4}	3^{hd}	$4^{\frac{1}{2}}$	$5^{3\frac{3}{4}}$	Guerra W A	2.90
17Nov84 8CD10	Grand Native	b	3	112	6	2	1^{hd}	2^{hd}	6^{8}	6^{10}	MacBeth D	26.60
17Mar84 5Aqu2	Carry It Full		5	121	2	7	7	7	7	7	Venezia M	18.70

OFF AT 4:13 Start good, Won driving. Time, :22⅖, :45⅗, 1:09⅕, 1:22⅗ Track fast.

$2 Mutuel Prices:				
	7-(H)-SENATOR BRADY	5.40	2.60	2.20
	5-(E)-SOLGNE		3.60	2.40
	4-(D)-ROMANTIC TRADITION			3.00

$2 EXACTA 7-5 PAID $16.80.

B. g, by Topsider—Admiring, by Hail To Reason. Trainer Miller Mack. Bred by Mellon P (Va).

SENATOR BRADY moved to the fore in hand after entering the turn, opened a clear lead into the stretch and remained clear under strong handling. SOLGNE, a forward factor from between horses, was clearly best of the others. A foul claim by the rider of GRAND NATIVE against SOLGNE for interference at the quarter-pole was not allowed. ROMANTIC TRADITION, eased back from the inside entering the turn, brushed with GRAND NATIVE entering the stretch when splitting horses but lacked the needed closing response. FIRST CONQUEST failed to

The path of least resistance limits play to improving three-year-olds of stakes quality. In any case, handicappers will likely face a stiff test of their skill. In the absence of top three-year-olds, better four-year-olds that have finished in-the-money in open stakes represent an alternative, provided they arrive at the race in sizzling form and are nicely suited to the distance and probable pace.

Keep an eye peeled for Ainslie's nicely bred, lightly raced, improving three-year-old that has done everything asked of it, except that it may have lost a Grade 1 or Grade 2 stakes in a good try. If the stakes try did not dull its form, the horse might romp home at attractive odds.

Grade 1 stakes   Advantage older

As recent seasons have shown and television understands, the outstanding exception to this norm often enters the definitive open races of the fall to do battle with the best older horses in the land. He enters the fray a national hero, the year's champion deluxe three-year-old.

By fall, this exceptionally sound and powerfully fast thoroughbred might be gunning for Horse-of-the-Year honors. If its top form has held, a crucial matter, the older division's standouts must be genuinely supreme to defeat it. They usually are. Secretariat was the exception proving the rule. Seattle Slew passed. Affirmed lost its form. Spectacular Bid lost to an older Affirmed.

Unless the older handicap division has been woefully depleted by injury, all but the most supreme of three-year-olds will be outrun in these definitive races.

Grade 2, Grade 3, and other open stakes   Advantage older

A few exceptions are noted. Grade 1 three-year-olds must be handicapped straightforwardly. During the second part of the season, these might stick out. Grade 2 three-year-olds that have won multiple stakes are acceptable, if their form is currently peak and their running style is well suited to the distance, footing, and probable early pace. Handicappers benefit if they remain strict. A third and interesting exception is a late-starting, lightly raced three-year-old that has impressively won an open stakes restricted to its age group and appears rampantly on the improve.

If that kind of upscale three-year-old enters an open stakes for older horses that is unlisted, it figures.

Conditioned stakes	Advantage threes

Since these races serve as stepping-stones to larger events, three-year-olds that have started recently and have been developing especially fast or well are preferred. More so if the conditions bar former stakes winners.

If the conditions bar only winners of specified amounts for specified periods, handicappers often must handicap previous older stakes winners straightforwardly. If older former added-money winners appear to be reaching peak form, these might pickle the three-year-olds. It depends. Handicappers variously favor horses of any age whose stakes titles have been more prestigious or whose purses won have been more expensive. If older horses' profiles do not apply, go to the younger horses on the improve. The races have been written for them.

Classified allowances, minimally restricted	Advantage older

When classified races specify restrictions involving relatively high purse values and multiple wins during relatively short time intervals, the race is not very restricted at all. A June 1 classified allowance event, offering $40,000 in prize money, might be restricted to nonwinners of $18,000 twice since April 8, less than sixty days past. Many of the top older runners on the grounds remain eligible. Several might be former stakes winners, perhaps within six months, or even three months. These hold a strong upper hand. To look competitive, three-year-olds should have looked impressive in an open stakes, preferably one having a relatively high value on the local purse schedule. Or, three-year-olds should have recently clobbered successive nonwinners allowance competition, and remain eligible today merely because those winner shares did not top the specified $18,000.

More inviting to owners and trainers of improving younger

horses are classified allowances whose restrictions involve wider, more inclusive boundaries. They know the conditions will eliminate most of the better older horses.

Classified allowances, highly restricted	Advantage threes

When classified events bar horses that have won one or two modest winner shares during relatively long time intervals, older horses that have accomplished anything impressive of late will be ineligible. Better three-year-olds that have started only recently and have been developing sharply often remain eligible. So might others that have been challenging their own age group in open stakes, but getting only second or third shares. The trainer might prefer an opportunity to run against older horses of the less exacting kind. If younger horses look more inviting than their older counterparts, they probably are.

An exception is the older added-money competitor that has been competing for stakes over an extended time, coming close enough, yet losing consistently. If its form remains sharp, the three-year-olds will find stiff competition after all. Another possible exception is the older stakes winner returning from a layoff. It might be preparing for added-money races, but if the distance, footing, and pace seem suitable, and its form sharp, it figures.

And certain three-year-olds are taboo, however restricted the classified conditions. Three-year-olds that have won nonwinners allowance races handily, but lose badly under stakes conditions, do not merit support against older horses under classified allowances.

Claiming races, all prices	Advantage older

No matter the distance, the time of season, or any restrictions embedded in the conditions, older horses dominate claiming races open to three-year-olds and up. They win more than their fair share, and 81 percent of the claiming races in which they encounter three-year-olds. Three-year-olds represent 26 percent of the horses entered in the races, but win only 19 percent of them. This trend should stand firm, as long as owners enter disappointing young horses in claiming races at unrealistic selling prices. Acknowledging that impulse, handicappers fare better by following its associated guideline. The higher the claiming price, even less the possibilities of three-year-olds.

A trickier handicapping problem arises when three-year-olds win claiming races limited to that age group, and next are entered to be claimed while trying older horses. How to translate the selling prices of the three-year-old races? A reduction is in order. Ainslie's *Encyclopedia of Thoroughbred Handicapping* recommends 20 percent. Use the recommendation, but remain flexible. Do not be afraid to reduce selling prices by as much as 50 percent, particularly if victory in races restricted to three-year-olds proved desperate or hard-fought.

If a three-year-old competing against older claimers has won only a maiden claiming race, handicappers should expect the creature to settle at a selling price approximately 50 percent below the price at which it entered the maiden event. Even at those slashed prices, such horses will probably get whipped to a frazzle unless they stay within their own age group.

To conclude our discussion of developing three-year-olds by pursuing an angle of interest to handicappers liking an unfamiliar edge, it long has been held that when three-year-olds that have been testing older runners return to competition with horses their own age, handicappers who collect charts or keep notebooks listing eligibility conditions can find glorious betting opportunities.

This they surely do. But as the preceding discussion shows, the truth is not so easily understood.

If they relate performances of both age groups to the kinds of eligibility conditions contested, when horses shuttle to and from races favoring one age group or another, handicappers will quickly learn to exploit the maneuverings.

Instead of lying in wait for three-year-olds that return to races limited to their own kind, try out the following guidelines related to age and the conditions of racing:

1. If a three-year-old loses to older horses under conditions which favor three-year-olds, mark it down when it returns to races limited to three-year-olds.

2. If a three-year-old wins or runs close to older horses when competing under conditions normally favorable to older horses, mark it up when again it engages only three-year-olds, even if moving up in class by a step.

3. If an older horse loses to three-year-olds under conditions

which favor older horses, it remains acceptable against similar older horses, but is not acceptable against similarly improving three-year-olds that are contenders.

4. If an older horse loses to three-year-olds under conditions which favor three-year-olds, do not penalize it under similar conditions if its toughest opponents figure to be older horses.

5. If an older horse beats three-year-olds under conditions which favor three-year-olds, mark the three-year-old losers down under similar conditions, but do not mark the older winner up when it moves ahead in class.

The guidelines do not apply to three-year-olds moving into or out of claiming races.

And unless the winner looked clearly best, any three-year-old that has lost to older horses under allowances for nonwinners once or twice other than maiden or claiming, particularly during the second half of the season, should hardly provide a thrill to handicappers when returned to those kinds of races—but now facing a field entirely its own age.

At this stage of his career trainer of stakes stars Charles Whittingham concerns himself almost exclusively with blue-blooded stock of high performance or potential, and the particular races he intends to win with them. His "peculiar" use of the condition book is illustrated in the accompanying piece.

The Handicapper's Condition Book Trainer Profile

Charles Whittingham

Trainer of champions Charles Whittingham prepares good horses for the stakes titles and monies their fashionable breeding portends and their well-appointed owners expect. All other racing goals and situations are decidedly secondary to him, including the winning of overnite races with developing horses of high potential. Whittingham also has a strong preference for the turf. To somewhat less extent, he prefers working with horses four and up, rather than with young horses.

Without understanding Whittingham's stakes preference and turf bias, handicappers of southern California would be unable to understand the trainer's peculiar use of the condition book. In this regard, Whittingham continually uses one or a series of races to prepare horses for later, bigger objectives. Nonwinners races to prep horses for initial stakes tries, minor stakes to tune horses finely for the major stakes.

As an extreme illustration of Whittingham's tendencies in these matters, in 1978 he used the Grade 1 Woodward Stakes to fine-tune his ace handicap horse Exceller for that star's major New York objective, Belmont Park's Grade 1 Jockey Club Gold Cup, to be run two weeks later. Whittingham practically conceded the important Woodward to Seattle Slew, in firm belief the race would better prepare Exceller for the even more prestigious Gold Cup, at one and one-half miles a quarter mile longer than the Woodward, and Exceller's best distance.

Few trainers would use Grade 1 fixtures as a kind of prep but in 1978 Whittingham's gambit was proved correct and justly rewarded. Coming from twenty-two lengths behind in the slop, and following perhaps the most dramatic stretch drive of the decade, Exceller prevailed over Seattle Slew by a nose. Had he done too little or too much in the Woodward, Exceller would have lost the definitive Gold Cup. Whittingham wisely knew that, and turned the knowledge into perhaps his greatest training triumph.

The Handicapper's Condition Book Trainer Profile

Lazaro Barrera

The argument that trainer Lazaro Barrera has become the most rounded, most accomplished conditioner of his time might be entered at several points, but in a book whose topic is eligibility conditions a surprisingly pertinent point of entry might be his winning

Lazaro Barrera has been as complete and versatile as any horseman in history. He wins with all kinds of horses in all kinds of races. A four-time Eclipse-winning trainer, a record, and his most prized achievements, Barrera has no discernible weaknesses and he moves developing horses ahead in class as surely as any trainer in history. He is seen here in Hollywood Park's walking ring with champion jockey Laffit Pincay, Jr.

more than $775,000 with the minor handicap horse Life's Hope. Unable to win anything but minor handicaps with him in New York or southern California, Barrera sent Life's Hope hither and yonder, to tracks and races where the gelding might do better. It worked. It usually does with Barrera.

Having completed the transition from the claiming game to the better races for better horses as quickly, surely, and successfully as anyone ever did, Barrera by 1980 had set new standards for other trainers to meet. He alone had won more than three million dollars in purses, and this twice, during 1978 and 1979, when the great Affirmed was three and four. During that two-year period, with Affirmed so overwhelmingly on his mind and schedule, Barrera produced an astonishing eighteen additional stakes winners, including the filly champion It's In The Air, champion sprinter J.O.

Tobin, and the syndicated horses Valdez, Star Spangled, and Barrera. Not a single horse in the stable, one of the nation's largest, suffered because Affirmed was there. The explanation includes Barrera's capacity for work and organization and his manipulation of horses and eligibility conditions. Lazaro Barrera moves improving horses ahead in class as successfully as is possible. By understanding his horses' individual needs, problems, capacities, and potentials, he gets the most out of each of them. No one else does that better, not even peers such as Angel Penna or David Whiteley, who work with smaller, more select stables filled with the generous bloodlines of highly exclusive clients.

Sometimes it seems Barrera suffers no weaknesses, no limitations. He wins with two-year-olds, with three-year-olds, with four and up, and with each age the Grade 1 titles consistently. He does equally superbly with fillies and with colts. He wins on the dirt, and on turf as well. He heads the standings on the west coast, and he leads them on the east coast too. He wins sprints and routes as well, and at both distances with the same horses. He wins with shippers, with foreigners, with first-time starters, and with horses returning from lengthy layoffs. In his 1985 computerized trainer study, which featured a six-year database and examined forty-one categories of performance, publisher Greg Lawlor summarized his data on Barrera succinctly: "no apparent weaknesses." His is the all-around game, to be sure, with little if any relief from the onslaught.

In 1982, Barrera relinquished control of Lou Wolfson's Harbor View Farm, thereby severing one of the strongest owner-trainer relationships in the annals of the sport. Wolfson preferred his base in New York. Barrera preferred to be based in southern California. In the bargain Barrera lost access annually to the progeny of the Harbor View foundation sires Raise A Native and Exclusive Native. The trainer has handled only a single champion since, the turf star Lemhi Gold, son of Vaguely Noble.

Into the breach has stepped the delightful Dolly Green, the Beverly Hills heiress now in the fourth year of building a first-rank racing and breeding operation. Mrs. Green buys nicely bred yearlings each season under Barrera's tutelage, but buying horses on the open market does not get the kind of classic results breeding to a foundation sire line does. Pride of profession is deeply rooted near the center of Barrera's character. He cannot accept defeat. The four consecutive Eclipse awards from 1978–81, the four consecutive money-won titles, the standards for purse monies, the several syndicated stallions, the relentless compilation of stakes and graded stakes—not all of this or more will be enough to dim the pride of performance that turns great ability into the highest order of achievement.

CHAPTER 11

Two-Year-Olds

THE DASHES

PRACTICED HANDICAPPERS KNOW that dashes for two-year-olds belong to the swift. The juveniles fly from the gate and run as hard and fast as they can for the five furlongs or five and one-half furlongs they must. Whether maidens or winners, with few exceptions, the fastest horses win.

Effective handicapping relies on appraisals of speed. Key indicators include final times, fractional times, workouts, and breeding. Among contenders, stables that win regularly with two-year-olds deserve credit. Handicapping subtleties involve track variants, fractional times, training styles, and betting patterns. To these we shall return quickly.

First, handicappers benefit if they rid themselves of remedies that do not apply.

Class matters in the most competitive of dashes, but routinely the classical qualities of willingness, determination, endurance, and courage hardly find room to operate. For this reason, when handicappers refer to the "class" horse in dashes, they had better be making fine qualitative distinctions among two-year-olds that have run the distance equally fast.

Of itself, form analysis rarely separates well-matched two-year-olds. No handicapper should wager on juveniles that do not train regularly and briskly. If workouts stop, or accumulate in suspiciously irregular patterns, or indicate tardiness, eliminate the juveniles. These are probably unsound, unwilling, or unable already.

While acknowledging that juveniles should be working out

sharply, handicappers best reserve their excitement until the promise has been delivered in the afternoon. As a basic check, if a three-furlong work has been recorded in :33 4/5 or such, look for a longer workout in fast time. When asked or permitted to do so, many ordinary two-year-olds can train at shorter distances with fanciful speed.

Pace analysis often does not reveal much about dashes that final time obscures. If handicappers note a two-year-old has attended fast fractions while positioned comfortably behind a speedball or two, then accelerates quickly when roused, and wins easily under wraps, its final time likely can be improved. Southern California handicappers that witnessed Flying Paster's debut at two knew they had seen something special once that youngster took off. The best kind of win at the dash, it looked like this:

Flying Paster		B. c. 2, by Gummo—Procne, by Acroterion				
		Br.—Ridder B J (Cal)		1978	1 1 0 0	$6,600
Own.—Ridder B J	120	Tr.—Campbell Gordon C				
27May78-6Hol 5f :221 :453 :573ft *6-5 118	52½ 32 1½ 15 Pierce D3		SMdn 92 FlyngPstr,Bchir'sLv,KngTtnkhmn 10			
•Jun 16 Hol 3f ft :38¹ h	Jun 11 Hol 4f ft :47 h	Jun 6 Hol 3f ft :34¹ h	May 22 Hol 5f ft :59⁴ h			

If two-year-olds can finish in twelve seconds or less at five furlongs, their final times might improve at five and one-half furlongs. Anything unable to survive rapid fractions at five furlongs is unlikely to do so at five and one-half. Improved form will not ordinarily help propel it much faster.

Jockeys are incidental. Gate ability helps, but all-out efforts by juveniles from wire-to-wire at these short distances hardly requires the finer riding skills of handling and timing.

If the fastest two-year-olds draw post positions of concern to handicappers, the horses will win regardless.

Two-year-olds can tote the 122 pounds they often bear in non-claiming dashes. Before weight is felt, the dash is over.

And eligibility conditions, our topic, which reliably guide the handicapping routine in all other races, have limited practical value when analyzing dashes for two-year-olds. If a five-furlong sprint will be contested for stakes money, a greater number of faster juveniles will compete. The handicapper's problem remains the same. Which is fastest?

In this regard, a brief digression. Absolutely the only place in handicapping for parallel-time speed charts is the two-year-old dash. Distances of six furlongs and beyond each demand expressions of racing qualities other than speed. These are not easily expressed in terms of final times projected for distance. Since dashes require only outlays of speed, however, handicappers can fairly use final times at dash distances to project final times at other dash distances.

However, handicappers who believe horses' final times at six furlongs can be used to estimate final times at a mile, or those of the mile to estimate final times at a mile and one-eighth, do so strictly as an article of faith. They cannot resort to reason or logic. No basis in fact, science, or experience supports such projections, and handicappers are not encouraged to seek profits from parallel-time charts.

Even at dash distances, parallel-time charts work best when applied to two-year-olds that were *not tiring* at shorter distances.

With such singular reliance on speed, is picking the juvenile dash winners as simple as it sounds? To be sure, many handicappers believe this the easiest pickings at any track. Talk to self-proclaimed experts about juvenile dashes, and they'll likely insist it's these races where they make their millions.

Wishing I could join their fun, I cannot. Handicapping truth is rarely simple, and is not as plain here as too many would pretend. To assert that two-year-old times are the most reliable recorded by racehorses is one thing. To follow that with assertions about the ease of handicapping or the making of money is another.

An illustration upcoming will serve the point.

It attaches to the first and most primary of five guidelines for handicapping two-year-old dashes.

1. Select the horse with the fastest final time at the distance.

If two contenders are equal, select horses with the fastest early speed.

By far the most important guideline, were this the only one handicappers would still be pressed hard to succeed. Two problems make the dashes difficult: (a) in many maiden races, several horses have not started and therefore have no recorded times and (b) final times do not estimate true speed nearly as well as adjusted final times, and these can be laboriously difficult to obtain.

Regarding the second difficulty, consider a classic case of a dash among juveniles that already had departed the maiden ranks. Analyze the field for the Cabrillo Stakes, carded at Hollywood Park, a few seasons back.

The contenders are Doonesbury, Parsec, and Murrtheblurr. I hope handicappers will agree the improving Stiff Diamond lacks sufficient early speed to overtake top two-year-olds in a race of less

8th Hollywood

5½ FURLONGS. (1.02⅕) 27th Running of THE CABRILLO STAKES. $40,000 Added. Colts and geldings. 2-year-olds. (Allowance) By subscription of $50 each, which shall accompany the nomination, $400 additional to start, with $40,000 added of which $8,000 to second, $6,000 to third, $3,000 to fourth and $1,000 to fifth. Weight, 122 lbs. Non-winners of a sweepstakes allowed 3 lbs.; two races other than claiming, 5 lbs.; a race other than claiming, 7 lbs. Starters to be named through the entry box by closing time of entries. Winners preferred in the main starting gate. A trophy will be presented to the owner of the winner. Closed Wednesday, June 27, 1979, with 18 nominations.

~~Cut the Cost~~

B. c. 2, by Amaspert—Cut It Short, by Nearctic

Br.—Meadowbrook Farms Inc (Fla) 1979 1 1 0 0 $4,950

Own.—Greene H F **115** **Tr.—Stute Warren**

14Jun79-3Hol 5f :22^{4} :46^{3} :58^{4}ft 4½ 116 2^{hd} 2½ 1^{hd} 1¾ McHrgueDG^{5} Mc25000 86 CutthCost,DltUnlimitd,InstntWhip 10

Jly 2 Hol 5f ft 1:02 hg Jun 11 Hol 4f ft :48^{1} bg Jun 3 Hol 5f ft 1:01 h May 29 Hol 4f ft :47^{1} h

California Ranger

B. c. 2, by What Luck—Goldlan, by Ridan

Br.—Szody G (Cal) 1979 1 1 0 0 $7,875

Own.—California Stable **122** **Tr.—Caton Dent**

22Jun79-11Sol 5½f :22 :45^{3} 1:04^{2}ft 3½ 113 7^{8} 4^{2} 1½ 1^{2} Ochoa A^{5} Sol Cty Fut 91 CliforniRngr,SlmSlmmr,BSoLucky 10

Jly 5 Hol 3f ft :35 hg Jly 4 Hol 4f ft :52^{2} hg Jun 18 Sol 4f ft :48^{4} hg Jun 6 GG 5f ft 1:00^{3} hg

Doonesbury

Dk. b. or br. c. 2, by Matsadoon—Vaguely Nice, by Vaguely Noble

Br.—Westerly Stud Farms (Cal) 1979 2 2 0 0 $16,525

Own.—Roberts-Roffe-Willis **122** **Tr.—Willis Barney**

5Jun79-8GG 5½f :21^{4} :44^{3} 1:03^{1}ft *1 117 1^{hd} 1^{1} 1^{6} 1^{12} Gomez R^{7} Tan Kindg 95 Doonesbury, Tiny Heller,Philarchus 9

31May79-6GG 5f :21^{3} :45 :57^{2}ft *8-5 118 74½ 53¾ 3½ 12½ Chapman T M^{9} Mdn 99 Doonesbury, Basit, Sparkle Fella 10

Jly 4 Hol 3f ft :36^{2} hg ●Jun 29 Hol 5f ft :58^{3} h Jun 24 Hol 5f ft :58^{2} h Jun 19 Hol 5f ft 1:02^{2} h

Stiff Diamond

B. c. 2, by Delta Judge—Firstbeam, by First Landing

Br.—Lamazor F P (Ky) 1979 4 1 1 1 $11,100

Own.—Lamazor F P **117** **Tr.—Fanning Jerry**

21Jun79-3Hol 5½f :22^{2} :45^{2} 1:04 ft *8-5 116 6^{5} 54½ 2^{hd} 1^{1} Shoemaker W^{9} Mdn 91 StiffDiamond,Owlwood,PostEntry 11

9Jun79-5Hol 5f :22^{2} :45^{1} :57^{3}ft 2½ 116 75½ 58½ 38½ 34½ Cespedes R^{8} Mdn 87 BAProspct,PostEntry,StiffDimond 10

2Jun79-5Hol 5f :22^{1} :45^{4} :58 ft 4½ 116 8^{10} 58½ 3^{6} 23½ Cespedes R^{2} Mdn 86 Encino, Stiff Diamond, Abyss 10

4May79-4Hol 5f :22 :45^{2} :57^{2}ft 6½ 115 6^{10} 5^{9} 56½ 58½ Toro F^{5} Mdn 85 Parsec, Valtat, Native Angle 6

Jly 4 Hol 3f ft :34^{3} h Jun 28 Hol 4f ft :47^{1} h Jun 16 Hol 5f ft 1:00 h May 29 Hol 4f ft :47^{2} h

Parsec

B. g. 2, by Wing Out—Grand Alma, by Aberion

Br.—Cardiff Stud Farm (Cal) 1979 2 2 0 0 $32,300

Own.—Jameson L **122** **Tr.—Knight Chay R**

6Jun79-8Hol 5f :21^{3} :45^{1} :58 ft 3½ 120 31½ 2^{2} 2^{hd} 1½ Lipham T^{1} First Act 90 Prsec,ExecutiveCounsl,Murrthblurr 7

4May79-4Hol 5f :22 :45^{2} :57^{2}ft 2½ 115 1^{2} 12½ 1½ 12½ Baltazar C^{4} Mdn 93 Parsec, Valtat, Native Angle 6

●Jly 4 Hol 3f ft :34^{1} h Jun 28 Hol 5f ft 1:00^{4} h Jun 22 Hol 6f ft 1:13^{1} h Jun 15 Hol 4f ft :48^{4} h

Murrtheblurr

B. c. 2, by Torsion—Princeton Pride, by Cornish Prince

Br.—Jones-Floyd-Jelsma (Ky) 1979 4 2 0 2 $40,833

Own.—Agnew D J **122** **Tr.—Fanning Jerry**

20Jun79-8Hol 5½f :22^{2} :45 1:03 ft 3½ 120 1^{1} 11½ 1^{2} 13½ Olivares F^{9} Haggin 96 Murrtheblurr, Encino, LoveIsBlue 10

6Jun79-8Hol 5f :21^{3} :45^{1} :58 ft 5½ 120 2^{hd} 1^{2} 1^{hd} 3^{2} Olivares F^{7} First Act 88 Prsec,ExecutiveCounsl,Murrthblurr 7

21Apr79-10TuP 5f :22 :45^{4} :58^{4}ft 3¾ 119 1^{hd} 21½ 33½ 34½† FrrDJr^{11} Phoenix Fut 78 Free Sea, ‡Brent, ‡Murrtheblurr 12

†21Apr79—Disqualified and placed third

11Apr79-9TuP 4½f :22^{1} :46^{1} :52^{2}ft 8-5 119 7 5^{3} 3½ 1no Frazier D Jr^{7} Fut Trl 90 Murrthblurr,ArizonMiss,SlmSlmmr 7

Jly 4 Hol 3f ft :36 h Jun 28 Hol 4f ft :47^{1} h Jun 13 Hol 5f ft 1:00^{3} h Jun 3 Hol 3f ft :34^{3} h

Traffic Pattern

Dk. b. or br. g. 2, by Top Conference—Basic Blue, by Bold and Brave

Br.—Maragar Stables (Cal) 1979 3 1 0 0 $5,800

Own.—Maragar Stable Inc **115** **Tr.—McBride H C**

20Jun79-8Hol 5½f :22^{2} :45 1:03 ft 86 115 10^{11} 8^{13} 8^{14} 8^{18} Mena F^{1} Haggin 78 Murrtheblurr, Encino, LoveIsBlue 10

1Jun79-5Hol 5f :22^{1} :46^{1} :58^{3}ft 14 114 2½ 2^{hd} 1^{hd} 1¾ Olivares F^{8} M28000 87 TrafficPttern,Teeker,SummerSilor 10

20Apr79-4Hol 5f :22^{2} :46^{3} :58^{4}ft 51 115 76½ 7^{7} 79½ 5^{9} Pierce D^{10} Mdn 77 Love Is Blue, Aspen Ridge, Basit 10

Jly 3 Hol 4f ft :47^{3} h Jun 27 Hol 5f ft :59^{4} h Jun 15 Hol 5f ft 1:01^{1} h Jun 8 Hol 5f ft 1:02^{1} h

Mojingo

B. c. 2, by Exclusive Native—Song Sparrow, by Tudor Minstrel
Br.—Roach Dr B (Ky)   1979   0 M 0 0

Own.—French & Beal   **115**   Tr.—Lukas D Wayne

Jly 2 Hol 5f ft 1:01 h   Jun 18 Hol 3f ft :35² hg   Jun 13 Hol 4f ft :47² h   Jun 6 Hol 4f ft :47⁴ h

Rich Doctor

Ro. c. 2, by Doc Scott J—Rich Return II, by Rich Gift
Br.—Houssels J K Sr (Cal)   1979   5 1 1 2 $11,144

Own.—J K Houssels Sr Estate   **117**   Tr.—Adams George D

16Jun79-3Hol	5f	:22¹	:45⁴	:58 ft	6½ 116	42¾ 31½ 2hd 1¾	Pierce D⁷		⑤Mdn 90	RichDoctor,TheCarpenter,DndyWit 8
31May79-5Hol	5f	:22¹	:45²	:58 ft	5¼ 116	42½ 46 45½ 31½	Olivares F¹		⑤Mdn 89	FleetTiming,Pergamum,RichDoctor 9
11May79-4Hol	5f	:22	:45²	:57³ft	36 115	6¹⁵ 5¹² 59½ 26	Olivares F⁵		Mdn 86	ExcutivCounsl,RichDoctor,NtvAngl 7
11Apr79-8TuP	4½f	:22²	:45⁴	:52 ft	15 119	3 77 79 56¾	Stallings WE³	Fut Trl	85	Fctory,Bell'sOwnSundy,PollyChck 10
28Mar79-3TuP	4½f	:23¹	:47	:53¹m	22 118	8 66½ 57 35½	Romero A⁷		Mdn 80	Free Sea, ArizonaMiss,RichDoctor 10

Jly 2 Hol 5f ft 1:00 h   Jun 25 Hol 5f ft 1:02² h   Jun 8 Hol 3f ft :39 h   May 27 Hol 5f ft 1:02¹ h

Buen Centavo

Gr. c. 2, by Catchpenny II—Guena Cosa, by Juanro
Br.—Howard Mymy (Cal)   1979   2 1 0 0 $4,950

Own.—Howard Mymy   **115**   Tr.—Moeller Glenn H

18May79-4Hol	5f	:22⁴	:46⁴	:59²ft	4½ 115	4½ 42 42 2hd	Frazier D Jr²	⑤M25000 83	‡DlwrThundr,BunCntvo,SummrSlor 9
18May79—Placed first through disqualification										
4May79-4Hol	5f	:22	:45²	:57²ft	30 115	5⁸ 6¹¹ 6¹² 6¹⁶	Frazier D Jr²	Mdn 77	Parsec, Valtat, Native Angle	6

Jly 1 Hol 4f ft :46⁴ h   Jun 25 Hol 4f ft :48² h   Jun 9 Hol 5f ft 1:02³ h   Jun 2 SA 4f ft :47⁴ h

than six furlongs. Its victory June 21 depended on front-runners' tiring, and that does not figure to recur here.

Which contender figures to win?

The blazing Doonesbury, correct?

The Hollywood crowd thought so, backing the Golden Gate shipper as its favorite at 8 to 5.

Many handicappers who "make millions" on the two-year-old dashes presumably lost a bundle on this one. These noted the following speed indicators:

- Golden Gate (GG) is a slower track than Hollywood Park.
- Doonesbury has recorded the fastest speed rating at five furlongs, a 99!
- When adjusted for typical track times, Doonesbury has recorded the fastest final time at five and one-half furlongs.
- Doonesbury has shown both early and late speed, winning on the lead and from behind the pace.
- When compared to the speedy Murrtheblurr, Doonesbury has overcome faster fractional times at five furlongs, and has set and maintained faster fractional times at five and one-half furlongs.

To dispense with Murrtheblurr, let's concede it has not arrived at the finish line as fast when forced to withstand a contested, rapid early pace. Its June 6 demise reveals a pace weakness. When forced to disengage another two-year-old in fast time early, it could not hold off the handy Parsec, a second late-comer, despite leading by two lengths after three furlongs. Murrtheblurr needs early daylight, and does not figure to earn it in the Cabrillo Stakes.

That leaves Doonesbury and Parsec. Don't Doonesbury's times stick out?

They do not.

To appreciate this, examine the fractional times recorded at Hollywood Park on June 6, the day Parsec annexed the First Act Stakes, earning a ninety speed rating.

For Sprints:			
1st Cl-12,500	7f	45 2/5	1:12
3rd Md Cl-20,000	6f	46 2/5	58 4/5
5th Cl-20,000	6f	46	58 2/5
8th Stk-2 yrs.	5½f	45	58
For Routes:			
2nd Cl-20,000	1 1/16m	47 1/5	1:12 1/5
4th Cl-25,000	1m	47 1/5	1:12 3/5
6th Alw-NW 1	1 1/16m (turf)	47 1/5	1:12
7th Alw-Nw 3	1 1/16m	46 3/5	1:11
9th Cl-25,000	1 1/16m	47 1/5	1:12 2/5

Not a collector of speed figures at the time, I cannot now reveal the class-distance par times for Hollywood Park during 1978–79, when the track was a mile oval, but I can assert the June 6 fractional times register as abnormally low.

Apparently, that understates the situation. On my arrival at Hollywood June 6, my neighbor announced, "I'm loaded for bear in the feature, and expect to make a killing. Parsec sticks out."

If Parsec truly figured, eventually I inquired as to how, considering Doonesbury's fractional and final times. A devotee of track variants, Frank Romano pointed out that June 6 had been the slowest day of Hollywood's season by a landslide.

"Tplus twenty-four," he informed me. That sounded like magic potion of the kind horse players are forever hoping to bottle.

Was it?

"Anything over plus twenty is very significant," said Frank. "This track was absolutely dead June 6."

I began to ponder Parsec. Not only does Romano keep useful track variants, he bets big. And he does so with the confidence of the good handicapper, which he is.

When the nine two-year-olds appeared for the Cabrillo Stakes, Frank Romano, who had not bet all day, counted out $1,000 and placed it on Parsec's nose.

By this time my own handicapping had boiled the race down to Doonesbury and Parsec. Parsec had shown speed, competitiveness, and versatility, coming from behind to win June 6, after staying close to the fastest fractions of the slowest day of the season. Not nearly as confident I would be backing an eventual winner, I joined Romano against the shipper from northern California when the odds persuaded me it was favorable to do so.

EIGHTH RACE
Hollywood
JULY 6, 1979

5 ½ FURLONGS. (1.02⅕) 27th Running of THE CABRILLO STAKES. $40,000 Added. Colts and geldings. 2-year-olds. (Allowance) By subscription of $50 each, which shall accompany the nomination, $400 additional to start, with $40,000 added of which $8,000 to second, $6,000 to third, $3,000 to fourth and $1,000 to fifth. Weight, 122 lbs. Non-winners of a sweepstakes allowed 3 lbs.; two races other than claiming, 5 lbs.; a race other than claiming, 7 lbs. Starters to be named through the entry box by closing time of entries. Winners preferred in the main starting gate. A trophy will be presented to the owner of the winner. Closed Wednesday, June 27, 1979, with 18 nominations.
Value of race $44,500, value to winner $26,500, second $8,000, third $6,000, fourth $3,000, fifth $1,000. Mutuel pool $407,049.

Last Raced	Horse	Eqt.A.Wt	PP	St	¼	⅜	Str	Fin	Jockey	Odds $1
6Jun79 8Hol1	Parsec	2 122	4	4	1hd	1hd	1hd	12	Shoemaker W	3.20
5Jun79 8GG1	Doonesbury	2 122	2	7	4½	3hd	3½	2½	Chapman T M	1.70
20Jun79 8Hol1	Murrtheblurr	2 122	5	3	22½	22½	22½	3¾	Olivares F	2.10
16Jun79 3Hol1	Rich Doctor	2 117	8	2	71½	64	53½	4nk	Pierce D	27.10
22Jun79 11Sol1	California Ranger	2 122	1	6	31	42½	4½	5hd	Ochoa A	58.80
21Jun79 3Hol1	Stiff Diamond	b 2 117	3	9	81½	87	6½	64	Pincay L Jr	11.20
	Mojingo	2 115	7	1	62	5hd	74	71	Toro F	9.00
20Jun79 8Hol8	Traffic Pattern	2 115	6	5	5hd	7hd	88	810	Delahoussaye E	82.80
18May79 4Hol1	Buen Centavo	2 115	9	8	9	9	9	9	Hawley S	58.90

OFF AT 5:34 PDT. Start good. Won driving. Time, :21 4/5, :44 4/5, :57 1/5, 1:03 2/5 Track fast.

$2 Mutuel Prices:			
4-PARSEC	8.40	4.00	2.40
2-DOONESBURY		3.60	2.60
5-MURRTHEBLURR			2.40

B. g, by Wing Out—Grand Alma, by Aberion. Trainer Knight Chay R. Bred by Cardiff Stud Farm (Cal).

PARSEC set or forced the pace inside of MURRTHEBLURR soon after the start and drew clear in the final sixteenth. DOONESBURY, never far back, rallied outside the leaders in the stretch but did not menace the winner. MURRTHEBLURR forced the early pace, drifted in and lightly brushed the winner in the upper stretch and weakened slightly near the end. RICH DOCTOR could gain little rallying on the rail in the final furlong. CALIFORNIA RANGER lacked a strong finish. BUEN CENTAVO bore out most of the trip.

Owners— 1, Jameson L; 2, Roberts-Roffe-Willis; 3, Agnew D J; 4, J K Houssels Sr Estate; 5, California Stable; 6, Lamazor F P; 7, French & Beal; 8, Maragar Stable Inc; 9, Howard Mymy.

Scratched—Cut the Cost (14Jun79 3Hol1).

Doonesbury started a little sluggishly and rushed up, which helped Parsec.

But the point is much larger.

In order to make millions in two-year-old dashes, handicappers at least must calculate par times and track variants and apply the variants to final times effectively. The adjusted final times account for differences in daily track speeds. Where speed is so important, the better estimates of true final time demand the extra effort.

Comparing final times, handicappers learn, does not consist of the studied glance at speed ratings. In the East, where shipping is commonplace, handicappers need to prepare variants and par times for local tracks, and after applying the variants they must often compensate still for track differences, which themselves are relatively unstable. It takes know-how and work. Nothing very useful can be accomplished at a glance.

The other big obstacle blocking handicappers that intend to make millions in juvenile dashes arises mainly in maiden races. Maiden dashes usually involve two-year-olds that have not started. These might have been working out impressively. Handicappers must decide whether a first-timer can run faster than the best times previously recorded. Our second and third guidelines help greatly in this dilemma.

2. Eliminate any experienced horse that has not earned a speed rating of eighty-seven or better at a distance within a half-furlong of today's.

3. Credit sharp-working two-year-olds whose breeding indicates high early speed.

The evidence on dosage associated in the popular literature with three-year-olds and classic distances has been extended persuasively by author Steven A. Roman to two-year-old racing. Roman has shown that among two-year-old winners of open stakes valued at $25,000 or higher, the average dosage indexes (DIs) decrease as the distance lengthens. But the general pattern is provocative, and greatly useful to handicappers.

Examine the graph of Figure 1, supplied by Roman for all two-year-old stakes winners of 1984.

The evidence shows unmistakably that as a group the important two-year-old winners at the dash distances have DIs that range from 10.50 or greater at five furlongs to 9.75 or so at five-and-a-half furlongs. These pedigrees are strongly prepotent with brilliance.

Note that at six furlongs the average DI has fallen slightly below 7.50, a rather steep two-point drop associated with a distance change of one-sixteenth of a mile. Sprints for two-year-olds really do differ from the dashes. Handicappers with access to the information will look longingly for relatively high DIs when analyzing first-starting juveniles at distances shorter than six furlongs.

In this context, handicappers should not discount local speed stallions whose runners rarely travel fast beyond six furlongs. The dash is considerably shorter than that, and speed counts most. At five furlongs, the local hotshot sire might outrank a national leader whose bloodlines depend more on qualities other than bountiful early speed. Handicappers give themselves an edge if they supplement the following list of leading national juvenile sires with the local rankings.

FIGURE 1. *Average Dosage Indexes by Distance for Two-Year-Old Open Stakes Winners at $25,000 or Higher*

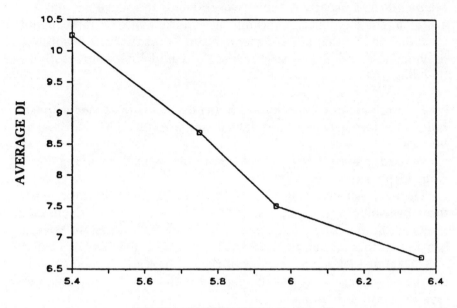

AVERAGE DISTANCE (furlongs)

Leading Juvenile Sires—Money Won
January 1—December 31, 1983

Juvenile Sire	Perf.	Win Perf.	Sts.	1st	2nd	3rd	Unp.	Purses
Alydar	16	4	45	15	11	5	14	$1,136,063
Faliraki	21	10	96	12	7	12	65	827,231
Halo	23	12	105	21	11	16	57	732,574
Tri Jet	24	16	162	29	16	20	97	671,664
Cox's Ridge	9	4	35	5	9	7	14	598,915
Seattle Slew	7	2	21	6	3	1	11	511,540
Vice Regent	22	11	92	19	15	9	49	481,491
Chieftain	13	5	50	9	12	5	24	472,862
Raja Baba	23	12	85	19	15	10	41	419,233
Timeless Moment	12	3	52	5	9	11	27	417,118
Avatar	25	10	115	15	11	15	74	410,658
Island Agent	1	1	8	5	1	1	1	360,495
Caro	10	5	29	8	4	5	12	345,002
Fire Dancer	28	15	211	18	31	31	131	331,528

Juvenile Sire	Perf.	Win Perf.	Sts.	1st	2nd	3rd	Unp.	Purses
L'Enjoleur	19	8	78	13	14	8	43	320,949
Table Run	22	12	130	17	21	20	72	311,574
Noholme II	15	5	46	10	9	5	22	310,157
Drone	10	6	39	10	7	4	18	304,670
Noble Table	15	7	90	11	9	12	58	304,163
Full Pocket	23	11	101	22	15	23	41	297,636
New Prospect	29	15	173	27	25	14	107	294,148
Draconic	17	7	83	19	9	9	46	292,616
Dock Robbery	7	5	86	22	10	11	43	290,348
L'Natural	21	11	96	17	16	19	44	286,750
Drum Fire	27	13	129	26	15	22	66	282,111
Topsider	12	7	46	12	10	11	13	277,201
Al Hattab	15	9	87	11	9	13	54	271,328
Smarten	9	3	48	6	7	7	28	262,762
Colonel Power	24	14	177	26	23	20	108	261,139
Sauce Boat	23	12	82	16	13	12	41	246,722
Cormorant	19	10	91	17	10	10	54	246,156
Well Mannered	16	8	103	16	9	18	60	244,518
Blushing Groom	9	6	49	11	6	10	22	241,931
Proud Birdie	26	12	161	20	16	18	107	239,831
Rollicking	17	7	86	15	13	8	50	238,401

Leading Juvenile Sires—Money Won
January 1—December 31, 1984

Juvenile Sire	Perf.	Win Perf.	Sts.	1st	2nd	3rd	Unp.	Purses
Danzig	12	10	73	22	10	15	26	$2,146,530
Exclusive Native	11	5	66	10	9	10	37	1,044,070
Buckaroo	18	9	122	19	21	15	67	829,009
Vice Regent	19	11	73	21	8	10	34	781,840
Valid Appeal	12	8	55	16	14	7	18	661,788
Mr. Prospector	7	4	22	5	7	3	7	522,990
Tilt Up	14	5	63	10	7	10	36	507,937
Alydar	20	7	58	13	8	3	34	500,714
In Reality	12	4	41	10	2	6	23	486,104
Clever Trick	25	17	107	34	15	15	43	478,409
Secretariat	18	5	58	9	9	3	37	431,738
Cutlass	20	13	88	22	20	9	37	430,450
Baldski	28	12	140	19	14	13	94	427,975
Roberto	11	1	25	2	3	3	17	413,017
Our Native	15	8	88	15	11	23	39	384,949
Run Dusty Run	17	8	77	10	9	8	50	384,913

Juvenile Sire	Perf.	Win Perf.	Sts.	1st	2nd	3rd	Unp.	Purses
Full Out	26	18	131	27	17	21	66	381,718
Le Fabuleux	6	2	23	6	1	3	13	380,421
Beau Buck	6	4	39	7	5	2	25	369,700
Top Command	14	3	56	6	6	4	40	336,554
Pirate's Bounty	14	6	73	8	18	11	36	330,007
Cougar II	11	1	35	2	3	3	27	323,675
Bob's Dusty	22	10	111	17	16	10	68	323,290
Overskate	9	3	36	7	5	4	20	315,853
Nijinsky II	10	4	36	7	5	2	22	310,694
Tri Jet	33	18	192	23	30	21	118	309,771
It's Freezing	17	9	76	17	11	9	39	308,229
Diabolo	12	4	64	8	4	14	38	300,822
Diplomat Way	40	12	239	20	21	27	171	281,457
L'Natural	21	8	92	15	10	7	60	274,472
Smarten	16	5	71	10	8	10	43	268,299
Matsadoon	26	14	106	18	14	13	61	267,336
Coastal	7	6	46	9	7	6	24	262,581
Table Run	12	6	61	11	11	6	33	260,638
Northern Prospect	15	7	94	10	15	10	59	257,751

1984 Leading Juvenile Sires
(Winning Performers)

Sire	Performers	Winning Performers
Full Out	26	18
Nalees Man	32	18
Tri Jet	33	18
Clever Trick	25	17
Great Above	27	15
Matsadoon	26	14
Apalachee	27	14
Exuberant	32	14
Cutlass	20	13
Bold Ruckus	19	13
Verbatim	28	13
On to Glory	24	13
Go Step	19	12
Forever Casting	18	12
Just the Time	19	12
Princely Pleasure	20	12
Baldski	28	12
Diplomat Way	40	12
Vice Regent	19	11
Search For Gold	19	11

Sire		Performers	Winning Performers
Brent's Prince	....	19	11
Draconic	....	16	11
El Rastro	....	16	11
Raise A Bid	....	24	11
Dactylographer	....	21	11
Family Doctor	....	19	11
Medieval Man	....	26	11
Gentle King	....	22	11
Topsider	....	14	10
Real Value	....	16	10
Sovereign Dancer	....	13	10
Danzig	....	12	10
Horatius	....	18	10
Hold Your Peace	....	19	10
Sevastopol	....	21	10
Colonel Power	....	20	10
Darby Creek Road	....	29	10
Bob's Dusty	....	22	10
Pacific Native	....	22	10
Ramirez	....	20	10

4. Credit impressive juveniles whose trainers' reputations derive from their handling of two-year-olds.

Some trainers specialize in accelerating or refining the early lick of two-year-olds. Their stables' juveniles win regularly, and often score in the earliest stakes at dash distances. That excessive early dosages of speed often interfere with the horses' later and better development is of no practical concern to handicappers, until that later time. The fastest two-year-olds figure to win the dashes. In close analyses, count on trainers who practice that specialty successfully.

5. Notwithstanding unexceptional differences in workout times, prepare to support any first-time starter which gets strong backing in the betting.

Guideline 5 recognizes stable help as the sole proprietors of unraced two-year-olds, and these people might want to bet on their good ones.

Good handicappers should collect worthwhile profits during any season of juvenile dashes. Patience makes all the difference. With so many stables sending out first starters earlier nowadays, handicappers must wait until all that speed has been recorded in competition. If local handicapping services that are forever doing so can provide reliable information and commentary about workouts and training races, handicappers might purchase the services profitably, as their precious edge in two-year-old dashes.

Concerning eligibility conditions and dashes for juveniles, handicappers must understand that maiden winners often move directly to stakes conditions. This is perfectly acceptable. There are not enough winners to fill a program of nonwinners allowance events. The early stakes boost the two-year-old programs, and keep owners-breeders in better spirits. Later on, handicappers can discount performances in these added-money events for the time-testing dashes they remain.

And if leading stables enter nicely bred, sharp-working first starters in these dash stakes, accept the maidens. These special juvenile prospects might just win in a breeze.

LONGER RACES

Responsible studies of two-year-old racing fail to tell handicappers much about predicting their route races. There are too few of them to permit generalizable findings. William Quirin's monumental computer analyses of past performance characteristics constructed par times for class-distance groups of horses of all ages, but Quirin begged off reporting on two-year-olds beyond six furlongs. "... it is impossible to make a valid statement concerning how fast a two-year-old can be expected to run a given route distance, and we will not attempt to do so."

Smart handicappers approach distance races for two-year-olds with an appreciation that the races are relatively unpredictable. Horses that win with speed in reserve at six furlongs might stretch out to middle distances at two, but they might not.

Dosage indexes can be helpful again when analyzing two-year-old routes, especially among the better horses. Handicappers should expect the juvenile route winners as a group will have DIs lower than the dash and sprint winners, yet the figures will remain higher than those of the better older horses.

Examine Figure 2, which reveals the average DIs for two-year-old, three-year-old, and older stakes winners at various times of the season.

While the indexes of the older horses remain relatively constant at different points in the season, and below those of two-year-olds at

FIGURE 2. *Change in Cumulative Average DI with Increasing Age (1982) of Winners of Open Stakes Valued at $25,000 or Higher*

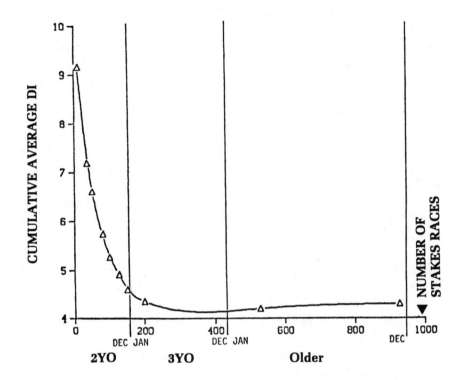

any time, the DIs of two-year-old stakes winners clearly become lower and lower throughout the second part of the year, when the routes begin.

Nonclaiming two-year-olds that win the dashes of spring are less likely to win the routes of fall, and increasingly less with every passing day. The two populations of juveniles differ in their racing characteristics and potential.

Importantly, there is no cutoff point that distinguishes two-year-olds that win sprints from those that win routes. The dosage data describe a pattern of lower DIs among two-year-old winners as distance increases, but several exceptions should be expected. The data do not mean that two-year-olds having DIs greater than 6.00 or 10.00 or whatever will not win at a mile and one-sixteenth; they will.

In this situation as well, the general tendency of two-year-olds to show striking improvement or steady deterioration in their form cycles might prove applicable on occasion. If two-year-olds have shown tremendous improvement and the next race is the first route, continued improvement can be expected. Also, really top two-year-olds with breeding that promises classic racing qualities usually do what is asked of them as juveniles. If a leading stable tries them at two turns under appropriate circumstances, they probably can complete the chore. Otherwise, distance races for two-year-olds are too tough until the horses have circled the course a time or two.

Races at six furlongs can be handicapped straightforwardly, with emphasis on pace handicapping. Accurate speed figures remain crucial. Not much more light can be shed on these races. Credit notable cycles of improvement. Do not excuse deteriorating form.

Here, finally, is a list of statistical findings (Quirin) that guide handicappers as they work with races at six furlongs or longer for juvenile maiden winners:

1. Maiden claiming winners that race for the same price at which they won or lower race at no disadvantage, but those that move into nonwinners once allowances are very likely to lose.

2. Maiden winners that show exceptional ability, in terms of time or style, are solid bets at profitable prices next time out.

This is because maiden winners are overbet as a rule, making the most exceptionally outstanding of two-year-old winners relative overlays. These show a profit when bet back.

3. Recent action is not as important as in races for older.

The absence of a race for more than thirty days does not diminish the two-year-old's chance to win.

4. If juveniles break the maiden in exceptional time at least two lengths faster than par for the race in which it next is entered, these are the best betting opportunities of all. The horses repeat the high speed, and often run even faster.

5. Be skeptical of maiden winners that won wire-to-wire without challenge at any call.

The quintessential contemporary horseman, trainer D. Wayne Lukas is not only the man for his times in racing, but the new leader of the pack. His money won ($11,155,188) and stakes won (70) records of 1985 astonished everyone in the industry. A partial explanation is his unprecedented success with juveniles and the talent he brings to selecting perfectly conformed yearlings at the Kentucky and Saratoga select sales.

A goal-directed individual, practically all that Lukas has left for himself is winning the Kentucky Derby. It's just a matter of time.

The Handicapper's Condition Book Trainer Profile

D. Wayne Lukas: One of a Kind

At $13 million, trainer D. Wayne Lukas became the disappointed underbidder to England's Robert Sangster at Keeneland Summer 1985 for the most expensive yearling ever sold at public auction. Sangster gave $13.1 million for the half brother by Nijinksy II to champion and leading sire Seattle Slew, and in the aftermath, Lukas second-guessed himself for not bidding upward of $15 million.

He was correct, of course, as the colt could have been syndicated for $10 million the next day and the first-year depreciation on the investment would have practically turned a paper profit quicker than the daddy could leave the post. If the precious colt someday won a Grade 1 stakes, the resulting resyndication would stop at $40 million or upward. A generation of yearlings, racehorses, broodmares, and stallions would follow. That represents millions more.

That's the way this game is played at the top and surely the central point not to be dismissed is that along with Sangster, Sheihk Maktoum, Stavros Niarchos, and the internationally bankrolled agents of the British Bloodstock Agency, the eight-year American trainer D. Wayne Lukas knows how to play the major league racing game and he knows how to win. This is rare air Lukas breathes, and relative to his training colleagues, it can be asserted categorically that his performance has been singular. No other trainer in the history of this sport has organized and managed a stable of thoroughbreds in the remarkably stylish, intelligent, and successful manner of D. Wayne Lukas. This man is so different in a contemporary, progressive way, it's begging the question to call him a new breed of trainer. He's more likely just one of a kind. Already his statistics have become their own points of reference, rather like Bill Shoemaker's did before he had been riding a decade. I have regularly referred to Lukas as a man for his times. It's becoming intensely clear he is instead a man for all times.

Lukas' strengths as a horseman go far beyond the ability to prepare a barnful of horses for stakes races and none supersedes his ability to appreciate dearly the value of his assets (horses). Lukas manages important money as well as the cleverest Wall Street portfolio analyst. His financial dealings are unmatched on any backstretch in the country.

To recall one unusual incident among many, years ago Lukas believed a young colt he did not train named The Carpenter was a Grade 1 prospect. He tried to buy the colt at a premium. No sale. So he tried to buy the dam at a premium. No sale. Finally, he *leased* the dam for five years at premium rates. The Carpenter soon won the

Grade 1 title. Lukas immediately moved the dam up in class—sending it to Nijinsky II and other nuts of the stud—and eventually sold the resulting yearlings for bonanza prices. That takes a special set of skills. How many other trainers can mimic Lukas on the matter?

The trainer's dominance with juveniles and young threes traces, to an educated eye for perfectly conformed yearlings, a rarified art Lukas practices on the loftiest plane with a handful of others and at which racetrack trainers as a class are greatly overrated. Structurally sound, the Lukas youngsters can better withstand the repeated concussion of hard racing, for which neither their physique nor temperament is suited. In this arena Lukas has benefited considerably from the times, the sport having drifted incessantly since the inflation of the seventies and the trainer's debut in 1978 toward the faster development and earlier racing of young thoroughbreds.

Of Keeneland's fifty highest-priced yearlings of 1985, Lukas signed for four. He paid $2.5 million for a Northern Dancer filly, ending a personal boycott of the great sire's progeny. When questioned about it, he simply pointed out that Northern Dancers flourished in Europe but not so terrifically here. Lukas took a second Northern Dancer that summer, another filly for $900,000. He took two royal colts, an Alydar for $975,000 and a Seattle Slew for $800,000. Lukas ranked 4th among Keeneland buyers, spending $9 million for eighteen yearlings. He led all American buyers.

On the track Lukas' numbers have improved impressively each year since 1978 but the great leap forward occurred between 1983 and 1985, when entrepreneur Eugene Klein financed a gigantic expansion of his thoroughbred holdings. Lukas led all trainers in money-won both seasons but the data for the two years document the amazing transformation that occurred. Consider the two lines below:

Year	Starts	1st	2nd	3rd	Pct.	Money–Won	Rank	(money)
1983	599	79	110	80	.13	$4,272,916	1	
1985	1,140	218	183	135	.19	$11,155,188	1	

In between (1984), Lukas led all trainers again with $5.8 million won but in 1985 he amassed $5.5 million with Klein's horses alone. The truly staggering statistic, however, shows the hammerlock Lukas has put on the stakes programs in the modern sport:

Year	Stakes Starts	1st	2nd	3rd	Pct.	Money–Won	Rank
1985	284	70	50	37	.25	$8,415,741	1

Lukas' stakes starters finished in-the-money 55 percent of the time! Favorites finish in-the-money 67 percent of the time.

To put this performance in deeper perspective, stakes runner-up in money-won, Charles Whittingham, banked $4.7 million, his best year ever. Woody Stephens won with 24 percent of his stakes starters, collecting $2.5 million. No one else earned that much in stakes races.

Whittingham also ranked second overall in money-won, yet his total of $5.8 million is *2.6 million below Lukas' stakes money only.* In more popular sports jargon, this is what is known as rewriting the record book.

With major divisions for 1986 and beyond in southern California, New York, the South, the Midwest, and minor platoons in northern California and elsewhere, the long-term tabulations may be unimaginable. Lukas now employs an astonishing 150-plus people. He manages the far-flung organization with a datacom network of computers that can talk to one another. In 1985, he and Klein constructed a full-facility off-site training center in north San Diego. And in 1986 Lukas purchased a private jet to fly from track to track at his convenience. Not unlike the managers of conglomerates and multinationals, Lukas wants personal control and he does what he must to secure it.

In the boxes and corridors of insiders at racetrackes, the knocks against Lukas suggest that he (a) wins because he is backed by big money and (b) breaks down too many horses by working them too hard too soon.

The first argument is specious. It turns reality upside down. Trainers do not win because they are blessed with rich clients. They enlist rich clients because they win. At some point an interaction begins, but essentially the big money is dependent on winning big, not vice versa. As soon as the winning big stops, so does the big money. His first season Lukas started 194 horses, won 37, earned $942,786, ranked 22nd in money-won. The numbers improved from year to year. In 1980, Lukas jumped to 5th in money-won. People noticed. The bigger money began to flow in.

On the second point, Lukas breaks down approximately as many horses as does any frontline trainer who concentrates on the younger divisions. The horses are plainly immature and many will not make it. Prior to the Kentucky Derby, Woody Stephens lost Devil's Bag, a colt he called the greatest two-year-old in racing history. Do critics think Devil's Bag received adequate care and supervision? Every step the colt took was carefully monitored. But he broke down nonetheless. At least one-half the Derby prospects go down annually.

Those looking to point the finger of blame can turn to the industry itself and racing associations that have brandished million-dollar pots to spur the two-year-old programs. It's a brand-new game. Lukas doesn't make the rules. He merely attempts to exploit them. The only way to prevent premature breakdowns is to change the rules and incentives of the modern sport. And that's a shopworn argument that has long since been lost.

A goal-directed individual, Lukas lists specific objectives each year and in 1986 will be shooting at $12 million in money-won and eighty stakes won. As this is composed, he is a quarter million ahead of the 1985 pace on money and four stakes in front as well. So far the Kentucky Derby has eluded him, though he has started ten horses and two favorites, and the trainer wants to win the roses badly. His tendency to buy yearlings having high dosage indexes has delayed him in the quest, but he has consciously altered that habit by a substantial degree.

The Kentucky Derby will be just a matter of time. After he wins it, a more ambitious goal is lying in wait for the right man. Lukas might consider it a personal ambition to become the first American trainer to win England's Epsom Derby. It would do wonders for international racing, a trend already well under way.

A gentleman, sophisticated in style and manner, and an enthusiastic articulate spokesman having a positive can-do attitude on matters great and small, Lukas' emergence as a national figure has worked admirably well for a sport having a horrendous public image. These contributions are hardly unimportant. In a difficult game for owners, breeders, horsemen, and bettors, Lukas sends forth a ringing message that just about anything is possible.

Recently he was invited to speak at the annual luncheon of the California Thoroughbred Breeders' Association (CTBA). He spoke extemporaneously for ninety minutes about success. The hall was palpably mesmerized. Afterward, Lukas sat down to rolling ovations and applause. It took only eight years.

References

AINSLIE, TOM. *Ainslie's Complete Guide to Thoroughbred Racing.* Simon and Schuster: New York, 1968, 1979.

————. *Ainslie's Encyclopedia of Thoroughbred Handicapping.* William Morrow and Company, Inc.: New York, 1978.

DAVIS, FRED. *Percentages & Probabilities: A Probability Study of Past Performance Characteristics.* Woodside Associates: Woodside, NY, 1973.

QUIRIN, WILLIAM L. *Winning at the Races: Computer Discoveries in Thoroughbred Handicapping.* William Morrow and Company, Inc.: New York, 1979.

ROMAN, STEVEN A. "An Analysis of Dosage," *The Thoroughbred Record,* April 1984.

Appendix 1:

Selection and Elimination Guidelines for Twenty Variations of Eligibility Conditions

THE GUIDELINES presented here represent a distillation of the larger text and are intended as a ready-reference to help handicappers distinguish horses well suited to the conditions of eligibility from horses that are not.

The standard array of races carded in major racing is examined as follows.

First, similar to what appears in the *Form*, the conditions of eligibility for each kind of race are written out in boldface. Immediately alongside these the basic handicapping requirements of the **Form** and **Distance** factors are given. Each horse in the race should satisfy the basic requirements. An exception to this format is races for maidens, where the basic requirements refer to the **Form**, **Jockey**, and **Speed** factors, but omit **Distance**. Experienced handicappers can modify the basic requirements as situations demand or new evidence indicates. Novices and others should interpret the basic requirements strictly.

The basic requirements normally will eliminate some horses from further consideration, thereby erasing errors of the grossest kind while easing the remaining handicapping burden.

Next, horses that qualify when judged on the basic requirements can be evaluated in four ways:

1. Do their records distinguish them as the kinds of horses **handicappers prefer** under today's conditions of eligibility?

2. Are they instead the kinds of horses handicappers **regularly eliminate** under today's conditions?

3. Do their records contain any **extra added attractions**?

4. Are there **special conditions** to consider for today's race?

To help handicappers answer the four questions, the Appendix presents its handicapping guidelines in list form under four headings:

Handicappers prefer

Regular eliminations

Extra added attractions

Special conditions

The selection profiles are presented in descending order of preference, but where several horses qualify as contenders practiced handicappers can consider the permissible profiles interchangeable. Final decisions can be informed by related factors, notably the odds line on each contender as post time nears.

The elimination guidelines are especially valuable for saving money on misplaced horses. Horses not well-suited to conditions or eligibility sometimes win, but generally they lose. They lose because the races were not written with them in mind. More important, consistent wagering on misplaced horses increases the customer's seasonal losses, and very unnecessarily.

On the final pages are more concrete definitions of the key abstract terms used throughout the appendix.

TYPES OF RACES

Maidens, for three-year-olds and up
Maiden claiming races, all prices, all ages
Maiden dashes, for two-year-olds

Allowance, three-year-olds and up, nonwinners other than maiden or claiming
Allowance, four-year-olds and up, nonwinners other than maiden or claiming
Allowance, three-year-olds and up, nonwinners two times other than maiden or claiming
Allowance, four-year-olds and up, nonwinners two times other than maiden or claiming
Allowance, nonwinners three times other than maiden or claiming, all ages
Allowance, nonwinners four times other than maiden or claiming, all ages

---

Conditioned stakes, for three-year-olds
Conditioned stakes, for three-year-olds and up
Grade 1 stakes, all ages
Grade 2 stakes, all ages
Lower grade and other open stakes, for three-year-olds
Lower grade and other open stakes, for three-year-olds and up

---

Classified allowance, three-year-olds and up, minimally restricted
Classified allowance, three-year-olds and up, highly restricted.

Claiming races, four-year-olds and up, all claiming prices
Claiming races three-year-olds, all claiming prices
Starter races, four-year-olds and up, all starting prices

MAIDENS

For three-year-olds, or
For three-year-olds and up. To identify contenders, the basic requirements. **Form:** horses must show regular, sharp workouts, with two or
more of high speed, and including at least one of five furlongs or longer
for sprints, of six furlongs or longer for routes. **Jockey:** to be ridden by a
national or local leader, or by the top apprentice, or by a regular stable
rider. **Speed:** if raced, has earned a speed rating of eighty-four or better
for sprints, of seventy-four or better for routes.

(During the first four months of the season, the basic requirements
and handicapping preferences below apply to races for horses four-
years-old and up.)

Handicappers prefer:

1. **a nicely bred, lightly raced three-year-old that finished second last
time out.**

2. **any three-year-old that finished second or third last out while demonstrating improved form and earning clockings at least within a length
or two of the acceptable speed ratings.**

In the absence of the above, prefer:

3. **first-time starting three-year-olds entered by reliable stables**, provided the horses are bred to show early speed, have recorded impressive
workout patterns, and appear calm and dry in the paddock and post
parade.

4. **a nicely bred, lightly raced impressive four-year-old from a leading
stable**, preferably of a kind that raced a few times at three, and satisfactorily, and is returning to action of late accompanied by a series of regular,
fast workouts.

Regular eliminations:

1. horses four-years-old and older, with the exception specified
above.

2. horses that have lost more than six maiden races, unless the latest

performance or two have been significantly improved, fall within the speed requirements, and the horses' records reflect other signs of improved form, that is, improved workouts, closer finishes, or favorable jockey changes.

3. first-time starters from stables whose win percentage has fallen below 15 percent, unless the workout pattern is sparkling and a leading jockey has been named.

4. horses that finished worst than third last time out.

5. horses whose workouts impress but whose races do not.

6. horses that raced green or rank last time, recording trouble lines that were self-induced.

Extra added attractions:

1. has high early speed, will be only pace-setter.

2. has good early speed, was pressed on pace last out, but figures to race clear today.

3. last time out recorded speed rating improved by five points or more.

4. gets jockey switch from journeyman to leader.

5. broke slowly, puts blinkers on.

Special conditions:

1. **In races restricted to state-breds, prefer:**

1.1 horses moving from acceptable performances in open races, notably those that show the second-place finish last out.

1.2 first-time starters sired by leading local sires whose get show high early speed, preferably those from leading stables and mounted by leading jockeys.

2. **at the route, prefer:**

2.1 horses that finished second or third last out in acceptable time at the same or related distances.

2.2 horses stretching out from a pair of sprints in which they raced evenly until the prestretch or stretch calls, and in one finished the final quarter in twenty-five seconds or less, without tiring.

3. **on turf, prefer:**

3.1 horses bred for turf and moving from previous races on dirt, notably if no other horses have raced impressively on grass.

3.2 horses that have raced more impressively on grass than on dirt, particularly those who show the recent second- or third-place finish.

MAIDEN CLAIMING RACES

For maiden claiming horses (all prices, all ages). To identify contenders, the basic requirements. **Form:** If raced within two weeks, no workouts necessary; if raced within three weeks, require at least one workout in satisfactory time; if raced within six weeks, require three or more workouts, with at least two in satisfactory time. **Distance:** in races of a mile or longer, require previous efforts at the same or related distances, with finishes within seven lengths of the winner. **Speed:** has a front-running or pace-pressing running style.

Handicappers prefer:

1. **horses moving from straight maiden races into maiden claiming conditions,** provided the basic form and speed requirements have been met in the open races.

Regular eliminations:

1. horses that have lost maiden claiming races previously; no excuses.

2. first-time starters, regardless of claiming price or stable-jockey connections.

3. horses moving from straight maiden events but exhibiting no early speed or recent dull form.

Extra added attractions:

1. any of the below, in combination.

2. a favorable jockey change.

3. improved workouts following the most recent race.

4. blinkers on.

Special conditions:

1. **horses without early speed that have run evenly or better in straight maiden races, provided they have earned one of the top two speed ratings in today's field, or have earned a pace rating higher than the other horses in the field.**

2. **at the route, sometimes prefer:**

2.1 horses that in straight maiden sprints ran evenly or better while earning a speed rating of seventy-eight or better, notably if no other horses in the field have demonstrated good early speed.

MAIDEN DASHES FOR TWO-YEAR-OLDS

For two-year-olds, at distances of five-and-one-half furlongs or less. To identify contenders, the basic requirements. **Form:** regular, fast workouts, with two or more at high speed, preferably at four furlongs or longer. **Distance-Speed:** If raced, has run at a distance within at least one-half furlong of today's while earning a speed rating of eighty-seven or better.

Handicappers prefer:

1. **the horse that has run the exact distance the fastest.**

2. **the horse that has run a distance shorter by one-half furlong the fastest while gaining rapidly and impressively in the stretch.**

3. **first-starters bred for high speed**, provided the horse is strongly supported in the wagering.

Regular eliminations:

1. experienced horses that have not earned speed ratings of eighty-seven or better.

2. first-starters not bred for high early speed.

3. horses that have run green or rank, particularly at the gate or on the turns.

Extra added attractions:

1. a high dosage index

2. a leading stable, or one whose record with two-year-olds has been outstanding.

3. alertness, poise, and calm manner in the paddock and post parade.

4. a leading rider or a favorable jockey change.

5. had gate problems, from sharp stable, puts blinkers on.

6. late tote action.

Special conditions:

1. **at five-and-one-half furlongs, when no horse promises high early speed, prefer:**

1.1 horses that finished fastest at five furlongs, provided they finished within two lengths of the winner and earned a speed rating of eighty-five or better.

1.2 first-starters from barns that excel with juveniles and having impressive workouts at six furlongs.

NONWINNERS ALLOWANCES

For three-year-olds, or
For three-year-olds and up, nonwinners other than maiden or claiming.
To identify contenders, the basic requirements. **Form:** has raced within six weeks, beating half the field and finishing within six lengths of the winner; sharp, regular workouts between races, including one within fourteen days of today. **Distance:** has earned acceptable speed ratings at same or related distance, or has run in-the-money at distances **both** shorter and longer than today's.

Handicappers prefer:

1. **a lightly raced, recent three-year-old winner that has run close once or twice in few tries and with sharp clockings (sprints eighty-five or better, routes seventy-eight or better) under similar allowance conditions.**

2. **any impressive three-year-old maiden winner last out,** preferably the nicely bred leading-stable kind that have broken maiden ranks first or second time out in fast time.

3. **any nicely bred three-year-old whose recent performances and clockings under similar conditions indicate dramatic or continued development.**

In the absence of the above, prefer:

4. **a lightly raced, late-developing four-year-old from a top stable whose latest races show significantly improved form and speed.**

5. **powerful winners of high-priced claiming races last out.**

Regular eliminations:

1. horses four-years-old and older whose past performances show six or more ordinary or unimpressive races under similar allowance conditions.

2. three-year-olds that have lost more than six consecutive races under similar conditions.

3. recent maiden winners having fast workouts but noncompetitive allowance races in which they failed to beat half the field.

4. recent maiden winners shipping from a minor track to a major track on the circuit.

5. horses that have been entered in claiming races without sharp success.

6. last out winners of maiden races completed in ordinary time or manner.

7. horses suffering a jockey change from leader to journeyman.

8. horses that race with a come-from-behind running style but record only ordinary speed ratings.

9. horses that have raced green or rank under allowance conditions.

10. horses favored in previous allowance races before losing badly or losing in ordinary time.

Extra added attractions:

1. already has demonstrated signs of superior class, notably combinations of high speed and determination.

2. a leading sire.

3. a notable jockey switch, preferably from journeyman to the leading rider at the meeting.

4. in sprints, has a front-running or pace-pressing running style.

Special conditions:

1. **when untried three-year-olds stretch out from sprints to middle distances, prefer:**

1.1 horses that can be rated kindly and should be favored by or at least comfortable with the probable early pace.

1.2 horses that finished the final quarter mile of their latest sprints in less than twenty-five seconds, without tiring.

1.3 leading jockey-leading trainer combinations.

1.4 horses drawing favorable post positions.

2. **on turf, prefer:**

2.1 recent maiden winners having well-established turf breeding, notably if the maiden win occurred on turf.

2.2 horses with previous turf experience, of even efforts or better.

NONWINNERS ALLOWANCES

For four-year-olds and up, nonwinners other than maiden or claiming. To identify contenders, the basic requirements. **Form:** has raced within thirty days, with regular workouts of three or more since, or has raced within sixty days and has a string of regular workouts, including two or more of fast time and at least one within a furlong of today's distance. **Distance:** has finished in-the-money or within three lengths of the winner at today's exact distance.

Handicappers prefer:

1. **a foreign-raced horse of Europe that has placed or finished close in a graded or listed stakes.**

2. **a lightly raced improving four-year-old from a top barn that recently broke maiden ranks impressively and has raced well in few tries under allowance conditions.**

3. **any foreign-raced horse that has won multiple races of allowance grade or better**, particularly if the import has high earnings resulting from close finishes in stakes or handicaps.

In the absence of the above, prefer:

4. **a consistent winner of higher-priced claiming races.**

Regular eliminations:

1. horses five-years-old and older.

2. regularly raced four-year-olds whose records show no recent and significant improvement.

3. horses entered more than once in claiming races without winning.

4. won wire-to-wire, quit when pressed on early pace.

Extra added attractions:

1. prior entry in a stakes or handicap.

2. regarding imports, a stable that wins consistently with them.

3. a jockey change to one of the three leaders in the standings.

4. consistent early speed.

Special conditions:

1. **on turf, prefer:**

1.1 foreign-raced horses that race regularly on grass, particularly those that have performed best at today's exact distance, or at closely related distances.

1.2 four-year-olds inexperienced on grass but having outstanding turf breeding.

NONWINNERS ALLOWANCES

For three-year-olds, or
For three-year-olds and up, nonwinners two times other than maiden or claiming. To identify contenders, the basic requirements. **Form:** has raced within six weeks, and since shows at least three workouts. **Dis-**

tance: has won or finished close at the exact distance or at related distances.

(Basic requirements and preferences below also refer to races for nonwinners of a specified winner's share two times other than maiden or claiming.)

Handicappers prefer:

1. **a nicely bred, lightly raced, improving three-year-old that in a few tries has won an allowance race smartly or determinedly in fast time and now is moving ahead in class by one logical step.**

2. **a foreign-raced four-year-old that has won or placed in a graded or listed stakes.**

3. **the same kind of three-year-old that has won an allowance race impressively and recently has lost no more than four races under nonwinners twice conditions while racing competitively in sharp time.**

4. **a lightly raced or late-developing four-year-old that once won an allowance race, has never been entered to be claimed, and has never been beaten badly under nonwinners twice conditions.**

In the absence of the above, prefer:

5. **consistent high-priced claiming race winners aged four or five that previously won an allowance race.**

Regular eliminations:

1. horses that have lost more than six consecutive races under similar conditions.

2. three-year-olds that have been entered for a claim since winning their first allowance race.

3. unimpressive recent winners under nonwinners once conditions.

4. three-year-olds that won an allowance race impressively, but have been soundly trounced in a stakes.

5. horses whose claiming races look significantly better than their allowance races.

6. horses aged six or older.

Extra added attractions:

1. even effort or better in a recent stakes.

2. bad race under similar conditions last time with an excuse, previous allowance races good.

3. highest speed ratings in allowance races, probable favorable pace today.

4. two wins in few tries, allowance win better than maiden win.

Special conditions:

1. **on turf, prefer:**

1.1 previous allowance race winners on turf.

1.2 horses moving from maiden win on dirt to nonwinners twice conditions on turf.

1.3 any horses inexperienced on grass that have top turf breeding and won a previous allowance race impressively.

NONWINNERS ALLOWANCES

For four-year-olds and up, nonwinners two times other than maiden or claiming. To identify contenders, the basic requirements. **Form:** has raced within thirty days, and since shows at least two sharp workouts. **Distance:** has won or finished within two lengths at the exact distance.

(Basic requirements and preferences below refer also to races for nonwinners of a specified winner's share two times other than maiden or claiming.)

Handicappers prefer:

1. **a nicely bred, lightly raced foreign-raced horse**, preferably a four-year-old, whose record shows either (a) a graded stakes win, (b) a listed stakes win, (c) few races and victories but relatively high earnings, or (d) multiple impressive wins under allowance or handicap conditions, and close finishes in graded stakes races.

2. **a late-developing or dramatically improving four-year-old that has never been entered for a claim and either won an allowance race last out or has raced well under conditions similar to today's in its latest races.**

In the absence of the above, prefer:

3. **consistent, high-priced claiming race winners aged four or five that previously have won an allowance race.**

Regular eliminations:

1. horses that have lost seven or more nonwinners twice allowance races.

2. unimpressive winners under nonwinners once allowances.

3. nonwinners of high-priced claiming races.

4. horses whose claiming races look significantly better than their allowance races.

5. foreign-raced horses in obviously dull or questionable form.

6. foreign-raced horses that have lost in the states when well supported in the betting.

7. foreign-raced horses moving from grass to dirt for first time.

8. horses aged six or older.

Extra added attractions:

1. even effort or better in a stakes race.

2. leading stable, highest speed rating at the exact distance.

3. switch from journeyman jockey to leader.

4. few races, relatively high earnings.

5. few races, previous impressive win, obviously improving form.

Special conditions:

1. **on turf, prefer:**

1.1 foreign-raced horses well-seasoned on that footing at the exact distance, notably in races at one and one-eighth miles or longer.

1.2 previous winners on grass, notably if that win looks best of the entire record.

1.3 lightly raced, previous allowance winner, bred for turf.

NONWINNERS ALLOWANCES

For nonwinners three times other than maiden or claiming, all ages. To identify contenders, the basic requirements. **Form:** has raced within thirty days, shows sharp regular workouts since; has not raced green or rank in its latest race. **Distance:** has won or finished within two lengths at the exact or related distances.

Handicappers prefer:

1. **a lightly raced three-year-old that has been a powerful winner of two allowance races and has run evenly or better when entered in an open stakes.**

2. **a consistent foreign-raced horse that has won a graded or listed stakes having a relatively high purse value.**

3. **multiple allowance race winners, aged three or four**, that recently have performed impressively and consistently in few tries under conditions similar to or better than today's.

In the absence of the above, prefer:

4. **highly consistent high-priced claiming horses**, preferably aged four or five, that formerly won two allowance races and recently have won or finished close while competing for purses comparable to or better than today's.

Regular eliminations:

1. horses that have lost more than four similar races.

2. horses that last out won under nonwinners twice conditions in ordinary time or manner.

3. three-year-olds badly beaten in stakes restricted to three-year-olds.

4. horses badly beaten in a conditioned stakes.

5. horses unfamiliar with the footing or unseasoned at the distance.

6. unexceptional claiming horses, and claiming winners below the highest selling prices on the local schedule.

7. shippers from a minor circuit that have not won a major stakes there.

8. horses that won their most impressive race last out, winning barely while engaging in an all-out drive or earning their highest speed rating while tiring in the stretch.

9. three-year-olds that once started in a maiden claiming race.

10. four-year-olds that have started for a claim since the second allowance win, regardless of its performance in that race.

Extra added attractions:

1. obvious signs of higher class under previous allowance conditions, i.e., successive powerful wins indicating ample reserves of power and speed, or high speed or acceleration and determination under pressure in the late stages of races.

2. an in-the-money finish in an open stakes.

3. has high early speed, rates kindly, figures to be the only pace-setter in the field.

Special conditions:

1. **in races open to three-year-olds and older, prefer:**

1.1 the nicely bred, lightly raced improving three-year-old from a good barn that has accomplished everything asked of it in fine style, especially a notable performance in a stakes race.

1.2 a similar four-year-old that qualifies well on all counts—distance, footing, form, pace, jockey.

2. **on turf, prefer:**

2.1 horses that have won or run big over grass in the past.

2.2 horses that have won or finished close in an open stakes on dirt, and are bred to race well on turf.

NONWINNERS ALLOWANCES

For nonwinners four times other than maiden or claiming, all ages. To identify contenders, the basic requirements. **Form:** has reached peak performance levels, through recent racing and workouts. **Distance:** has won at exact or related distance.

Handicappers prefer:

1. **a stakes winner**, preferably of an open stakes.

2. **an increasingly powerful winner of three allowances races that has finished in-the-money or close to the winner in an open stakes.**

3. **horses that have won three nonwinners allowance races impressively in no more than six tries and are competing under today's conditions for the first or second time.**

Regular eliminations:

1. horses four or older that have never beaten half the field in an open stakes.

2. horses that failed to finish in-the-money when entered in a conditioned stakes.

3. horses that have not yet won three allowance races.

4. horses that have previously been entered to be claimed.

5. nonstakes-winning three-year-olds trying the distance or footing for the first time.

Extra added attractions:

1. has won an open stakes race.

2. multiple allowance winners aged four that are dropping from classified allowance conditions where they have won or finished close while competing for a purse higher than today's.

Special conditions:

1. **on turf, prefer:**

1.1 horses that have won more impressively on turf than on dirt.

1.2 stakes winners or contenders on dirt, well bred for turf.

STAKES AND HANDICAPS

Conditioned stakes, for three-year-olds, nonwinners of a sweepstakes or nonwinners of a specified amount since a specified date. To identify contenders, the basic requirements. **Form:** has raced within six weeks, regular sharp workouts since. **Distance:** has won or finished close at the exact distance or a related distance; if sprint to route, finished sprint final quarter in twenty-four seconds or less without tiring, can be rated kindly, and does not figure to be severely contested on the early pace.

Handicappers prefer:

1. **horses that have finished in-the-money in an open stakes in which previous stakes winners competed**; the better the open stakes, the better.

2. **any nicely bred, lightly raced improving horse that has beaten successive nonwinners allowance conditions easily or powerfully in quick time,** notably if the horse finished with obvious reserves of speed and power.

Regular eliminations:

1. horses once entered to be claimed.

2. horses that won two nonwinners allowance races in ordinary time and manner and have never been seasoned against stakes horses, or have been beaten badly in an open stakes.

3. horses that struggled in average time to win a nonwinners three times other than maiden or claiming allowance race.

4. horses moving ahead in class and to a distance longer by a quarter-mile or farther, unless after staying reasonably close to the pace of the shorter race the horse finished the final quarter with impressive speed and power.

Extra added attractions:

1. from leading stable, switch to leading jockey.

2. only horse favored by probable early pace.

Special conditions:

1. **during first three months of year, prefer:**

    1.1 nicely bred, sharp-working maidens entered in sprints by leading stables that have won stakes with maidens in the past.

    1.2 horses that broke preliminary conditions at two impressively and are making their first three-year-old start.

2. **on turf, prefer:**

2.1 previous impressive turf winners.

2.2 impressive multiple allowance winners on dirt, bred for turf.

STAKES AND HANDICAPS

Conditioned stakes, for three-year-olds and up, nonwinners of a sweepstakes or nonwinners of a specified amount since a specified date. To identify contenders, the basic requirements. **Form:** has raced within six weeks, regular sharp workouts since. **Distance:** if four, has won at exact distance; if three, has won or finished close at exact distance or at related distance.

(During the first four months of the season the above requirements and preferences below apply also to races restricted to four-year-olds and older.)

Handicappers prefer:

1. **a three-year-old that has finished in-the-money or run close in a Grade 1 or Grade 2 stakes for its own age.***

2. **a four-year-old that has finished in-the-money in an open listed stakes for older horses.**

3. **any lightly raced, rapidly improving three-year-old that has won successively and impressively under nonwinners allowance conditions.**

In the absence of the above, prefer:

4. **the three- or four-year-old that has recently run the most impressive race in an open stakes open to older horses.**

5. **any highly consistent four-year-old, including horses entered in claiming races, that have won two of their latest six while competing for winner shares just below any specified prices in the stakes conditions.**

Regular eliminations:

1. horses six-years-old and older.

2. any five-year-old that does not compete regularly in stakes, and has been unable to finish first or second when entered in conditioned stakes.

3. previous open stakes winners returning to action after layoffs of nine months or longer, notably if workouts are short, irregular, or unimpressively easy, and the distance and footing are not just right.

4. unexceptional looking three-year-olds, and three-year-olds previously entered to be claimed.

---

* Foreign-raced horses from South America, Australia, New Zealand, and South Africa are not acceptable in U.S. stakes races *unless* they have run consistently in Grade 1 events, and have won two or more of the races.

Extra added attractions:

1. a second-place finish in a stakes last time out.

2. a favorable jockey switch **combined with** a change to a more favorable distance or footing.

3. aged three or four, lightly raced, improved form and record recently after several dull efforts, much-improved workouts since showing better form.

Special conditions:

1. **on turf, prefer:**

    1.1 previous turf winners, with preference to four-year-olds.

    1.2 highly impressive three-year-olds with top turf breeding, especially if no horses four and up have won smartly on turf under nonwinners twice allowance conditions or better.

STAKES AND HANDICAPS

Grade 1 stakes, all ages. To identify contenders, the basic requirements. **Form:** most recent races and workouts signify best efforts. **Distance:** has won a stakes race at exact or related distance.

Handicappers prefer:

1. **a national or regional champion, or a local division leader that has won a Grade 1 stakes.**

In the absence of the above, prefer:

2. **multiple Grade 2 stakes winners that have placed or finished close in a Grade 1 race.**

3. **a developing three-year-old that has won a Grade 2 stakes or important open stakes definitively, suggesting still greater class in reserve.**

Regular eliminations:

1. horses that have not won a Grade 1 race, the exceptions above withstanding.

2. Grade 1 winners in questionable form.

3. All other horses

Extra added attractions:

1. Grade 1 horse that lost last out when favored to win, notably if that losing race was used as a prep for today's Grade 1 objective.

2. stable or trainer that wins Grade 1 races consistently.

Special conditions:

1. **at distances of a mile and one-quarter or beyond, prefer:**

1.1 horses having a dosage index of 4.0 or below.

1.2 older horses that have won at the exact distance.

2. **on turf, prefer:**

2.1 previously graded stakes winners on turf.

STAKES AND HANDICAPS

Grade 2 stakes, all ages. To identify contenders, the basic requirements. **Form:** has raced within sixty days, condition remains in the improvement cycle, as indicated by latest races and workouts. **Distance:** has won or finished second in an open stakes at the exact or related distance.

Handicappers prefer:

1. **a Grade 1 stakes winner.**

2. **a Grade 2 stakes winner that has finished close this season in Grade 1 events.**

3. **any recent listed stakes winner, the higher the purse, the better.**

Regular eliminations:

1. **horses that have never won an open stakes**, unless no such winners have been entered.

2. horses that previously have won a conditioned stakes but have never finished in-the-money when entered in an open stakes.

3. horses aged four and up that do not compete regularly in open stakes, and satisfactorily.

4. horses that have won a single stakes but today are not particularly well-suited to the distance or footing, or to the probable early pace.

5. all claiming horses.

Extra added attractions:

1. a recent second-place finish or close finish in a Grade 1 stakes.

2. consistency, especially two wins in the latest six stakes efforts.

3. leading stable, leading rider combination.

Special conditions:

1. **races limited to three-year-olds, prefer:**

1.1 the nicely bred, lightly raced improving horse from a leading barn that has done everything asked of it in smashing style and now is moving into graded stakes competition.

2. **on turf, prefer:**

2.1 previous stakes winners on turf, preferably horses four-years-old or older.

3. **at distances of a mile and one-quarter or farther, prefer:**

3.1 horses having a dosage index of 4.0 or below.

STAKES AND HANDICAPS

Lower grade and open stakes, for three-year-olds. To identify contenders, the basic requirements. **Form:** has raced within six weeks, sharp regular workouts since, including two at five furlongs or farther in quick time; in latest effort did not race rank or green. **Distance:** has won at exact or related distance; if moving from sprint to route, must have won at shorter distance with evident reserves of speed and power, must be favored today by probable early pace.

Handicappers prefer:

1. **a previous winner or close runner-up in an open listed stakes.**

2. **a nicely bred, lightly raced, impressively improving horse that has won at least two nonwinners allowance races, and powerfully, such that it might be among the best in the division.**

3. **horses that during the three-year-old season have won any stakes previously, even the conditioned kind, easily or powerfully.**

4. **any horse that has won successive nonwinners allowance races in improving time and manner.**

Regular eliminations:

1. horses that at any time have been entered to be claimed.

2. horses that have not yet won two allowance races.

3. horses that have won a conditioned stakes but since have lost badly in open or graded stakes.

4. any horse that has engaged in three or more successive driving finishes within weeks under allowance and stakes conditions, unless it won all the races.

Extra added attractions:

1. won a stakes race last out.

2. royal breeding, still improving.

3. dramatically changed form, resulting in unexpected big win last out.

4. fastest finish at distance, notably if done in less than twenty-four seconds.

Special conditions:

1. **at distance of a mile and one-quarter and farther, prefer:**

1.1 horses that have looked most powerful in the stretch at middle distances.

1.2 horses having dosage indexes of 4.0 and below.

1.3 horses whose breeding suggests greater stamina at long distances.

1.4 horses from leading stables, handled by leading trainers.

2. **on turf, prefer:**

2.1 previous big winners on grass.

2.2 multiple allowance winners on dirt, bred for turf.

STAKES AND HANDICAPS

Lower grade and open stakes, for three-year-olds and up. To identify contenders, the basic requirements: **Form:** has raced within six weeks, sharp regular workouts since; latest races among best efforts. **Distance:** if four or older, has won at exact distance; if three, has won at exact distance or related distance.

(During the first four months of the season the above requirements and preferences below apply also to races for four-year-olds and up.)

Handicappers prefer:

1. **a horse that has won a Grade 1 or Grade 2 stakes within the past three months.**

2. **horses that recently won an open listed stakes having a purse value similar to or better than today's.**

3. **any three-year-old that won an open stakes powerfully when entered against its own age group.**

In the absence of the above, prefer:

4. **recent runners-up in listed graded or open stakes**, especially horses that have won a classified allowance race easily since.

5. **highly consistent, higher-priced claiming horses**, provided they remain in peak form, are perfectly suited to the distance and footing, and will be favored by the probable early pace.

Regular eliminations:

1. horses four-and-up that do not compete at least occasionally and satisfactorily in open stakes and handicaps.

2. horses five-and-up that have never won a stakes.

3. three-year-olds that have been unable to win an open stakes when so entered against their own age group.

4. horses four-and-up that won a conditioned stakes at age two or three but since have not finished in-the-money of an open stakes open to older runners.

5. three-year-olds that are stakes winners against that age group but have been unable to finish fourth or better in open stakes open to older runners.

6. foreign-raced horses that have not won a Group 2 or Group 3 stakes overseas.

7. inconsistent allowance horses, unexceptional claiming horses.

Extra added attractions:

1. won a stakes race last out.

2. highest earnings by comfortable margin.

3. coming up to peak effort today.

4. third or fourth outing for previous stakes winner following lengthy layoff, notably if comeback race was a good but losing effort under classified allowance conditions at wrong distance or on wrong footing.

5. previous losing race designed as a prep for today's major stakes objective.

Special conditions:

1. **purse of less than $50,000 and none of the preferred profiles can be found, prefer:**

1.1 multiple winners of classified allowance purses this season.

1.2 any horse whose recent consistency (two wins in latest six races) indicates best form of its career.

2. **on turf, prefer:**

2.1 previous stakes winner on turf.

2.2 impressive classified winners on turf.

2.3 still-improving three- or four-year-olds whose latest race, on turf, was best yet, by large margin.

3. an in-the-money finish in a conditioned stakes does not qualify three-year-olds for consideration in an open stakes open to older runners.

CLASSIFIED ALLOWANCES

Classified allowance, three-year-olds and up, minimally restricted, that is, nonwinners of two or more races offering to the winners the highest amounts of the overnite (nonstakes) purse schedule* during the past sixty racing days. To identify contenders, the basic requirements. **Form:** if stakes winners, have raced within sixty days, and have recorded at least four workouts since; if not stakes winners, have raced within three weeks, with at least two impressive workouts since. **Distance:** have won at the exact distance during this season or last.

Handicappers prefer:

1. **a Grade 3, listed, or open stakes winner in acceptable form,** notably if it won a race having a winner's share higher than today's specified amount within the past three weeks or so.

2. **any nonclaiming horses whose recently demonstrated class, as indicated by purse values, eligibility conditions, and quality of competition of its latest best efforts, is superior to today's conditions,** provided their form remains sharp or continues in the improvement cycle, and the horses remain eligible today only because they have not raced frequently enough recently, or they have raced well recently while losing to better; the better the recent class, the better.

In the absence of the above, prefer:

3. **horses that since the specified date have one fewer win than the permissible number in the conditions and/or winning or strong performances in races having winner shares just slightly below the amounts specified in the conditions, notably if their records just prior to the specified date in today's conditions would make them ineligible today.**

Regular eliminations:

1. previous Grade 1 and Grade 2 winners returning to action following lengthy layoffs, such that they are not expected to be in winning condition, or are not well meant, particularly if their running styles will not be nicely suited to the distance and footing.

(* For example, at Santa Anita the highest overnite purse is currently $45,000, the winner's share $24,750. If classified conditions there specified "for nonwinners of two races of $22,000 or more . . ." that restriction would intend to bar only multiple winners of the best overnite races at the track, or of two stakes races, or of one of each. Thus, the conditions can be considered minimally restricted. They intend to bar only the top horses on the grounds.)

2. allowance horses that have raced regularly since the specified date for comparable or smaller purses, but have not won or have not won frequently enough.

3. undistinguished three-year-olds moving from nonwinner allowances to classified allowances, or from out-of-the-money finishes in conditioned stakes to classified allowances.

4. all horses whose current form looks questionable or deteriorating, including previous stakes winners.

5. all allowance and claiming horses that have been competing for purses having winner shares smaller than today's specified amount by $5,000 or more.

6. all claiming horses that have never won a classified race, or have not finished in-the-money in an open stakes this season.

Extra added attractions:

1. an in-the-money finish in a recent open stakes; the higher the purse, the better.

2. peak form, a previous satisfactory performance in an open stakes, a strong finish last out, and today switching to a more suitable distance or footing.

3. strong comeback race within past fourteen days, record prior to today's specified date better than today's conditions would permit.

4. to be handled by a jockey that has achieved best results with the horse in the past.

5. the highest speed rating at the distance and footing during this season under classified conditions or better.

6. beats all but the top horses, today facing a top horse returning from a layoff and not well suited to the distance or footing.

Special conditions:

1. **on turf, prefer:**

1.1 previous classified and stakes winners on turf; the higher the purse, the better.

1.2 three-year-olds that have been impressive winners of nonwinner allowance races on turf, in opposition to older stakes winners on dirt that have raced unimpressively on grass.

(Author's note: Conditions of eligibility for classified allowance races at major tracks vary according to the number and value of horses' victories since a specified date. In general, the greater the number of permissible victories, the higher the winners' share specified, and the shorter the time intervals specified, the greater the number of better horses that will remain eligible to compete.

On these pages and the next few, this variation in classified conditions is considered to range from "minimally restricted" to "highly restricted." Specific guidelines aside, as a general rule minimally restricted conditions bow to class, and highly restricted conditions bow to form. These guidelines are intended to be consistent with that generality.)

CLASSIFIED ALLOWANCES

Classified allowance, three-year-olds and up, highly restricted, that is, nonwinners of a race offering to the winner a relatively moderate amount on the overnite (nonstakes) purse schedule since a specified date that includes a period of ninety calendar days or longer. To identify contenders, the basic requirements. **Form:** has raced within thirty days, at least two workouts since; if a previous stakes winner and has not raced since the specified date, must show a pattern of eight to twelve regular workouts, with at least three at distances of five furlongs or farther in acceptable times. **Distance:** has won at exact or related distances in satisfactory time.

Handicappers prefer:

1. **horses of improving form and moving from less restricted to more restricted classified conditions;** that is, from conditions permitting more than one recent victory to conditions permitting only a single recent win; from a higher specified winner's share to a lower specified amount; from a shorter specified time interval to a longer time interval.

2. **nonclaiming horses whose recent records fall barely within the boundaries of today's classified conditions;** that is, just within the permissible number of wins, specified winner's share, and specified time interval.

3. **lower grade and other open stakes winners returning from lengthy layoffs and recording the kind of workout pattern described in the above requirements of Form**, provided the distance and footing are nicely suitable and nothing about the probable pace figures to nullify any basic class and form advantages.

In the absence of the above, prefer:

4. **consistent (two wins in last six attempts) higher-priced claiming horses perfectly suited to the distance, footing, and probable early pace.**

Regular eliminations:

1. better stakes horses entered for conditioning or for preparation for richer purses and better stakes.

2. nonclaiming horses that combine questionable current form with any disadvantages related to distance, footing, pace, jockey and post position.

3. horses that have run regularly since the specified date without winning while competing for purses comparable to today's.

4. inconsistent claiming horses moving up.

Extra added attractions:

1. peaking form, well suited to the distance, footing, and probable pace.

2. improved recent form, drop in class from nonclaiming race having a purse better than today's.

3. nicely bred, improving three-year-old of late summer or fall moving from win under nonwinners twice allowances to highly restricted classified allowances open to older horses.

4. won for better purse just prior to specified date, sparkling workout pattern and one recent satisfactory race.

5. drop from even effort in stakes last out, switch to one of top three jockeys in the standings.

Special conditions:

1. **during fall, prefer:**

1.1 three-year-olds that started in midsummer or later and have moved through preliminary nonwinners allowance conditions impressively.

1.2 four-year-olds that have competed regularly in nonclaiming races and are now returning from layoffs that began just prior to the specified date.

2. **on turf, prefer:**

2.1 younger, lightly raced horses that have recently won successive nonwinners allowance races and are bred for turf.

2.2 previous turf race winners of higher purses than today's.

CLAIMING RACES

For four-year-olds and up, all claiming prices. To identify contenders, the basic requirements. **Form:** last race acceptable, that is, beat half the field and finished within six lengths of the winner; if entered for $20,000 or more, has raced within past thirty days, with three workouts since; if entered for below $20,000, has raced within past twenty-one days, has worked out since. **Distance:** has won at the exact distance, or has finished within two lengths at today's distance this season.

Handicappers prefer:

1. **any horse dropping 30 percent or more in claiming price;** the better its previous race, the better.

2. **horses having the highest speed figures or fastest adjusted times.**

3. **horses dropping in claiming price that combine early speed with one of the field's top three speed ratings at the distance,** obtained by averaging the *Form* speed ratings for the last two races.

4. **horses having high early speed and improving form.**

5. **horses that won their previous race by three lengths or more.**

6. **horses that follow a winning race or a significantly improved performance with a rise in claiming price to a level where they have previously won or where they will not be outclassed.**

7. **off-pace horses that have the highest pace ratings in the field plus improving form.**

Regular eliminations:

1. horses indicating deteriorating form in their latest races.

2. horses unable to satisfy the requirements of the class or form or distance factors **in combination with** unacceptable weight, jockey, footing, trainer, or post position.

3. horses that are among the bottom half of the field on speed figures or pace ratings.

4. horses without early speed that do not figure to benefit from a pace battle among the front-runners, unless such horses have a pronounced class edge and run at tracks that do not strongly favor speed horses.

5. horses that appear in long, front tendon bandages for the first time.

6. horses that appear sore or lame in the walking ring, or that appear unusually washy or nervous or reluctant during the paddock and prerace ceremonies.

Extra added attractions:

1. a leading trainer of claiming horses or a repeatedly successful training pattern of any acceptable trainer.

2. improved form last out, dropdown today, switch to a leading rider.

3. has won two of last six races, or has won three of last ten.

4. when the higher of its latest two speed ratings is considered, has earned one of top two speed figures in the field.

5. four workouts in the past twenty days.

Special conditions:

1. conditioned races, for nonwinners of a number of races since a specified time, prefer:

1.1 improving horses having few recent races and one recent win fewer than the permissible number of victories; the higher the top claiming price of the recent win, the better.

1.2 a consistent winner at a claiming price within the range of today's top specified price, but **exempted** from today's restrictions.

1.3 horses returning to action with sparkling workouts and having an impressive record at comparable claiming prices just prior to the specified time interval.

2. conditioned races, for nonwinners at a specified distance for a specified time interval, prefer:

2.1 a consistent router at today's claiming price having few recent races and one less recent win than is permissible by the conditions.

2.2 a sprinter that has recently won at today's top claiming price or better and is stretching out, provided it can control or survive the probable early pace.

2.3 a consistent winner at a lower claiming price that has won recently and has been exempted from today's restrictions.

CLAIMING RACES

For three-year-olds, all claiming prices. To identify the contenders, the basic requirements. **Form:** even effort or better last race at comparable or higher claiming prices; has raced within six weeks, three workouts since. **Distance:** has won or finished in-the-money at exact or related distances; if stretching out from sprint to route, finished strongly at shorter distance and not moving ahead in class today.

Handicappers prefer:

1. horses dropping into claiming races following an even effort that beat at least half the field under nonwinners allowances.

2. previous winners at today's top claiming price or higher, provided recent form remains acceptable.

3. any horse that has been lowered successively in claiming price and last time out demonstrated much-improved form and competitiveness, particularly if today's entered price is lower than its latest entered price.

4. horses rising in class by as much as 50 percent in claiming price following a powerful win which indicated the winner possessed reserves of speed and power.

Regular eliminations:

1. horses dropping in class following a dull or listless effort, particularly horses that have dropped down previously.

2. horses rising in class by 50 percent or more following an unexceptional win or an easy win accomplished in ordinary time.

3. any horse that won impressively last out but has not raced or worked out for twenty-one days since.

4. horses without early speed.

5. lackluster form and dull recent races, especially if only win occurred under maiden claiming conditions.

6. any horse entered in a claiming race following the maiden win, unless its speed and pace ratings are superior to anything in the field.

Extra added attractions:

1. first start in a claiming race, last race had an excuse, and latest allowance races were even efforts or better.

2. much-improved form last out, dropping in claiming price today.

3. returning to a previous winning claiming level following a much-improved performance last out.

4. figures to control or to survive the early pace.

5. recently claimed by a leading claiming trainer, has shown improved form since.

6. switch to a leading rider.

7. has never been entered in a maiden claiming race.

Special conditions:

1. **races open to older horses, prefer:**

    1.1 older horses.

    1.2 those few three-year-olds that have recorded clearly superior class and pace ratings.

2. **on turf, prefer:**

    2.1 previous winners on turf.

2.2 horses bred for turf that have demonstrated a liking for the distance.

2.3 maidens bred for turf.

STARTER RACES

For four-year-olds and up, all starting prices. To identify contenders, the basic requirements. **Form:** has raced within thirty days, has recorded two workouts since. **Distance:** has won at exact or related distance.

(During the final four months of the year the basic requirements and preferences below apply also to races for three-year-olds and up.)

Handicappers prefer:

1. **the horse that previously has won or finished close at the highest selling price in open claiming races.**

2. **any horse that gained eligibility last time out by dropping in class to today's starting price,** provided its recent races against better claiming horses were even efforts or better and no horse of superior class has dominated the series.

3. **any horse that has won in the starter series this season.**

Regular eliminations:

1. horses that have not won at a claiming price higher than today's starting price.

2. repeat losers in the starter series.

3. horses dismounted by leading riders.

Extra added attractions:

1. high consistency in this season's starter series.

2. versatile runner, in relation to running style, footing preference, and pace preference.

3. from a leading claiming stable.

4. able to carry high weight repeatedly.

Special conditions:

1. **under handicap conditions, prefer:**

    1.1 high-weighted horses that have already won in the series.

    1.2 horses of higher weight that gained eligibility last race.

2. **on turf, prefer:**

2.1 horses that have won previously on turf.

2.2 impressively improving three-year-olds bred for turf.

DEFINITIONS OF TERMS AND PHRASES

1. **Acceptable speed ratings, acceptable time, respectable clockings**—an index of speed that varies with the conditions of eligibility and the distance of races; the speed ratings below indicate acceptable performance for the horses and distances specified:

90—sprints under stakes and classified allowances

88—routes under stakes conditions

84—routes under classified allowance conditions

87—sprints for nonwinners allowance conditions

85—sprints for claiming conditions at $20,000 and above

80—sprints for claiming conditions below $20,000

78—routes for nonwinners allowance conditions

75—routes for claiming conditions at $20,000 and above

70—routes for claiming conditions below $20,000

2. **Average time**—typical running times for that class at the distance, usually called **par** times.

3. **Conditioned stakes**—a stakes race that bars previous stakes winners or horses that have won a specified amount of first money (amount awarded to the winner) since a specified date.

4. **Even effort**—maintains running position or margin behind the leader at each point of call in the past performances.

5. **Fast finish, finished fastest**—ran final quarter-mile of a race in twenty-four seconds or less.

6. **Graded stakes**—an open stakes of relatively high quality, rated either Grade 1 (highest), Grade 2, or Grade 3.

7. **High-priced claiming horses**—selling prices among the most expensive on the local schedule of claiming races.

8. **Highly consistent**—has won two of last six allowance races, or three of last ten claiming races.

9. **High speed, high early speed**—able to set or press the pace until the prestretch or stretch calls, as indicated by ones, twos, and threes at the first points of call in the past performances.

10. **Inconsistent**—unable to win a race in thirteen or more consecutive attempts.

11. **Leading rider, leading trainer, leading stable**—one that appears on the list of leaders in the track's daily program; one whose winning rate is 15 percent (12 percent in New York or southern California) or higher.

12. **Lightly raced**—fewer than ten races lifetime.

13. **Open stakes**—a stakes race that invites all comers.

14. **Powerful winner, wins powerfully**—was close to pace at the stretch call, gained two or more lengths in the stretch while winning handily.

15. **Ran close, finished close**—within two or three lengths of the winner.

16. **Related distance**—within a furlong of today's.

17. **Satisfactory performance**—beat half the field; finished within seven lengths of the winner.

Appendix 2:

A Compilation of the Graded and Listed Stakes of Canada, England, France, Germany, Ireland, Italy, and the United States by Grade Designations, Purse Values, and Eligible Ages

NOTE: In this compilation of the most prestigious stakes races conducted by the seven countries whose programs are evaluated annually by the International Pattern Committee or the North American Graded Stakes Committee, the grade designations, purse values, and eligible ages are provided. *Daily Racing Form* provides additional crucial information in its past performance tables, such as track, distance, and footing.

Purse values of foreign races are the dollar equivalents as of January 31, 1983. They can be accepted as relatively stable. U.S. purses are current as of January 31, 1985.

NUMBER AND PERCENTAGE OF BEST RACES BY COUNTRY*

Country	Total Races	Black-Type Races	Group-Graded Stakes	Grade 1 Races	Pct. of Group-Graded Stakes
England	2,844	178	101	18	3.5
France	4,174	178	80	23	2.5
Germany	1,978	96	29	5	1.4
Ireland	720	71	34	8	4.7
Italy	3,251	191	49	12	1.5
North America	69,738	2,031	281	93	0.4

* As indicated by International Cataloguing Standards, 1981–(   ).
Note: All Purse Values are 1983 amounts and represent added-money only. They do not include nomination, entry, and starting fees.

The importance of the stakes races in this compilation can be appreciated by consultation with the table below. It reveals the small percentage of the graded stakes on the national calendars. If a stakes race is listed here, and another is not, handicappers can be confident the listed stakes is almost certainly the better race.

CATALOG OF STAKES RACES

Canada

RACE	PURSE	AGE
GRADE 1		
Rothman's International	$405,000	3up
GRADE 2		
E.P. Taylor S.	$162,000	3up
GRADE 3		
British Columbia Derby	$100,000	3yo
Dominion Day H.	81,000	3up
Grey S.	60,750	2yo
King Edward Gold Cup H.	60,750	3up
Natalma S.	48,600	2yo
Niagara H.	81,000	3up
Summer S.	48,600	2yo
BLACK TYPE, Listed		
Canadian Oaks (R)	$101,250	3yo
Queen's Plate (R)	121,500	3yo
Achievement S.	55,000	3yo
Alberta Derby	60,750	3yo
Alberta Futurity	60,000	2yo
Ballerina H.	50,000	3up
Belle Mahone S.	85,000	3up
Bison City S.	70,000	3yo
Breeder's S.	100,000	3yo
British Columbia Premier's Championship H.	100,000	3up
Bull Page	60,000	2yo
Bunty Lawless	60,000	3up
Canadian Derby	125,000	3yo
Claredon S.	55,000	2yo
Connaught Cup	65,000	4up
Dutchess S.	40,500	3yo
Eclipse S.	48,600	4up
Fanfreluche	40,500	2yo
Fury S.	48,600	3yo
Glorious Song S.	40,500	2yo
Hendrie S.	40,500	3up
Highlander S.	40,500	3up
Horometer S.	40,500	3up

RACE	PURSE	AGE
Jacques Cartier S.	40,500	4up
Jammed Lovely	40,500	3yo
Kingarvie S.	48,600	2yo
La Prevoyante S.	48,600	3yo
Lady Angela S.	48,600	3yo
Maple Leaf S.	48,600	3up
Marzarine S.	48,600	2yo
My Dear S.	40,500	2yo
Nandi S.	48,600	2yo
Nearctic S.	40,500	3up
New Providence S.	48,600	3up
Ontario Debutante S.	60,750	2yo
Ontario Fashion H.	60,750	3up
Ontario Lassie S.	60,750	2yo
Ontario Matron S.	60,750	4up
Prince of Wales S.	60,750	3yo
Princess Elizabeth S.	48,600	2yo
Queenston S.	40,500	3yo
Seagram Invitational H.	40,500	3up
Seaway S.	40,500	3up
Selene S.	48,600	3yo
Shady Wells S.	48,600	2yo
Shepperton S.	48,600	3up
Sir Barton S.	48,600	3yo
Speed to Spare Championship S.	44,550	3up
Stampede Futurity	40,500	2yo
Star Shoot	40,500	3yo
Toronto Cup S.	40,500	3yo
Valedvictory S.	40,500	3up
Vandal S.	40,500	2yo
Victoriana S.	48,600	3up
Whimsical S.	40,500	3up
Wonder Where S.	48,600	3yo
Yearling Sales	60,750	2yo

England

RACE	PURSE	AGE
GRADE 1		
Benson and Hedges Gold Cup	$165,000	3up
Coral Eclipse S.	107,250	3up
Coronation Cup	90,750	4up
Derby S.	165,000	3yo
Dubai Champion S.	165,000	3up
Gold Cup	89,100	3up
King George VI and Queen Elizabeth Diamond S.	244,200	3up

RACE	PURSE	AGE
King's Stand S.	66,000	3up
Oaks	107,250	3yo
One Thousand Guineas	99,000	3yo
St. Leger S.	165,000	3yo
Sussex S.	115,500	3up
Two Thousand Guineas	99,000	3yo
William Hill Cheveley Park S.	53,625	2yo
William Hill Dewhurst S.	53,625	2yo
William Hill Futurity	53,625	2yo
William Hill Middle Park S.	53,625	2yo
Yorkshire Oaks	74,250	3yo
GRADE 2		
Coronation S.	$41,250	3yo
Coventry S.	24,750	2yo
Flying Childers S.	26,400	2yo
Geoffrey Freer S.	49,500	3up
Gimrack S.	44,550	2yo
Goodwood Cup	56,100	3up
Great Voltigeur S.	66,000	3yo
Hardwicke S.	49,500	4up
John Porter S.	41,250	4up
King Edward VII S.	41,250	3yo
Laurent Perrier Champagne S.	41,250	2yo
Lowther S.	36,300	2yo
Mecca-Dante S.	74,250	3yo
Mill Reef S.	28,050	2yo
Nassau S.	52,800	3up
O.L.L. Richmond S.	16,500	2yo
Park Hill S.	41,250	3yo
Prince of Wales S.	41,250	3up
Princess of Wales S.	42,900	3up
Queen Elizabeth II S.	41,250	3up
Queen Mary S.	24,750	2yo
Ribblesdale S.	41,250	3yo
Royal Lodge S.	37,950	2yo
St. James Palace	49,500	3yo
Sun Chariot S.	41,250	3up
Vernons Sprint Cup	81,675	3up
Waterford Crystal Mile	61,050	3up
William Hill Sprint Championship	82,500	3up
Yorkshire Cup	49,500	4up
GRADE 3		
Anglia Television July S.	$24,750	2yo
Bisquit Cognac Challenge S.	41,250	2up
Brigadier Gerard S.	41,250	4up

RACE	PURSE	AGE
Cherry Hinton S.	24,750	2yo
Cheshire Oaks	33,000	3yo
Chester Vase	38,775	3yo
Child S.	33,000	3up
Clerical Medical Greenham S.	33,000	3yo
Cork and Orrery S.	33,000	3up
Cornwallis S.	23,100	2yo
Crauen S.	26,400	3yo
Cumberland Lodge S.	33,000	3up
Dee S.	26,400	3yo
Diadem S.	33,000	2up
Doncaster	41,250	3up
Duke of York S.	41,250	3up
Earl of Sefton S.	33,000	4up
Esal Blue Riband Trial	31,350	3yo
Esal Bookmakers Oaks Trial	NA	3yo
Gainsborough Stud Fred Darling S.	33,000	3yo
Gordon S.	37,950	3yo
Guardian Classic Trial	36,300	3yo
Henry II S.	41,250	4up
Hoover Fillies Mile S.	28,050	2yo
Horris Hill S.	24,750	2yo
Hungerford S.	37,950	3up
Jersey S.	33,000	3yo
Jockey Club Cup	39,600	3up
Jockey Club S.	39,600	4up
King George S.	37,950	3up
Lancashire Oaks	41,250	3yo
Lockinge S.	33,000	3up
May Hill S.	24,750	2yo
Molecomb S.	28,050	2yo
Mono Sagaro S.	33,000	4up
Musidora S.	41,250	3yo
Nell Gwyn S.	26,400	3yo
Norfolk S.	24,750	2yo
Ormonde S.	36,300	4up
Palace House S.	33,000	3up
Princess Elizabeth S.	26,400	3yo
Princess Royal S.	33,000	3up
Queen Anne S.	33,000	3up
Queen's Vase	33,000	3up
Salisbury Two Thousand Guineas Trial	26,400	3yo
Seaton Delaval S.	26,400	2yo
September	33,000	3up
St. Simon S.	33,000	3up
Temple S.	41,250	3up

RACE	PURSE	AGE
Waterford Candelabra S.	28,050	2yo
Westbury S.	41,250	4up
White Rose S.	26,400	3yo
BLACK TYPE, Listed		
Aberant S.	$ 9,800	3up
Acomb S.	13,200	2yo
Alciydon S.	19,800	3up
Autobar Victoria Cup H.	24,750	3up
Beeswing S.	24,750	3up
Blue Seal S.	11,550	2yo
Bonusprint Easter	16,500	3yo
Bonusprint Sirenia	16,500	2yo
Bradford and Bingley H.	33,000	3up
Cecil Frail H.	33,000	3yo
Champagne S.	13,200	2yo
Champion Two-Year-Old Trophy	12,375	2yo
Chesham S.	18,150	2yo
Clive Graham S.	23,100	4up
Doonside Cup	24,750	3up
Duchess of Montrose H.	13,200	3yo
Duke of Edinburgh S.	11,500	2yo
Extel H.	33,000	3yo
Fern Hill S. H.	11,550	3yo
Firth of Clyde S.	16,500	2yo
Galtres S.	13,200	3yo
Garrowby H.	19,800	3yo
Gerry Feilden Memorial S.	13,300	3yo
Greaves of Sheffield	24,750	3up
Gus Demmy Memorial S.	18,150	3yo
Harry Rosebery Challenge Trophy S.	24,750	2yo
Haydock Park Spring Trophy S.	16,500	3up
Heathorn S.	16,500	3yo
Houghton S.	16,500	2yo
Hyperion S.	11,500	2yo
John of Gaunt S.	33,000	3up
John Smith's Magnet Cup H.	41,250	3up
Jubilee H.	24,750	4up
Ladbroke Chester Cup H.	28,050	4up
Ladbroke European Free H.	33,000	3yo
Ladbrokes (Ayr) Gold Cup H.	41,250	3up
Land of Burns S.	19,800	3up
Lanson Champagne S.	18,150	2yo
Leisure S.	13,200	3up
Lupe S.	16,500	3yo
Mecca Bookmaker's Scottish Derby	33,000	3yo
Miner's Northumberland Plate H.	49,500	3up
National S.	9,900	2yo

RACE	PURSE	AGE
NMT Ebbisham	19,800	3yo
Oak Tree S.	23,100	3yo
Old Newton Cup H.	33,000	3up
Peter Hastings S. H.	16,500	3up
Portland H.	16,500	3up
Pretty Polly S.	13,200	3yo
Prince of Wales S.	13,200	2yo
Princess Margaret S.	11,550	2yo
Queen Alexandra S.	16,500	4up
Rochford Thompson Newbury	13,200	2yo
Royal Hunt Cup H.	26,400	3up
Salisbury One Thousand Guineas Trial S.	14,025	3yo
Schroeder Life Predominate	23,100	3yo
Sir Charles Clore Memorial	16,500	3yo
(For Sirenia, see Bonusprint)		
Solario S.	24,750	2yo
Somerville Tattersall S.	19,800	2yo
St. Catherine's S.	11,550	2yo
St. Hugh's S.	13,200	2yo
Strensall S.	11,550	3up
Tote Cesarewitch H.	49,500	3up
Tote Ebor H.	49,500	3up
Valdoe S.	19,800	3up
Virginia S.	24,750	3up
Ward Hill Bunbury Cup	19,800	3up
Warren S.	9,900	3yo
Washington Singer S.	11,550	2yo
William Hill Cambridgeshire H.	49,500	3up
William Hill July Cup	82,500	3up
William Hill Lincoln H.	33,000	4up
William Hill Stewards' Cup H.	49,500	3up
Windsor Castle S.	16,500	2yo
X.Y.Z.H.	24,750	3yo

France

RACE	PURSE	AGE
GRADE 1		
Abbaye de Longchamp	$ 76,500	3up
Arc de Triomphe	637,500	3up
Cadran	76,500	4up
Diane Hermes	204,000	3yo
Foret	76,500	2up
Ganay	114,750	4up
Grand Criterium	127,500	2yo
Ispahan	114,750	3up

RACE	PURSE	AGE
Jacques Le Marios	89,250	3up
Jockey Club	140,000	3yo
Lupin	127,500	3yo
Marcel Boussal	76,500	2yo
Morny	76,500	2yo
Moulin de Longchamp	102,000	3up
Paris	114,750	3yo
Poule d'Essai des Poulains	127,500	3yo
Poule d'Essai des Pouliches	127,500	3yo
Robert Papin	76,500	2yo
Royal-Oak	76,500	3up
Saint-Alary	114,750	3yo
Saint-Cloud	255,000	3up
Salamandre	76,500	2yo
Vermeille	178,500	3yo

GRADE 2

RACE	PURSE	AGE
Astarte	$ 51,000	3up
Conseil de Paris	76,500	3up
Cote Normande	51,000	3yo
Criterium de Maisons-Laffite	51,000	2yo
Criterium de Saint-Cloud	51,000	2yo
Deauville	63,750	3up
Dollar	63,750	4up
Eugene Adam	76,500	3yo
Evry	76,500	4up
Greffulhe	63,750	3yo
Harcourt	51,000	4up
Hocquart	76,500	3yo
Jean de Chaudenay	76,500	3up
Jean Prat	51,000	4up
Jean Prat	63,750	3yo
Kergorlay	51,000	3up
Malleret	51,000	3yo
Maurice de Gheest	51,000	3up
Maurice de Nieuil	76,500	3up
Noailles	63,750	3yo
Opera	51,000	3–4yo
Pomone	51,000	3up

GRADE 3

RACE	PURSE	AGE
Arenberg	$40,800	2yo
Aumale	40,800	2yo
Barbeville	40,800	4up
Berteuk	40,800	3yo
Bois	40,800	2yo
Calvados	40,800	2yo
Chemin de Fer du Nord	40,800	4up

RACE	PURSE	AGE
Chenes	40,800	2yo
Chloe	38,250	3yo
Cleopatre	40,800	3yo
Conde	40,800	2yo
Corrida	40,800	4up
Daphnis	38,250	3yo
Eclipse	40,800	2yo
Edmond Blank	40,800	4up
Esperance	40,800	3yo
Exbury	40,800	4up
Fille de L'Air	40,800	3up
Flore	40,800	3up
Fontainbleau	40,800	3yo
Foy	40,800	4up
Gladiateur	40,800	4up
Gontaut-Biron	40,800	4up
Gros-Chene	40,800	3up
Grotte	40,800	3yo
Guiche	40,800	3yo
Ionchere	40,800	3yo
La Coupe de Maisons-Lafitte	40,800	3up
La Coupe	40,800	3yo
La Rochette	40,800	2yo
Lutece	40,800	3yo
Lys	40,800	3yo
Meautry	40,800	3up
Messidor	40,800	3up
Minerue	38,250	3yo
Muguet	40,800	4up
Niel	40,800	3yo
Nonette	40,800	3yo
Palais Royal	40,800	3up
Perth	40,800	3up
Petit Couvert	40,800	2up
Porte Maillot	40,800	3up
Prince d'Orange	40,800	3up
Psyche	40,800	3yo
Quincey	40,800	3up
Reservoirs	40,800	2yo
Ris Orangis	38,250	4up
Rond-Point	40,800	3up
Royallieu	40,800	3up
Royaumont	40,800	3yo
Saint Roman	40,800	2yo
Saint Georges	40,800	3up
Sandringham	40,800	3yo
Seine-Et-Oise	40,800	3up

RACE	PURSE	AGE
Thomas Bryon	40,800	2yo
Vanteaux	40,800	3yo
Vichy	63,750	3up
BLACK TYPE, Listed		
Agence Francaise	$22,950	2yo
Alencon	33,150	3up
Andre Carrus	33,150	4up
Armand de Jumilhac	33,150	4up
Automne	25,500	3up
Avre	25,500	3yo
Bagatelle	28,050	3yo
Bel Air	33,150	3yo
Belle de Nuit	20,400	3yo
Belles Filles	33,150	3yo
Bellevue	33,150	3up
Bordeaux	51,000	3up
Boulogne	22,950	3up
Butte Mortemart	22,950	4up
Cabourg	22,950	2yo
Cagney	32,150	3up
Calonne	28,050	3yo
Camargo	25,500	3yo
Carrousel	28,050	4up
Castries	33,150	3up
Cent Cinquantenaire de la Societe d'Encouragement	76,500	3up
Chapelle	33,150	4up
Chenettes	33,150	3yo
Chevilly	33,150	3up
Clairefontaine	25,500	3up
Cluny	33,150	3up
Compiegne	30,600	3up
Compiegne	33,150	3up
Conseil General des Alpes-Maritimes	38,250	4up
Coronation	25,500	3yo
Cote d'Azur	33,150	3up
Courcelles	25,500	3yo
Creil	22,950	3up
Criterium de Bernay	22,950	2yo
Dangu	33,150	3up
Deauville	38,250	3up
Derby de l'Ouest	30,600	3yo
Derby du Midi	38,250	3yo
Djebel	20,400	3yo
Dormans	28,050	4up
Duc d'Aoste	33,150	3yo
Ecuries	33,150	4up
Elevage	33,150	3up

RACE	PURSE	AGE
Epernon	33,150	3yo
Epinettes	33,150	3yo
Esplanade	33,150	4up
Evry	33,150	4up
Federations Regionales	22,950	3up
Finlande	30,600	3yo
Fleche	20,400	2yo
Floals	28,050	2yo
Francois Andre	33,150	3up
Geoffroy de Waldner	33,150	4up
Gravilliers	33,150	4up
Handicap d'Ete	33,150	3up
Handicap de Cloture	22,950	4up
Handicap de l'Essonne	33,150	3yo
Handicap de la Seine	33,150	3up
Handicap de la Tamise	33,150	3up
Handicap de Printemps	33,150	4up
Handicap de Saint-Cloud	33,150	4up
Hedouville	30,600	4up
Henri Greffulhe	33,150	3up
Herod	20,400	2yo
Honfleur	33,150	3up
Imprudence	20,400	3yo
Joubert	30,600	3yo
Jouvence	33,150	3up
Juigne	25,500	3yo
La Coupe G3	40,800	4up
La Moskowa	33,150	4up
Lac	33,150	3yo
Liancourt	25,500	3up
Lilas	25,500	3yo
Lizy	33,150	4up
Lyon	51,000	3up
Major Fridolin	33,150	3yo
Manche	35,700	3up
Mandinet	33,150	4up
Marseille	76,500	3up
Marseille-Vivaux	51,000	4up
Matchem	30,600	3yo
Max Sicard	38,250	3up
Menneval	28,050	3yo
Montenica	22,950	3yo
Municipalite et du District	33,150	4up
Nabob	35,700	3up
Nantes	63,750	3up
Obelisque	22,950	2yo
Omnium	38,250	3up

RACE	PURSE	AGE
Omnium II	25,500	3yo
Ouilly	28,050	3up
Pepiniere	25,500	4up
Perray	33,150	3yo
Pharel	22,950	2yo
Pin	25,500	3up
Plaisance	33,150	4up
Point du Jour	25,500	4up
Pontarme	25,500	3yo
Pontchartrain	33,150	3up
Porte de Passy	28,050	3up
Provinces	51,000	3up
Ranelagh	25,500	3yo
Reine Marguerite	33,150	4up
Reux	28,050	4up
Reves d'Or	20,400	2yo
Ridgway	28,050	3up
Rieussec	33,150	4up
Saint-Cyr	28,050	3yo
Salverte	33,150	3up
Sassy	33,150	3up
Seine	25,500	3yo
Seine-et-Marne	33,150	3up
Soya	22,950	2yo
Strasbourg	33,150	3up
Suresnes	25,500	3yo
Table	33,150	3up
Theve	22,950	3yo
Tourelles	22,950	3up
Tuileries	28,050	3yo
Vallee d'Auge	22,950	2yo
Ville de Toulouse	51,400	3up
Ville de Touville	28,050	3yo
Yacowlef	25,500	2yo
Yearlings	25,500	2yo

Germany

RACE	PURSE	AGE
GRADE 1		
Aral-Pokal	$ 67,200	3up
Baden	126,000	3up
Berlin	71,400	3up
Deutsches Derby	126,000	3yo
Europa	168,000	3up

RACE	PURSE	AGE
GRADE 2		
Badische Wirtschaft	$64,260	4up
Diana	50,400	3yo
Dusseldorf	37,800	4up
Hansa	42,840	3up
Henckel	37,800	3yo
Hertie International	52,500	3yo
Moet & Chandan-Zukunfts	45,360	2yo
Thier-Deutsches St. Leger	42,840	3yo
Union	50,400	3yo
GRADE 3		
ARAG-Schwarzgold	$42,840	3yo
Badener Meile	37,800	4up
Bayerisches Zucht	42,840	3yo
Consul-Bayeff	25,800	3yo
Deutscher-Stutenpreis	29,400	3yo
Dortmund	25,200	3up
Furstenberg	37,800	3yo
Goldene Peitsche	37,800	3up
Herbststuten-Preis	29,400	3–4yo
Hessen-Pokal	29,400	3up
Land Nordrhein-Westfalen	29,400	3up
Ludwig Goebels	25,200	3yo
Oettingen	37,800	3up
Ostermann-Pokal	33,600	3up
Spreti	37,800	4up
Stadt Gelsenkirchen	21,420	4up
Steigenberger-Hotelgellschaft	21,420	3yo
Winterfavorit	29,400	2yo
BLACK TYPE, Listed		
Alexander	$12,600	2yo
Allianz-Pokal	14,700	3up
ARAG-Junioren	8,400	2yo
Badener Jugend	17,136	2yo
Benazet	19,278	3up
Berberis	7,140	2yo
Busch-Memorial	13,600	3yo
Casino Baden-Baden	14,994	3yo
Casino Travemunde	14,700	3up
Dillmann-Memorial	5,040	3yo
Dusseldorfer Industrie	13,600	3up
Dusseldorfer Stutenpreis	8,400	3yo
Festa	9,240	3yo
Fruhjahrs Stuten-Preis	8,400	3yo
Gerling	31,500	4up
Gontard	14,994	3&4

RACE	PURSE	AGE
Hamburger Ausgleich	12,600	4up
Hamburger Criterium	8,400	2yo
Hammonia	8,400	3yo
Hennessy et Chandon Cup	14,700	3up
Hessen	29,400	3up
Hoppegarten	9,240	3yo
Horster Criterium	8,400	2yo
Jacobs-Kaffee	19,278	3up
Jacobs-Pokal	17,220	4up
Jahrlingsauktion	14,994	2yo
Jan Wellem	13,600	4up
Kolner Fruhjahrs-Ausgleich	14,700	4up
Moormann	12,600	4up
Nereide	6,426	3yo
Oleander	17,136	4up
Oppenheim	21,420	2yo
Otto Schmidt	12,600	3yo
Philips	13,600	4up
Ratibor	21,420	2yo
Rheinboden	6,300	3yo
Robert Pferdmenges	17,220	3up
Rudolf Oetker	8,400	2yo
Scherping	17,136	3yo
Schlenderhan	19,278	3up
Schwarzwald	9,282	2yo
Sierstorpff	17,220	2yo
Silberne Peitsche	8,400	3up
Silbernes Band der Ruhr	17,250	3up
Spreti-Memorial	14,700	3up
Stadt Baden-Baden	14,994	3up
Stadt Berlin	13,600	3yo
Stadt Mulheim a.d. Ruhr	21,420	4up
Union Klub-Pokal	19,278	3up
Vogelpark Walsrode	31,500	4up
Winterkonigin	17,850	2yo

Ireland

RACE	PURSE	AGE
GRADE 1		
Airlie/Coolmore Irish Two Thousand Guineas	$42,000	3yo
Goffs Irish One Thousand Guineas	28,000	3yo
Heinz Phoenix S.	21,000	2yo
Irish Guinness Oaks	35,000	3yo
Irish Sweeps Derby	70,000	3yo
Irish St. Leger	42,000	3up

RACE	PURSE	AGE
Joe McGrath	28,000	3up
Moyglare Stud	42,000	2yo
GRADE 2		
BBA/Goffs National	$19,600	2yo
Blandford	16,800	3up
Gallinule S.	14,000	3yo
Nijinsky	14,000	3up
Panasonic Beresford	28,000	2yo
Pretty Poly S.	16,800	3yo
Rogers Gold Cup Ballymoss	16,800	3up
GRADE 3		
Ashford Castle	$14,000	2yo
Athasi S.	11,200	3yo
Ballsbridge-Tattersalls Angcesey	14,000	2yo
Ballyogan S.	11,200	3up
Brownstown	11,200	3up
Curragh	11,200	2yo
Desmond	11,000	3up
Gilltown Stud	16,800	3up
Greenlands	11,200	3up
Larkspur	11,200	2yo
McCairns Trial S.	11,200	3yo
Mulcahy S.	11,200	3yo
Pacemaker International Whitehall	16,800	3up
Park S.	14,000	2yo
Railway	14,000	2yo
Royal Whip	11,200	3up
Seven Springs Sprint	16,800	3up
Silken Glider	11,200	2yo
Tetrarch S.	11,200	3yo
BLACK TYPE, Listed		
April Fillies	$ 8,400	3yo
Ardenode Stud	14,000	2yo
Azalea S.	11,900	3yo
Ballycorus	7,000	3up
Ballylinch & Norelands Studs S.	11,200	3yo
Bass Gold Cup H.	11,200	3up
Birdcatcher Nursery H.	8,400	2yo
Carna Filies S.	11,200	3up
Castleknock Sprint S.	14,000	3up
Coolmore Godswalk S.	8,400	3yo
Coolmore Hello Gorgeous S.	14,000	3up
Coolmore Pas de Seul S.	14,000	3up
Coolmore Try My Best S.	14,000	2yo
Cornelscourt	8,400	3up
Gladness S.	8,400	3up

RACE	PURSE	AGE
Goffs Sales	8,400	2yo
Hennessy H.	11,200	3up
Hennessy V.S.O.P.S.	7,000	2yo
Herbertstown	7,000	3up
Irish Cambridgeshire H.	14,000	3up
Irish Chorus	8,400	2yo
Irish Lincolnshire H.	8,400	3up
Kilruddery S.	11,200	3up
M.C. Collins Marble Hill	8,400	2yo
Madrid H.	8,400	3yo
Maher Nursery H.	7,000	2yo
Marwell S.	8,400	2yo
McDonogh H.	12,600	3up
Midsummer Scurry H.	9,800	3up
Mooresbridge	7,000	4up
Oldtown Stud S.	8,400	2yo
Paribas Cesarewitch H.	16,800	3up
Philips Electrical	21,000	3up
Saval Beg	8,400	4up
Stackallen S.	7,000	3up
The Minstrel	7,000	3yo
Trigo S.	7,000	3up
Tyros S.	8,400	2yo
Ulster Harp Derby	7,000	3yo
Waterford Crystal Nursery	8,400	2yo
Waterford Testimonial	11,400	2up
Youghal	16,800	3up

Italy

RACE	PURSE	AGE
GRADE 1		
Derby	$154,000	3yo
Emilio Turati	84,000	3up
Gran Criterium	77,000	2yo
d'Italia	92,400	3yo
Jockey Club (Also Coppa d'Oro or Gran Premio)	140,000	3up
Lydia Tesio	70,000	3-4yo
Di Milano (Gran Premio)	140,000	3up
Oaks d'Italia	92,400	3yo
Parioli	77,000	3yo
Presidente della Repubblica	70,000	3up
Regina Elena	77,000	3yo
Roma	84,000	3up

RACE	PURSE	AGE
GRADE 2		
Chiusura	$49,000	2up
Dormello	46,200	2yo
Emanuele Filiberto	46,200	3yo
Federico Tesio	49,000	3up
Legnano	42,000	3–4yo
Melton	42,000	3up
Principe Ameded	46,200	3yo
Ribot	49,000	3up
St. Leger Italiano	53,900	3yo
Tevere	53,900	2yo
Umbria	42,000	2up
Vittorio di Capua	49,000	3up
GRADE 3		
Ambrosiano	$35,000	3up
Aprile	28,000	4up
Bagutta	30,800	3yo
Buontalenta	38,700	3yo
Carlo Porta	38,700	3yo
Cascine	28,000	4up
Citta di Napoli	35,000	3up
Citta di Torino	28,000	4up
Coppa d'Oro di Milano	42,000	4up
Criterium di Roma	38,500	2yo
Criterium Femminile	30,500	2yo
Criterium Nazionale	46,200	2yo
Ellington	35,000	4up
Estate	38,500	3yo
Lazio	38,500	3yo
Natale di Roma	28,000	4up
Nearlo	38,500	3yo
Omenoni	42,000	3up
Pisa	46,200	3yo
Primi Passi	38,500	2yo
Roma Vecchia	35,000	3up
Royal Mares	35,000	3up
Toscana	30,800	2yo
U.N.I.R.E.	35,000	3up
Virginia Curti Criterium	30,800	2yo
BLACK TYPE, Listed		
(Purse values for listed races are first money only. NA indicates "Not Available.)		
A. de Giovine	$12,250	3up
Agnano	10,500	4yo
Albano	14,000	3up
Alfonso Doria	NA	3yo

RACE	PURSE	AGE
Allevamento	NA	3up
Aniene	NA	2yo
Apertura	10,500	4up
Arconte	NA	3yo
A. Ricchi	12,250	4up
Aringo	NA	3up
Aurora	NA	2yo
Avvenire	NA	2yo
Baggio	NA	3yo
Bersaglio	NA	3up
Bimbi	NA	2yo
Boschetti	NA	3yo
Botticelli	NA	3yo
Campidoglio	NA	3up
Campobello	NA	2yo
Castellini N.	NA	4up
Castello Sforzesco	8,750	2yo
Ceprano	NA	3yo
Certosa	NA	3up
Chiesa C.	NA	3up
Cino del Duca	NA	3up
Citta' di Varese (Gran Premio)	14,000	3up
Coppa del Mare	14,000	3up
Corriere dello Sport	NA	3yo
Corsa Dell'Arno	21,000	3up
Criterium Labronico	NA	2yo
Criterium Partenopeo	NA	2yo
Cumani S.	NA	3yo
Daumier	NA	3yo
Degli Occhi C.	NA	3yo
Dei Proprietari	14,000	3up
Dei Tre Anni	10,500	3yo
Del Dado	NA	2yo
Del Piazzale	NA	3up
Della Moda (Gran Premio)	10,500	4up
Delle Scuderie	8,750	3yo
Delleana	NA	2yo
Divino Amore	NA	2yo
Duca d'Aosta	NA	3up
Eupili	NA	2yo
F. Schelbler	NA	3yo
Fausta	NA	3up
Firenze	10,500	3yo
Fiuggi	NA	2yo
Fiume	10,500	3up
G.G. Trivulzio	NA	3yo
Giovanni Falck	NA	3yo

RACE	PURSE	AGE
del Giubileo	21,000	3up
Grosseto	NA	3yo
Guidonia	NA	3up
Handicap D'Autunno	21,000	3up
La Novella	NA	3yo
Le Marmore	NA	2yo
Locatelli M.	NA	4up
Lombardia	17,500	3up
Mediterraneo	NA	2yo
Merano	NA	3yo
Mergellina	NA	3up
Minerva	NA	3yo
Miradolo	NA	3up
Montecitorio	NA	4up
Monterosa	10,500	3up
Nastro d'Argento	NA	3up
Niccolo dell'Arca	NA	3yo
Novella	NA	2yo
102 Anniversario	17,500	4up
Ostia Antica	NA	3up
Palmieri	NA	3up
Palmieri	14,000	3yo
Perrone	NA	2yo
Peyron	NA	2yo
Po	8,750	3up
Repubbliche Marinare	NA	2yo
Resegone	NA	3yo
Rumon	NA	2yo
Saccaroa	NA	3yo
Sambruna A.	NA	3up
Seregno	NA	3yo
Sette Colli	10,500	2yo
S. Gennaro	9,800	3yo
Signorino	NA	4up
Speranza	NA	2yo
Tor di Valle	12,250	4up
Torricola	NA	3yo
Trenno	21,000	3up
T. Righetti	12,250	3yo
Tudini	NA	3up
Tupini	NA	4up
Vanoni	NA	4up
Verziere	NA	3yo
Villa Borghese	NA	3yo
Viminale	NA	4up
Zanoletti di Rozzano A.	NA	3yo

The United States

RACE	PURSE	AGE
GRADE 1		
Acorn S.	$150,000	3yo
Alabama S.	125,000	3yo
American Derby	125,000	3yo
Apple Blossom H.	250,000	4up
Arkansas Derby	500,000	3yo
Arlington Classic	100,000	3yo
Arlington H.	100,000	3up
Arlington-Washington Futurity	150,000	2yo
Arlington-Washington Lassie	100,000	2yo
Beldame S.	200,000	3up
Belmont S.	350,000	3yo
Blue Grass S.	150,000	3yo
Bowling Green H.	175,000	3up
Brooklyn H.	250,000	3up
Budweiser Million	1,000,000	3up
Californian S.	300,000	3up
Century H.	200,000	3up
Champagne S.	250,000	2yo
Charles H. Strub S.	300,000	4yo
Coaching Club American Oaks	200,000	3yo
Cowdin S.	100,000	2yo
Delaware H.	100,000	3up
Demoiselle S.	100,000	2yo
Dwyer S.	125,000	3yo
Fantasy S.	250,000	3yo
Flamingo S.	365,000g	3yo
Florida Derby	300,000g	3yo
Flower Bowl H.	100,000	3up
Frizette S.	150,000	2yo
Futurity S.	100,000	2yo
Gamely H.	100,000	3up
Gazelle H.	100,000	3yo
Gulfstream Park H.	175,000	3up
Haskell Invitational H.	200,000	3yo
Hempstead H.	125,000	3up
Hialeah Turf Cup H.	150,000	3up
Hollywood Derby	250,000	3yo
Hollywood Futurity	1,000,000g	2yo
Hollywood Gold Cup	500,000g	3up
Hollywood Invitational H.	300,000g	3up
Hollywood Oaks	150,000	3yo
Hollywood Starlet	500,000g	2yo
Hollywood Turf Cup	500,000g	3up
Hopeful S.	100,000	2yo

RACE	PURSE	AGE
Jerome H.	150,000	3yo
Jockey Club Gold Cup S.	500,000	3up
Kentucky Derby	350,000	3yo
Kentucky Oaks	150,000	3yo
La Canada	150,000	4yo
Ladies H.	100,000	3up
Laurel Futurity	100,000	2yo
Man o' War S.	250,000	3up
Marlboro Cup Invitational H.	400,000	3up
Manhattan H.	100,000	3up
Maskette S.	100,000	3up
Matriarch S.	200,000	3up
Matron S.	75,000	2yo
Meadowlands Cup H.	500,000	3up
Metropolitan H.	250,000	3up
Monmouth H.	250,000	3up
Mother Goose S.	150,000	3yo
Norfolk S.	200,000	2yo
Oak Leaf S.	200,000	2yo
Oak Tree Invitational H.	400,000g	3up
Pan American H.	125,000	3up
Peter Pan S.	75,000	3yo
Preakness S.	200,000	3yo
Remsen S.	200,000	2yo
Ramona H.	125,000	3up
Ruffian H.	150,000	3up
San Antonio H.	200,000	4up
San Fernando S.	125,000	4yo
San Juan Capistrano Invitational H.	400,000g	4up
San Luis Rey S.	200,000	4up
Santa Ana H.	100,000	4up
Santa Anita Derby	250,000	3yo
Santa Anita Handicap	1,000,000g	4up
Santa Barbara H.	150,000	4up
Santa Margarita Invitational H.	250,000	4up
Santa Susana S.	150,000	3yo
Secretariat S.	125,000	3yo
Selima S.	100,000	2yo
Spinaway S.	75,000	2yo
Spinster S.	150,000	3up
Suburban H.	250,000	3up
Sunset H.	200,000	3up
Super Derby Invitational	500,000g	3yo
Swaps S.	200,000	3yo
Sword Dancer S.	200,000	3up
Top Flight H.	100,000	3up
Travers S.	200,000	3yo

RACE	PURSE	AGE
Turf Classic	400,000	3up
United Nations H.	150,000g	3up
Vanity H.	200,000	3up
Vosburgh H.	100,000	3up
Washington, D.C., International S.	250,000g	3up
Whitney H.	150,000	3up
Widener H.	125,000	3up
Wood Memorial S.	150,000	3yo
Woodward S.	200,000	3up
Yellow Ribbon S.	400,000	3up
Young America S.	500,000g	2yo
GRADE 2		
Ak-Sar-Ben Cornhusker H.	$150,000	3up
Alcibiades S.	150,000g	2yo
American H.	150,000	3up
Arcadia H.	80,000	4up
Arlington Matron H.	75,000	3up
Ashland S.	100,000	3yo
Astarita S.	75,000	2yo
Ballerina S.	75,000	3up
Bay Meadows H.	300,000	3up
Bernard Baruch H.	75,000	3up
Beverly Hills H.	100,000	3up
Black Helen H.	125,000	3up
Black-Eyed Susan S.	100,000	3yo
Bougainvillea H.	50,000	3up
Breeders' Futurity	150,000g	2yo
California Derby	200,000	3yo
Carleton F. Burke H.	100,000	3up
Carter H.	100,000	3up
Cinema H.	100,000	3yo
Del Mar Debutante	125,000	2yo
Del Mar Derby	125,000	3yo
Del Mar Futurity	150,000	2yo
Del Mar Invitational H.	200,000	3up
Del Mar Oaks	125,000	3yo
Diana H.	75,000	3up
Dixie H.	100,000	3up
Donn H.	75,000	3up
Eddie Read H.	150,000	3up
El Camino Real S.	100,000	2yo
Excelsior H.	125,000	3up
Fall Highweight H.	100,000	3up
Firenze H.	75,000	3up
Forego H.	75,000	3up
Fountain of Youth S.	100,000	3yo
Gallant Fox H.	75,000	3up

RACE	PURSE	AGE
Gardenia S.	200,000	2yo
Golden Harvest H.	200,000	3up
Gotham S.	150,000	3yo
Hawthorne Gold Cup H.	200,000	3up
Hawthorne H.	60,000	3up
Hollywood Juvenile Championship S.	100,000	2yo
Jersey Derby	150,000	3yo
Jim Dandy	100,000	3yo
John B. Campbell H.	125,000	3up
Landaluce S.	75,000	2yo
Las Palmas H.	100,000	3up
Lawrence Realization S.	75,000	3yo
Lexington S.	75,000	3yo
Long Island H.	125,000	3up
Long Look H.	100,000	3up
Longacres Mile H.	150,000	3up
Longfellow H.	100,000	3up
Louisiana Derby	200,000g	3yo
Malibu S.	100,000	4yo
Massachusetts H.	150,000	3up
Matchmaker S.	300,000g	3up
Mervyn Leroy H.	150,000	3up
Michigan Mile and One-Eighth H.	150,000	3up
Milady H.	100,000	3up
Molly Pitcher H.	100,000	3up
Monmouth Oaks	100,000	3up
Nassau County H.	75,000	3up
New Orleans H.	200,000	4up
New York H.	75,000	3up
Oaklawn H.	250,000	4up
Ohio Derby	200,000g	3yo
Orchid H.	125,000	3up
Paterson H.	150,000	3up
Pegasus H.	200,000	3yo
Pennsylvania Derby	200,000	3yo
Queen Charlotte H.	100,000	3up
Red Smith H.	125,000	3up
Round Table H.	75,000	3yo
Rutgers H.	150,000	3yo
San Bernardino H.	100,000	4up
San Carlos H.	80,000	4up
San Felipe H.	100,000	3yo
San Luis Obispo H.	125,000	4up
San Marcos H.	80,000	4up
San Pasqual H.	100,000	4up
San Raphael S.	100,000	3yo
Sanford S.	75,000	2yo

RACE	PURSE	AGE
Santa Maria H.	100,000	4up
Sapling S.	200,000	2yo
Saranac S.	100,000	3yo
Saratoga Special S.	60,000	2yo
Schuylerville S.	60,000	2yo
Seneca	75,000	3up
Seminole H.	50,000	3up
Sheepshead Bay H.	100,000	3up
Sheridan H.	75,000	3up
Shuvee H.	100,000	3up
Silver Screen H.	75,000	3yo
Sorority S.	200,000	2yo
Stars and Stripes H.	100,000	3up
Stuyvesant H.	100,000	3up
Sword Dancer S.	200,000	3up
Test S.	100,000	3yo
Tidal H.	100,000	3up
Tom Fool S.	100,000	3up
Tropical Park Derby	125,000	3yo
W.L. McKnight H.	100,000	3up
Washington Park H.	125,000	3up
Wilshire H.	75,000	3up
Withers S.	75,000	3yo

GRADE 3

Adirondack S.	$75,000	2yo
Affectionately H.	75,000	3up
Affirmed H.	75,000	3yo
Ak-Sar-Ben Board of Governors' H.	50,000	3up
Ak-Sar-Ben Omaha Gold Cup S.	150,000	3yo
Ak-Sar-Ben President's Cup H.	50,000	3yo
Ak-Sar-Ben Queen's H.	100,000	3up
Alibhai H.	60,000	3yo
Anoakia S.	60,000	2yo
Arlington Oaks	75,000	3yo
Assault H.	75,000	3up
Athenia H.	75,000	3up
Balboa S.	50,000	2yo
Barbara Fritchie H.	100,000	3up
Bay Meadows Derby	100,000	3yo
Bay Shore S.	100,000	3yo
Bed o' Roses H.	75,000	3up
Ben Ali H.	50,000	3up
Bewitch S.	50,000	3up
Boiling Springs S.	50,000	3yo
Bold Ruler S.	75,000	3up
Bonnie Miss S.	75,000	3yo
Brighton Beach H.	50,000	3up

RACE	PURSE	AGE
Budweiser Tampa Bay Derby	150,000	3yo
California Jockey Club S.	125,000	3up
Canadian H.	75,000	3up
Christmas Day H.	50,000	3up
Chrysanthemum H.	50,000	3up
Chula Vista H.	75,000	3up
Citation H.	100,000	3up
Clark H.	50,000	3up
Comely S.	75,000	3yo
Cotillion S.	100,000	3yo
Dahlia H.	75,000	3up
Discovery H.	60,000	3yo
Display H.	75,000	3up
Distaff H.	50,000	3up
El Dorado H.	60,000	3yo
El Encino S.	80,000	4yo
Equipoise Mile H.	75,000	3up
Everglades S.	50,000	3yo
Fair Grounds Classic	100,000	4up
Fair Grounds Oaks	150,000	3yo
Falls City H.	50,000	3up
Fayette H.	50,000	3up
First Flight H.	60,000	3up
Fort Marcy H.	50,000	3up
Gallorette H.	75,000	3up
Gold Rush Futurity	100,000g	2yo
Gold Rush S.	100,000	3yo
Golden Gate H.	300,000	3up
Governor's Cup H.	100,000	3yo
Gravesend H.	60,000	3up
Grey Lag H.	75,000	3up
Hawthorne Derby	100,000	3yo
Hill Prince S.	60,000	3yo
Hillsborough	100,000	3up
Honeymoon H.	100,000	3yo
Hutcheson H.	60,000	3yo
Illinois Derby	200,000	3yo
Inglewood H.	100,000	3up
Jamaica H.	75,000	3yo
Jim Beam Spiral S.	300,000	3yo
Juvenile S.	75,000	2yo
Kelso H.	100,000	3up
Kentucky Jockey Club S.	50,000	2yo
Knickerbocker H.	60,000	3up
La Brea S.	60,000	4yo
La Jolla Mile S.	75,000	3yo
La Prevoyante H.	100,000	3up

RACE	PURSE	AGE
Lamplighter H.	50,000	3yo
Landaluce S.	75,000	2yo
Laurance Armour H.	75,000	3up
Linda Vista H.	60,000	3yo
Long Branch S.	50,000	3yo
Longacres Derby	100,000	3yo
Los Angeles H.	75,000	3up
Louisiana Downs H.	200,000	3up
Mahubah H.	50,000	3up
Marylander H.	50,000	3yo
Miss Grillo S.	75,000	2yo
Nashua S.	75,000	2yo
National Jockey Club H.	100,000	3up
National Sprint Championship	150,000	3up
Native Diver H.	100,000	3up
Next Move H.	75,000	3up
Oceanport H.	50,000	3up
Palomar H.	60,000	3up
Pennsylvania Governor's Cup H.	50,000	3up
Phoenix Gold Cup H.	100,000g	3up
Pilgrim S.	75,000	2yo
Poinsettia S.	65,000	3yo
Post-Deb S.	50,000	3yo
Princess S.	60,000	3yo
Pucker Up S.	50,000	3yo
Queens County H.	60,000	3up
Railbird S.	60,000	3yo
Razorback H.	100,000	4up
Riggs H.	50,000	3up
Roamer H.	75,000	3up
Rolling Green H.	125,000	3up
Roseben H.	75,000	3up
Salvator Mile H.	50,000	3up
San Diego H.	75,000	3up
San Gabriel H.	80,000	4up
San Gorgonio H.	80,000	4up
San Vincente S.	75,000	3yo
Santa Monica H.	75,000	4up
Santa Ynez	75,000	3yo
Sierra Nevada H.	100,000	4yo
Silver Belles H.	100,000	3up
Sixty Sails H.	150,000	3up
Stymie H.	75,000	3up
Suffolk Downs Sprint H.	100,000	3up
Sunny Slope S.	60,000	2yo
Suwannee River H.	65,000	3up
Swift S.	75,000	3yo

RACE	PURSE	AGE
Swoon's Son H.	50,000	3up
Tanforan H.	100,000	3up
Temptes S.	75,000	2yo
Toboggan H.	60,000	3up
Tremont S.	60,000	2yo
True North H.	75,000	3up
Vagrancy H.	75,000	3up
Violet H.	100,000	3up
Volante H.	75,000	3yo
Westchester H.	75,000	3up
Will Rogers H.	60,000	3yo
Woodlawn S.	50,000	3yo
Yerba Buena	125,000	3up
BLACK TYPE, Listed		
A Gleam H.	$60,000	3up
Ak-Sar-Ben H.	100,000	3up
Ak-Sar-Ben Oaks	100,000	3yo
Albany H.	60,000	3up
Albany H.	50,000	3yo
Alex M. Robb S.	60,000	3up
All-American H.	75,000	3up
Alsab S	50,000	2yo
Anita Peabody	55,000	3up
Anne Arundel H.	50,000	3yo
Aqueduct H.	60,000	3up
Ascot H.	75,000	3yo
Ashley T. Cole S.	50,000	2yo
Astoria S.	60,000	2yo
Auld Lang Syne S.	100,000	3up
Bachelor S.	50,000	3yo
Baldwin S.	60,000	3yo
Bastonera Invitational H.	50,000	3up
Bay Meadows Lassie S.	50,000	2yo
Bay Meadows Oaks	50,000	3yo
Bayou H.	50,000	4up
Beaugay H.	60,000	3up
Bel Air H.	150,000	3up
Belle Roberts H.	75,000	3up
Berlo H.	60,000	3up
Bertram F. Bongard H.	100,000	3up
Bewitch H.	50,000	3up
Bing Crosby H.	50,000	3up
Bolsa Chica S.	60,000	3yo
Boojum H.	60,000	3up
Bouwerie S.	60,000	3yo
Bradbury S.	60,000	3yo
Broadway H.	60,000	3up

RACE	PURSE	AGE
Busanda S.	60,000	3yo
Busch S.	50,000	3up
Busher H.	60,000	3yo
Cabrillo H.	50,000	3up
California Breeders' Champion S.	100,000	2yo
California Breeders' Champion S.	100,000	3yo
California Miss Sires S.	150,000g	3yo
California Oaks	75,000	3yo
Camilla Urso H.	50,000	3up
Cascade S.	50,000	2yo
Catskill S.	60,000	3yo
Charles Hatton S.	50,000	3up
Chicago Land S.	50,000	3up
Chief Penneck S.	50,000	3up
Children's Hospital H.	50,000	3up
Choice H.	75,000	3yo
Cicada S.	50,000	3yo
Cinderella S.	50,000	2yo
Citation Invitational H.	80,000	3up
Cleveland Gold Cup H.	50,000	3yo
Cliff Hangar H.	50,000	3up
Coal Town S.	50,000	4up
Colonial Cup International Steeplechase	50,000g	4up
Color Me Blue H.	50,000	3yo
Columbian H.	50,000	3up
Correction H.	60,000	3up
Count Fleet H.	50,000	4up
Countess Fager H.	100,000	3up
Courtship S.	50,000	2yo
Daddy's Datsun Invitational H.	50,000	3up
Damon Runyon S.	60,000	2yo
Dark Mirage S.	50,000	3yo
Debonair S.	60,000	3yo
Derby Trial S.	50,000	3yo
DeWitt Clinton S.	100,000	3yo
East View S.	50,000	2yo
El Cajon S.	50,000	3yo
El Camino Real Derby	200,000	3yo
El Conejo H.	60,000	4up
El Monte S.	65,000	4up
El Rio Rey S.	60,000	2yo
Empire S.	60,000	2yo
Escondido H.	50,000	3up
Essex H.	50,000	4up
Evan Shipman S.	60,000	3up
Evening Out S.	50,000	2yo
Fairmount Derby	100,000	3yo

RACE	PURSE	AGE
Fall Festival Juvenile S.	75,000	2yo
Fashion H.	50,000	2yo
Federico Tesio S.	75,000	3yo
First Act S.	50,000	2yo
First Lady H.	50,000	3up
Flash S.	50,000	2yo
Fleur de Lis H.	50,000	3up
Florida Stallion S.	50,000	2yo
Florida Stallion S.	85,000	2yo
Florida Stallion S.	85,000	2yo
Florida Stallion S.	350,000	2yo
Florida Stallion S.	350,000	2yo
Florida Turf Cup H.	50,000	3up
Friendship S.	100,000	2yo
Garden City H.	50,000	3yo
Geisha H.	50,000	3up
Glass House H.	50,000	3up
Glassboro H.	50,000	3up
Golden Poppy H.	75,000	3up
Golden Rod S.	50,000	2yo
Golden State Breeders Sires S.	150,000	3yo
Goodwood H.	100,000	3up
Governor's Buckeye Cup H.	50,000	3up
Governor's Lady H.	50,000	3up
Great American S.	50,000	2yo
Grey Flight H.	50,000	3up
HITS Parade Invitational Derby	100,000g	3yo
HITS Parade Invitational Futurity	100,000g	2yo
Haggin S.	50,000	2yo
Hail Hilarious Invitational H.	75,000	3up
Happy New Year Invitational H.	50,000	3up
Hazel Park H.	50,000	3up
Hialeah Sprint Championship H.	65,000	3up
Hoist the Flag	50,000	2yo
Hollie Hughes H.	60,000	3up
Hollywood Express H.	60,000	3up
Hollywood Prevue S.	100,000	2yo
Hudson H.	60,000	3up
Hyde Park H.	60,000	3up
Illini Pricess H.	50,000	3up
Illiniwek S.	50,000	2yo
Illinois Breeders Futurity	55,000	2yo
Illinois Coronet H.	50,000	3up
Imp S.	50,000	3up
Imperatrice H.	50,000	3up
Interborough H.	60,000	3up
Iroquois S.	60,000	3up

RACE	PURSE	AGE
Jack R. Johnston Memorial H.	50,000	3up
Japan Racing Association H.	50,000	3yo
Jeanne d'Arc S.	50,000	3&4
Jennings H.	50,000	3up
Jersey Blues H.	50,000	3up
Jockey Hollow H.	50,000	3up
Joe Gottstein Futurity	50,000	2yo
Joe Palmer S.	60,000	3up
Juvenile Championship S.	50,000	2yo
Juvenile H.	50,000	2yo
Juvenile S.	60,000	2yo
Kings Point H.	60,000	3up
Kingston S.	60,000	3up
La Centinela S.	60,000	2yo
La Habra S.	60,000	3yo
La Puente S.	60,000	3yo
Lady Sponsors' S.	50,000	2yo
Lafayette S.	50,000	3yo
Lamb Chop H.	50,000	3yo
Land of Lincoln S.	50,000	3yo
Lansing H.	50,000	3yo
Las Cienegas H.	60,000	4up
Las Flores H.	60,000	all
Las Virgenes	80,000	3yo
Laurel Turf Cup H.	60,000	3up
Level Best S.	50,000	3yo
Little Silver H.	50,000	3yo
Los Feliz S.	60,000	2yo
Louisiana Downs Futurity	100,000g	2yo
Louisville Allowance S.	50,000	3up
Lucky Draw S.	50,000	3yo
Magnolia S.	50,000	3yo
Manta H.	60,000	3up
Marion H. Van Berg Memorial H.	50,000	3up
Mark's Place H.	65,000	3up
Mark's Place Invitational H.	75,000	3up
Martha Washington S.	50,000	3yo
Maryland Juvenile Championship S.	100,000g	2yo
Mayflower S.	75,000	2yo
Meteor H.	50,000	3up
Michigan Breeders' H.	50,000	3up
Michigan Futurity	50,000	2yo
Miller High Life Cradle S.	125,000	2yo
Miss America H.	100,000	3up
Mistletoe H.	50,000	3yo
Modesty H.	50,000	3yo
Mohawk S.	60,000	2yo

RACE	PURSE	AGE
Monrovia H.	60,000	4up
Montauk S.	60,000	3yo
Moonbeam H.	50,000	3up
Morvich H.	60,000	all
Mount Vernon S.	60,000	3up
Native Diver S.	50,000	3yo
Nebraska Racing Hall of Fame S.	50,000	3up
New Jersey Futurity	50,000	2yo
New York Breeders Futurity	50,000	2yo
New York Derby	100,000	3yo
New York OTB Big Apple H.	60,000	3yo
Noor Invitational H.	50,000	3up
Orange County H.	50,000	3up
Osunitas S.	50,000	3up
Palisades S.	50,000	3yo
Palos Verdes H.	80,000	all
Pasadena S.	60,000	3yo
Paumonok H.	60,000	3up
Pearl Necklace S.	50,000	3yo
Pelham H.	50,000	3up
Pelican State S.	50,000	2yo
Petrify H.	60,000	3up
Phoenix H.	50,000	3up
Pippin S.	50,000	4up
Pomona Invitational H.	75,000g	3up
Preston M. Burch H.	50,000	3up
Prince John S.	50,000	2yo
Prioress S.	50,000	3yo
Providencia S.	60,000	3yo
Queen City Oaks H.	50,000	3yo
Quivira S.	50,000	3up
Rancho Bernardo H.	50,000	3up
Rare Perfume S.	60,000	3yo
Rebel H.	100,000	3yo
Red River S.	50,000	3up
Regret H.	50,000	3yo
Resolution H.	50,000	3up
Riverside S.	50,000	3yo
Rockaway S.	60,000	3yo
Rosedale S.	50,000	2yo
Rosetown S.	50,000	3yo
Round Table H.	50,000	3yo
Ruffian S.	50,000	3yo
Ruthless S.	60,000	3yo
Sag Harbor S.	50,000	3yo
San Clemente S.	50,000	3yo
San Francisco Mile H.	75,000	3up

RACE	PURSE	AGE
San Jacinto H.	80,000	4up
San Joaquin Invitational H.	50,000	3up
San Marino H.	80,000	4up
San Miguel S.	60,000	3yo
San Simeon H.	80,000	4up
Santa Catalina S.	60,000	3yo
Santa Lucia H.	65,000	4up
Santa Ysabel S.	60,000	3yo
Schenectady H.	60,000	3up
Sea O'Erin H.	50,000	3up
Seabiscuit Invitational H.	50,000	3up
Seabiscuit S.	100,000	3up
Searching S.	60,000	3yo
Seattle H.	50,000	3up
Senorita S.	60,000	3yo
Shecky Greene H.	50,000	3up
Sierra Madre H.	60,000	4up
Silky Sullivan Invitational H.	60,000	3up
Silver Spoon H.	60,000	3up
Sorrento S.	50,000	2yo
Spectacular Invitational S.	50,000	3up
Sport Page H.	60,000	3up
Sporting Plate H.	60,000	3up
Sportsman's Spring H.	50,000	3up
Spotlight H.	60,000	3yo
Star Ball Invitational H.	60,000	3up
Stephen Foster H.	50,000	3up
Stroh's H.	50,000	3up
Susan's Girl H.	50,000	3up
Sutter H.	50,000	3yo
Telly's Pop Invitational H.	75,000	3up
Texas Open Futurity	150,000	2yo
Thanksgiving Day H.	50,000	3up
Thomas A. Edison H.	50,000	3up
Thomas D. Nash Memorial H.	50,000	3yo
Ticonderoga H.	60,000	3up
Tizna H.	65,000	3up
Treetop S.	50,000	2yo
Triple Bend H.	60,000	3up
Turf Paradise H.	100,000g	3up
Twilight Tear S.	50,000	3up
Vallejo S.	50,000	3yo
Walter Haight H.	50,000	3up
West Point S.	60,000	3up
Whirlaway S.	60,000	3yo
White Skies H.	50,000	3up
Woodhaven S.	50,000	3yo

RACE	PURSE	AGE
Yaddo S.	60,000	3up
Yankee H.	75,000	3yo
Youthful S.	50,000	2yo
Yuletide H.	50,000	3up